SOUTHEAST EUROPEAN STUDIES
VOL. 1

巴尔干研究

(第一辑)

梁占军／主编

世界知识出版社

图书在版编目（CIP）数据

巴尔干研究. 第 1 辑 / 梁占军主编. -- 北京：世界知识出版社，2020.1
ISBN 978-7-5012-6151-2

Ⅰ.①巴… Ⅱ.①梁… Ⅲ.①巴尔干半岛—历史—研究 Ⅳ.①K540.7

中国版本图书馆 CIP 数据核字（2020）第 018868 号

责任编辑	狄安略
责任出版	赵 玥
责任校对	张 琨

书　　名	巴尔干研究（第一辑） Baergan Yanjiu（Diyiji）
主　　编	梁占军
出版发行	世界知识出版社
地址邮编	北京市东城区干面胡同 51 号（100010）
网　　址	www.ishizhi.cn
电　　话	010-65265923（发行）　010-85119023（邮购）
经　　销	新华书店
印　　刷	北京虎彩文化传播有限公司
开本印张	720 毫米×1020 毫米　1/16　23¾印张
字　　数	410 千字
版次印次	2020 年 4 月第一版　2020 年 4 月第一次印刷
标准书号	ISBN 978-7-5012-6151-2
定　　价	80.00 元

版权所有　侵权必究

《巴尔干研究》

出版单位：首都师范大学文明区划研究中心

主　　编：梁占军

副 主 编：李建军

学术顾问（以姓氏笔画为序）：
马细谱　武　寅　徐　蓝　钱乘旦

编 委 会（以姓氏笔画为序）：
王洪起　孔凡君　刘文明　刘作奎　朱晓中
张　丽　赵　刚　柯　静　高　歌　梁占军
Alexandre Kostov　Božo Repe　Florian Bieber
Ivan Ilchev　Ljubodrag Dimić　Tvrtko Jakovina

特约编辑：Zvonimir Stopić

发刊词

"巴尔干"一词的本义源自土耳其语的"山脉",泛指欧洲东南部亚得里亚海和黑海之间的半岛山地。但是,自19世纪末以来,"巴尔干"这个词逐渐与"战争""动乱""纷争"等词语联系在一起,甚至成为"欧洲火药桶"的代名词。事实上,从20世纪初的两次巴尔干战争到1914年"萨拉热窝刺杀"引发第一次世界大战,从第二次世界大战期间的反法西斯抵抗到冷战中两大阵营的分裂与对立,从冷战后南斯拉夫的解体到其继承国之间后续的一系列内战和冲突,等等,20世纪以来的巴尔干经历的是一百多年的战端频发、血火交织的历史,巴尔干被称作"欧洲火药桶"可谓名副其实。

不过,在这百年战乱纷呈的背后,人们常常忽略的是巴尔干悠久的历史文明与多彩的文化形态以及其先天的地缘政治优势。作为现代欧洲文明的发源地,巴尔干地区自古以来就是多民族、多宗教、多文化的交汇之地,古代希腊罗马的遗迹和思想流传至今,影响巨大。与此同时,由于巴尔干地处欧亚结合部,是连接欧亚、推进东西方贸易和文化交流的重要交通枢纽,无论古代的丝绸之路,还是今天的"一带一路"倡议,巴尔干地区都是其中不可或缺的重要组成部分。也正是如此,巴尔干地区自古以来就是帝国统治或大国争夺的对象,而且内部各民族反抗外族压迫的纷争不断,至今仍是国际社会关注的热点地区。长期以来,欧美各国的学者对于巴尔干问题的关注和研究热情持续高涨,"巴尔干学"早已成为一门国际显学。

但是,限于种种历史和客观条件的制约,中国人对于巴尔干地区的了解普遍都很薄弱,无论是历史、现状、宗教、民族、政治、文化、习俗等都所知甚少。由于懂得当地语言的研究人员十分稀缺,相关的研究也很不系统。总体上看，我国的巴尔干研究起步晚，基础弱，研究队伍分散。虽然随着"一带一路"倡议的推进，近年相关研究取得了不少进展，但客观上讲，目前的研究存在以下"三多三少"：

第一，关注现实问题多，剖析历史根源的少

众所周知，历史是过去的现实，现实是将来的历史，从长时段看，二者的转换犹如一个硬币的两面。实际上，由于历史具有各时段相对稳定的阶段性特点，现实中每一个问题便都有一条历史的尾巴可寻，抓住这条尾巴，就可以沿着历史的脉络顺藤摸瓜，揭示出现实问题的来龙去脉。事实上，研究现实问题必须了解历史，否则就无法深刻理解现实，也无法预测未来走向。但就现实中的巴尔干研究而言，历史研究与现实研究基本处于割裂状态，历史学和政治学背景的两拨人马各自为战，少有交集：从事历史研究的几乎不碰现实，关注现实的很少钻研历史，由此造成一些认识的割裂和盲区。英国著名巴尔干学家马克·马佐尔在他的《巴尔干五百年》一书中曾明确指出："要了解巴尔干就必须去关注历史本身，历史并不是一面让我们掩饰过去、自照美德的镜子。"① 因此，在巴尔干研究中应注重把历史与现实有机结合起来，以现实问题为导向，深入探索问题的历史根源。这样既可以发挥出历史研究的优长、学以致用，也有助于透过错综复杂的表象来揭示现实问题的真相，进而准确把握事态发展趋势，提出合理的对策建议。

第二，分散的专题研究多，贯通的整体性研究少

目前我国的巴尔干研究由于队伍分散，基本上是各自为战的零碎研究，缺乏贯通性的整体或系统研究。比如从历史研究的视角看，2018年末马细谱先生和余志和先生的《巴尔干百年简史》② 的出版是自2007年陈志强先生的《巴尔干古代史》③ 问世十年后有关巴尔干历史的最新著作，极大地充实了巴尔干近现代史的著述。但迄今为止，贯通古今的巴尔干通史仍付之阙如，这种断代的研究无法弥补体系化研究的缺失，也不利于巴尔干研究的深入。这里强调贯通的整体研究不是要忽略局部的重要性，而是因为局部必须依托整体才能更好地体现其价值。换句话说，就是局部的研究是为整体的贯通提供砖瓦，而整体的研究可为局部的研究提供方向。这一点，钱穆先生在《晚学盲言》开篇曾讲

---

① 马克·马佐尔：《巴尔干五百年》，中信出版集团2017年版。
② 马细谱、余志和：《巴尔干百年简史》，中国青年出版社2018年版。
③ 陈志强：《巴尔干古代史》，中华书局2007年版。

得非常清楚："有'整体',有'部分'。但应先有了整体,才始有部分;并不是先有了部分,乃始合成为整体,如先有了'天',乃始有春、夏、秋、冬。非是有了春夏秋冬,乃始合成一'天'。"简言之,整体与部分二者相对存在,离开整体参照的部分实际就不再是部分,而是一个整体,这种意义上的多个整体可以合成一个新整体。故二者"和之则两美,离之则两伤"。要全面系统地了解某一个研究对象,必须整体与部分兼顾。目前我国的巴尔干研究关注具体的、局部的问题较多,缺乏整体贯通的构想和研究,这对于我们从整体角度搞清复杂多变的巴尔干情势是极为不利的。

第三,研究队伍语言学科背景的多,其他专业的少

近年来随着"一带一路"倡议的提出,国内的巴尔干研究方兴未艾。但是,由于对象国语言的限制,相关的专业人才比较稀缺,且学科背景单一,相关研究的深度和广度均有待拓展。目前从事巴尔干研究的主力军是为数不多的通晓对象国语言的中老年专家学者,青年学者也大多是语言学专业背景,他们依托自身的语言优势,在获取一手信息方面占尽先机,对于热点问题的跟踪和解读快速而具体,相关研究大多集中在语言文学、时事热点问题方面。总体上讲,历史、政治、经济、法律等专业背景的研究人员极少,这极大地限制了我国巴尔干研究的深度和广度。一句话,现有的研究状况并不足以支撑我国对"一带一路"沿线国家的国情进行全面了解的现实需求,也不能充分满足中国推进"一带一路"倡议的时代需求。

在此背景下,作为教育部批准的首批国别与区域研究基地,首都师范大学文明区划研究中心以推动中国巴尔干学的发展为己任,自2015年起开始,依托我校世界史学科的两个优势方向:全球史与国际关系史,聚焦巴尔干地区,重点研究巴尔干地区多元文明之间的交流与互动。历经三年多的时间,我们先后与巴尔干地区的多数国家的大学和研究机构建立了合作关系;聚集了一批高水平的国内外专家;成功加入国际东南欧学会,成为亚洲除日本外的第二个集体会员;积极谋划和创办中心刊物《巴尔干研究》。当前,国内有关国别区域研究的期刊除了传统的《欧洲研究》《美国研究》《日本研究》等外,还涌现出不少研究中心创办的不定期出版的系列辑刊,如《国别和区域研究》[①]《土

[①] 罗林主编:《国别和区域研究》(2018年第2期,总第6期),中国社会科学出版社2018年版。

耳其研究》①《巴基斯坦研究》②《中东研究》③等，这些学术辑刊在推进相关领域研究方面发挥着独特的作用。本中心创办的《巴尔干研究》将是国内第一部专门聚焦巴尔干研究的学术辑刊，其目的是为国内外有志于巴尔干研究的学者提供一个以文会友的交流平台，并进而为增进中国和巴尔干国家的相互了解、切实推进"一带一路"背景下的文明互鉴贡献一点力量。

本辑刊的宗旨是要努力打通历史研究与时政研究之间的壁垒，兼容巴尔干研究的历史与现实，使二者相互借鉴融合，从而推进和拓展我国巴尔干学研究的领域。这是我们通过对中国巴尔干研究的现实观察而得出的办刊思路。基于以上考虑，本辑刊的栏目重点突出"时政研究"与"历史研究"两大类，同时辅以"史料选译""学术信息"等栏目，对国内外学者的研究成果兼容并蓄，一视同仁。第一期共收集15篇中外学者的专题论文，其中特稿3篇、时政7篇，历史研究5篇，此外还有档案选译及相关文章，这是本中心成员和国际巴尔干研究学者的集体智慧和结晶。作为一本追求国际化的刊物，本辑刊采用中英双语的形式，对所刊文章尽力保持原貌，以期最大限度地体现作者的观点，方便同行之间的交流和批评。

我们相信，在国内外同行专家的共同支持与呵护下，《巴尔干研究》这朵初绽的小花一定会释放出夺目的光彩！

梁占军
2019 年 2 月 27 日

---

① 李秉忠主编：《土耳其研究》（2018 年第 1 期，总第 1 期），社会科学文献出版社 2018 年版。
② 孙红旗主编：《巴基斯坦研究》（第 2 辑），中国社会科学出版社 2017 年版。
③ 西北大学中东研究所主编：《中东研究》（2018 年第 2 期，总第 8 期），社会科学文献出版社 2018 年版。

序言 巴尔干研究，大有可为

欣闻首都师范大学文明区划研究中心创办的《巴尔干研究》第一辑即将出版，作为首师大历史系毕业的校友，我感到由衷的高兴。这是国内第一本聚焦巴尔干问题的学术刊物，具有拓荒的性质，它表明首师大在开拓新的学术增长点方面又迈出了坚实的一步。也正因为如此，当中心主任梁占军邀请我为刊物写序时，我欣然应允。

无论是从世界历史研究的角度，还是从当代国际关系和全球化发展的角度来看，巴尔干地区的重要性都毋庸置疑，它有必要成为国家重点关注和研究的战略要地。从地缘上看，巴尔干地区连接欧亚交通，战略地位十分重要。目前除塞尔维亚、克罗地亚、斯洛文尼亚、波黑、黑山、北马其顿等前南斯拉夫解体后的6个继承国家外，还有希腊、阿尔巴尼亚、保加利亚、罗马尼亚、匈牙利等中东欧国家。这一地区历史上曾经长期处在帝国的统治和压迫之下，多民族交织，宗教信仰各异，多元文化交杂，百多年来纷争和战乱不断，被公认为欧洲的火药桶。在许多与国际风云和人类命运息息相关的重大事件中，都能看到这里的影子。在作为一个极其重要的角色历经了一战、二战和冷战后，今天的巴尔干地区依然是大国窥视和争夺的焦点地区。当今我国提出的"一带一路"倡议能否如愿实现，巴尔干地区起着关键性的作用。

在学术研究领域，巴尔干研究是亟待加强的薄弱环节。历史上，中国和巴尔干地区的交集并不多。近代以来，随着全球化程度的不断加深，中国对巴尔干地区的了解也在不断增多。改革开放以来，双边的交往开始加强，中国对巴尔干地区的关注度大大提高，但相关的国情和基础研究总体上还不够深入，许多具体的事物都语焉不详，对巴尔干各国的研究远远跟不上形势的发展。

今天，中国改革开放的大门正在以更大的力度向世界敞开，作为一个负责任的大国，中国对世界的认知不能仅仅局限于几个大国和几个地区。加强对世界其他国家和地区的了解已经是大势所趋，是中国处理一切重大国际事务的基础和前提。在推进"一带一路"和构建人类命运共同体的愿景下，中国需要更加深入地开展与巴尔干国家和人民的交互往来，为此必须加强对巴尔干各国历史和现状的深层了解。巴尔干地区特殊的地理位置、历史经历和复杂的宗教文化现实使得它的研究价值日益凸显。事实上，从多元文明互动与共生的角度去研究巴尔干地区的民族、国家和文化认同、历史上的各类冲突及其化解、宗教信仰的对立与互鉴等，对于我们秉持合作共赢的理念，促进世界各国和平相处、共同发展具有非常重要的现实意义。

首都师范大学文明区划中心把巴尔干地区作为研究的重点，并针对目前我国还没有聚焦巴尔干问题的专门期刊这一现状，创办了专门的辑刊《巴尔干研究》，填补了这方面的空白。这是一个顺应时代发展、谋求学以致用的积极举措，体现了学术界助力国家发展重大需求的使命感。该中心作为首批教育部国别和区域研究培育基地，一直是建设高校智库的倡导者和践行者之一。2015年以来，中心着力聚焦巴尔干地区的问题研究，是国内第一家注重从历史和现实的双重视角来研究巴尔干问题的中心。近五年来，中心本着一手信息、一手人脉、一手史料的原则，与国内外大学和智库开展合作，聘请了中国社科院、中联部、新华社等国家级智库的人员作为兼职研究员，如中国社科院世界历史研究所的资深巴尔干研究专家马细谱先生，即为该中心的首席专家。同时中心还聘任了两名年轻的克罗地亚籍的研究人员，创办了中心的微信公众号，第一时间发布巴尔干国家的重大新闻，挖掘其来龙去脉，传播信息，努力建设国内独家的巴尔干信息库，并且与巴尔干国家知名高校联合培养国别区域研究的人才，等等，做了大量的基础工作。

首都师范大学文明区划中心在巴尔干研究方面，始终依托其世界史研究的学科优势，注重发挥其全球史和国际关系史研究的特长，呈现出良好的发展势头。我相信，首都师范大学在引领国别区域研究特别是巴尔干研究方面，一定会大有作为！

祝《巴尔干研究》出版顺利！祝首都师范大学文明区划研究中心不负众望！

武　寅

中国社会科学院前副院长、研究员

目 录

发刊词 …………………………………………………… 梁占军 / 1
序言　巴尔干研究，大有可为 ………………………… 武　寅 / 5

特别专栏：
关于"巴尔干"的一场争论

作为历史空间的欧洲巴尔干 ………… [德] 赫姆·尊德豪森 著　孔烨 译 / 3
作为研究范畴的"巴尔干"：界线、空间、时间
　　……………… [保加利亚] 玛莉亚·托多洛娃 著　王冰钰 译 / 23
巴尔干：为差异辩护 ………… [德] 赫姆·尊德豪森 著　刘晨 译 / 42

时政研究

巴尔干国家差异性、复杂性及其对"17+1"合作的影响 ………… 孔寒冰 / 58
俄罗斯在西巴尔干的经济存在及政治影响 ………………… 朱晓中 / 72
Policing the Peace after Yugoslavia: Police Reform between External Imposition
　　and Domestic Reform ………… [卢森堡] 弗洛里安·比伯 / 87

Slovenes between the Balkans and Central Europe
······························ ［斯洛文尼亚］博佐·雷佩 / 110

Montenegro's Foreign Policy between the EU and Russia
······························ ［克罗地亚］白伊维 / 131

BRI—Potential for Economic Cooperation between China and the Western Balkans:
　The Case of The Republic of North Macedonia
　　····················· ［北马其顿］安娜·布拉热斯卡 / 144

No Escape from Balkan?: The "Balkans" in the Contemporary Croatian Scientific
　Thought ······ ［克罗地亚］左立明、［克罗地亚］高山·久尔杰维奇 / 162

历史研究

Bosnia and Herzegovina in the First World War, 1914-1918
·· ［波黑］兹雅德·塞西奇 / 192

保加利亚中学教科书中关于十月革命评价的变化
·················· ［保加利亚］伊斯克拉·巴耶娃 著　马细谱 译 / 251

二战期间中国进步报刊论巴尔干人民的反法西斯斗争和铁托
　——以《新华日报》和《解放日报》为例 ············· 马细谱 / 255

波黑：失落的"出生证明" ······························ 陈慧稚 / 266

斯洛文尼亚分离主义活动的宣传话语 ······················ 杨　东 / 276

学术论坛

我译《保加利亚中短篇小说集》 ·························· 余志和 / 292

关于巴尔干的七个观点 ⋯⋯⋯⋯⋯［英］蒂莫西·雷斯 著　邓灿等 译 / 299

史料选译

意大利、巴尔干与二战之始：法文档案选编 ⋯⋯⋯⋯⋯ 杨紫桐 编译 / 304

学术信息

罗马尼亚东南欧研究所简介 ⋯⋯⋯⋯⋯⋯⋯⋯⋯⋯⋯⋯⋯ 武　垚 / 322
保加利亚巴尔干学研究所成立50年及其学术活动 ⋯⋯⋯⋯ 马细谱 / 326
喜读《巴尔干百年简史》⋯⋯⋯⋯⋯⋯⋯⋯⋯⋯⋯⋯⋯⋯ 李建军 / 334
Katalog Osmanskih Dokumenata（I）/ Catalogue of Ottoman Documents,
　　prepared by Azra Gadžo-Kasumović, Gazi Husrev-Bey Library in Sarajevo,
　　2018, 448 pg. ⋯⋯⋯⋯⋯⋯⋯⋯⋯⋯［波黑］尼哈德·多斯托维奇 / 337
评艾莱兹·比贝莱的《阿尔巴尼亚与中国：不对称的联盟》
　　⋯⋯⋯⋯⋯⋯⋯⋯⋯⋯⋯⋯⋯⋯⋯⋯⋯［克罗地亚］白伊维 / 340
新书速递（九本）⋯⋯⋯⋯⋯⋯⋯⋯⋯⋯⋯⋯⋯⋯⋯⋯⋯⋯⋯⋯ / 342

征稿启事 ⋯⋯⋯⋯⋯⋯⋯⋯⋯⋯⋯⋯⋯⋯⋯⋯⋯⋯⋯⋯⋯⋯⋯ / 364

特别专栏：
关于"巴尔干"的一场争论

编者按

  本专栏介绍的是1999—2003年玛莉亚·托多洛娃（1949—）和赫姆·尊德豪森（1942—2015）对巴尔干历史认识的争论。两位教授都是巴尔干研究领域的资深学者，了解二人关于巴尔干的学术探讨对我们来说非常重要。托多洛娃论述了作为西方"他者"和意境地图中的巴尔干，尊德豪森分析的是具有文化联系但历史空间独特的欧洲巴尔干。探讨时托多洛娃依托人类学、文学、游记、象征和文化理论等领域的知识，而尊德豪森注重史料、事件、政治史和哲学知识。他们对巴尔干的争论因各自取径和方法的不同，引起了不同国家学者、作家、记者的热烈回应，内容不断被引述和讨论。虽然这次学术探讨已过去将近20年，但并未过时，因为他们讨论的主题都是开放性的。因此我们在本辑翻译了德语原文，介绍给中国学者，这样有助于我们增强对巴尔干界限、时间、空间、差异性和多样性的理解。

作为历史空间的欧洲巴尔干*

[德] 赫姆·尊德豪森 著　孔烨 译

内容提要　本文将巴尔干作为欧洲的历史空间来进行考察，并对这种研究取径进行了说明，对空间界限和塑造空间的八个特征进行了分析。在这种视角下，尊德豪森反驳了托多洛娃在其著作《想象巴尔干》中的一些认识，包括"巴尔干主义"、作为"他者"的巴尔干和理性解决巴尔干冲突等概念和观点。
关 键 词　巴尔干　欧洲巴尔干　历史空间　边界
作者简介　赫姆·尊德豪森，德国柏林自由大学东欧学院教授
译者简介　孔烨，首都师范大学外国语学院德语系研究生

在 20 世纪最初 20 年里，巴尔干给外界留下的印象越来越晦暗，直至难以辨识。1903 年 6 月一支由塞尔维亚军官组成的小团体对塞尔维亚国王亚历山大·奥布雷诺维奇及其夫人的谋杀、1908 年的波斯尼亚危机、国家秘密组织的颠覆活动、马其顿问题、1912—1913 年的巴尔干战争、在此期间首次被系统收集的有关"民族清洗"（ethnische Säuberung）的信息、新巴尔干国家之间无数次的看似近乎无法解决的领土冲突，以及 1914 年 6 月 28 日奥匈帝国王位继承人弗朗茨·斐迪南在萨拉热窝遭遇的暗杀，将巴尔干钉在了滋生暴力和"欧洲火药桶"的耻辱柱上。

美国人约翰·冈瑟（John Gunther）写道："这些可怜、令人不快的巴尔干

---

* 本文发表于 1999 年德国第四季度的《历史与社会》（Holm Sundhaussen, "Europa balcanica, Der Balkan alshistorischer Raum Europas," *Geschichte und Gesellschaft*, 25. Jahrg., H. 4, Ostdeutschlandunterdem Kommunismus 1945-1950, Oct.-Dec., 1999, pp. 626-653）。译文省略大部分注释。

小国之间确实存在足以引发世界大战的矛盾，这是对人类本性与政治本性不可容忍的冒犯。大约15万年轻的美国人因1914年萨拉热窝事件引发的战争而丧失。巴尔干政局中那些令西方读者难以理解的、令人厌恶的吵嚷至今依然对欧洲和平，乃至世界和平至关重要。"

早在19世纪末，欧洲的政治家就已对巴尔干的政治家及其争吵感到恼火。俾斯麦称希腊人、塞尔维亚人和保加利亚人为"偷羊贼"；奥匈帝国外交大臣卡尔诺基伯爵严厉地斥责那些"巴尔干无产者"。"巴尔干化"这一概念在第一次世界大战末才在政治新闻学中出现。该概念似乎精当地概括出该地区当时最新的发展趋势，并很快在欧洲其他地区和欧洲以外的世界传播开来。它指的是"对较大经济政治体的分割，以及由此带来的相关地区的政局动荡"。

在不足一个世纪内，人们对巴尔干的感知彻底改变了。如果说这种感知在浪漫主义时期（Zeitalter der Romantik）和第一次反奥斯曼解放战争时期，仍然受到人们对古希腊罗马时期留下的遗产、对自由的热爱、对巴尔干人民英雄气概以及对他们"民族精神"本真的赞叹的影响，那么自19世纪末以来，巴尔干的形象愈加被原始性和暴力倾向所替代，有时甚至伴有种族主义的刻板形象。不曾改变的只有人们对巴尔干普遍匮乏的了解。阿加莎·克里斯蒂精准地将这无知反映在她的作品中。她在1925年用以下文字简明扼要地勾勒出了由她创造的国家"黑塞斯洛伐克"（Herzoslovakia）："那是巴尔干国家之一……主要河流，未知。主要山脉，同样未知，但为数众多。首都，艾卡勒斯特（Ekarest）。人口，主要是强盗。爱好，暗杀国王以及进行革命。"

在一段与阿加莎·克里斯蒂同时期的英国人莱尔（Archibald Lyall）和一位波斯长老会教徒在雅典进行的谈话中，后者问他："您为什么想去阿尔巴尼亚，我亲爱的先生？那儿没什么可看的，只有黑石头。而且没有房子，只有充满裂缝和破洞的小堡，来复枪从那儿窥视着；阿尔巴尼亚人，他们坐在那儿然后砰砰砰。比狂野的西部还糟糕。那是廷巴克图（Timbuctoo）①，我亲爱的先生，廷巴克图的最中央。我告诉您，我亲爱的先生，上帝在和他的岳母打了一架之后创造了阿尔巴尼亚人。"

来自保加利亚、现居美国的历史学家玛莉亚·托多洛娃在其1997年出版的《想象巴尔干》（*Imagining the Balkans*）一书中搜集了塑造巴尔干形象的大量丰富材料，其中许多形象都是负面的。从这些巴尔干的刻板印象中流露出的

---

① 指遥远、未知、难以到达的地方。——译者注

无知和傲慢，往好处讲是令人发笑的，往坏处讲则是让人厌恶的。我们不难理解托多洛娃的悲痛结论："由于巴尔干在地理上与欧洲不可分割，文化上却被塑造为欧洲之中的'他者'，因此巴尔干一直以来都背负了来自外部的政治、意识形态和文化方面的挫败。这些挫败源于巴尔干外部地区及社会固有的紧张和矛盾，而西方却因此豁免于一系列的指控：种族主义、殖民主义、欧洲中心主义以及基督徒对伊斯兰教的不宽容……巴尔干和东方一样成了积累负面特征的储藏室；'欧洲'和'西方'的正面、自我庆贺的形象正是在其与巴尔干的对立中被建构出来的。随着作为独立语义价值的东方和东方主义[①]再次出现，巴尔干地区却仍未摆脱欧洲的掌控，成为其反文明、第二自我和阴暗内心的象征。"

那么，巴尔干只是一个"欧洲人"和"西方"为了神话自己而创造出来的充满偏见的虚构概念吗？还是说，除人们的固有印象之外，巴尔干具有其他特征，可以让人们将其理解为一个独特的地区？

一个区域若要称得上独特，那么构成这一空间的各个部分必须能形成一个（无论何种类型的）整体，且该整体包含的要多于这些部分的简单相加。基于这个整体，该地区能通过具备"自身"特征或不具备"外来"特征，以此区别于其他地区或大区。因为这里同样适用：没有他者，就没有认同。关于巴尔干是否是"欧洲内部的他者"，"欧洲"以及"他者"是如何定义的，这些问题尚可讨论。但无可争议的是，任何一个认同的过程都以区别他者为前提。无论对个体或群体，还是对地区来说，自我指涉的认同都不存在。因此，空间构建永远是在一个或多或少高度抽象的层面上展开的、通过跨越空间以及在空间内部进行比较得出的结果。空间构建的目的是把空间（此即欧洲）划分为有结构意义的统一体，这些统一体同时又是对子统一体的概述。划分欧洲空间所用的特征取决于观察者的专业兴趣或研究议题。可能涉及自然地理、人类学地理、政治、经济、人文科学、结构历史或者其他特征或特征组合。普遍适用的是：对同一空间所采用的分类特征数量越大，空间概念就越明确。反而言之：特征越广泛、越与其他大空间的特征交叠，地区轮廓就越模糊，直至在极端情况下完全消失。

分类在科学研究和日常使用中都是一种常见的系统化处理方式，不可或缺也难以消除。不过，系统化的方法究竟能为人们认识事物提供多大助益，取决于两个评判标准：一是重要度，二是可信度。只有当鉴定标准能被赋予长远的

[①] 即欧洲为西方，非欧洲为东方。——译者注

(影响历史的)、解释的意义，历史的空间概念（historische Raumbegriffe）才是有意义的概念——下文也正是在这个意义上使用这一概念。

我们将目光聚焦于选定的现象 ["事实"（Fakten）及其影响] 来建构空间。聚焦某些特定现象的做法一向是利弊并存：焦点之外的，陷入视野之外；处于焦点的，则会受到过度曝光。其结果或被指摘为"简化主义"或被批为"简单化"。玛莉亚·托多洛娃充分利用了这种批评的做法。不过，她也无法提供实用的其他选择。毕竟，复杂的社会现实一向仅能部分被理解。这不仅适用于空间建构：每个感知都以（通常为无意识的）筛选和聚焦为基础。这项不足无论是"建构主义者"还是"解构主义者"都不能逃脱。将我们的感知分解成无数的无定形信息中，这种想法不仅是不现实的，也是不实用的。建构的概念总会有意识或无意识地，以这种或那种形式一次次地潜入我们的感知。因此，问题不在于空间概念是否是一个建构的概念，这个概念与简单化和信息丢失是否有关——这些都毋庸置疑，问题在于，感知过滤器如何使用，以及它的分析结果是否具有解释现象的能力。科学的、因此也是有意识的建构之优势在于能对筛选标准进行阐释，从而证伪。也就是说：结果可检验，还可以根据情况被证实、修改，或摒弃。

我们所说的一个区域的基本特征不是绝对固定的，也不能被清晰界定（当然，这不意味着，这些特征仅仅存在于我们的设想之中，缺少非语言的真实性）。对于历史结构和关系空间以及与之相关的特征集群的建构基于实证（从历史人口统计学到政治、经济、文化指标）和认知事实（例如，基于在涉及区域中宗教、文化和政治精英的阐释模式）。然而，鉴于邻近空间之间长达数百年的、纷繁复杂的相互影响，除了主导特征外，或多或少还有显露其他空间特征的扩展，更不用提共生与融合。因此，没有人会真的声称，历史上的巴尔干空间有固定的边界和永久不变的特征。特征是历史进程的结果：它们形成、变化、消逝。因此，历史空间不是通过突然的时间断裂或线性边界（后者只是方向性指导），而是通过逐步的过渡呈现出来的。不仅国界和空间边界有时会瓦解（另一方面，这能导致国家的破裂）——空间边界本身也随着时间变化，并且最终能够完全丧失其影响力。但是，这在几年或几十年内不会发生。有时甚至几百年后都不会发生。

社会和政治学家斯坦·罗坎（Stein Rokkan）——他本人不曾受到"怀有历史偏见"等诸如此类的指责——在一次演讲中指出了如何建立比较宏观社会学的方法。他发现，为了能够解释现代西方社会中政治参与的不同形式，必须诉诸所谓的"历史事实"。"为了理解在当下一系列结构中可观察的变化,我决定去分析那些对于政治体系起关键作用的联盟和协议发生了哪些重大变化。通过研究欧洲国家的选举历史,'持久'的意义——在每个国家历史的进程中,决策和同盟建立的长远影响——越来越让我印象深刻。……我尝试在这些变化背后发现一种阐释逻辑,并且我认为,这种逻辑已在国家发展路径类型学中找到:为此我必须联合一系列历史变量,从宗教改革开始,直到边缘族裔解放的最后阶段。"

由于目前流行"后结构"模式,因此,倘若使用"持久"或结构的研究模式,则首先需要一番自我辩护。费尔南·布罗代尔(Fernand Braudel)写道:"社会观察者认为,结构是现实和社会集体力量之间的一种秩序构造、一种关联和足够牢固的关系。对我们历史学家来说,结构无疑是一种配合、一种构造,更是一种很少随时间损耗及迁移的现实。一些生存长久的结构成为世世代代的稳定因素:这些结构通过限制历史来阻断历史,也就是说它们决定历史进程。其他结构则解体得快得多。但所有结构都既是支撑也是障碍。"即使是批评布罗代尔"结构功能主义"过于呆板且忽略了行为者(Akteure)的人,也很难不承认历史形成的结构、感知模式和行为模式的存在。被后结构主义历史观推到聚光灯下的主体和行动者——尤其是不计其数的小行动者——他们并非在历史和文化真空中活动,而是被放进了社会组织中。这种社会组织仅有一部分(甚至可能是很小的部分)由经历着的(erlebend)主体自身创造;其余的部分则作为现实或传统(可证实的或虚构的传统),被主体有意识或无意识地经历、经受和复制。所有行动者和主体同时也是被困者和客体。他们的行动和改变空间始终受到历史结构、规范和价值体系、文化感知模式以及行为准则的限制。虽然这些可变迁、可转变,但其转变速度通常很慢。

结构在很多因素的共同作用下得到强化。如此一来,主体想要使结构发生改变就变得困难,但并非不可能。结构主要因自身的动力(Eigendynamik)而变迁。而该动力能通过行动者的文化实践(他们的认同及意义赋予、"集体记忆",诸如此类)被减慢。只有当结构的固有变迁和重要行动者的转变意愿恰好相同,才涉及通常所说的"革命"。这种革命不是精英之间的权力转移,而是使社会发生根本转变的革命。相反,如果变迁和转变不兼容,那么结构和行动者就会牵制彼此。布罗代尔所说的历史的"封锁",所指无它,正是这一点。换句话说:行动者的感知、阐释及行为模式不是主观意愿或"理性选择程序"的产物,而或多或少受社会化过程、集体经验和经历或其"回忆"及加工的影响。尽管如此，这些模式不受严格决定论的左右，而是给人留出了做决定的余地——不论这种余地是否真的被采用。

如何勾勒一个历史空间取决于我们所关注的关系。依据我们关注的焦点——统治关系和社会同盟、生产及分配模式、价值及规范体系等的不同，空间界限划定有不同的结果。理想情况是，大量重要的关系体系（Beziehungssystem）在很长的时期里能够重合。这在历史实践中仍是例外。因此，我们只得不断接近历史空间的构建；这种构建有助于我们组织认知兴趣。历史区域是工作概念（或规定），必须检测其有效性，如有必要，须进行修改。

下面来谈谈巴尔干。已故匈牙利中世纪研究学者斯苏兹（Jenö Szücs）曾对欧洲的历史区域做了杰出的划分和勾勒，将其分为西欧、中东欧和东欧，但巴尔干却被他排除在外，因为东南欧"在中世纪末期同逐渐衰弱的拜占庭一起脱离欧洲结构五个世纪"。但巴尔干地区受奥斯曼人长达四五百年的统治就等同于该地区"脱离""欧洲结构"了吗？"鲁米利亚"①或"欧洲土耳其"只是欧洲内的异类吗？取代了拜占庭的奥斯曼帝国难道没有把拜占庭的许多机构和制度沿用下去，而仅做了细微的改动吗？巴尔干地区的典型居住模式不是在中世纪就已存在，在奥斯曼统治时期仅经历过一次动荡吗？同样，我们如何对待那些在国家机器下得以延续，并且决定性地塑造了大部分公民思维及行为模式的前奥斯曼制度（尤其是基督教）呢？正因为奥斯曼的长期统治，不更应该将该地区及其丰富多元性视为"欧洲结构"中的一部分吗？让西方文化和文明之"摇篮"所处的空间"脱离""欧洲结构"，这样做妥善合理吗？最后："欧洲结构"是什么？去掉奥斯曼元素，这些结构岂不缺少统一且前后矛盾？

把巴尔干排除在欧洲历史区域之外，这从很多角度讲都不可接受且过于随意。首先，巴尔干——按照托多洛娃的表述——"在地理上与欧洲不可分割"。因此，我们先转向该区域的地理、划界和变换的命名。巴尔干地区的西、南、东面临界五片海域：亚得里亚海、爱奥尼亚海、爱琴海、马尔马拉海和黑海。在这点上，学界基本意见一致。有激烈争议的是该地区的名称及北界。主要有两种命名："巴尔干"和"东南欧"。

1808年，受柏林地理学家奥古斯特·措伊内（August Zeune）影响，"巴尔干半岛"这一名称代替了此前普遍的"（欧洲）土耳其"或"鲁米利亚"两种命名。作者从传统观点出发：作为连绵不断的山脉，巴尔干山脉，旧称

---

① 土耳其语，奥斯曼帝国在巴尔干半岛的领地。——译者注

"Mons Albanus, Scardus 或 Hämus",在黑海和斯洛文尼亚阿尔卑斯山之间的整个陆地上伸展,并且正如亚平宁山脉对意大利半岛一样,该山脉对整片地区有着相似的重要意义。因此,措伊内追随古希腊地理学家(斯特拉波、托勒密等)的设想,他们关于连贯的中心链(Zentralkette)的观点在文艺复兴时期重新焕发生机。但是实际上,被称作巴尔干(Balkan,源自土耳其语,意为"山脉")的山脉(保加利亚语:"Stara Planina" = 老山)只伸展了420千米(平均宽度30—50千米),并且将保加利亚分为北部(多瑙河平原)和南部(罗多彼山地)。和百年前的猜测不同,巴尔干没有与东南欧其余山脉形成连贯的地貌体系。该错误被旅行学者指出后〔其中最著名的是奥地利地质学家阿米·博(Ami Boué,1794-1881)和奥古斯特·格里瑟巴赫(August Grisebach)〕,"巴尔干半岛或 Hämus 半岛"的概念遭到越来越多的批评。奥地利领事约翰·乔治·冯·汉①熟知塞尔维亚人、阿尔巴尼亚人和希腊人的定居区,是主张在"欧洲土耳其"修建铁路的先驱者。在他1861年出版的《从贝尔格莱德到萨洛尼卡的旅行》中,他遗憾地表示,"东西欧中心链的地理学神话"仍一直活跃着,而且阻碍其铁路工程的实现。对于"欧洲东南隅的整片三角地带",汉提出了"东南半岛"这一概念。足足30年后(1893年),地理学家费舍尔(Theobald Fischer)着手研究汉的提议,他提出了"东南欧半岛"的说法,并将其北界移至萨瓦河—多瑙河一线。

然而关于东南欧的命名和扩展的讨论一直持续到20世纪。1918年,塞尔维亚学者斯维伊奇(Jovan Cvijić,1865-1927)的人类地理学先锋著作《巴尔干半岛,人文地理学》在巴黎问世。该书的出版使已稳固确立的巴尔干概念得到了进一步的发展。不仅学术语言如此,日常语言应用中也是如此。不仅有"巴尔干"航空公司、"巴尔干"酒店等,而且还有"巴尔干"科学研究所(比如,在贝尔格莱德、索非亚和萨洛尼卡)以及过去和现在都很多的"巴尔干"杂志〔其中有《巴尔干》(Balcania)、《巴尔干》(Balcanica)、《巴尔干斯拉夫》(Balcanoslavica)、《巴尔干档案》(Balkan-Archiv)、《巴尔干研究》(Balkan Studies)、《巴尔干研究》(Études Balkaniques)等〕。在该区域之外,"巴尔干"也在科学机构、杂志、单一出版物和词典中占有稳固地位。

另一方面,巴尔干概念成为议题不单单由于其地理上误导性的起源,还由于此概念带有贬义。为避免使用带贬义的概念,学者们尝试(尤其)在该地区

---

① 奥地利外交官、阿尔巴尼亚学家,1869年起任奥地利驻雅典总领事。——译者注

以外的研究中找寻一个无贬义的名称。"东南欧"一词很合适，尽管名称的变换没能改变该地区冲突不断的状况和外界对该地区的感知。不仅如此，巴尔干概念已深入人心，难以被取代。北界仍有争议，因为对其的确定没有各方均接受的地理、种族地理或历史标准。因此，将"巴尔干"等同于"东南欧"的处理方法与将狭义的巴尔干概念和广义的东南欧概念进行区分的处理方法相对立。狭义巴尔干空间的北界迁移至（包括下文会提及的一些波动）萨瓦河与多瑙河下游河道。与之相反，东南欧的北界从北部的亚得里亚海，沿东阿尔卑斯山脉、小喀尔巴阡山脉和贝斯基德山脉，随德涅斯特河直到注入黑海。也就是说：依照这种（尤其在匈牙利不被接受的）理解，除了巴尔干国家外，喀尔巴阡空间或前圣伊什特王国（及其邻国）——也就是斯洛伐克、如今的匈牙利、克罗地亚、伏伊伏丁那、罗马尼亚的巴纳特和特兰西瓦尼亚——以及前罗马尼亚侯国瓦拉几亚和伏尔塔瓦（包括比萨拉比亚）也属于东南欧。整个"卡尔帕索斯—巴尔干"包括大约100万平方千米的面积，1亿居民（1980年中期）。此种广义的东南欧概念主要建立在以下事实基础上，即萨瓦河与多瑙河沿岸并没有形成显著稳定的地理、种族地理或政治史方面的障碍。这导致了各种干扰的形成。斯维伊奇——权威性地参与一战后南斯拉夫国家建立的学术（首先是种族地理学）合法化——对萨瓦河—多瑙河一线作为巴尔干空间北界只持保留意见。他的主要顾虑是，这条分界线的两侧都居住着南支斯拉夫人。为了不在萌芽阶段就破坏南斯拉夫国家的建立，萨瓦河边界，以及多瑙河边界的一部分必须被相对化。巴尔干北界的其他地点也是类似的情况。因为种族居住情况、语言相似关系、现代国界以及历史演变结构——这些会在之后谈到——等因素在不同地区并不完全一致，因此所谈空间的定义和分界就会出现多种重叠和前后不一致。比如以前的罗马尼亚侯国伏尔塔瓦和瓦拉几亚就是如此。它们曾被划归到广义的东南欧概念之下，然后又归于狭义巴尔干概念。在巴尔干半岛最西北存在两种分界的变体。库帕河偶尔会被视为巴尔干的西北界，但大多数情况下，被当成巴尔干西北界的是乌纳河（二者均为萨瓦河支流）。第一种情况下，克罗地亚高原或者说克罗地亚前军事分界地区（直到1995年都有大量塞尔维亚居民）属于巴尔干，第二种情况下则不属于。

尽管有些地区的边界并不明显，乌纳河、萨瓦河与多瑙河南部空间仍呈现出独立的历史文化区域。其面积大约48万平方千米（明显比德国大，但也明显比法国小），包括波斯尼亚—黑塞哥维那、塞尔维亚（包括科索沃地区，但不包括伏伊伏丁那）、黑山、瓦尔达尔马其顿、保加利亚、多布罗加、土耳其欧洲部分、希腊和阿尔巴尼亚。由于周围有五片海域，因此这一带理应被称为半岛。为了和广义的东南欧概念区分开，下面称这部分地区为"巴尔干半岛"或"巴尔干"。半岛南北向伸展大约1300千米，东西向北部大约1000千米，南部大约300千米。易跨越的博斯普鲁斯和达达尼尔海峡将巴尔干半岛与邻近的小亚细亚分隔开。宽阔的北部像梯形，而南部——实际上是希腊半岛——则狭窄得多，并且被大量深入陆地内部的海湾分开。巴尔干半岛西部受希腊狄娜里克山脉体系的影响，该体系从西北部朱利安阿尔卑斯山脉越过狄娜里克断层块、北阿尔巴尼亚阿尔卑斯山脉和品都斯山脉，直至半岛南部，从这里越过伯罗奔尼撒和爱琴海半岛，延续至小亚细亚。在西部狄娜里克山脉和东部巴尔干山脉之间坐落着罗多彼山脉所在的色雷斯地带。在多瑙河以南，较大型的平原和盆地只出现在北保加利亚、阿尔巴尼亚沿海区域、马其顿以及巴尔干山脉以南的马里卡山谷（Marica）和东色雷斯山谷。

　　巴尔干地区建立了中欧和西南亚之间的桥梁。在北部，该地区没有太大地质物理方面的阻碍，逐渐变为匈牙利平原，通过多瑙河与欧洲中央大陆相连。由多瑙河、摩拉瓦河与马里卡河道形成的向东南方的延伸——从贝尔格莱德，越过尼什至伊斯坦布尔——以及在尼什分叉、沿摩拉瓦河和瓦尔达尔低地的贝尔格莱德—萨洛尼卡链接轴，这些连接在中欧和小亚细亚之间、中欧和北非（苏伊士运河）之间贯穿起距离最短的交通干线。因此，贝尔格莱德，萨瓦河与多瑙河交汇处的"白色城堡"，既是巴尔干半岛、地中海东部地区和西南亚的北门，同时也是被多瑙河横穿的潘诺尼亚平原及其山丘的东南山口。作为军用和贸易公路，贝尔格莱德—君士坦丁堡/伊斯坦布尔轴从罗马时期，历经之后几百年直到（最近的）现在，都没有丧失其重要的交通政治意义。类似的情况还有在尼什分叉、通往爱琴海和萨洛尼卡的路段，该路段与南塞尔维亚和马其顿一道横贯巴尔干半岛中央部分。从都拉斯越过萨洛尼卡通往君士坦丁堡的古老的厄纳齐雅大道（Via Egnatia）也是如此。马其顿枢纽自古希腊罗马时期，历经中世纪拜占庭、保加利亚和塞尔维亚的国家建立，直至1912—1913年的巴尔干战争以及二战，这期间一直都是国际争夺的对象，如今仍继续被视为潜在矛盾源。与从西北至东南伸展的自然交通线不同，由于迪纳拉断层块，从亚得里亚海岸至巴尔干半岛内部的南北连接引起巨大问题。虽然亚得里亚海提供通往西巴尔干外围的便捷通道，并且一直是外国商人和殖民者的入口，但是紧随其后的山脉屏障使海岸边缘与其后方的连接更加困难。只要不把深受罗马—威尼斯影响、有自己城市文化的亚得里亚海沿海地区（Küstensaum）完全排除

11

在巴尔干空间之外,那么就不能否认其作为亚地区的特殊身份。

巴尔干半岛多山、地表切割强烈,有广阔的通道通往周边地区,中欧与小亚细亚之间的桥梁,这些因素自古以来都为外来移民和军事侵占提供了便利,同时也给国家制度在地区内部中的平稳推行造成了困难。在很长一段时间内,巴尔干都属于大帝国(罗马帝国、东罗马/拜占庭帝国、奥斯曼帝国),这些帝国的根源或在巴尔干地区之外,或远远超出其范围。

20世纪80年代中期,巴尔干居住人口超过4200万人,他们来自不同的国家、族群,有不同的宗教信仰、不同的语言。由于地理框架条件,平均人口密度为87人/平方千米,比西欧和中欧低。与此相应,城市网也较稀疏。

自古希腊罗马时代末期或自斯拉夫殖民以来的巴尔干半岛历史(始于6世纪末)并不适用于西方历史的时期划分模式。这样看来,斯苏兹判决巴尔干空间从欧洲结构"脱落"这一点丝毫不难理解。在巴尔干历史中,中世纪与近代以及近代早期与现当代的分界从未被详尽讨论过。近代始于巴尔干空间并入奥斯曼帝国这一观点既未能让人们就此达成共识,也不令人信服。暂且把古希腊罗马时代末期之后该地区的历史粗略分为以下时期:1.大约近千年的拜占庭帝国和前奥斯曼巴尔干国家时期;2. 400—500年直接或间接的奥斯曼统治时期;3. 自19世纪初以来的民族国家和民族建立时期。

那么,巴尔干空间长远的、结构塑造的特征是什么,以及它区别于其他历史空间的特征何在?将巴尔干与欧洲其他地区进行比较是一条合适的取径,因为如果巴尔干"地理上与欧洲不可分",那么在确定其特征时,欧洲其他部分也应该作为参考体系。此前需明确的是,巴尔干国家的史学就此并未做出值得一提的贡献。虽然在30年代就已有人要求展开一项雄心勃勃的——跨学科、比较性质的——巴尔干研究,但至今都未得以实现。像以前一样,不同国家的史学都聚焦在自己的历史上。对邻国的无知和傲慢不比托多洛娃所抱怨的西方对巴尔干空间完整性的傲慢少。因此,接下来提出的观点只是探索性(完全不充分的)尝试,提纲挈领地将巴尔干定性为一个历史空间。

1. 民族与民族间关系不稳定、狭小空间内族群混居带来的不稳定(Gemengelage)。由于小亚细亚和中欧之间的桥梁位置以及通往外围的开放通道,自古以来,巴尔干半岛就经历了诸如人口迁移、族裔交叉、同化过程和认同转换等剧烈的变化。斯拉夫殖民前后、多瑙河下游早期拜占庭王朝保卫崩溃之后,一直有游牧民族侵入该空间。由于战争以及拜占庭和奥斯曼时期系统推行的强制迁移,还由于经济或社会所决定的、从平原到山脉的迁移,和从山脉到平原的迁移，以及（对于其来源有激烈争议）瓦拉几亚直至近代广泛扩散的游牧业，这些因素都导致巴尔干地区大部分族群结构处于不断波动中。倘若当地居民面对奥斯曼侵略者选择躲进山区，那么农民成为牧人；而一旦人口压力或经济灾难迫使山区居民迁移至收成更好的平原，那么牧人又变为农民。这些"无定向的（metanastasisch）迁移"（源自已经提到的塞尔维亚人类地理学家斯维伊奇）为不断更新宗法文明模式和保存远古习惯法做了巨大贡献。

各类迁移之中，17、18世纪的塞尔维亚人北迁具有尤其突出的意义。当时摩拉维亚—瓦尔达尔盆地、科索沃、伊巴尔地区（Ibar-Region）和东塞尔维亚地区的大部分居民分几批离开他们祖先的居住地，越过萨瓦河与多瑙河，向北迁移，在哈布斯堡王朝领地安家。来自迪纳拉山脉地区的一部分阿尔巴尼亚人、一部分南斯拉夫人接着来到因迁徙而人口密度降低的这片地区。斯维伊奇及其学生进行的民族志学领域的研究，是否让我们更好地了解了在很多塞尔维亚及其临近地区子空间人口的来源和定居点呢？[①] 研究阐明，在19世纪，只有少部分塞尔维亚居民是土生土长的。这在摩拉维亚盆地以及在瓦列沃和波德里涅地区不超过20%，极端情况下，世代居住者只占总人口的极小部分。在10个接受民族志学调查的塞尔维亚子区域中，一共只有4.3%受调查的家庭（或家族）是土生土长的；34.2%是18世纪末之前迁入的，61.5%是19世纪才迁入的。

很遗憾没有对巴尔干空间其他子区域的相似密度的微观分析。但是总的来说，可以确定：奥斯曼领土在欧洲土地上的每次扩张或萎缩，都伴随着强烈的人口移动和迁移。与拜占庭一样，奥斯曼统治者以边界安全或复兴生产和商业为目的，或多或少一次又一次让大规模人群定居、迁出、迁移。因此，与西欧不同，在民族迁移时期之后，人口相对稀疏的巴尔干半岛的居住状况从未能持续巩固。

希腊人、阿尔巴尼亚人和一支古希腊罗马时代被罗马化的民族的剩余居民（瓦拉几亚人或弗拉赫人的一部分）属于巴尔干半岛最古老的居民。自6世纪末南斯拉夫人——部分与游牧民族（阿瓦尔人、保加利亚原住民、哈扎尔人等）关系紧密——到来，新的游牧民族和"撒克逊人"（后者在西巴尔干矿业地区）随之而来。土耳其人、犹太人、吉卜赛人、亚美尼亚人、鞑靼人、切尔

---

① 1902年斯维伊奇创立了"塞尔维亚民族志收藏"（Srpski etnografski zbornik），由塞尔维亚科学协会出版，当时有100余卷。

克斯人、"埃及人"等属于最年轻的人口阶层。关于单个群体的族群形成存在激烈的争议，由于相关资料贫乏，该问题变得扑朔迷离。随着在"漫长的19世纪"，种族首次成为现代国家建立与合法化的根本因素，灾难出现苗头。因为这样一来，关于"我们"这一群体的建构、排行、真实性和纯粹性的竞赛就开始了。后奥斯曼国家致力于其合法化，来"分解"所继承的族群、语言、宗教信仰的冲突局势。其结果是1875年以来的四大"清洗浪潮"。第一次与后奥斯曼国家建立直接相关；第二次包括从1912年巴尔干战争开始到1923年希腊土耳其和平协定这一时期；第三次由1941年希特勒的巴尔干战争触发，直到40年代末；第四次是1991—1999年在四分五裂的南斯拉夫的战争时期。

2. **古希腊罗马时代遗产的遗失和之后的接受**。巴尔干属于欧洲"2000年前就已经'有历史意义'"的那部分。希腊被视为西欧的"摇篮"，巴尔干半岛不仅融入罗马帝国，而且贡献了许多位罗马皇帝和将军。首次罗马法编纂也在位于巴尔干空间与小亚细亚交界的东罗马帝国的君士坦丁堡实现。然而，自中世纪初（或自拜占庭时期）起，"古老欧洲"的古希腊罗马高度文明逐步黯然失色，最终彻底被湮没。而对古希腊罗马文化的重新发现直到19世纪仍仅限于西方（"新欧洲"），并未扩展到巴尔干地区。这也包括对罗马法的接受和实施（以及由此产生的社会和经济后果）。在拜占庭，由查士丁尼编纂的罗马法不久就陷入被遗忘的境地，几百年后被天主教会接受，在漫长、复杂的过程后，成为整个西方法律体系的基础，而直到19—20世纪才重又"再出口"回其拜占庭原产地。这实属历史奇观。

3. **拜占庭东正教遗产**。罗马帝国首都于公元330年由罗马迁至君士坦丁堡，以及罗马帝国划分为东西两部分（公元395年）之后，东罗马帝国开始了拜占庭千年史。东西罗马的行政界线从中间穿过西巴尔干中部（斯库台子午线），紧靠后来罗马和君士坦丁堡之间教祖管辖区的司法管辖边界。直到现在，这条著名界线的意义改变甚微（代表性的是波斯尼亚）。"拜占庭模型"及其国教东正教对巴尔干半岛大部分地区的历史产生了重要影响。罗马教会与君士坦丁堡教会的疏离是一段漫长、痛苦的历史，它在9世纪后半叶阜丢斯（Photius）大主教时期达到第一个顶峰，并最终走向1054年的"教会大分裂"，分裂的根源更多在于个人虚荣，而非神学争议。即使理由很可笑，"教会大分裂"仍成为东西方之间几百年深刻疏离的象征。为了防止误解：这里谈到的欧洲的宗教信仰分裂，并不涉及——至少不是首要的，也不单单是——神学或教条历史。对历史空间的确定而言，重要的是几个世纪以来教会在赋予意义方面垄断和神父的跨语境解释权（transkontextuelle Deutungsmacht）。"在前资本主义社会，教士的教阶高低是知识占有量的标志，教阶越高，有权支配的智识类知识越多。即使不是每个知识分子都是神父，并且不是每个神父都是知识分子，但是承载着宗教的超验性目的的教阶，将知识划分成了不同的等级。"其他对历史空间的确定产生影响的因素，还包括政治神学以及教会的活动空间；教会一方面受到外围环境的影响，另一方面也在影响着外围环境。这涉及宗教和世俗权力的形象，还涉及参考体系，该体系融合两种模式：一是"拜占庭模式"，二是"西方模式"。

此处本文只能诉诸一些关键词和简化的二分法，而无法展开详述：在东罗马帝国，基督教吸纳了古希腊罗马关于"皇权神授"（Gottkaisertum）的观念，教会和国家组成了"交响曲"；而在西罗马帝国，世俗和宗教权力处于对抗中（即优西比乌和奥古斯丁提出的相互矛盾的方案）。自4世纪以来，东罗马帝国的统治目标和东正教并不完全吻合，但彼此却紧密相连。这种"交响曲"与5世纪末以来西方的格兰西"双剑学说"① 形成强烈对比。

此外，一方面涉及在拜占庭东正教（"希腊的"）空间的新柏拉图世界观，另一方面涉及在西方（"拉丁的"）空间经过经院哲学改造后的亚里士多德思想传统［也就是说，涉及格里高利·帕拉马斯（Gregorios Palamas）与托马斯·阿奎那的矛盾概念］。最后，还涉及以下两个方面：一是拜占庭的皇权（Kaiserrecht）超越了查士丁尼时代而得以延续，罗马法的影响力也随之减弱；二是几百年后，《民法大全》② 在西方重见天日。

这里出现了三个方面——统治、神学/哲学和法律，其组织与传授主要由教会或信仰共同体承担，而且在所有公共生活领域都有重大影响：统治的合法化、社会内部个人及群体的位置、政权或国家与社会的关系、所有权的形成、权利与司法的理解、哲学和科学的发展等。几个世纪以来，政治、社会、经济和文化都受拜占庭与西方、君士坦丁堡与罗马不同模式的影响。例如分权理论或所有权在西方得到发展，这是偶然吗？人们在研究等级制国家、城市、启蒙运动与世俗化、近代制度建立的历史，或对欧洲（东/西）教育史（Bildungsgeschichte）进行对比研究时，总会一再触及东正教与西方教会（天主

---

① 格兰西（Gratian），12世纪本笃会修道士，博洛尼亚教规学者。格兰西以"物质之剑"比喻武力，以"精神之剑"比喻主教的劝告和祈祷。——译者注
② 6世纪东罗马帝国皇帝查士丁尼一世下令编纂的一部汇编式法典，是罗马法的集大成者。——译者注

教与新教）之间的分界线，尽管二者有时存在相交或界限模糊之处。在几个世纪中，尽管有些地方的分界线一会向西，之后又向东蜿蜒移动，其"主要据点"却惊人地稳定。这需要解释。宗教信仰边界能提供解释。这可能不是唯一的解释，甚至可能是错误的，但迄今还没有其他更具说服力的解释。

事实上，那些深刻影响了西欧形象的历史发展在东正教或东正教自主教会的地盘上或者未产生影响，或者仅仅作为边缘现象出现，比如世俗权力和宗教权力之间几百年来的斗争，以及那些或多或少都与教会和神职人员在意义赋予和阐释上的垄断（Sinngebungs-und Deutungsmonopol）相关的大规模运动：文艺复兴、人文主义、宗教改革、反宗教改革、启蒙运动等。不论在西方模式还是在拜占庭模式中，都有一些偏离主流趋势的潮流（且它们彼此影响），而这些潮流也被视为偏离，它们或在自身发展过程中受阻，或仅能发挥微弱的作用。尽管巴尔干空间也有启蒙运动的先驱［奥布拉多维奇（Dositej Obradović）、伏尔加里斯（Eugenios Vulgaris）、科拉伊斯（Adamantios Korais）、丘伦达尔斯基（Paisij Chilendarski）等］，但是那句格言"孤燕不成夏"① 也适用于此。

巴尔干半岛与西、中欧之间一直持续到19世纪的文化距离不单单是奥斯曼帝国统治的结果（尽管距离因此而延续），而是在东、西教会长久疏离的过程中，以及在第四次十字军东征后产生的"拉丁憎恨"（君士坦丁堡的掠夺、拜占庭帝国的瓜分，以及1204年"拉丁统治"的确立）下就已经形成了。"拉丁憎恨"在1453年奥斯曼帝国占领君士坦丁堡时期就已经如此活跃，以至于同罗马的教会联盟相比，伊斯兰教的统治看起来还没那么糟。"西方"不能克服对"教会分立论者"的偏见和轻视。尽管奥斯曼帝国的东正教徒与天主教势力（尤其是哈布斯堡和威尼斯）之间多次合作，巴尔干基督徒与"西方"的关系在随后的时期仍然是矛盾的，并且在拒绝和钦佩之间摇摆不定。这点在后奥斯曼时期，自从巴尔干开始"欧洲化"或"西化"就很少改变："西方人"和"反西方人"一直势不两立；如今还有人如此。

4. **奥斯曼伊斯兰遗产**。巴尔干半岛持续500年（从近14世纪末直至20世纪初）的奥斯曼帝国统治长远地影响了该地区，并加深了其与西欧的隔绝。奥斯曼帝国的统治伴随着新居民群体［尤鲁克人、西班牙/葡萄牙籍犹太人（Sephardim）、切尔克斯人等］的定居，并通过"土耳其战争"加剧了本就复杂化的种族、语言、宗教信仰的冲突局势。早前边界的废除产生了一个内部空

---

① 解释为不要凭个别现象草率判断。——译者注

间，其使移民和居民群体互相渗透变得简单。奥斯曼帝国的统治导致了城市以及一部分乡村人口的伊斯兰化（尤其在阿尔巴尼亚人定居区、保加利亚人的部分定居区以及波斯尼亚）。多种族、多文化的城市与分割化、基本自给自足的城郊农村的差别越来越大。同时，奥斯曼帝国帮助非伊斯兰宗教（基督教和犹太教）获得虽从属于伊斯兰、但同样突出的意义（类国家的任务）。奥斯曼帝国废除了中世纪巴尔干的封建等级（只要不皈依伊斯兰），然而，帝国不仅给皈依者，也给那些被容忍的宗教的主要代表以及犹太教、东正教和亚美尼亚商人提供意想不到的晋升机会。帝国不仅让高级（逐步希腊化的）神职人员，也让低级（通常是未受教育的）神职人员在受到平等对待的东正教民中上升至领导阶层，并巩固了教士阶层的权利。当欧洲广大地区向专制统治形式过渡之时，"苏丹世袭统治"（马克斯·韦伯）的内部权力结构受到侵蚀，变为半无政府状态。与专制主义在西方国家的成功渗透相对立的是奥斯曼帝国衰亡时期的瓦解效应以及巴尔干半岛"奥斯曼治下的和平"的崩塌。

　　由于通常奥斯曼帝国的行政机构不渗透到地方上（不在低地，更别提在山区），当地村庄自治的古老形式、习惯法的准则（从血仇到家庭法）和家庭侍从网络得以发展和复制。从西、中巴尔干（在北阿尔巴尼亚、黑山和黑塞哥维那部分地区直至19世纪、部分直至20世纪存在生命力旺盛的结构）的牧区山区出发，在几个世纪的移民过程中，宗法文化模式蔓延至半岛广大（即使不是所有）地区。在有父系制度和人权秩序的、对欧洲来说独一无二的"巴尔干家庭家政"中，在"英雄式生活方式"的培养中，在鲜明的荣辱观中，以及在深深植根的"民族文化"和宗教风俗习惯中，这些宗法文化模式都得以体现。"民间信仰的世界……事实上，用杜尔哈姆（Edith Durham）的话说，是'过去的土地'；是还未经历马克斯·韦伯所说的'觉醒'的世界。这里，魔法和仪式不是作为迷信的遗物或落后的铁证，而是作为想象力持续性胜利的可见标志而继续存在，然而荒唐的是，它们继续竭尽全力去寻找我们在自然及宇宙中位置之谜的答案"。巴尔干的生活方式尤其在不受国家管制的地区（这些地区远离政治中心，且有自然屏障保护）得到广泛传播，在这些地区，部落、氏族、农村社区和大家庭共同构成了关乎存亡、功能多样的基本组织形式。在奥斯曼帝国统治结束很长时间之后，传统元素在巨变时期依然会被当作"资源"重新激发，以此来进行自我保护与自我证明。

　　5. **现代"落后"的社会和经济。**在拜占庭帝国黄金时期显现的、欧洲东南部较之西欧的文化及文明落差，自中世纪盛期以来逐渐颠倒过来。由于继承了拜占庭帝国东正教和奥斯曼帝国伊斯兰教的遗产，巴尔干的经济和社会发展走上了一条偏离西、中欧的小路。西方的巨大创新和发展（中世纪农业革命、财产权的实施、国际贸易及信用体系的动力、农业的商业化、原始工业化等）很长时间都完全没有到达巴尔干，或者只有微弱影响。直到18、19世纪，农业生产还停留在中世纪水平。此外，西欧—大西洋经济空间繁荣发展，而与此同时，古时地中海地区的"世界经济"却在逐步失去其原有的地位。

与东欧其他地区或东方一样，在巴尔干（暂不考虑亚得里亚海子区域）也很少有拥有自治和独立、自己的机构和法庭的城市合作社。尽管在拜占庭帝国晚期和奥斯曼帝国统治时期，一些城市或特定的城市居民阶层被赋予了特权，但是无论在前奥斯曼还是在奥斯曼时期，都没有形成法律划定的、能反对统治暴力的城市协会。而直到奥斯曼帝国统治末期或在摆脱了其统治以后，资本主义经济模式与市民阶层发展的萌芽才产生，且在随后的时间里——伴随着仅仅是局部的、被多次中断的现代化进程——其发展也是阻碍重重。

类似的情况还有国家与社会的分离。虽然奥斯曼上层政府完全容许一定的社会自治，但是这种自治要么具有当地（村庄社区或部落）特征，要么具有宗教信仰特征（米勒特制①）。两种社会组织形式都对保留传统负有义务，并且都极端敌视创新。直至后奥斯曼时期，坚持传统宗教世界观和东正教牧师的反启蒙、反解放行为都阻碍了市民社会结构的形成。

巴尔干地区社会经济的停滞和倒退只是（或首先是）"土耳其压迫"的结果（如同通常声称的那样）这一点很难去证实或反驳。亚洲生产方式，包括"传统再分配"（Konrád/Szelényi）的一种特有形式，是否随奥斯曼帝国统治引入欧洲，或者奥斯曼人是否只延续了拜占庭传统，这些问题还需要进一步澄清。只需回顾一下俄罗斯的经济史和社会史，人们就足以明白应谨慎对待这些问题。

6. 民族国家及民族的建立。自19世纪头十年以来，巴尔干地区现代国家的建立通过奥斯曼帝国或大或小领土的逐步分离而实现。巴尔干基督徒的起义最初有复辟的特征。其目的是重建被奥斯曼中央政府或地区统治者破坏的古老秩序——而不是建立新的秩序。这个目的是倒退的，不是前进的。同时在西方——通过巴尔干散居社区和商人获得的——思想的影响下，国家建立过程还包含了一个新的元素。因为在巴尔干空间历史中，种族在19世纪第一次被宣

---

① 奥斯曼帝国时期的宗教自治制度。——译者注

告为国家建立及国家合法化的原则。与长期巩固的领土国家不同，年轻的后奥斯曼国家因此承受巨大的合法化压力。民族先驱者争取各自人民的竞争也相应地激烈。东正教徒被击溃，语言界限被划定清晰，民族神话被创造出来，对种族而言具有决定性意义的传统被"民族化"，并且所有不符合新编纂出的民族文化的因素一概被剔除，尤其是几个世纪的奥斯曼遗产以及随着新国界的确立同时被制造出来的少数民族遗产。具有严重后果的民族划界和排外的过程摧毁了巴尔干跨种族及多种族的漫长（并且总体和平的）时期。一种奇特的混合再次出现：一方面是采纳自西欧的现代原则（自决权），另一方面是巴尔干过去的神话（尤其是论资排辈及永久性的概念（Ancienniät-Permanenzvorstellungen）和对权利的索取，这些权利是巴尔干民族在奥斯曼人侵略之前的某个有利时机争取到的）。为了阐释领土要求，民族主义者见机行事，时而引用"历史权利"（historische Rechte），时而又引用民族自决权，并且依兴致和心情掺杂两者。随着潘多拉的盒子被打开，一大波巴尔干问题便暴露在光天化日之下（"马其顿问题""阿尔巴尼亚问题""塞尔维亚问题""色雷斯问题"等）。后果在上面（第一点中）已经提到。

7. 精神气质和神话。定居巴尔干空间的不同群体的思维和行为模式之间是否具有明显的相似之处，或者说过去或现在是否存在一种巴尔干特有的精神气质，这依然饱受争议。一方面，这是因为对精神气质概念的不同定义，另一方面是因为很难有方法、依据经验、令人信服地证实精神气质。自 1918 年斯维伊奇在研究中引入"巴尔干精神气质"这一概念，学者们便做出了各种尝试去证实或摒弃一种（或若干）巴尔干气质的存在。最新的尝试之一来自希腊历史学家帕斯查理斯·M. 吉特洛米利德斯（Paschalis M. Kitromilides），他对现代国家建立前巴尔干地区东正教居民的精神共性进行了研究。他得到了这样的（所罗门王式的）① 结果："在上述 18 世纪巴尔干社会符号宇宙的草图中，我尝试在以上概述的 18 世纪巴尔干社会的象征宇宙中确定巴尔干体验（experience）的三个组成部分，即东正教文化、奥斯曼统治和欧洲思想，它们（即这三个组成部分）形成了交流框架，该框架与清晰可辨的政治背景相连，可以被阐释为一种独特的、从历史角度看可信的'精神气质'。我不完全确定以下结论从方法角度是否合理，但这种历史上、政治上特定的一系列独特思维特征应该等同于广泛的人类学意义的'精神气质'。"

---

① 即英明的。——译者注

父权制、民俗和神话在多大程度上塑造了巴尔干居民的精神气质,对此暂时还没有明确结论。但无可否认的是,巴尔干地区出产了如此之多的神话、英雄与殉道者,多到它自己都难以消化。与"土耳其压迫"神话和对伊斯兰教的仇视形成鲜明对比的是前奥斯曼"黄金"时代的神话,民族"纯洁、自然、质朴"的神话,民族再生的神话,科索沃神话,巴尔干海杜克(Haiduken)① 神话和牺牲者神话,这些神话在现代国家建立的准备及后续阶段起了出乎意料的颠覆性作用。哲学家许布讷(Kurt Hübner)说:"神话思维是命运思想所特有的……普遍和特殊、整体和部分在其中融为一体……它不了解过去、现在、将来的时间维度之区别;一切本质都是持续的现在。"作为完整世界及自我理解的特别形式,神话总能进入公共话语和政治文化精英的宣传机构中去。从民族意识角度获得重新解读的民俗传统也一直参与其中。贝尔格莱德文化人类学家在 1992 年末说:"如今在前南斯拉夫——尤其在塞尔维亚、黑山、克罗地亚以及波斯尼亚和黑塞哥维那——政治演讲和著作的作者喜欢运用民间文学的文学形式、主题和形象,其意图明显是唤醒爱国和战斗的情感。然而,在南斯拉夫新的政治话语中,民俗形式和主题的基本功能是提出想法……在由这种语言传递的讯息和情感中,民众的声音引起共鸣,民众的意愿得以表达。"

8. 巴尔干作为强权的猎物。从 17 世纪末开始的奥斯曼政权的逐步衰落唤醒了欧洲强国对"博斯普鲁斯病夫"的遗产的贪欲。俄国和哈布斯堡王朝追逐巴尔干空间的领土利益,而英国和法国却首先追求经济和策略利益。在 19—20 世纪,欧洲强国(除了已提到的外,还有后来的德国和意大利)一直不断大肆干涉巴尔干国家的内部事务。因此,巴尔干国家的政客和知识分子非常乐意看到、也几乎仅仅看到了自己扮演的牺牲者角色。同时,为了取得比邻国更稳固的地位,年轻的后奥斯曼国家一直不断寻求强国的支持。除了少数几次为期短暂的共同对外的合作,巴尔干国家由于种族国家间的竞争和互相排除的"历史权利"而激烈争执,并且曾经渴望得到外界的——视目的而定的——干预,之后又为之懊悔。

一些这里——列举并不完整——提到的参数(例如东正教、经济落后、种族冲突局势)不是巴尔干半岛仅有的特点。其他特点并未对巴尔干所有地区都有相同的影响,有时甚至完全没有(例如中、东保加利亚的"巴尔干家庭家

---

① 海杜克,本意为"强盗"或"土匪",指 15—19 世纪巴尔干人民反抗奥斯曼帝国统治的游击战士。巴尔干流传着很多他们的故事和歌谣,至今仍是民俗的组成部分。——译者注

政")。一些特征转移到其他东南欧地区,例如种族亲缘关系、语言相似关系、暂时的奥斯曼帝国直接或间接的统治或霸权(在匈牙利中部、斯拉沃尼亚、罗马尼亚的多瑙河侯国,或者在特兰西瓦尼亚)。尽管存在单个参数的不同偏差,仍然可以得出一个有坚实实证基础的特征集群,该特征集群赋予了巴尔干空间不可替代的、迷人的、间或可怕的面貌。

最后还要再强调一次:历史区域不会永恒存在。这些区域是漫长历史波浪和其感知的结果。像所有历史对象一样,也遭受变迁。巴尔干空间也在几个世纪中发生了深远的改变。拜占庭模式被修改、补充、覆盖、削弱。这一过程的后拜占庭结果也与西方模式阶段推移的(phasenverschobene)重复和适应不同。转变发展得很慢。偶尔的加速和行动阶段过后,是停顿和倒退阶段。即使在政治史大事件发生以后——在革命、完全崩溃或卡里斯马型①的动员之后——新的开端也仍会被历史遗产——不论有无意识,愿或不愿,以这种或那种形式——赶上,并受其塑造。

最后同样重要的是,并非所有负面的巴尔干形象仅因其负面性就都是错误的。玛莉亚·托多洛娃在其材料丰富、富有启发性和挑衅性的研究结尾处就当时的南斯拉夫战事写道:"如果可以不再把南斯拉夫(不是巴尔干地区的)危机描述成巴尔干幽灵(Balkangeistern)、旧巴尔干敌对关系、有因果关系的(ursächlich)巴尔干文化模式和众所周知的巴尔干化,而是按照西方用在自己身上的合理标准的话,情况就会好很多。西方自己专用的标准包括:自决问题还是不可侵犯的现状问题,公民权和少数群体权利,种族和宗教自治问题,独立的可能性和局限性,大民族、国家和小民族、国家之间的平衡,国际机构的角色。"这些句子反映出托多洛娃的美好愿望。她提出的要求意味着,除了外部观察者外,当地行动者也尤其要做好理性行动和辩论的准备。理性的标准是有逻辑的、可预见的。这些标准不是"命运般的",也不是"整体的",而是可讨论、可协商的。南斯拉夫冲突各方的辩论模式显示了另一种品质:这些辩论模式充满了神话以及末世论那种非黑即白的立场——要不全盘接受,要不彻底否定,这些立场毫无商量的余地,毕竟你没法在(所谓的)是与否、生与死的问题上与人讨价还价。把敌人从特定的区域驱逐,摧毁一切会让人想到以前的东西,还要肃清现在和过去并改变历史,这些愿望几乎不可能与托多洛娃的标准取得一致。这种理性与感性、理智与激情的灾难性混合体也存在于欧洲的

---

① 即个人魅力型。——译者注

其他地方。然而在巴尔干空间，许多因素汇集在一起——复杂的种族起源、种族冲突局势、"历史权利"的引证、种族国家基础之上的国家及民族建立、公民社会不可避免的弱点、"神话的浩劫"和"不愿流逝的过去"，这些因素的组合在一起，形成了一个解不开的线团，使得理性解决变得困难，同时这些因素也被部分政治及文化精英用来动员和操纵民众。

　　巴尔干形象是一个由多重形象组合而成的综合体，这些形象在当地被创造出来，用于当地居民相互间进行争执、诽谤和诋毁。"东方主义"在欧洲的任何地方都不像在巴尔干空间那样活跃。具有代表性的是身兼作家、学者身份的塞尔维亚临时总相弗拉丹·乔尔杰维奇（1844—1930）于1913年出版的小册子。其中谈到"真正的"阿尔巴尼亚人："阿尔巴尼亚人又瘦又小，他们有吉卜赛人和腓尼基人的特点。阿尔巴尼亚人不仅让人想到腓尼基人，还让人想起那些把尾巴缠在树上睡觉的原始人……"乔尔杰维奇的"阿尔巴尼亚人想象"并非作家的闹剧，而是阻碍阿尔巴尼亚国家建立的檄文。文章的措辞让人想起那些在20世纪80年代末米洛舍维奇（Slobodan Milošević）在塞尔维亚组织的"会议"上出现的口号（关于"怪胎""非人"等）。这些也是"巴尔干人想象"的一部分；这些也是真实世界的一部分，这个世界不是被"西方"观察者，而主要是由那些当地的亲历者建构出来的。

作为研究范畴的"巴尔干":
界线、空间、时间[*]

[保加利亚] 玛莉亚·托多洛娃 著　王冰钰 译

内容提要　本文以巴尔干为例,考察意境地图的研究范畴——界线、空间和时间,以历史遗产、"平凡化"等构想来回应尊德豪森在《作为历史空间的欧洲巴尔干》一文中的探讨和争论。
关　键　词　巴尔干　意境地图　界线　空间　时间
作者简介　玛莉亚·托多洛娃,美国伊利诺伊大学历史系教授
译者简介　王冰钰,首都师范大学外国语学院德语系研究生

本文首先旨在进一步考察对意境地图（Mental Maps）起决定性作用的研究范畴。论述时以巴尔干半岛为例,有意将相关观点和带有批评色彩的评论以一种较为尖锐的形式呈现出来,以便引发进一步的讨论。意境地图泛指对人的印象的形塑,也有作者使用"提纲"（Skripte）、"框架"（frames）或"模式"（Schemata）等指称。意境地图这一构想阐明了一种"主动创造性",这是人类试图赋予世界秩序和意义的核心要素。

即使地理工作者和制图员也将他们的工作理解为一种"测量世界"的方法,"但（这些工作）不只是测量,而是将测量塑造成可以跨越人、时间、空间交流的方法。""制图没有受限于数学的维度,它也可以是一种精神的、政治

---

[*]　本文发表于 2002 年德国第三季度的《历史与社会》（Maria Todorova, Jurgen Scheunemann and Stephanie Warnke, "Der Balkan als Analysekategorie: Grenzen, Raum, Zeit," *Geschichte und Gesellschaft*, 28 Jahrg., H. 3, Mental Maps, Jul.-Sep., 2002, pp. 470-492）译文省略大部分注释。

的或者道德的方法。"①

如前文所述，感知某种东西不仅意味着吸收和接纳成熟的外部印象，更确切地说，我们的印象从一开始就被建构了——这已是共识。我们把我们接触到的信息模式化，这种模式是我们自己在感知过程中引入的。海登·怀特（Hayden White）称之为"有计划的、对事实进行安排和整理的仪器"，"隐含的塑造手段"。这同样适用于下一级，在这一级我们将自己的感知作为认识和知识表达出来，这种认识就会被其他的接收者吸收，并按照他们自己的精神体系来整理。因此在研究意境地图的时候，对于其内涵和产生、接受意境地图的大脑，人们应给予同样的关注。

一、西方意境地图中的"巴尔干主义"（Balkanismus）

在《想象巴尔干》中，笔者论证了文中称其为"巴尔干主义"的一种特有的话语，这种话语塑造了人们对巴尔干的看法与意图。巴尔干主义可以被看作是顽固的"框架"或者意境地图的一种，有关巴尔干的信息在其中被加工和表现出来，它首先出现在传媒、政治和文学领域。在这里被称为巴尔干主义的事物，逐步产生于巴尔干被发现和臆想的18、19世纪。确切的感知模式形成于巴尔干战争和一战时期针对巴尔干特有的话语和意境地图中，在之后的几十年里，又加入了一些新的、本来不太重要的元素。泛泛的巴尔干主义一直处于推广和传播的过程中，并经历了詹姆斯·克利福德（James Clifford）称其为"话语上的硬化"（diskursive Verhärtung）的阶段。

笔者继而论证了巴尔干主义与东方主义（Orientalismus）的区别。后者描述了一种主观臆想的对立：东方和西方是作为无法兼容的两种体系出现的，是两个彼此对立、互相封闭的世界，而前者则包含着一种歧义性。所以巴尔干一直是一种桥梁或者交叉点的形象，位于东西方之间，位于不同的发展阶段之间。这种形象引起了"半发达""半殖民""半文明"或"半东方"等诸如此类的人们对巴尔干过时的想象。巴尔干作为东西方的桥梁这一理念以及它作为

---

① 对此有一种极具启发性的情况，在过去的十多年中，地理工作者一直在逐渐摆脱仅仅从事对地理事实的物质性研究工作，而在逐渐靠近历史事实的非物质性。与此同时，他们还在反抗历史（作为一种关于时间关系的科学）与地理（作为一种关于空间关系的科学）原则之间的严格边界。

"基督教堡垒"（antemurale christianitatis）的形象，这些令人印象最为深刻的语言表述，可理解为欧洲的一种特殊的（sui generis）意境地图。意境地图在不同的时期，会从某一个欧洲地区、民族或国家转移到下一个地方，比如：匈牙利、奥地利、德国、波兰、罗马尼亚、克罗地亚、希腊、塞尔维亚、保加利亚、俄罗斯、巴尔干半岛、斯拉夫地区、中欧地区、东正教地区。"中间性"作为巴尔干地区一种暂时的属性，可能会让其成为不完全的他者。与此相对的是东方，东方被理解为完全的他者。但是巴尔干地区被构想成一个独立却不完整的个体，原因有两个：宗教和"种族"（Rasse）。

尽管天主教和东正教之间存在着历史悠久的强烈的敌意，但基督教（包括从其中分裂出来的东正教）和伊斯兰教之间的障碍和阻隔也被认为是无法逾越的。在针对巴尔干地区的具体研究中，人们猛然发现了两种西方观点奇特的传播过程：一种观点是关于宗教的，一种是关于阶级的。人们对待伊斯兰教的态度从拒绝逐步变成了进步性地接受，不过伊斯兰教还是被明确地看作是异类，与此同时，人们对奥斯曼帝国的态度却是二元的。这就引起一种特殊的阶级巩固，尤其是与穆斯林的、奥斯曼的统治者之间的结合，因为他们构成了贫穷粗俗的上升阶层的对立面——即便后者是基督教徒。描述这种情况的话语和描述西方世界下层社会的话语几乎是一致的，所以在伦敦东区和欧洲"东区"（East End）之间产生了一种相似的情况。不过鉴于东欧剧变的背景之下英国的没落和美国的崛起，以纽约曼哈顿下东区作类比似乎更加合适，那里有贫穷、有知识，也有活跃的潜力。

种族问题需要更为复杂的研究。

一方面，存在着许多关于巴尔干"混血"（Promenadenmischung）居民的思想观念。巴尔干地区复杂的族裔组成被看作是半岛不稳定和冲突的原因，还被描述成"多样性的弊端"。但往往被忽略的是，引发族裔争端的本质原因并不是族裔多样性［族裔（ethnisch）是一个常常与种族（rassisch）混用的概念］。毕竟只有在理想状态下的一个以族群同一性为目的的单一民族国家里，才有可能爆发族裔冲突。

另一方面，人们一直把巴尔干地区划归给西方世界，尽管存在族群的模糊性及森严的内部等级：白人对有色人种，印欧语系族群对其他族群。这也解释了为何人们在前南斯拉夫战争的研究中倾注了大量精力，尽管同时期在世界的其他地方还存在着更严峻、更血腥的冲突。如同关于污名化的社会学研究中体现的那样，"差异是类型化过程的核心，简而言之，差异就是类别之间或者之内的变体"。于是，论点可以这样表达：东方主义区分了两种人们构想出来的类型，而巴尔干主义则强调其中一种类型内部的差异。

巴尔干已然不能在地理上摆脱欧洲，可是在文化上却被视作"他者"，因此，巴尔干吸收了其他地区和社会政治上的、思想上的和文化上的敌对情绪。随着时间的推移，巴尔干主义逐渐替代东方主义，为西方减轻了情绪上的罪责感（emotionale Entlastung），将西方从对种族主义、殖民主义、欧洲中心主义和基督教对伊斯兰教的不容忍的指责中转移出来。毕竟巴尔干还是欧洲的一部分，那里的居民也大多是白人和基督徒，因此，投射到他们身上的失望就可以避免被当作种族和宗教上的偏见并成为众矢之的。和东方一样，巴尔干也充当了负面特征的"储藏室"，这对欧洲和"西方"自我满足的积极形象的形成是十分必要的。随着作为独立语义价值的东方和东方主义再次出现，巴尔干仍然是欧洲最受压制的、反文明的"黑暗面"。以电影来类比的话，巴尔干就是埃米尔·库斯图里卡（Emir Kusturica）的《地下》（*Underground*），那里有着无休止的战争。

巴尔干主义作为从一战以来就被利用的概念，在接下来的几十年中，并没有持续地出现，仍然只是在特定的政治性的重要时刻、由不同的重要人物引发（比如在二战时期，或作为60年代反殖民冲突的比照）。直到1989年，巴尔干主义这个概念才开始被大量使用，并在修辞层面衍生出了两个平行的发展方向：其一，有关曾经的中东欧社会主义国家，他们成功地与巴尔干保持距离；其二，能言善辩的政治家把南斯拉夫内战夸大为"巴尔干战争"，并为大众所熟知。

在《想象巴尔干》中，我之所以有意识地没有指责学术，原因之一是，这涉及一个尚未深入研究的复杂命题，如此也能避免陷入诸如"在巴尔干主义中，学术话语是否存在以及在多大程度上存在"这类泛泛而谈的危险。此处无需再次引述萨义德（Said）的观点，也就是东方主义（或者是这里的巴尔干主义）的话语拥有一种包罗万象而又无处不在的特质。我的出发点不如说是，科学知识的诞生极少伴随着大众神话的诞生。不过不排除有许多从事巴尔干研究的科学家，在私下里怀有令人担忧的成见，学术讨论的规则迫使他们有所保留。如同"是什么"和"怎么样"这两个问题在科学阐述领域一样，这些规则毫无疑问是重要的。

将"什么是巴尔干？"这个问题与德里达的论断——"文本之外，无物存在"（Il n'y a pas de hors-texte）——连接在一起而产生的讽刺性改写——"本文之外是什么？"（Qu'est-ce qu'il y a hors du texte?）——没有什么严肃的意义。巴尔干主义的哲学推论让人想起柏拉图式的理想主义，想起一种信念，相信天生的思想可以赋予头脑能力，来完全地反映外部现实。与之相反，后现代主义以一种讽刺的方式让人们想起英国经验主义（Englischer Empirismus）的假设——尽管这是从一个完全不同的角度出发——我们完全无法获知我们的意识感知范围之外的事物。这种观点隐含着对认识的否认。在《想象巴尔干》中提及的"巴尔干本体论"（Balkan-Ontologie）并没有要求，世界"本身"和在这里被描绘的世界取得一致。一些人在评论、信件或者注释里赞扬道，我的阐述成功地超越了萨义德的文本性（Textualität），不过其中一些人认为，在我对巴尔干存在主义的重建中接受了这样一种一致。事实并非如此，我只是提出了另一种科学研究惯例中的意境地图，在我看来，这种意境地图更适合架构认识。

"边界"（Grenzen）长期以来都是热门的研究课题，尤其在有关同一性和其"定位"的研究中。边界是一种适宜的研究进路，因为在这里，在边界处，可以展开对实体的区分和辨析。因为同一性和可变性有共生的关系，它们最准确的定义和特性在界线上是清晰可见的。后来"区别"（Differenz）变成了一个社会经验和社会研究的基本类目，并在过去的几十年里对历史研究产生了巨大影响。"界线"当然也是首要的困难选择，不仅因为它会不断变化并随着政治、社会和文化标准的变化而变化。更重要的是，对边界的过度关注会过分强调"分殊"（Unterscheidung）和"差异"（Differenz）这样的主题。

最近有这样一种明确的趋势：关注度逐渐从边界研究转向了空间这一类别，这是一个全新的或者说是重新流行的研究方向。这种研究意向对系统内部闭合的过程和结构给予了必要的关注。它一方面带来了有价值的研究成果，另一方面也引来了一些问题。其中最重大的一个当推本质主义（Essentialismus）。本质主义和理论关系不大，地理学家已对理论做过透彻的思考和修正。他们强调知识、权力和空间之间的关系并同时指出了"空间"在隐喻和物质上的意义。这种新的本质主义的出现，某种程度上归咎于人们在具体的历史研究中，往往过于仓促、不加反思地使用"空间"这一范畴。①

相反，我一直主张"历史遗产"（historische Erbe）的构想。依我看，没有

---

① 这里有一篇有关保加利亚历史编纂学的有趣文章，以此为例。作者通过采用"空间"这个研究类别并不加批判地与未研究过的"保加利亚人"类别连接起来，将研究工作不由自主地理解为一种新的科学语言外表下的统计学和民族主义的要求。

把它替换成空间计划,而是让它保留了空间分析中有价值的元素,同时也融入了时间因素并从历史的角度详细说明。最终,如同一部有关冷战的著名戏剧——《林中漫步》(A Walk in the Woods) 所说的,"历史只是延展到时间上的地理学"。倘若人们只将注意力放到时间元素的对等关系上,那么该如何回答一个让人误认为简单的问题呢:"巴尔干是什么?"

欧洲东南部曾广泛地影响整个欧洲,比如古希腊罗马时期、古希腊文化、古罗马政权等。纵观不同的历史传统,其中有两种起到了决定性的作用:其一是拜占庭时期根本的政治、习俗、法律、宗教和大众文化的影响,其二是持续半个千年的奥斯曼政权。它们的名称来源于地名,建构了它们曾经历过的最长时间的政治统一。在这个时期欧洲东南部接受了一个新名字,其中包含奥斯曼元素或者人们所以为的奥斯曼元素。这也是引起现今对巴尔干的定式思维最强的因素。在这一点上,不夸张地说,巴尔干事实上就是奥斯曼帝国的历史遗产。

究竟将奥斯曼的历史遗产当作一种连续性还是一种感知,这一点对《想象巴尔干》的论述十分重要。① 前一方案,即视历史遗产为一种连续性,有别于一般意义上的奥斯曼体系或者奥斯曼时期的特性。它是一个过程,当奥斯曼帝国在特定地区不复存在、继而在这些地区有新的国家形成时,这一过程便启动了。从根本上说,这种方案涵盖了所有形成于18和19世纪并自此流传下去的特质。倘若对奥斯曼历史遗产在政治、文化、社会和经济领域不同程度的影响进行研究,则不难发现,除了在人口统计学的发展和大众文化方面外,巴尔干各国几乎刚一取得政治独立,奥斯曼历史遗产的影响便出现断裂。随着一战的结束,这种断裂也结束了。之后,奥斯曼的历史遗产也只在感知的层面上继续产生影响了。与之相对的是,奥斯曼的历史遗产还在人口统计学的关键领域持续了较长的一段时间,更重要的是,这种历史遗产之后与土耳其这个单一民族国家混为一体并在其影响之下有所改变。

与此相反,作为感知的奥斯曼历史遗产,指的是过去与几代人的感知之间相互作用的关系。人们重新定义了自己对过去的评价。过去不断地流变、丰富化,人们的感知也处于持续的发展与增长中。用一句话来概括,这不是对过去

---

① 这种特性不应该被当作"真实"和"想象"来理解。"连续性"的特性往往是独立于感知的。或许人们可以更好地定义这种差别,通过指明这两种情况描绘了社会现实但都不同地远离了经验。"感知"是社会现实,但又离直接的现实远了那么一点,人们或许可以将社会中相互作用的状况与文化或文本上的状况相比较。

的重建，而是对过去的建构。被看作感知的历史遗产拥有在巴尔干民族主义话语中的牢固地位，同时也是最重要的政治支柱之一，它指出了所有巴尔干国家明确的相似之处。恰恰是因为这些历史遗产对于如今社会秩序的稳定十分重要，尤其是使这些国家具有了合法性，所以未来人们必然会复制这种历史遗产。①

在过去的一个世纪中，作为感知的奥斯曼历史遗产渐渐衰落。那些被定义为"巴尔干"的国家，也就是之前处于奥斯曼帝国领土内的国家，一直在不断地远离这种历史遗产和"巴尔干主义"。在这样的背景下，今天的我们就是历史的见证者，见证着族群的多样性和共存这一帝国的历史遗产是如何在巴尔干半岛上逐渐消失殆尽的，又是如何被制度化的族群一致性的系统所取代的。这可能是此地区欧洲化进程的最后一个阶段，也意味着历史中的"奥斯曼的"巴尔干的终结。1913年，一位英国外交官在给卡耐基基金会的报告中写道："人们可以大胆地断言，在亚洲和拜占庭对巴尔干几百年的压迫之后，欧洲文化仅存的基础和欧洲文明仅有的那么一点倾向就是民族主义的意识。"他还写道："在巴尔干，不论是在何时何地，民族意识觉醒的时候，文明就有了起源；又因为这种意识产生的最佳路径可能就是战争，所以战争是巴尔干取得和平的唯一途径。"这篇报告是在一战爆发数月前写就的，如今看来确是一种赤裸裸的讽刺。当时的巴尔干民族主义被看作是唯一的"欧洲"元素，不过后来人们认识到，巴尔干民族主义与西方市民的所谓文明化的民族主义有着内在的差异。

几十年后，西方轻易地就忘记了他们肃清族群、宗教和政治的传统，这其中有一些肃清的"顶点"，比如西班牙的收复失地运动（Reconquista）、宗教战争和两次世界大战。现在，以这种方式被"清洗"过的西方，也可以为这种事态的发展道歉，他们已经开始借助全球性的传媒运动来进行政治性道歉。西方想要建造族群多样性的"民族博物馆"（Volksmuseen）——不过是在自己的边界之外。他们甚至准备放弃自己对民族主义的"著作权"。帕尔塔·查特杰（Partha Chatterjee）如此说道："民族主义如今被看作是一种本性上黑暗、原始、不可预见的力量。这种力量威胁到了文明生活中有秩序的平和。从前看上

---

① 为了实际的目的，我在《想象巴尔干》中运用了所有必要的评定手段，将以下这些国家划入"巴尔干半岛"的范畴：希腊、阿尔巴尼亚、保加利亚、罗马尼亚，除斯洛文尼亚之外的所有前南斯拉夫国家，以及土耳其的部分地区。不过今天我想把斯洛文尼亚也划分进去，因为没有整个南斯拉夫地区的20世纪巴尔干历史是没有意义的。需要强调的是，这完全不是按照一个纯粹的地理标准或者随意的历史或文化标准来划定的。

去被排挤到世界外缘的东西，现在想要穿过哈布斯堡、沙皇和奥斯曼的帝国中被遗忘的地区，寻找自己返回欧洲的路。它就像是第三世界的副产品，如同毒品、恐怖主义和非法移民一样引起了西方的不满，但也无法被阻止。"

尽管奥斯曼的历史遗产很重要，但要否认最新的——哪怕是时间最短的遗产，而且否认恰恰出自那些坚持维系先前帝国传统的人，也颇成问题。① 我指的当然是社会主义和共产主义的遗产。我想公开表达一种观点，在东欧寻找社会主义遗产是荒谬的，"东欧"这个词本身就是社会主义的历史遗产。不论是谁，在1989年亲身经历过东欧剧变应该都会赞同。只有当人们把东欧理解为欧洲共产主义，也就是华沙条约的政治同义词的时候，这种想法才有意义：有无数个关于希腊和土耳其的笑话流传着，有关他们是否归属西欧，以及，如果乔治·马歇（Georges Marchais）和恩里科·贝林格（Enrico Berlinguer）分别赢得了法国和意大利的大选，② 那么东西方的地缘政治差异将会发生怎样的变动。共产主义实验所开展的地理空间，正是"东欧"一词曾清晰指涉的对象。

当时，社会主义时代在继续多层次地延展。不过在1989—1990年前后，这个时代结束了，它也变成了历史遗产。我此前对奥斯曼时代和其历史遗产的讨论也可以应用在共产主义的遗产上。在将传统看作连续性的这个范畴，人们可以观察不同领域中社会主义历史遗产的运行模式，比如政治、经济、社会和思维模式等领域，它们在后共产主义国家还都十分明显地相似。不论我们喜欢与否，对于绝大多数"转型研究者"来说，东欧就是最优先的、理所当然的研究起点。社会主义传统在各个领域和国家的保留程度不尽相同，不过就像所有的传统一样，它们都将不复存在，之后就会转移到感知领域。

社会主义的历史遗产是一系列传统的最后一个，就像之前解释过的一样，在上世纪80年代末90年代初共产主义时代走向终结的时候，社会主义也就变成了一种历史遗产。这种传统本身也是一种较大规模的现象的次类别，就像有些人可能会论证的那样，它已经变成了历史遗产，不过另外一些人却把它看作

---

① 这种所谓的哈布斯堡怀旧风（Habsnurg-Nostalgie）大部分都出现在中东欧的科学和文化产业中。首先出现在匈牙利，在捷克和波兰就没那么明显。有趣的是，相应的涉及奥斯曼传统的怀旧风却让人难以看出。诚然这与哈布斯堡人或奥斯曼人的内在特性关系不大，当然和他们一个是基督教帝国，另一个是穆斯林帝国更没关系。更多的是因为奥地利还有德国在二战之后获得了巨大成功，如果人们牵扯其他记忆和评价的情况没有发生的话，如果人们没有更强调差异并让反德的雄辩术再次流行的话。

② 乔治·马歇，法国共产党总书记（1972—1994）。恩里科·贝林格，意大利共产党总书记（1969—1984）。——译者注

是一个仍在持续的过程。当然，我在这里所指的是，按照专业术语应该描述为"资本主义的世界体系"（伊曼纽尔·沃勒斯坦）、"资本主义的生产方式"（马克思）或者现代社会的"铁笼"（马克斯·韦伯）。在齐格蒙特·鲍曼（Zygmunt Bauman）看来，现代社会带着其对启蒙的宣告——资本主义和社会主义"永远联系在一起"——正将自身发展为一种传统，因为我们现在正站在十字路口，面对着一条"难以描述"的路。

从以上论述中可以得出的最重要的结论是，历史遗产不会永远存续，就算继续存在，也可能已经完全改变了最初的形态。基于"历史遗产"这个研究范畴的同时性、学科交叉的特点，且其影响力不断减弱，因此我们才有可能强调历史进程的可塑性。在巴尔干地区这一特殊问题上，历史遗产的研究范畴有助于我们对该地区形成丰富细腻的认识，从而避免在时间和空间上将该地区边缘化。假定存在一个固定不变的文明断裂带，并在这一断裂处将巴尔干地区的特点进行本体化，这种假说在历史学家的研究中几无立足之地。在这个基础上就产生了如今的政治辞令，在其中，巴尔干主义以意境地图的形式通过强有力的方式重新出现了。

二、差异悄悄地本体化了？

接续前文的论述，笔者认为以下有必要通过具体的例证，就"巴尔干作为独立空间"这一问题展开讨论。比如，赫姆·尊德豪森刊于《历史与社会》中的一篇文章对《想象巴尔干》一书做出了回应。在许多方面，我都同意他对巴尔干的观点。但在另一些方面，我们产生了分歧，或者说我们的侧重点不同，这也体现了我们在方法或理论上的差异。尊德豪森很显然加入了对"巴尔干主义"的批评，他总体的研究意向是不存在争议的。他将巴尔干确定为一种历史中的空间概念，并尝试阐明其定义。他还谨慎地指出，对历史空间的建构只是其中一种研究进路，有利于知识的积累。空间是必须要重新研究和修改的方案：这一点我完全认同。事实上我很惊讶，他会这样反问道："巴尔干只是一个'欧洲人'和'西方'为了神化自己而创造出来的充满偏见的虚构吗？还是说，除人们固有印象之外，巴尔干具有其他特征，可以让人们将其理解为一个独特的地区？"我书中的最后一章，特别研究了巴尔干是如何在奥斯曼历史遗产的影响下被重新构建为一个历史空间的。尊德豪森在自己的文章中没有评论这一章。简而言之，我不认为巴尔干是一种虚构，更没有把它看作是一种杜撰。① 尽管我接受尊德豪森文章中谨慎而又明确的问题意识，但我认为问题意识的展开方式值得商榷。

赫姆·尊德豪森提出了八种对地区起决定性作用的因素或者特征。第一个是"民族与民族间关系不稳定、狭小空间内族群混居带来的不稳定"。与西欧相反，巴尔干半岛人民之间的关系好像从未巩固过。原则上，我对这个论断没有什么好反对的。我自己也认为，恰恰在人口统计学方面，帝国的特征得到了最长久的体现。从奥斯曼帝国解体直到今天，在巴尔干有过四次重要的"清洗浪潮"——在这一点上，我与尊德豪森的看法一致。不过在他看来，清洗浪潮是巴尔干有别于西方的特点。而我认为，欧洲最大规模的一次人口迁移是二战的直接后果，并没有发生在巴尔干半岛上。我要批评这第一种特点的表达。不谈两个特定空间中人口发展的矛盾性，即西方的稳定性和巴尔干的不稳定性，人们或许还可以这样表达：至少从15世纪开始，巩固欧洲国家王朝、宗教、族群同一化的进程就已经开始了。更直接地说，人们可以把这个进程称作族群和宗教清洗。民族国家的建立及巩固是一个动态的进程，这个进程已在欧洲持续数百年并且至今还未停止。从地理和时间的角度来看，这个进程始于西欧，之后逐步向北部、中部、南部和东部扩散，最后来到东南部也就是巴尔干地区。我们称为西方的稳定性的东西，在某种程度上也可以定义为这种进程较早达成的、矛盾的结果。

笔者提出这一建议，并非出于满足政治正确的要求，而是因为此乃研究方法的要义所在。如果说，第一种说法的出发点是，有两种在地理和历史上不同的空间存在，那么第二种说法则是将巴尔干置于一个更大的、共同的、长久的进程中进行考察。后者将巴尔干重新定义为一个自我发展的共同空间（欧洲或全球）的一部分。这个空间的一大特点是政治单位的同一化，确切地说，是其在想象中的同一化。这也就导致了对"西方"概念的解构：从一个静止的模型到一个动态的元素，以不均匀的方式长时间地经受这一历程。

我完全明白，这里可能会有方法论上的反对意见：提到这个从15世纪持续到20世纪的进程的时候，人们可能会指责我认定了一种决定论的

---

① 这不意味着把巴尔干当作是杜撰就不是一个有价值的主题了，比如维斯娜·古兹沃斯（V. Goldsworthy）在自己的书《创造鲁里坦尼亚：想象的帝国主义》（*Inventing Ruritania: The Imperialism of the Imagination*）中就把巴尔干看作是杜撰。我个人对产生感知的地点很感兴趣，不过要在感知完全脱离感知对象并变成观念（Vorstellung）的玩物之前。

(deterministisch)、目的—进化论（teleologisch-evolutionär）的发展，这种发展在"被清洗过的"民族国家的形成过程中达到顶点。人们当然不能预设，后起者不过是迟到了，他们能理解先行者在理想的实验顺序中积累起来的经验。此外，20世纪末和15世纪末是不同的，因为先行者是当今人类经济上、政治上最成功的一部分人。他们的行为在数百年尚能被人们接受，在今天则不可能。想要反驳这一观点，有两种可能。

驳论之一针对以下问题：把如此长期的发展阶段总结到一个概念里，到底合不合适？在工业化问题上，我们都面临相似的挑战。因为几个世纪内，工业化在整个欧洲进行着，甚至在工业化的核心区域——英国持续了好几个世纪，直到国家的不同地区和所有行业都完成了工业化才完全结束，也就是从18世纪到19世纪末——也有观点指出，是从16世纪到19世纪。当然工业化进程的运作体制，以及各地区和时期的社会支出是不同的，先行者和后起者都会遇到同样的问题，但没人追问过，把所有这些复杂情况纳入一个普遍进程的框架中进行考察，从认识论的角度而言是否合宜？简而言之，广泛的和长期有效的范畴一直都包含本质论、目的论和决定论的危险。人们可以通过对特定地区、特定时间的细致研究来避免这种问题。但是，作为研究者，我们有义务给予读者最低限度的一致性。要么我们将这一范畴（及其量化手段）用于对巴尔干或对其他正在经历类似进程的地区的研究中；要么我们完全摒弃这种范畴，无可避免地引发唯我论（Solipsismus）并落入认识论的虚无之中。

驳论之二针对决定论的指责以及行动问题（Handlungsproblem）。对此存在一种隐含的观点，如果说巴尔干的民族国家建立和族群同一化是注定的，那么是否就没有别的可能性了？鉴于这个理论的说法，我并不支持这种还原式的决定论，我更推崇的是研究各个历史节点的可能性的发展。就实际情况而言，很多因素都足以让人们认为，处于等级序列中的小国家和民族，其行动空间极为有限。想想维也纳会议后的君主立宪时期，人们关于霸权的争论及其在政治实践中的运用；想想自此之后，人们往往视帝国为反常，视民族国家的建立为常态；再想想如今的"自由市场的民主"，这件"束身衣"被国际货币基金组织、世界银行和领先的经济强权所推崇，且没有其他的选择。一个更难、更严肃的问题是：我们是否在强调这些小国家、小民族行动空间受限的同时，忽略了他们应承担的责任？有关这一点，后文有详述。

在尊德豪森所主张的观点中，还有两个与巴尔干空间的基本特点有紧密联系：一个是第六个特点，即民族国家及民族的建立；另一个是第八个特点，即巴尔干作为强权的猎物。最后这个特点本来间接地触及了我在前文强调的点，但它关注的主要是心理学层面的后果，因它强调政客和学者的受害者心态（Opfermentalität）。不过我不愿用"过于片面的"来描述这一特点。在尊德豪森看来，巴尔干地区民族国家的形成并非以建立新秩序为目标，而是为了恢复前奥斯曼时期的状态——对此，我找不到什么实证的根据。希腊民族运动的景象出人意料地共和、民主，19世纪60年代和70年代的保加利亚民族运动以及罗马尼亚统一运动也是如此。类似地，土耳其为了建立共和国而进行的民族独立运动也积极献身于现代化，即使他们对民主并不十分感兴趣。尊德豪森推断，1804年的塞尔维亚大起义成为了星星之火，之后逐渐扩展到整个巴尔干半岛。我觉得在这一节较大的问题依然存在，那就是把欧洲空间机械性地划分为两个各有特点的形成空间：一是以带来了现代的原则和自决为标志的西欧空间，二是以被迫创造了历史神话为特点的巴尔干空间。这种二分法把问题简化了，不仅没有考虑到西欧对建国神话的大量研究和生产、对民族形成的研究以及历史—文学的虚构等因素，而且也忽略了那些新巴尔干国家为获得历史的合法性不得不做的努力，恰恰回应着西欧的这样一种焦虑：将"历史的"民族和"非历史的"民族的生存权区别开来。尊德豪森说过"采纳自西欧的现代原则"，显然他拥有一种普遍的、常规的看法：像是启蒙运动、民族独立和独立人权这样的思想自然都是来自西方的，然后在东方这块陌生的土地上生根发芽。其实这些思想可能也是逐渐以不均衡的步伐在西方逐渐落地生根的。接受这些想法的农民不只逐渐转变为希腊人、塞尔维亚人或者保加利亚人，也转变为了法国人，正如尤金·韦伯（Eugene Weber）说明的那样。

这种二分法影响最大的是拜占庭东正教遗产（第三个特点）。这本来是我最初想在我的书中处理的问题，但是我读这方面的内容越多，我越确信，"拜占庭主义"（Byzantinismus）这个主题值得拿来单独研究。① 19世纪的时候曾有过一系列努力，想要挖掘拜占庭文明的核心，可是如同一些类似的尝试，困难依旧重重。黑格尔对拜占庭历史有一段很普及的精准表述："拜占庭的历史是一系列持续千年的犯罪、衰弱、卑劣、丧失气节的行为。"反之，其他人则关注一些关键特征，首当其冲的就是教会和国家之间的关系。"政教合一"

---

① 许多研究者已经开始这项工作了；接下来的论点基于安格洛夫（D. G. Angelov）未发表的文章《拜占庭主义的形成》(*The Making of Byzantinism*)，展示于1999年2月12—13日在哈佛大学冈茨堡欧洲研究中心（Minda de Gunzburg Center for European Studies）举办的 Sokrates Kokkalis 博士生工作坊，主题为"通往东南欧的新途径"（New Approaches to Southeast Europe）。

特别专栏：关于"巴尔干"的一场争论

（Caesaropapismus）是由信仰新教的一位来自哈勒的教授于18世纪在一场反对教皇和拜占庭的论战中提出的，19世纪的时候成为理论性的纲领，这就完全足够解释东西方之间的差异。在拜占庭人发表了可以让中世纪学学者接受的、令人信服的反驳之时，类似"政教合一""拜占庭式独裁"和"停滞的社会关系"等刻板印象在其他科学和教科书中广泛流传，流行的文献和著作却对这点避而不谈。尊德豪森的分析恰恰反映出了这一趋势。这也解释了，为何在对比巴尔干和西方对待古希腊罗马遗产的方式时，尊德豪森不能得出深刻的见解（第二个特点）。此处不能涉及更多细节，但是我想说明，我认为，把一个持续千年的、多方面的、动态的时期缩小成一个模式，实在是太机械了。（他用一种新柏拉图式的世界观称之为"拜占庭模式"，与来自亚里士多德传统的西方模式不同。）我不禁自问：这些特征对于研究今天的世俗化社会（其中有些在很大程度上属于非宗教性质）是否能带来启发。

现在我们谈谈精神气质和神话（第七个特点）。我们不难接受这样一种普遍的预设：精神气质是一个充满争议的范畴；"这个"巴尔干的"这种"精神气质——人们不可能就这种独一性达成共识。倘若有，那么也只能用于特定的时期和特定的群体。且即便如此，为何在诸多特征中，单单抽取精神气质作为研究范畴，这一点仍旧存疑。显然尊德豪森相信，巴尔干独有的精神气质是存在的，尽管它被描述成对神话的偏爱。神话中包含前奥斯曼"黄金"时期，土耳其的压迫，淳朴自然的民族，民族的重生，科索沃，海杜克（Haiduk）以及受害者的神话。把这些神话系统地区分开对我来说实在太难了。比如，古希腊罗马的"黄金"神话、中世纪的神话、30年代的纽伦堡法案的神话及其实践和血统论（ius sanguinis）；比如，民族意识形态中的罗马、罗马共和国和教皇统治的神话；又比如法国普瓦捷（Poitiers）战役（8世纪和14世纪）、女武神（Walküre）之战以及一战前和战时被敌人封锁的德意志帝国的神话，都很难区分。强调巴尔干神话过度的作用一般又是基于如今南斯拉夫的异常形势——之前还在进行内战，现在已经分裂了。

对奥斯曼伊斯兰遗产（第四个特点）进行的短暂考察由一种奇特的联系组成，一个是对持续500年的奥斯曼政权的百科全书式概览，一个是对巴尔干特色家庭形式中延续更久的古老模式的详细介绍。这个特点的分析的结构给人造成这样一种印象：后者是奥斯曼时期和巴尔干空间最重要、最有意义的历史遗产——即使在括号中已经做出限定，这种形式仅存在于19世纪和20世纪部分时期的北阿尔巴尼亚、黑山共和国和黑塞哥维那部分地区。既然在19世纪，这种形式无论在地理上还是统计上都没能占主导地位——更遑论在今天，那么我们不得不问：为何作者在对巴尔干的概述中，独独在这一特征上花费笔墨；显然，因为他们下意识地被看作是对巴尔干独特生活方式的解释：它有父权制的传统、威望很高的长者和对英雄主义的向往，因而被看作是真正的"战士和牧人的瓦尔哈拉神殿"。对此，我曾在我之前有关历史人口统计学的著作中详细地研究过。

与奥斯曼历史遗产息息相关的是巴尔干空间的最后一个特点：现代"落后"的社会和经济（第五个特点）。一方面，作者认为，拜占庭东正教和奥斯曼的传统在巴尔干不一致的发展进程，使得此区域继续与西欧隔绝。另一方面，他否定了自己之前的看法，对一种说法表示怀疑：是否奥斯曼时期要为此地区社会经济的停滞和倒退负主要责任。毫无疑问，巴尔干地区在过去的几个世纪一直在奋力追赶西方。但既然如此，为何作者仍然把这一点当作巴尔干地区独特的、本质的特征，认为在与资本主义中心的关系问题上，这一点将巴尔干与其他（半）边缘地带区别开来了呢？赫姆·尊德豪森非常明确地意识到了这个问题，他说，这些特点中有许多并不是巴尔干独有的。巴尔干独有的是这种特征集群，明确地体现了其鲜明的特点。在这一点上，我完全同意他的看法，历史中的地区不是永恒的，漫长的历史浪潮和其感知的结果才是永恒的。不过在这一点，我们又有一些分歧。他认为，"拜占庭模式"和"西方模式"好像都是在这种历史浪潮中诞生的，并非出自思想上分门别类的建构——那种关于一分为二的文明的意境地图，正是基于这种建构。

在尊德豪森文章的结尾，他评论了我的批评——"如果可以不再把南斯拉夫（不是巴尔干地区的）危机描述成巴尔干幽灵、旧巴尔干敌对关系、有因果关系的巴尔干文化模式和众所周知的巴尔干化，而是按照西方用在自己身上的合理标准的话，情况就会好很多。西方自己专用的标准包括：自决问题还是不可侵犯的现状问题，公民权和少数群体权利，种族和宗教自治问题，独立的可能性和局限性，大民族、国家和小民族、国家之间的平衡，国际机构的角色。"显然他认为这是一种空想：不仅是外界的观察者，巴尔干地区的活跃分子也应理性行事。这自然是与战争参与者的极端行径相对的，尊德豪森总结道："把敌人从特定的区域驱逐，摧毁一切会让人想到以前的东西，还要肃清现在和过去并改变些，这愿望几乎不可能与托多洛娃的标准取得一致。这种理性与感性、理智与激情的灾难性混合体也存在于欧洲的其他地方。然而在巴尔干空间，许多因素汇集在一起……形成了一个解不开的线团……"

我觉得这似乎是一种不寻常的对理性的定义。换句话说：只有在假定人类本身就是不理性的情况下，我才可能会赞同这个观点。战争和其委婉的近似物——防卫，都是持续伴随人类出现的现象，它们也是广阔历史中最重要的雇主；即使在今天，它们仍然在现代国家财政预算中占据着巨大的份额。希波的奥古斯丁则支持"正义战争"的想法（令人意外的是，他不是东正教的圣人）。① 文明诞生之初，人类社会中就存在族群清洗。所有敌对的男人都被杀死，女人被奴役——这种基本的行为自古希腊时期就存在，那里也就是"西方文明的摇篮"。不论年龄和性别的无差别的大屠杀首先就是一种现代现象，虽然不是唯一的，西方在这件事上走得最远。或者换句话说，为什么人们可以在谴责希特勒的同时还能够对希特勒现象进行分析并尝试做出解释？比如，探查在严峻的社会和经济危机背景下，一个社会中不同群体针对一种激进的意识形态有哪些不同的反应？为什么在米洛舍维奇（Milosevic）政权这里就不可能？为什么会把非理性当作这个地区的特点？

本文提出这些问题并非为了得出这样一种明显的推论：暴行是可以比较的或者在对西方和巴尔干地区的评论中存在双重标准。后者是我假设的。更应该说清楚的是，理性或者非理性不是研究对象固有的、内在的特质。它们存在于旁观者的眼中，是它们意境地图中的隐藏部分。赫姆·尊德豪森提醒道，"并非所有负面的巴尔干形象仅因其负面性就都是错误的"。我非常赞同。我还想更进一步指出（事实上也的确这样做了）：定式思维——不论正面还是负面的——未必都是错的；它们往往建立在真实可考的特征之上。我想探查的并非这些特征的具体内容，而是它们作为定式思维的身份和作用。也就是说，人们将个体或集体的（即便是真实的）某些特征进行了过度的概括并使其固定下来，而后又把这些特征当作一种工具，用以分析个体和集体的行为。简而言之，要被批判的不是语音（Phonetik），而是句法（Syntax）。

赫姆·尊德豪森在其文章的最后举了一个例子，那就是曾经的塞尔维亚王国首相、作家、科学家——弗拉丹·乔尔杰维奇（Vladan Đorđević）。他在1913年的一部作品中演绎过针对阿尔巴尼亚人的、公开的种族主义攻击。尊德

---

① 圣奥古斯丁的这个学说是在"神权政治"（Der Gottesstaat）中逐渐发展起来的。教皇乌尔班二世在1097年第一次十字军东征前的讲话中运用了这个学说，企图为这场针对异类（比如东正教徒）的战争辩白。这个学说之后也成为了接下来的十字军东征的合法认可，不论是针对穆斯林还是针对东正教徒的战争。与此相对的是，在拜占庭帝国并没有"正义战争"的思想，在这里，战争是统治者的而非教会的特权。

豪森将其与上世纪80年代和90年代在塞尔维亚发生的、米洛舍维奇领导的反阿尔巴尼亚种族主义攻击明确地联系在一起。这是一种历史的方法，说明了塞尔维亚话语的连续性。这是他对意境地图的一种选择。这当然是一种合理的选择，但不是唯一的选择。不过我更愿意把分析的空间拓展到当时欧洲的学术地图上。在19世纪后半叶到20世纪中期这个时期，人们可以把弗拉丹·乔尔杰维奇与戈宾诺（Gobineau）、休斯敦·张伯伦（Houston Chamberlain）、瓦格纳、希特勒归为一类，他们来自欧洲种族主义的其他空间。这使得乔尔杰维奇也没有那么令人反感了。相对而言，从一个适当的角度来看，应当将巴尔干纳入共同的欧洲或全球空间中，而非把它缩减为一种历史的、空间上的延续。①

三、政治结论

这就回到了我在书中提出的观点所带来的政治影响。尽管我谴责过分的巴尔干政客，但是当我选择了一个比较的视角进行论述时，难道不是潜在地否认了政治行为的一次性，不是将恶相对化了吗？不过看起来无害的、对描述方式的选择承载了太多意义。对此，没有人可以控制自己的文章和其应用。我的文章是否会被民族主义者或者巴尔干地区的反对西方者滥用？理论上来说，这种可能性是不能被排除的。事实上，在我的书出版并被翻译成整个半岛的所有语言之后，并没有发生这种情况。可能是因为这个论点过于复杂和过于详细，无法满足宣传者对明确、简单和类似食谱的判断的要求。毕竟这本书不是为民族主义的读者量身打造的。该书首先是面向西方读者，和吸收了西方产生的话语与定式思维的巴尔干地区学者。中心思想是"我们自己有罪，并不是环境有罪"，它承担着一项崇高的要求：与所谓属于巴尔干的消极的特点做斗争，同时摆脱尊德豪森生动描述的对受害者群体的操纵。

我没有隐瞒我的政治目的：我拒绝对巴尔干半岛的隔离（Ghettoisierung）。从我的角度，我只是想尝试发掘，这种隔离背后有怎样一种智识上的支持。同时我也没有幻想，这项研究能立刻带来另一种政策。正如前文所述，对巴尔干

---

① 我想在此强调，当我运用"共同的欧洲空间"这一想法的时候，我没有把欧洲变成不可变更的前提条件。这也不是一种方法论的确定，让人们不得不在政治上转化为融入"共同的欧洲房屋"（戈尔巴乔夫）的愿望。这只是反映了一个事实，从广泛的关系来说，欧洲是自然的历史和地理背景，在其中的一些区域基于这个背景发展成长着。

的隔离既可以采用原始的巴尔干主义的形式，这很容易被揭露，还可以采用客观的学术描述和分析的形式。笔者不揣浅陋，仍想提醒读者诸君：在意识形态和认知上，学术研究永远不可能价值中立。"'描述'意味着，意义更明确地命名一个地点，构建一个知识对象，并产生知识，通过描述性建构的行为相连"。当然就像每一篇文章一样，不论是我的还是尊德豪森的，都会下意识地表现自己的想法和疏忽。但不论我在他的文章里多么仔细地寻找，也很难发现他有类似的意识，很难找到真正暗示出他自己观点的文字。

学术研究得出的结果，在政治层面上往往容易遭遇过度阐释、引发争议。类似的例子足可写一本书，笔者在此也无意赘述，仅举一例。亨廷顿关于西方基督教世界与东正教世界之间文明之墙（Zivilisationsmauer）的理论，曾激起听者（比如希腊人，他们是欧洲的成员）的震惊和抗议。然而在我看来，他的表述只停留在文化层面而非其他——不论在其理论遭遇攻击期间还是之后）。不过人们轻易地就忘记了，他在数十年前发表过这样一种论断：美国对越南的轰炸促进了当地的现代化发展。类似的论断人们还从未听闻过，比如：1999年北约对塞尔维亚、阿尔巴尼亚和其他相关的巴尔干国家的空袭是有益的。

最后还应该探究一种刚兴起的趋势，一种唯名论（Nominalismus）的奇特形式，有人把"巴尔干"这个空间的名字替换成所谓更中立的"东南欧"。"巴尔干"这个概念里没有什么意识形态的东西：作为一个名称，它不可能更中立或是更谨慎，因为它只意味着"山"。事实上"巴尔干"这个名字已经有了消极的意味；不过也没有理由去相信，如果人们把能指（signifiant）改变了，就能让所指（signifié）摆脱消极的定式思维。① 除了消极的意义外，"巴尔干"在许多巴尔干国家也有积极的和中立的意义。在保加利亚尤其如此。那里甚至有很多人以"巴尔干"为姓。因此，置换概念是不实际的，也是不可能的。如果想要解放那些在集体认知里，因为使用"巴尔干"这个概念而自卑和觉得受辱的巴尔干人，唯一的解决方法是解放这个概念，而不是磨灭这个概念。不过即使可能的话，外界对巴尔干半岛社会的意图也不会有什么变化。这更可能产生一种状况，就是即便不出现"黑鬼"（Neger）这个词，也是一种种族主义。"东南欧"这个组合词作为替代品，却大大偏离了非意识形态的初衷，尽管他们觉得这听起来是客观的地理描述。完全相反的是，这个词也有一段令人不快

---

① 能指与所指是结构语言学的一对范畴。"能指"指语言的声音、形象，"所指"指语言所反映的事物的概念。——译者注

的历史：纳粹曾在20世纪30年代到40年代使用这个概念，意为在东南部的欧洲"大经济区"的"天然的经济与政治整体"。

假如人们忘记了纳粹曾使用过该词，那么不论是西方还是巴尔干本土的科学家和政治家，都会把这个词看作是中立的概念。不过还有一个事实，即使用最无辜的名字来标记某些东西，也并非就是无辜的行为。为了运用语言学家的术语，复杂的理念比如地区、民族、种族、性别等都是社会建构的系统，包含被标记的和未被标记的范畴。欧洲的复杂理念也由被标记的和未被标记的范畴组成。"东欧"是一个被标记了的范畴，在西欧和美国的大学的授课内容里，它会被当作是欧洲历史的一个类属。"中欧""中东欧""东南欧"的历史和文学有时也被标记为这个地区的下属类目。欧洲的其他部分不会用"东北欧""西南欧"或者"中西欧"，甚至是"西欧"这样的范畴来代表，而是会简单地用"欧洲"来代表。这些都是未被标记的范畴。在这里出现了以下这种情况：被标记的范畴被定性为偏离的，而那些未被标记的范畴则被当作标准表述，其余范畴必须对其自身定位。因为是那些未被标记的范畴在现实中占有主导地位，看起来不显眼的那些就站在一般认知的中心。

我促请，让巴尔干地区"平凡化"，从而正常化。我认为，这个呼吁在德国应该更容易被理解。毕竟在几代人之前，对德国历史的大部分解读都带有武力和军国主义的传统：不是从条顿森林时期[①]开始，就是从三十年战争时期开始的。长期以来，人们一直从"特殊道路"的视角解读德国历史的基质。但从不久前开始，研究的重心转移了，现在德国历史不再被看作"异常"，而是被看作普遍的欧洲历史的一个版本。用一句话来说，正常化了。可能有人会反对：之所以会这样，是因为德国自己正常化了。不过重点是，正常化是一个复杂的、辩证的过程，外界的感知和行为作为重要因素混杂其中。

在方法论的角度上，我支持一条处于以下两者之间的折中路线：一种是历史目的论，这其中包含着人为建立的关联性；另一种是强调不兼容性、不可化约性的文明模型——当然这同样包含人为因素。这种方法的预设是，人类有一个基本的整体，它为普遍性创造了条件，从而避免完全分离、分裂或相对主义的陷阱。因此我们应该做一些仔细的地理和历史上的研究，强调结构、发展和

[①] 条顿森林战役是公元9年罗马帝国与日耳曼人在今德国西南黑森林（Schwarzwald，又称条顿森林）进行的战役，以前者的失败告终。此役使强大的罗马停止扩张，被认为是日耳曼人的立国之战。——译者注

结果的复杂多面性。不仅是为了欧洲其他部分,也是为了巴尔干空间。毕竟巴尔干是一个理念,连接了每个局外人的感知,也就是处于这个空间之外,也不是这里的居民的那些人。另外,这种复杂多面性不应该针对同一的、稳定的(西)欧洲模式,这种模式忽略了欧洲这一部分的许多方面。巴尔干地区对于整个世界政治没有太大的意义——在这一点上,人们可以达成共识。[1] 它特别吗?我想,不是的。它特别邪恶吗?在某些时期,是的,但也不与其他地区在其他时期的恶相等。它另类吗?当然是的,但只是与其他的有所区别而已。当然我看到了一种差别,我想运用一个诗意的比喻来描述,节选于海涅的诗[2]:

>世界上有两种老鼠,
>饿着的和吃饱的。
>吃饱的安居家中心满意足,
>饿着的出门远游不见归途。

---

[1] 这其中甚至包括1999年的那场轰炸,通过在北约50周年这一天为北约的成立辩白,解决了这个问题(除了许多不同的原因外)。我对此事件的看法在以下这篇文章中:玛莉亚·托多洛娃:《巴尔干半岛:从发现到介入》(*The Balkans: From Invention to Intervention*),载于《科索沃,在介入巴尔干地区问题上的争议之声》(*Kosovo, Contending Voices on Balkan Interventions*),Grand Rapids 出版社,2000年,第159—169页。

[2] 19世纪德国诗人海涅的诗歌《游历鼠》(*Die Wanderratten*),本文作者稍做改动,将原本在后面的诗句放在了原诗篇的第一段最后一句,由此形成本文的结尾。——译者注

巴尔干:为差异辩护[*]

[德] 赫姆·尊德豪森 著 刘晨 译

内容提要 尊德豪森把欧洲作为参考系统,回应与托多洛娃关于巴尔干的三个主要差异观点,分析巴尔干区别于其他地区的差异性和多样性。

关 键 词 巴尔干 差异 历史特征 欧洲的历史 空间

作者简介 赫姆·尊德豪森,德国柏林自由大学东欧学院教授

译者简介 刘晨,首都师范大学外国语学院德语系研究生

近年来,针对东欧概念的研究常涉及空间观念的解构,并且涉及以下问题:对于"东欧"的理解是如何随着时间的推移逐渐变化的?空间是如何发现的?人们如何建构空间形象以及人们如何在政治上利用空间形象?如今,人们十分热衷于研究"意境地图"。由于东西方政治矛盾的消失以及全球化进程的推进,人们在此前便已对这个问题多加关注,而当下人们越来越想统一欧洲,清除一切分裂的事物。在现实中的"墙"倒塌之后,人们开始寄希望于去除"思想上的墙",也因此人们愈加关注"意境地图"的研究。最终,连后现代主义也凭借着他们对解构的狂热为瓦解"现实"做出了贡献。

南斯拉夫联邦解体以及1991年至1999年的后南斯拉夫战争也使更远的区域——东南部欧洲和巴尔干地区——再次进入学术领域的辩论中。玛莉亚·托多洛娃于1997年在她的《想象巴尔干》一书中叙述了"西方"的巴尔干形象。

---

[*] 本文发表于2003年德国第四季度《历史与社会》(Holm Sundhaussen, "Der Balkan: Ein Plädoyer für Differenz," *Geschichte und Gesellschaft*, 29 Jahrg., H. 4, Protestantismus und Nationalsozialismus, Oct. - Dec., 2003, pp. 608-624)。译文省略大部分注释。

一方面，她探讨了巴尔干形象产生以及自18世纪晚期以来的变化；另一方面，她探讨了巴尔干形象在目前对于政界的影响和作用。两年后，我针对巴尔干地区作为欧洲的历史空间可以如何被定义的问题提出了一个建议。这是两个彼此触及但互不渗透的不同的问题意识。在前者中，"意境地图"、"西方"社会的定式思维及它们的作用是讨论的中心。在后者中，巴尔干地区及巴尔干人民眼中的自我形象则是研究对象。而只有在托多洛娃讨论"现实"［文本之中有什么（Qu'est-ce qu'il y a de hors-texte）］①的章节中，我们的研究对象才彼此重合。

托多洛娃在其早年文章《作为研究范畴的巴尔干》（*Der Balkan als Analysekategorie*）中便已明确澄清了，她并不将巴尔干地区"视为一种虚构"，并且也"从未将其当作虚构进行研究"。她对历史空间做出了区分：一是作为启发式理念的历史空间，一是作为意境地图的历史空间。此外，她还区分了作为本体的巴尔干和作为感知（Perzeption）的"巴尔干主义"。但是这种区分并未在读其著作的读者那里得到好评。而且此书的德文版书名用词不专业，极易令读者产生误解。②托多洛娃并没有在想象巴尔干，而是致力于巴尔干地区的发现以及巴尔干形象的构想。她并不认为巴尔干地区是一个想象空间，而是对在"西方"社会中空间的真实写照以及"西方"的感知模式和感知过滤（Wahrnehmungsmuster und-filter）感兴趣。自20世纪初以来这种感知模式及感知过滤产生了消极的巴尔干形象。因此有必要澄清一下。

我和托多洛娃的观念之差异涉及：1. 巴尔干形象于"西方"社会自我意识的意义；2. 对于巴尔干空间的历史"现实"的选择与权衡；3. 由选择与权衡引起的或明确或含蓄的评价。首先，我要对托多洛娃的论题提出疑问，她认为巴尔干被"西方"理解为"第二自我和阴暗内心的象征"。"西方"对后古希腊和后拜占庭帝国的巴尔干空间的兴趣在几个世纪后变得微不足道，并且这种兴趣在冲突局势中只维持了很短时间，此后很快便再次消退。她认为，"巴尔干和东方一样成了积累负面特征的储藏室；'欧洲'和'西方'的正面、自我庆贺的形象正是在其与巴尔干的对立中被建构出来的"，对于这种说法托多

---

① 这里的法语原句与上一篇文章《作为研究范畴的"巴尔干"：界线、空间、时间》中引用的"Qu'est-ce qu'il y a hors du texte?"只是表达不同，意义是一致的。——译者注

② 在此尊德豪森提及的是托多洛娃《想象巴尔干》一书的德文版，即《巴尔干地区的创造：欧洲先入为主的偏见》（M. Todorova, *Die Erfindung des Balkans: Europas bequemes Vorurteil*, Darmstadt, 1999）。尊德豪森认为此书德文版书名用词有误，与其想表达的主题不符。——译者注

洛娃并没有给出以客观事实为依据且令人信服的证据。这是什么时候发生的？关于1912年至1913年的巴尔干战争的报道或者关于90年代的后南斯拉夫战争的报道都没有塑造出"西方"的自我形象。这也不能证明"认知地图"（kognitiver Landschaft）的根深蒂固。[①] 与那些两极化的划分方式如"欧洲和俄罗斯""欧洲和亚洲""基督教和伊斯兰教""西方和东方""资本主义和社会主义"等不同——在这些两极分立中，巴尔干可以是其中任何一极，总之不是中心，"欧洲和巴尔干"这对臆想的对立对于欧洲的身份认同没有什么助益——不论这对概念中的后者是什么。可以确定的是：任何尝试去定义或者想象"西方"的人，在没有确定界线的情况下都是无法做到的。因为定义这件事情从字面及方法上的意义来看就是确定界线。但是巴尔干在"西方"的定义和塑造认同上没有以负面形象出现。它在近代，在危机与战争之外，在"西方"社会的长期认识中，既不扮演着消极的角色又不扮演着积极的角色。它曾经和现在都无关紧要。"西方"对巴尔干地区的缺乏兴趣——也就是不仅使欧洲外的世界，而且还使一些欧洲国家和地区淡出视野的"欧洲中心主义"——是一种挑战，而不是巴尔干半岛的一幅依旧染过色的图景。

赫尔德[②]、歌德[③]、格林兄弟[④]对于"原始民族"的热忱和他们的文学作品以及亲希腊思想（Philhellenismus）都曾使巴尔干地区在短时间内成为了"西方"的（积极的！）"第二自我"，但是这些都没有给"西方"对巴尔干地区的缺乏兴趣带来根本和长期的改变。连卡尔·麦（Karl May）[⑤]也没能做到这点。巴尔干地区是一片空白，这片空白在发生冲突的情况下会或多或少被常见的、陈词滥调的说明模式所填充，就像这些模式也会用在世界上其他的"白色"地区。"欧洲"公开承认，巴尔干地区过于陌生，过于微不足道，以至于不可能成为"第二自我"。它不适于"西方"模式且一点也不适于"普遍"历史的模板。它是欧洲中被遗忘的、陌生的且不能作为他者的部分。当在冲突局势中需

---

① 后者（似乎）只要获得了新的养分，就会保持活跃的状态。否则它们就会逐渐消失（至少在很短的时间之后）并且会被新的"意境地图"所替代。必要时，将会重新激活那些适合于解释当前事件的概念或者发明一些新的概念。此后它们才能发挥作用。

② 约翰·哥特弗雷德·赫尔德（1744—1803），德国哲学家。——译者注

③ 约翰·沃尔夫冈·冯·歌德（1749—1832），德国思想家、作家。——译者注

④ 即雅各布·格林（1785—1863）和威廉·格林（1786—1859），两人是19世纪德国历史学家、语言学家、民间故事和古老传说的搜集者，共著有著名的《格林童话》。——译者注

⑤ 卡尔·麦（1842—1912），德国探险小说作家，其所写的关于美国西部的冒险故事对欧洲人影响深远。——译者注

要解释某些东西时，那些对巴尔干地区不甚了解，并且有着过高要求的"欧洲人"就会直截了当地认为，这种解释是费力且令人厌烦的。

证明"巴尔干主义"是"西方"的负面形象的证据是如此的贫乏，而证明"东方主义"是巴尔干社会的负面形象的证据却是如此的毋庸置疑。"土耳其的困厄"，对于"在不同文化间徘徊的漫游者"的憎恨，对于"被土耳其化者"（Vertürkten）和"叛教者"的憎恨（也就是那些皈依伊斯兰教的巴尔干基督教徒），对于阿尔巴尼亚的、波斯尼亚的和其他土生土长的穆斯林的憎恨，"亚洲专政"和穆斯林的"落后"的范例等都是自19世纪以来政治出版界、科普文学、一部分专业文献和塑造民族认同感的虚构文学的固定组成部分：从"塞尔维亚的歌德"佩塔尔·彼得罗维奇·涅戈什（Petar Petrović Njegoš），到使保加利亚"重生"的诗人伊凡·沃佐夫（Ivan Vazov），再到当代最著名的阿尔巴尼亚作家伊斯梅尔·卡达莱（Ismail Kadare）。各种书籍、文献里充斥着"东方主义"的证据，以及由东方主义引发的、基督教—巴尔干民族运动针对"东方"与"土耳其"的"文明化传教"，后者发端于1844年科列蒂斯（Kolettis）提出的"伟大理想"（或大希腊主义）。部分巴尔干精英将他们学到的"西方"傲慢的优越感，再加上基督教—东正教的传教思想，一并运用于他们那穆斯林的邻居。不过此处无法展开对比的系统的研究。[①]

定义是用语言手段划定界线。也就是说，从某个固定的上下文中排除一个定义项不是必然的。定界和排斥并不一样。它们可以重合，但它们不必重合。在这个问题上常会产生误解和混乱。不仅如此，"认知地图"和更大或更小范围内的空间概念也会因此受到影响。什么是"欧洲历史"？什么是"德国历史"？什么是"保加利亚历史"？所有这些宏观历史的核心都是概念，这些概念以各自研究对象的或明确或含蓄的定界为基础。

玛莉亚·托多洛娃在其《想象巴尔干》一书中，带着显而易见的好感改写了奥斯卡·哈雷奇（Oscar Halecki）[②]针对"欧洲历史"的论述。但是哈雷奇的"欧洲历史"并不是地理意义上的欧洲历史，而是源于古希腊历史遗产和基督教的结合。来自匈牙利的研究中世纪欧洲的学者斯苏兹（Jenö Szücs）在他

[①] 虽然存在针对在西方文学中的"巴尔干主义"的研究，但是还没有出现针对在巴尔干文学或其他文章中的"东方主义"的研究，这一点之于研究状况来说是很典型的。

[②] 奥斯卡·哈雷奇（1891—1973），波兰历史学家，著有《西方文明的边境：中东欧史》（*Borderlands of Western Civilization: A History of East Central Europe*, New York: The Ronald Press Company, 1952)。——译者注

的关于《欧洲的三大历史区域》的概要中遵循了哈雷奇的论点并做了更为细致的论证。在他看来,"欧洲历史"的动机(das Movens)是灵活多变的时空发展:从西欧到中欧,再从中欧到东欧,并且在后一过程中停滞不前。

在人们如此理解的"欧洲历史"的概念中,特征是定义,而空间则是变化不定的。"去空间化"让以下情况成为可能:欧洲地理的某个部分在某些时候逐渐消失在"欧洲历史"之外或者"欧洲历史"的中心向外部转移并且由此离开了地理意义上的欧洲。当这样一种情况持续了过久的时间时,再去谈论"欧洲历史"就毫无意义了。哈雷奇坚持不懈地想将"欧洲时代"和随之到来的"大西洋时代"做出区分。

哈雷奇以及斯苏兹认为,巴尔干地区在奥斯曼帝国的统治下已经脱离了"欧洲历史"。在这件事上,它脱离到何处去并不十分清楚。在哈雷奇的定义下伊斯兰教并不从属于"欧洲历史"。它是一个闯入者:在摩尔人统治下的西班牙和在撒拉逊人统治下的西西里岛以及在奥斯曼帝国统治下的巴尔干地区。在一些当代人看来,时至今日,脱离欧洲历史者的名单仍在加长——关于波斯尼亚的讨论就是明证。哈雷奇曾经在美国生活过,所以他坚决排斥现实存在的社会主义。而斯苏兹则是一位在实行现实社会主义制度的刚果①生活过的学者,于是他便更加谨慎地表述自己的思想,避免直接反驳哈雷奇的言论。简单来说:伊斯兰教和社会主义——至少是那些前社会主义国家的社会主义——不属于"欧洲历史"。

我不想在这里深入这个主题,但毫不掩饰地说,相对于哈雷奇意义上的"欧洲历史"(Europäische Geschichte),我更喜欢"欧洲的历史"(Geschichte Europas)。我认为欧洲的历史是发生在一个具体地理空间内的历史:伴随着它的所有的多样性和历史变迁。在这里空间意味着定义,而特征则是变化不定的。也就是说,和"欧洲历史"恰恰相反。以特征为导向的方法与以空间为导向的方法彼此对立。因为以特征为导向的方法在没有空间的情况下无法施展,而以空间为导向的方法在没有特征的情况下也无法发挥,所以在"欧洲历史"和"欧洲的历史"之间存在多种多样的重合之处。然而,方法上的不同也深刻影响着这个问题,哪些属于欧洲历史的范围,哪些不属于。虽然地理意义上的欧洲概念也不能做到在所有方面都明确清晰,但毫无疑问的是,巴尔干地区属

---

① 即刚果人民共和国,为刚果共和国于1970—1991年的国名,其为非洲第一个社会主义国家。——译者注

于欧洲。因此，巴尔干半岛的历史也属于欧洲历史的一部分。

这种论断不仅仅适用于前奥斯曼时代和后奥斯曼时代——在这方面是毫无异议的，而且适用于其间的四百到五百年。更何况从14世纪末到19世纪或20世纪的500年间并不单单是奥斯曼帝国及其制度的历史。它并不只是"土耳其战争"和一次"文明的冲突"的历史。它也是那些在奥斯曼帝国的欧洲部分生活的人的历史。在这些人中，不仅有本土和外来的穆斯林（他们从"欧洲历史"中脱离出去了），还有与之相互影响的基督教徒（这些基督教徒一如既往地代表了居民中的多数人），还有犹太人以及属于其他信仰群体的人们。这是由不同形式的宗教、族群、政权产物互相影响产生的历史，是由不同宗教思想文化的融合与对立产生的历史。排除法和"脱离"的论点并不符合事实情况，尤其是因为其没有令人信服的原因，就将欧洲的过去只归结于国家与统治体系的历史中去。

令人惊愕的是，在西方的历史编纂学中，巴尔干半岛在东罗马帝国灭亡后便很少出现，并且较之于"欧洲的历史"这一前提，巴尔干地区的人们更认同"欧洲历史"。这种观点足以说明，为什么类似"回归欧洲"和"欧洲化"的说法不仅在后奥斯曼时期而且在后社会主义时期都十分受欢迎。当人们不是通过地理意义而是通过特定特征去定义欧洲时，这种说法才有意义，而那些特定特征则排除了在"土耳其的"和"社会主义的"统治下的巴尔干地区，并将其视为"非欧洲的"。从地理上来说阿尔巴尼亚和保加利亚等国家是无法回归欧洲了，因为它们一直在欧洲境内。而令人惊奇的是，玛莉亚·托多洛娃赞同了哈雷奇的思想，并支持他的论断，即巴尔干在长达四五百年的时间里被"欧洲的历史"排除在外，同时却不遗余力地谴责斯苏兹。她接受在奥斯曼帝国统治下的巴尔干空间从"欧洲"的脱离（在"意境地图"的意义上）并且完全赞同哈雷奇的见解。而与之相反的是她对斯苏兹的观点嗤之以鼻。与哈雷奇不同的是，斯苏兹强调基督教欧洲的宗派分裂的意义（天主教和新教 VS 正教）。稍后会详细介绍。

在巴尔干历史的研究上，托多洛娃表示支持与空间范畴相连的"历史遗产"的概念。她认为，两种历史传统曾经对于巴尔干空间的历史是"至关重要"的：拜占庭帝国延续千年之久的政治、制度、法律和宗教的影响；延续近500年的奥斯曼帝国的统治。在《想象巴尔干》一书中托多洛娃也用以下言论着重指出了拜占庭帝国历史遗产的意义：虽然在拜占庭帝国统治下的千年间半岛在政治上是支离破碎的，但随着基督教以希腊东正教的形式从君士坦丁堡传播，斯拉夫人对罗马法的适应，拜占庭文学和艺术的影响，一言以蔽之：对拜占庭文化和政治模式的模仿，形成了一个文化上的实体——即便不是政治上的统一。但是由于她对拜占庭历史遗产的一切看法都听上去像是一种口头上的承认，而这种口头承认——一经说出——即可被付诸实践，因此可以断定"巴尔干地区事实上就是奥斯曼帝国的历史遗产"。①这听起来就好像是奥斯曼人磨灭了拜占庭的传统并使其在后奥斯曼时代失去了所有意义。

这让我想到了我与托多洛娃之间的主要争论点，主要在于历史特征——并不是想象！——长期性和短期性以及历史特征的权衡和评价。首先我要探讨的是第一个观点。我对于托多洛娃的论断——历史遗产不会一直延续——毫无异议。在《巴尔干欧洲》（*Europa Balcanica*）一书中我反复地强调过，一个历史空间的形成是"历史进程的结果"，这些形塑的过程出现、变化并消失，并且着重指出历史区域并"不会无穷无尽"的存在。"本质主义"（Essentialismus）和"悄无声息地让差异上升到本体的地位"更是根本谈不上的。由此这个问题就归结到了传统和历史遗产的持续性上。

托多洛娃（含蓄地）假设到，拜占庭模式并不有助于人们理解"今天的世俗化社会……（其中有些在很大程度上属于非宗教性质）"。她的这个假设并没有说服我。因为这并不关乎于当今社会的虔诚，也不关乎于神学或者教义史或者这个哈雷奇已提出过的问题：天主教与新教之间的神学差异是否不比天主教和东正教之间的差异大。这也不仅仅关乎教会史学。这关乎着几个世纪以来，拉丁—罗马的和希腊东正教的传统是否塑造了我们社会的规范和价值观，以及在塑造的过程中产生了何种程度的影响，它们是否影响了各种文化的定型以及影响达到了什么程度。毕竟，宗教直到"不久前"仍非私人事务。就算在巴尔干空间内的当今社会百分之百地世俗化了，这也不能成为反对宗教在建构历史经验文化空间中的重要性的有力观点。我要以另一种方式并且带着故意的挑衅重新表述这个事实：在巴尔干空间内的社会是否有自己的文化？如果有的话：那么这些文化是如何产生的？它们被哪些元素影响？通过哪些方式表达出来？以希腊东正教形式存在的宗教是否对文学、绘画、建筑学等来说毫无意义？此外这种宗教是否也对巴尔干社会以及其他东正教社会的认同毫无意义？

---

① 我认为（托多洛娃）这里可能想表达的不是巴尔干地区，而是巴尔干形象，特别是因为在此句前谈到了"巴尔干地区的刻板印象"。另一方面来说，此观点与应受东南欧"影响"的"历史传统"有关联。

特别专栏：关于"巴尔干"的一场争论

基督教和东正教的分裂是否曾经只是一个在世俗化道路上被解决的神学问题？如果是这样的话，巴尔干地区同"西方"的差异要比我曾经假设并且敢于去表述的那样更加强烈。卡斯帕尔·冯·格雷耶兹（Kaspar von Greyerz）在其最近发表的专著中描述了近代早期西欧的宗教史及文化史。他在参考了托马斯·卢克曼（Thomas Luckmann）的观点后认为，宗教就是社会塑成的象征系统。他认为宗教是一种文化现象，这种文化现象除了对宗教信徒产生影响外也会对社会关系产生影响，而这些社会关系虽然也会被宗教影响，但并不会全身心地投入到宗教活动中去。即便在世俗化开始后，"西方"文化在理念上也并未完全改变——尽管"西方文化"是与宗教的斗争中逐渐被塑造出来的。它并不是启蒙运动及市民革命的唯一产物。

尽管我对此持有怀疑态度，但是晚于"西方"陷入世俗化漩涡中的巴尔干地区的社会，在如今或者说至少到1989年——确实可能比或曾经比——"西方"社会更加世俗化。但这并不意味着人们会因此遗忘宗教在激发身份认同感方面的意义。这一点适用于东正教也适应于伊斯兰教。①但是让我们先来看一下东正教。希腊、塞尔维亚以及其他信仰东正教的19世纪和20世纪的神学家及思想家，他们针对"西方"、针对启蒙运动和法国大革命的理想，针对个人主义和资本主义，并且针对"欧洲文明的可怕疾病"的反西方论战是否只描述了边缘人的思想。除了精英阶层的欧洲人之外，他们是否回溯在社会各部分引起共鸣的态度和价值观？以反现代主义形式，深深植根于"西方"的反西方主义塑造了在巴尔干精英中的争论中至关重要的基本特点。"欧洲恐惧症"（Europaphobie）就如同"亲欧洲主义"（Europaphilie）一样，有制造话语的能力。不仅是"西方"妖魔化巴尔干地区，巴尔干地区也会妖魔化西方。因此，是不是必须将"想象巴尔干"与"想象西方"等同起来，因为对差异（Alterität）的感知不是单行轨道，而是交互相错又相互映照的互相联系。难道人们找不到大量证据以证明"西方"文化（包括"西方"哲学）——自19世

---

① 在巴尔干空间的早期民族塑造（Nationsbildung）中，在波斯尼亚，人们可以将宗教（这里指的是伊斯兰教）的双重作用视作信仰和塑造文化的特征进行范例研究。当波斯尼亚的穆斯林在20世纪60年代末70年代初被承认为一个民族时，不仅在国外而且在早期的南斯拉夫引起了混乱。人们用大写的"M"标记作为一个民族的穆斯林，用小写的"M"标记作为一个宗教团体的穆斯林，而这种拼写上的区分对人们的启发很小。也有些人为这个于1993年接受了"波斯尼亚人"称谓的穆斯林民族辩护，他们拒绝或者无感于伊斯兰教，但是他们并没有放弃奥斯曼帝国—伊斯兰教历史遗产——被他们视为塑造民族认同感的特征——以及波斯尼亚的前奥斯曼帝国遗产。伊斯兰教对于"穆斯林民族"——其曾在波斯尼亚的社会中占有极高的比例——以及对波斯尼亚人来说是不可或缺的文化"标记"。

49

纪以来已被部分巴尔干空间内有文化教养的精英阶级所接纳——是如何不加区别地被谴责为"无神的、不人道的、反基督教的以及肆无忌惮的"吗？希腊民族主义者德拉古密斯（Lon Dragoumis）在1904年写道，"我们无论如何也想模仿两样东西，为了能成为这样的人：1. 古人（古希腊人），2. 异乡人，法兰克人，欧洲人"。"古人未曾有害于我们，异乡人却严重危害我……欧洲文明让我们非常困惑……折磨我们的不是俄罗斯人、保加利亚人、罗马尼亚人、奥地利人、意大利人和土耳其人。这些人的侵入和他们的强盗行径并不算什么。现代思想带着它的共济会、博爱主义和团结精神被强加于我们头上……这种现代文明的入侵，而不是保加利亚人和意大利人的入侵，败坏我们，感染我们，同时准备着瓦解我们。正如尼采所说，这就是让我们成为兽群中的动物的文明。"

但是，这个影响了在巴尔干空间内的社会文化认知的历史遗产，既不是拜占庭帝国的，也非奥斯曼帝国的——人们普遍反对这一说法，或者是社会主义的历史遗产，那么它到底是什么呢？是类似于在哈雷奇看来，与宗教相关的普世教会合一运动，或者世俗化的"西方"以及"市民社会"，或者那些被偶像化的、走进了民族创建神话（Gründungsmythen）和记忆文化的"人民"？

让我们把论战放到一边。鉴于拜占庭帝国统治下的近千年时间，我还未使用类似"政教合一""拜占庭独裁者"或者"停滞不前的社会关系"的表述。当然，我曾说过"拜占庭模式"。我将一个非常多元化的千年时代归结于一种模式，对此托多洛娃十分恼火，而我无法理解她的这份恼火。一种模式并不是一段发展历史。除此之外，托多洛娃本人曾说过"拜占庭文化和政治模式"。也许只是因为我使用了"模式"这个词的单数形式，所以使她感到困扰？这很容易解决。只要我们两个人都统一使用模式这个词的单数形式或者复数形式就可以了。这样一来，我们两人同时都会受到诟病，人们会认为我们对问题进行了化约。

我认为，托多洛娃在"作为连续性的历史遗产"和"作为感知的历史遗产"中做出的区分，过于僵化或者说——仅就托多洛娃而言——过于机械。拜占庭模式和西方模式是历史遗产和感知。它们既在"路径依赖"（Pfadabhängigkeit）的意义上，同时也作为"意境地图"而变得历史悠久。不论西方人对"希腊的教会分裂者"的诽谤，还是拜占庭地区的人对"会拉丁文的人"和"法兰克人"进行的攻击，均深刻地影响了政治决策乃至历史的走向——比如说支持或反对一个教会联盟，包括往一个方向或另一个方向做出

特别专栏：关于"巴尔干"的一场争论

决定所导致的后果——而且同时影响了另一方的感知。感知是决定过程的一部分，做出的决定会加深感知并使其继续传递下去——直到如今。人们首当其冲会想到塞尔维亚的科索沃神话（Kosovo-Mythos）或者2000年发生在希腊的反对教皇访问的抗议活动。一项历史遗产是否更多地以"路径依赖"形式，以物质或非物质的遗产（制度）[Überreste (Institutionen)] 或作为记忆文化（Erinnerungskultur）有效地展现出来，将会是一个吸引人的研究命题。但是这个问题对于确定历史空间来说并不重要。由于先前的决定、事件与后来的决定和事件之间存在或正面或负面的联系，因此路径依赖的范式可以让人避免将历史视为孤立的点（Punktualität），同时也促使人对历史"断层"进行反思。托多洛娃特别强调了在拜占庭时期和奥斯曼时期之间的断层，以及在奥斯曼时期和后奥斯曼时期之间的断层。此外，我还将关注点放在了所有"断层"的连续性元素。连续性并不是静止的状态，而是适应和重塑的过程。看似矛盾的是，断层和连续性总是相互伴随着出现并且这两个概念是不相称的。在社会历史中并不存在真正的"零时刻"（Stunde Null）；每一个现在都是它过去的一部分。奥斯曼帝国的历史遗产并非简单接替了拜占庭帝国的历史遗产，而是继续发展和改变了它。换句话说：奥斯曼帝国的历史遗产属于拜占庭帝国的历史遗留的一大部分。这听起来很矛盾，但事实却正是如此；不仅是因为奥斯曼人以只是略微修改的形式采用了许多在其欧洲行省上已存在的制度，更多的是因为奥斯曼帝国这个多等级国家（der osmanische Überschichtungsstaat）将拜占庭帝国的历史遗产的许多元素保存了下来，就像储存在一个带盖的乳酪盒中一样——从实际层面上以及从感知层面上来说。东正教会和教士保护了苏丹的基督教臣民以防他们失去其文化认同，这件事成为了巴尔干地区历史编纂学上的常规部分。所有人都认同，大部分本地人民是从前奥斯曼帝国的历史遗产中获取的集体自我认知。并且有足够证据证明，后奥斯曼帝国及其认同的缔造者承袭了前奥斯曼帝国的历史遗产，他们试图去引起连续性或者创造连续性，即便我们可以证实这并不存在。新建构和创建神话一直在揭示着或多或少被创造出来的连续性的基本特征。没有一种创造是无中生有。所有人都以这种或那种方式将它和熟悉的事物联系起来。另外，玛莉亚·托多洛娃也表达过对"连续性"和"感知"概念的不适。总的来看，相较于给人的印象来说，我们的观点在这方面也许相差并不太远。

差异和评价的方面表现不同，二者密切相关。托多洛娃曾提醒大家，"不要过分强调'分殊'（Unterscheidung）和'差异'（Differenz）这样的主题"。

这也说明了她对"界线"有所保留。而模糊的是,"过分"强调差异和"过度关注界线"到底意味着什么。首先我要复述一下,每个定义都是界线的划定,无论其是关于一个物质客体、一个概念或是在空间和时间内的历史研究对象:欧洲的历史、"西方"的历史、巴尔干地区的历史或者保加利亚人、德国人的历史等。差异的强度很大程度上依赖于观察者与其研究对象的距离。这种强度是动态的,没有固定的大小。近距离观察给人带来的强烈差异会因为从上往下的角度观察而减弱或者完全消失。如果人们从巴尔干空间内部进行观察的话,就会只见树木,不见森林。而如果人们以总体角度去观察巴尔干空间的话,那么就无法感知到巴尔干地区与欧洲其他部分或者与世界的差异。在关于巴尔干地区作为历史空间或分析类别的讨论中,这两个研究角度都不适合。在这里我涉及的是中间距离,具体地说:将欧洲作为参考系统。

巴尔干空间的居民不是"外星人"。没有什么事情是发生在这个空间内,而没有以这样或那样的形式在欧洲其他部分和欧洲之外的空间发生过。我们是否应该而且必须点到为止呢?在一个可重构历史的时间内巴尔干地区的人在其基本行为方式上并未改变。他既没有变得更好也没有变得更坏,既没有变得更聪明也没有变得更愚笨。倘若不同时间与空间中的人是相同的——在永恒的形式(specie aeternitatis)方面相同——或者只在很少的方面上存在不同,那么我们就不需要研究历史了。我们可以将这个领域托付给人类学家和社会心理学家。时间、空间和差异就会自行解体。一切都是人性化的,一切都是正常的。即使那些看上去异常的事物也是以平庸方式正常着。最终只会留下少许"自然的"二分法。如果我们与自然的二分法之间的距离足够大,那么连这样一种二分法都会随之消失。为什么是"德国历史"?为什么是巴尔干空间的历史?为何要宣传那些"纪念地"(Erinnerungsorte)?为什么是历史学家之争?这一切(以及还有更多)都是多余的。甚至也许是有害的,因为它与定义和"差异"永远都脱不开关系。

再重复一遍:没有什么事情仅发生在巴尔干空间内,却没有以这样或那样的形式在欧洲其他部分和欧洲之外的空间发生过。我同托多洛娃一样拒绝"隔离巴尔干地区"。我在《巴尔干欧洲》中使用了特征集群以确定历史空间。我假设,通过使用集群概念可以避免引发评价以及其带来的情绪的误解。显而易见这没有成功。为了进一步说明:集群的各个元素不是独特的,也不只是适用于巴尔干地区,而是它们的时空组合和由此产生的历史特异性。集群的不同元素分散在不同的范围内——时间上的和空间上的——并且同其他元素一起塑造出以不同方式组合而成的压缩区（Verdichtungszone）。认为复杂的族裔分布和其带来的争论是巴尔干空间的唯一特殊之处，这种观点是愚蠢的。断定拜占庭帝国—东正教的和奥斯曼帝国—伊斯兰教的历史遗产仅存在于巴尔干地区是错误的。①但是只有在同一个区域内——欧洲内外的其他任何地方——这八个我曾在《欧洲巴尔干》中列举过的特征——当然，这并非定论，仍有待探究——才能归结为同一个集群。这个集群就是"巴尔干地区"。

玛莉亚·托多洛娃说过，"文明诞生之初，人类社会中就存在族群清洗"。至少当人们回溯种族清洗的定义时这是无可争议的。相同的事物也以普遍形式适用于国家的[或前国家的（vornational）]趋同化努力（Homogenisierungsbestrebungen）或者适用于种族主义。如果种族清洗不是在同一时间点上在欧洲其他部分成为主题，以及种族主义不是在同一时间点上在德国及在不同西方社会中成为主题，是否谈论在巴尔干空间内的种族清洗和种族主义是不正确的？只要种族清洗和种族主义是研究的核心主题，那么自然应当采用跨区域的研究视角。但在关于《欧洲巴尔干》的讨论中，种族清洗并不是第三标准（tertium comparationis）。

这些主题在巴尔干历史编纂学中迄今未得到关注。业内有许多关于德国种族主义的研究，但是至今还没有关于巴尔干空间种族主义的研究。可能种族主义从未出现在巴尔干空间，如此一来，人们也就无法研究它。但确实是这样的吗？②是否巴尔干地区不同于"西方"？或者我们必须再次回到时间和空间，也就是回到史学的坐标系统的话题上去吗？

如果普遍可观察的基本行为表现为不同的时空形式和格局，那么历史学仍然是不可或缺的。任何强调过程和情境并拒绝决定论的人，都无法满足于过程结果的比较，而他必须使过程本身，包括其流变形式、特征、矛盾或非同时性成为研究对象。这样一来，仅仅断定诸如法国在很长一段时期内推行了深度的趋同化，以及后南斯拉夫国家在20世纪末也做过相同的事情，这是不够的。我们还应该更近距离地观察时间、空间和情况，观察要素的各个组态及其一系列原因。人们努力在已经改变的框架条件下，将巴尔干空间内的趋同化进程或

---

① 拜占庭帝国和奥斯曼帝国的历史遗产远远（朝不同方向）超过本文涉及的空间。但是与俄罗斯和与巴尔干地区相比，拜占庭帝国的历史遗产经历了一个截然不同的变化过程。而分散在三大洲的奥斯曼帝国的历史遗产同样在不同区域有着明显的不同。

② 有证据表明，巴尔干空间内的种族主义主要针对穆斯林，而反伊斯兰主义则扮演了反犹太主义的角色。

者——举个其他例子——工业化进程缩减到短短几十年，这种努力已经得到了回报，而这种进程在欧洲其他地区却延续了好几个世纪，关于这一点值得进行研究。如果权力（Gewalt）具有情境和程序的因素（eine situative und prozessuale Komponenten）——超出所有人行使权力的能力与意愿，那么就有必要去研究、命名每个特殊情况。我所采用的时空特征集群，其意义正在于此。

托多洛娃猜测，我的文章中总是隐含着价值评断，或者说她带入了自己的评价。这表明了她的攻击性，但这并不是我的意图。在19世纪及20世纪时，本地的精英阶层曾表述过一些目标（如"欧洲化"），这些目标是否实现了又实现到了何种程度？我虽然在不同的文章中探讨过该问题，但其仅仅涉及了目标实现的程度，而没有涉及评价。而为什么那些被本地精英阶层搁置在巴尔干地区的西方化目标只是部分地实现，并且有时是根本没有实现，则是人们关注的焦点。这个问题有理有据并且亟待解决。与托多洛娃，还有许多也在进行巴尔干空间研究的同行不同的是，尽管存在交互关系和迁移的历史（Transfergeschichte），我的研究仍然以欧洲不同的历史路径为出发点。与此同时，我采用了"历史路径"而非"发展路径"的概念，因为后者含有目的论的成分。这些不同的历史路径（具体有多少种暂且不去讨论）属于历史财富和欧洲大陆上的多样性。但是没有差异就没有多样性。没有多样性也就没有定界，转移历史有可能是令人印象深刻的，但转变的标志或定义也有可能是不明确的。因此我们可以得出这样一个结论：任何不想定界的人都不应该谈论多样性。

波斯尼亚的哲学家穆罕默德·菲利波维奇（Muhamed Filipovic）曾有"不同事物之间多样化的统一"这样的提法。他所指的是在其故乡波黑的"统一中的多样化"。这也适用于欧洲。而令我困惑的是从欧洲的历史（Geschicte Europas）中消失的差异结构。所以相对于普遍性话语，我更主张一种具有包容性的、差异的话语。因为假设出来的普遍性（Postulierte Universität）是以西欧为中心的元语境的结果。这种普遍性与历史无关且渐有目的论色彩。托多洛娃批评道，人们并非自始至终将巴尔干置于"西方"的范畴内进行阐释。我也这样认为。或者换句话说：我对生搬硬套地强求巴尔干空间的历史适应一种"普遍的"模式——也就是"西方的"或者"欧洲的"历史模式——提出批评。相比一个迟来的、被"奥斯曼帝国的历史遗产"所中断的、被篡改的和在时间上被聚集在19世纪或20世纪的"欧洲的历史"的变体来说，巴尔干空间的历史更像某些其他东西。"变体理论"不仅是错误的，因为它预设了一种尚未得

特别专栏：关于"巴尔干"的一场争论

到一致定义的基本模式的假设——早期现代化理论就是一例——只有或多或少将较长的历史时期从这一基本模式中"剥除"，或从这一基本模式中进一步区分出多种多样的"特殊道路"，该模式才有可能成立。而且这种变体理论也不会带来新的研究成果，因为如果巴尔干空间的历史只是一个从"西方"的角度来看并不是特别成功的"普遍"历史的变体，那么研究它就没有任何吸引力，甚至比迄今为止的情况更不受重视。

如果托多洛娃所要求的巴尔干地区的"正常化"或"平凡化"旨在打击90年代战争期间盛行的"妖魔化"，那么我就没有异议。但如果她的要求旨在使差异面目全非，把"常态"（Normalität）和"规范化"（Nomartivität）等同起来，那么我就无法认同。巴尔干地区作为一个历史空间既不"正常"也不"非正常"。它是与众不同的，而它的这份与众不同值得受到关注。即使在古希腊罗马结束和东罗马帝国的鼎盛时期之后，巴尔干地区逐渐开始失去其在欧洲的文化优势，该地区的历史也随时准备着重要的历史经验，而巴尔干地区的"普遍"历史学和历史编纂学的代表学者却很少或根本就未意识到其历史经验的重要性。而值得探讨的是：为什么奥斯曼帝国的欧洲行省在很长一段时间内对他人十分容忍——比当代西方国家更能容忍，为什么没有驱逐犹太人、胡格诺派等，为什么没有三十年战争，没有农奴制？寻找伊斯兰教的特殊欧洲变体，寻找在奥斯曼帝国统治下的东正教的普世教会运动或在巴尔干空间的近代非集权社会的变体（Varianten neuzeitlicher akephaler Gesellschaften），或者分析多族群现象、文化融合和杂糅的特殊形式，这些研究方向是十分吸引人的。此外值得探讨的问题还有：在后奥斯曼帝国统治下的巴尔干国家的"现代化"是如何进行的，为什么它一部分是成功的，一部分是不成功的。充满悖论的是，人们对巴尔干地区几十年前就出现的问题迟迟未着手研究，直到对发展中国家进行研究之时，才提出这些问题。

"正常化"在于承认多样性（因为多样性是常态），而不在于拒绝和禁忌。但差异本身在全球化的时代"落后了"。它不仅涉及现在或将来，而且显然也涉及过去。任何为差异命名的人，都必须首先为自身辩护。我们在努力跨越文化与社会之间的障碍时，经常遇到解构、界线和空间的流动、差异的消解等，简言之：我们面对的是后现代主义的后果，即一切事物或多或少都是相像的。在任何地方我们都能发现市民社会的元素，即使它们如此短暂，并且我们认为可以利用理性选择方法（rational-choice-Verfahren）来解释一切。但是如果某些差异或变体不能被否定，它们就会变得微不足道。一些人高度赞扬多样性和多元文化现象，但同时它们也被视为禁忌：具有讽刺意味的是，往往是这些人都有着相同的热情。任何违反禁忌的人都面临着来自"思想中的墙"的伪论据。尽管我们在日常生活中时不时地就会探讨多样性、混合性、身份和差异性，自我和他人的问题，但在如今，研究差异仍不是政治正确的。我们将无力再负担这种自相矛盾了。

时政研究

巴尔干国家差异性、复杂性及其对"17+1"合作的影响

孔寒冰

内容提要 在世界区域研究中，巴尔干半岛占有独特的地位。自古及今，巴尔干地区因其重要的地缘政治和地理位置而成为东西方大国的角逐场所。大国和大国博弈留给了巴尔干地区多样的、复杂的甚至冲突的遗产。因此，比起中东欧的另外两个次区域，巴尔干国家在国情上的差异性大，内部关系和外部关系复杂性强。巴尔干国家在"一带一路"倡议和"17+1"合作中占有重要地位，它们的这些差异性和复杂性在其中的影响不可低估。

关 键 词 巴尔干国家 差异性 复杂性 17+1合作 中东欧

作者简介 孔寒冰，北京大学国际关系学院教授

引　言

在区域研究中,巴尔干地区是最复杂的。其表现,一是外部和内部对所谓的巴尔干地区认同度低;二是历史上大国争霸留下的各种遗产仍然时起时伏地影响着这个地区的社会发展。然而,巴尔干并不是一个由来已久的区域概念,其确切的范围界限到底在哪儿,从古至今都有分歧。① 不仅如此,全部疆域都在巴尔干的希腊却不被算作巴尔干国家,更不用说虽然只有小部分在巴尔干但历史上长期影响该地区的土耳其了。如果截屏2018年,人们会清楚地看到巴尔干地区的国家不仅数量多,而且异质性强,在从20世纪90年代开始的社会转型、新国家构建和社会发展三个主题上的差别特别大。斯洛文尼亚、克罗地亚、罗马尼亚、保加利亚都已经是北约和欧盟的成员,其中,斯洛文尼亚还加入了欧元区和申根区。阿尔巴尼亚和黑山只是北约的成员,而其他国家还都远近不同地站在欧洲的大门口。在国家建构上,有的国家还面临着很难摆脱甚至无法摆脱的困境。比如,波黑的塞尔维亚、克罗地亚和穆斯林三大民族缺乏对统一国家的认同,在科索沃问题上塞尔维亚与许多国家存在着矛盾,斯洛文尼亚和克罗地亚等相邻国家之间还有领土纠纷等。另外,北马其顿的国名一直与希腊等国有争议,直到2018年6月两国才就定名北马其顿达成一致。基于上述考虑,本文将聚焦点放在当前巴尔干国家的差异性和复杂性及其成因上,在此基础之上分析它们对"一带一路"倡议和"17+1"合作的影响。

---

① 陈志强:《巴尔干古代史》,中华书局2007年版,第1—2页。马克·马佐尔著,刘会荣译:《巴尔干:被误解的"欧洲火药库"》,天津人民出版社2007年版,第1—2页。

一

"一带一路"沿线所及的65个国家和地区中,中东欧国家有17个[①],即捷克、斯洛伐克、匈牙利、波兰、斯洛文尼亚、克罗地亚、波黑、塞尔维亚、黑山、北马其顿、阿尔巴尼亚、保加利亚、罗马尼亚、希腊、立陶宛、拉脱维亚和爱沙尼亚。在中东欧17个国家中,巴尔干地区的有10个,它们是斯洛文尼亚、克罗地亚、波黑、塞尔维亚、黑山、北马其顿、阿尔巴尼亚、保加利亚、罗马尼亚和希腊。单从数量上看,巴尔干国家在"一带一路"和"17+1"合作中的地位和影响就不可低估。中东欧17国并不是一个内聚性极强的区域,

---

[①] 中东欧是一个内涵不准确的概念。综合字面上的地理位置、内容上的地缘政治等方面因素,中东欧至少有三重的空间范围。第一,从地理位置上看,中东欧的范围就是欧洲的中部和东部,包括中欧的德国、波兰、捷克、斯洛伐克、匈牙利、奥地利、列支敦士登和瑞士8国,东欧的俄罗斯的欧洲部分、白俄罗斯、乌克兰、摩尔多瓦、立陶宛、拉脱维亚和爱沙尼亚等7国。这15个国家合起来就是地理位置上的中东欧,但是,无论在国际政治的实践中还是学术研究的理论上,这样组合的中东欧是从来都不存在的。第二,由地缘政治上的东欧演变而来的中东欧。1944年10月,斯大林和丘吉尔通过秘密会谈就苏联和西方盟国战后各自活动的区域、范围和程度的划分达成了默契,形成了后来所谓的"巴尔干百分比"。据此,中欧东部的匈牙利、捷克斯洛伐克和波兰,东南欧(巴尔干半岛)上的南斯拉夫、阿尔巴尼亚、保加利亚、罗马尼亚属于苏联的势力范围。西欧、中欧的西部、北欧和东南欧的希腊则属于西方盟国的势力范围。后来,德国一分为二,民主德国(东德)和联邦德国(西德)分属于苏联和西方阵营。但是,所谓的东欧并不在欧洲的东边,是在中东欧的东半部和东南欧;所谓的西欧也不只在欧洲的西边,而是除欧洲西边之外,还包括中欧的西半部、北欧和东南欧的希腊。地缘政治上的东欧指的是与苏联结盟,实行共产党一党制、指令性的计划经济和马克思主义一元化的意识形态的社会主义模式。从1989年开始,由于内外部多重原因,东欧国家发生了社会制度的快速变化,共产党都失去了执政地位,社会主义制度不复存在,马克思主义也不再是社会的主导思想。更为重要的是,苏联自身也发生了社会制度的变化,而且于1991年年底解体。这些本质性的特征都没了,地缘政治上的东欧也就消失了。于是,在称谓上,各种相关研究文献中出现了"中欧""新欧洲""中间地带""中东欧"和"后社会主义"等各种说法。在这些取代地缘政治上的东欧的概念中,为中外学术界所普遍认可并常用的就是"中东欧"。与原来的东欧相比,中东欧的空间范围及其这里的国家都发生了比较大的变化。一是民主德国和联邦德国合并,二是捷克斯洛伐克1993年分裂为捷克和斯洛伐克两个国家,三是南斯拉夫在1991—2006年间先后分裂为斯洛文尼亚、克罗地亚、波黑、北马其顿、塞尔维亚和黑山等6个国家。这样一来,加上国家结构没有发生变化的匈牙利、波兰、阿尔巴尼亚、罗马尼亚、保加利亚和希腊,中东欧地区一共就有了14个国家。但在地理位置上,这些国家仍然分属于中欧的东部和东南欧,而没有一个东欧国家。第三,"17+1"合作机制意义的中东欧。这个合作机制是中国外交部2012年提出来的,中东欧的空间范围除了由地缘政治上东欧演变而来的14国之外,又增加了从苏联独立出来的立陶宛、拉脱维亚和爱沙尼亚3个波罗的海国家。在冷战期间,前14国属于东欧,后3个国家属于苏联,相互之间没有任何联系。

实践上包括了三个差别较大的次区域以及1981年就加入欧共体的希腊。捷克、斯洛伐克、匈牙利和波兰属于中欧，一体化程度非常高，其标志就是它们组建的"V-4"集团。立陶宛、拉脱维亚和爱沙尼亚属于东欧，几乎从古到今都是"抱团生存"。巴尔干国家属于第三个次区域，但特征与前两者完全相反，这里的10个国家对本地区的认同度和相互之间的认同度都特别低。从根本上说，"一带一路"倡议和"17+1"合作都建立在各种差异基础之上的，因而不可否认这些差异对"一带一路"倡议和"17+1"合作的影响和制约。就中东欧的三个次区域来说，巴尔干国家在差异性和复杂性方面是最典型的。

有学者深刻地指出："近代以前的巴尔干半岛就是一个经济、政治、宗教、文化、民族多样性突出的地区，是一个多样性因素没有经过历史合理协调整合并逐渐形成整体利益的地区，因此是一个地区内部差异性超过了地区共同性的地区。"[①] 近代之后，虽然有相同或相近的历史发展进程，但是，这里的民族和国家依旧没有形成稳定的区域共同体，冷战期间的"东欧"也只是共同受制于苏联的地缘政治区域，在根本性的政治体制、经济体制和对外关系方面没有差异或者差异很小。冷战结束后，地缘政治上的东欧消失，其表现，一是社会制度发生了根本性的变化，即由苏联模式转向西方模式；二是苏联的控制不复存在，这些国家转向了西方国家。

对巴尔干国家来说，除了以上两点之外，还有一个重要的变化，那就是统一的南斯拉夫社会主义联邦共和国（简称南联邦）在血雨腥风中解体。1991年，斯洛文尼亚、克罗地亚、波黑和北马其顿宣布独立，塞尔维亚和黑山组建了南斯拉夫共和国联盟（简称南联盟）。南联盟先于2003年改称塞尔维亚和黑山（简称塞黑），后于2007年正式分离为两个独立国家。至此，南联邦一分为六。在这过程，原为塞尔维亚自治省的科索沃于2008年宣布独立，成为事实上的独立国家。由于中国尚未承认，本文没有把它计入巴尔干国家之列。

巴尔干国家之间在许多方面都有非常大的差异。

第一，领土面积大小和人口多少上的差异，参见表1。

---

① 陈志强：《巴尔干古代史》，前言，第3页。

表1 巴尔干国家领土面积和人口

国家	领土面积（单位：平方千米）	排序	人口总数（单位：万人）	排序
罗马尼亚	238391	1	1970.0	1
保加利亚	111001.9	2	712.8	2
塞尔维亚	88300	3	705.8	3
克罗地亚	56594	4	417.4	4
波黑	51200	5	351.7	5
阿尔巴尼亚	28700	6	287.6	6
北马其顿	25713	7	208.1	7
斯洛文尼亚	20273	8	206.5	8
黑山	13800	9	62.2	9

数据来源：中国外交部官网（http://www.fmprc.gov.cn），世界银行数据库（http://www.worldbank.org）。

领土和人口是国家构成的基本要素，它们的大小或多少影响着国家的规模，而国家规模所产生的影响则是多方面的。相对而言，规模大的国家在国际关系中的地位就比较重要，话语权和影响力就比较大，而规模小的国家的话语权和影响力比较小甚至没有。从自身角度看，巴尔干国家在经贸往来和人员交流等方面的输入需求（也就是自身市场容量）和输出能力（向市场提供产品的数量）相差悬殊。相对而言，规模大的国家输入需求大且输出能力强，反之就小和弱。这些方面的差异一方面会影响巴尔干国家利益和诉求的整体性，另一方面会影响它们同中国合作的规模和程度。

第二，民族和宗教上的差异。

巴尔干国家不仅民族数量多，而且使用不同的语言和信奉不同的宗教，因而构成非常复杂。仅就主要民族的语言来说，东欧民族就有分属印欧、乌拉尔等两个语系，拉丁、斯拉夫和阿尔巴尼亚等四个语族，南斯拉夫、阿尔巴尼亚和东拉丁等四个语支，有塞尔维亚—克罗地亚语、斯洛文尼亚语、马其顿语、保加利亚语、阿尔巴尼亚语、罗马尼亚语等语种。如果再将其他少数民族的语言考虑在内，巴尔干国家的语言种类还要更多。宗教是一种与人们对超自然力量的信仰相适应的社会文化现象，其社会功能除了可以解除人们的精神紧张，调节人们的思想、意识和行为之外，还可以整合社会。巴尔干主要民族所信奉的是天主教、东正教和伊斯兰教。在中东欧17国的主要民族中，有的民族内部也有少数人由于种种原因信奉与本民族主要信仰不同的宗教，如一些塞尔维亚人信奉伊斯兰教，一些阿尔巴尼亚人信奉天主教或东正教。但是，大多数民族整体信仰的宗教是一样的。参见表2。

表2　巴尔干国家信奉不同宗教居民的比例①

国家	天主教（%）	东正教（%）	伊斯兰教（%）
罗马尼亚（2011年）	10.7	81.9	0.9
保加利亚（2011年）	1.7	59.4	7.8
塞尔维亚（2011年）	6.0	84.6	3.1
北马其顿（2002年）	0.4	64.8	33.3
阿尔巴尼亚（2011年）	10.0	6.8	56.7
波黑（2013年）	15.2	30.7	50.7
克罗地亚（2011年）	86.3	4.4	1.5
斯洛文尼亚（2002年）	58.7	2.3	2.4
黑山（2011年）	3.4	72.1	19.1

语言和宗教对民族一方面可以强化民族的构成因素，通过共同的语言和共同的信仰，人们可能增进对同一个民族的认同感。但另一方面，它们又强化了民族的排他性，催生了不同民族之间的对立和冲突。比较起来，宗教由于自身的特点在这两方面的负面作用更为明显。处于天主教、东正教和伊斯兰教的交汇处的巴尔干地区是宗教力量此消彼长的典型场所，从而使这一地区各民族间的关系比较紧张。同样，巴尔干国家民族与宗教上的复杂性产生的直接后果，就是它们作为一个整体缺乏内在的或"软性的"认同感和凝聚力，形成不了单独的文明区域。不仅如此，不同的地缘文明还和各自大致相同的文化记忆和发展程度高低不同的经济、政治整合，导致巴尔干国家之间有许多隐性和显性的、历史与现实的矛盾和冲突。

第三，经济发展水平上的差异。

经过近三十年的社会转型和发展，在经济发展水平上，巴尔干国家以私有

---

① https://www.cia.gov/library.

制为基础的市场经济都已经确立起来,但发展和完善的程度并不相同,在此基础之上呈现出的经济发展状况也不一样。如果从领土面积和人口多少上说,巴尔干国家是中小国家并存,那么,从 GDP 总量和人均 GDP 上说,它们则是富国穷国并存。GDP 指标虽然不能说明全部问题,但基本上可以表明这些国家经济的发展程度和规模,参见表3。

表3 巴尔干国家GDP 总量和人均GDP(2016年)①

国家	GDP 总量（单位：亿美元）	排序	人均 GDP（单位：美元）	排序
罗马尼亚	1875.9	1	9522.8	3
保加利亚	532.4	2	7469.0	4
克罗地亚	507.2	3	12149.2	2
斯洛文尼亚	447.1	4	21650.2	1
塞尔维亚	383.0	5	5426.2	5
波黑	169.1	6	4808.4	7
阿尔巴尼亚	118.6	7	4125.0	8
北马其顿	109.0	8	5237.1	6
黑山	43.7	9	7028.9	9

GDP 总量从很重要的方面反映出国家的经济实力,而经济实力同样是支撑一个国家在国际舞台上地位、话语权和影响力的重要因素。巴尔干国家在这方面的悬殊差别同样决定着它们的利益与诉求不一样,在同中国的经贸合作和文化交往中接受能力和输出能力也有别。从人均GDP 上看,上表中超过1 万美元的只有2 个国家,但都是小国,GDP 的总量并不大。但是,这些国家的发达程度、现代化程度以及开放程度都比较高,基础设施比较好,服务业也很完善。在这些方面,巴尔干国家的实际差距也非常明显。相比之下,在GDP 总量小而人均GDP 又低的国家,基础设施都有待于完善,服务业不太发达。这种差距同样制约着它们利益诉求和行为能力的整体性。

第四,"回归欧洲"方面的差异。

巴尔干国家在摆脱了苏联模式和苏联控制之后,几乎无一例外地都以"回

① 世界银行数据库(http://www.worldbank.org)。

归欧洲"为社会发展的目标,只是程度上有所不同。如前所述,"回归欧洲"主要是从社会发展模式角度说的。虽然都是"回归欧洲",但是,巴尔干国家的具体情况差别很大。保加利亚、罗马尼亚、阿尔巴尼亚是第一种类型。它们的国家结构没有发生变化,社会转型的内容就是否定苏联模式的合法性,在此基础上转向西方式社会发展模式。保加利亚、罗马尼亚、阿尔巴尼亚的社会转型主要是受波兰、匈牙利等国社会剧变的冲击,转型之前量变积累相对不充分,其去苏联模式化及后西欧模式的重新确立都较仓促并且充斥着动荡甚至暴力,所需时间也相对长些。斯洛文尼亚、克罗地亚、波黑、黑山、北马其顿是第二种类型。它们都是南斯拉夫社会剧变和国家解体过程中新独立的国家。在社会主义时期只是南斯拉夫的共和国或者苏联的加盟共和国,从其母体(南斯拉夫)那里继承的国家遗产很少甚至没有。所以,作为一个独立的主权国家,它们的内政和外交机构需要重新建构。对这些国家而言,社会发展的内容除了去苏联模式外,更为重要的是构建新的国家。国家虽然是新建的,但赖以建立的基础却是苏联模式的废墟。其中,斯洛文尼亚、克罗地亚、黑山和波罗的海三国转型前的经济发展程度、民主化程度都比较高,历史上与西方的关系较为紧密,转型条件准备较充分,按新社会发展模式进行的国家构建比较顺利。波黑、北马其顿和黑山主要受困于民族、宗教矛盾、地区政治或国际政治,构建统一国家的历程比较艰难或曲折。与此相适应,它们的社会转型也不顺畅。塞尔维亚是第三类。它虽然也是新独立的国家,但因为是南斯拉夫的唯一继承者,几乎不存在独立建国的问题。也正因为它完整地继承了南斯拉夫的遗产,因而去苏联模式化和新制度构建的任务繁重。

社会转型的内容常常依据不同的标准划分成不同的类别,如经济转型、政治转型、文化转型等。不仅是不同的国家,就是在同一个国家,这些不同方面的转型不仅不是同步的,而且差别比较大。但总体来说,社会转型是相对短暂的。它只是社会发展中的某一个过渡性或连接阶段,但不同方面的转型所需要的时间并不一样。对巴尔干国家来说,政治上去苏联模式化的时间比较短,甚至可以说就是社会剧变本身。在剧变过程中,这些国家都很快地实行了议会制、通过宪法确立了新的政治制度、进行了多党制的选举等。经济上的去苏联模式化主要是通过私有化、市场化实现的。总体上说,经济转型的时间要远远长于政治转型,而且各国之间的差别也很大。但是,外交上的转型不仅所需时间长,而且差别更大。参见表4。

表4 巴尔干国家回归欧洲的程度

国家	加入北约时间	加入欧盟时间	加入申根区时间	加入欧元区时间
罗马尼亚	2004年	2007年		
保加利亚	2004年	2007年		
斯洛文尼亚	2004年	2004年	2007年	2007年
克罗地亚	2009年	2013年		
塞尔维亚		2010年申请		
北马其顿				
波黑				
黑山	2017年			
阿尔巴尼亚	2009年	2009年申请		

巴尔干国家的"回归欧洲"实际上包括社会转型、新国家构建和社会发展三方面内容。在这三方面，这些国家有共性，但地区性和个性也很突出。所谓共性，指的是这些国家都具有的特征，即去苏联模式化和西方模式化。所谓地区性，指的是巴尔干地区不仅国家多，而且异质性强，发展差别明显。斯洛文尼亚、克罗地亚、罗马尼亚、保加利亚都已经是北约和欧盟的成员，阿尔巴尼亚和黑山只是北约的成员，而其他国家还都远近不同地站在欧洲的大门口。除了去苏联模式化的共性和多样化的地区性之外，巴尔干国家最近三十年在社会转型、新国家构建和社会发展上受自身的历史传统和政治文化影响比较大，因而都在不同程度上凸显自己的个性特征，在社会发展方面几乎一国一样。

二

除了这些差异之外，这些巴尔干国家的内部关系和相互之间的关系还非常复杂，其表现主要有以下几方面。

第一，四重认同程度比较低。

所谓四重认同，指的是区域认同、民族认同、国家认同和政治认同。它们有区别又有联系，而且不同国家又各有侧重。

区域认同，指的是这些国家对由它们组成的巴尔干区域的态度。应当说，在与中国合作的"17+1"机制中，巴尔干国家是有认同的，并且在各方面都取得了很大的成就。但在这个合作机制之外，这些国家对巴尔干地区是缺乏认同的。西北的斯洛文尼亚和克罗地亚甚至不认为自己是巴尔干国家。而东部的保加利亚和罗马尼亚已加入欧盟。西巴尔干地区除了阿尔巴尼亚之外都是通过争吵甚至战争从前南斯拉夫分裂而成的，对共同的区域的认同比较低。

民族认同，指的是相同民族的人对本民族特有政治文化、风俗习惯的态度。而国家认同，指的是公民对本国的态度。民族是一种文化地域上面的概念，而国家是更广的政治地理上的概念。除了民族数量众多之外，巴尔干国家的民族交叉分布和跨境分布状态十分突出。一个国家有多个民族，一个民族又生活在不同的国家里。在巴尔干地区，民族认同和国家认同的正负效应往往是相伴的。比如，阿尔巴尼亚人是一个跨界民族，除了阿尔巴尼亚之外，北马其顿、希腊、黑山、科索沃也有数量不等的阿尔巴尼亚人。除了塞尔维亚之外，塞尔维亚人还分布在克罗地亚、波黑、黑山。在这种情况下形成的民族认同往往会使一国之内民族关系错综复杂，对国家的统一建构和社会发展非常不利。比如，北马其顿的马其顿族和阿尔巴尼亚族，波黑的塞尔维亚族、克罗地亚族和穆斯林，都缺乏对统一国家的认同，而非主体民族的外倾性非常强。在波黑，塞尔维亚人认同的主要不是波黑这个国家，而是塞尔维亚。在北马其顿，阿尔巴尼亚人认同的主要不是北马其顿这个国家，而是阿尔巴尼亚。在波黑这样的国家里，由于受国际社会的约束，塞尔维亚人、克罗地亚人和穆斯林虽然相处一国，但在新国家的体制构建以及内外政策上，他们在统一国家中的地位和作用上都存在着不同程度的分歧和矛盾，而这些分歧和矛盾也影响到波黑的对外关系上。

政治认同，指的是一国之内的政党和民众对国家体制和内外政策的态度。巴尔干国家实行的都是政党政治，多党竞争，轮流执政。在这样的政治框架之内，再加上复杂的民族认同和国家认同问题，不同政党及其代表的民众各有各的政治认识，具体的内政外交政策也不尽相同，延续性不强，认同度不高。多党竞争最突出的特点就在于相互间治国理念和方针政策的不认同甚至对峙，这虽然是政党政治的常态，但对"17+1"的有效合作来说，却是必须加以考虑的因素。

上述四个认同问题分属于不同层次，具体表现在巴尔干各国则是各有侧重。但不能否认的是，在这四个认同上的差异同样不仅制约着它们同中国交往与合作的整体性，也制约着各国同中国交往与合作的延续性。

第二，国家关系多纠结。

巴尔干国家不仅民族数量多，而且交叉和跨境分布。这种状况与各民族的历史记忆相叠加，使巴尔干地区内的国家关系更为复杂。巴尔干地区民族跨境现象的产生，有历史上民族迁徙的原因，也有周边强大民族影响的原因，但更多的是大国关系和国际体系造成的，是它们的"副产品"。巴尔干地区的近代民族国家都是大国关系和国际体系的产物，领土疆界都是大国主导划定的。在这个过程中，大国主要是按自己的利益和要求，同时也为了协调大国关系和便于对中东欧国家的控制，制造并强化了这个地区民族分布的"马赛克现象"。比如，阿尔巴尼亚领土疆域的划定和阿尔巴尼亚人散落在巴尔干地区的其他国家，这主要是1912年六大国外长伦敦会议决定的。西巴尔干地区的民族跨界格局也是由国际社会主导的《代顿协议》决定的。在大国制定的国际体系里，巴尔干地区的民族和国家是不可能有任何突破的，但民族跨界的种种负面效应却都存在。

由于上述这些历史或政治上的原因，巴尔干一些相邻国家的关系就显得错综复杂，在不同程度上影响着这个地区的合作与稳定。比如，塞尔维亚与克罗地亚两国关系就一直受困于现代历史上的矛盾和南联邦解体时的武装冲突。克罗地亚之所以在2013年才加入欧盟，重要原因之一就是它与斯洛文尼亚的领土纠纷。阿尔巴尼亚与塞尔维亚在科索沃地位问题上尖锐对峙。阿尔巴尼亚是第一个承认科索沃独立的国家，而塞尔维亚至今也不放弃对科索沃的主权。北马其顿与希腊主要在北马其顿国名问题上存在矛盾，与保加利亚在领土问题上存在争端，与塞尔维亚在教会问题上存在分歧，等等。这些矛盾、争端和分歧对巴尔干地区的民族关系和国家关系的影响是负面的，虽然成为历史的跨境民族问题有时也会成为相关国家开展合作的契机，但更多情况下其导致国家关系冷漠。

总的来看，随着时间的推移和在国际社会的干预下，因民族跨界而产生的这些冲突、争执和分歧会不断地淡化，有的可能得到解决。但是，它们很难彻底消除，特别是有着光荣与悲哀的记忆的历史是挥之不去的。

第三，与大国关系的远近亲疏不同。

在某种意义上可说，巴尔干国家的前生今世都离不开大国。大国是巴尔干近代民族国家的"接生婆"和"保姆"，而巴尔干从来都是被罩在东西方大国的阴影之下生存和发展的。甚至可以说，中东欧国家的这种命运直到今天依然如此。但问题在于，它们所倚重的不是一个大国，而是不同甚至相互对峙、竞争的大国。因此，巴尔干国家的复杂性还体现在它们与大国的关系上。它们同欧盟、美国、俄罗斯、土耳其等大国的关系并不等量齐观，亲疏远近各有侧重。

在与欧盟关系方面，巴尔干国家的梯次性还是十分明显的。斯洛文尼亚于2004年，罗马尼亚和保加利亚于2007年，克罗地亚于2013年成为欧盟的成员。阿尔巴尼亚和塞尔维亚先后于2009年和2010年向欧盟提出了加入申请。北马其顿、波黑和黑山也在积极努力。与欧盟关系远近的不同制约着巴尔干国家的内外政策，更制约着它们的一致性。进入欧盟的国家就与"老欧洲"平起平坐，不仅不需再看欧盟脸色行事，甚至还可以在欧盟的框架内说"不"。但是，那些正在加入欧盟途中的国家，还得忍气吞声，努力满足欧盟的要求。在与美国关系方面，出于"回归欧洲"和摆脱俄罗斯的需要，巴尔干有的国家同美国站在一起。但由塞尔维亚和黑山构成的南联盟在科索沃问题上受到美国为首的北约的狂轰滥炸。独立成国之后，塞尔维亚也长期与美国主导的西方阵营对峙。在与俄罗斯关系方面，一般而论，与欧盟和美国走得越近的国家，同俄罗斯的关系越疏远。在地理位置方面，离西欧越近的国家，同俄罗斯的关系越疏远。在宗教文明上，天主教文明圈的国家，同俄罗斯的关系比较疏远。如果将这些前提条件反过来，那么，这样的国家同俄罗斯的关系就走得近些。不过，由于冷战之后世界格局发生了根本性的变化，美国独大，俄罗斯实力大不如前，巴尔干国家"回归欧洲"的趋势不可逆转，所以，它们同俄罗斯的亲疏都是有度的。塞尔维亚、黑山和保加利亚等与俄罗斯走得相对比较近，但也不会超越欧盟、北约划定的界限。在与中国关系方面，总体上说，由于"17+1"合作机制，巴尔干国家与中国的关系都比较好。但是，上述那些中东欧国家在各方面的差异性和复杂性在客观上都会影响到它们同中国合作关系的密切程度。那些规模比较大、影响力比较大、市场需求量比较大和提供产品能力比较强的国家，在同中国合作中所占的地位就比较重要。另外，巴尔干国家同中国关系还受一些不确定的因素影响，如美国和欧盟因素、政党政治因素以及各国的自身利益，等等。

三

综上所述，巴尔干地区的复杂性是民族宗教、历史文化、国内政治、地区政治、国际政治和国际影响等诸多因素综合作用的结果，形成的时间长，短时期内难以彻底消除。这些"老病"虽然在不同程度上为"回归欧洲"的大势所遮掩，但对这些国家作为一个整体的内聚性、对外关系的一致性的影响是不言而喻的。中国在"17+1"框架内同它们的合作要想顺利地前行，不仅要认清这些差异性，而且必须超越它们。稍有不慎，"17+1"合作机制就会失灵，其负面效应也会波及"一带一路"。

中国与巴尔干国家合作就是建立在这种多样、复杂和差异基础之上的，范围涉及多种领域和多个层次。良好的并且定位很高的政治关系，是落实"17+1"合作机制的基本前提和可靠保证。它可以通过首脑互访、领导人峰会以及各种会议、论坛来进行整体性的构建、升级，相对来说成本也比较低，构建起来难度不大。但历史经验证明，政治关系往往又是脆弱的和易变的，受其他多重因素的影响比较大。巴尔干国家都是政党政治，党派和首脑频繁更替会在一定程度上影响国家内政外交方面的具体政策的延续。与此相联系，巴尔干国家在与中国交往过程中会在不同程度上受到国内政治、地区政治和国际政治的干扰。政治关系需要坚实而牢固的经贸关系来支撑，因此，中国发展同巴尔干国家的友好关系时，要特别考虑到并超越它们多元的利益诉求和易变的内外政策。

比如，在具体的经贸合作上，中国不太可能将巴尔干国家作为一个整体，而是要面对一个个具体国家，根据它们的差异来确定与每个国家具体合作的领域、总量和档次等，以便进行"精准性"的合作。所谓"精准性"，主要是指中国同巴尔干国家在各方面的合作要找好契合点，真正是互需互补，规模和档次适度。做到这些的基本前提是对巴尔干国家的多样性和中国与它们的差异性进行详细、深入的分析和考察，而不是脱离这些而进行政治论证或学术论证。虽然差异性大、经济贸易、文化交流等方面的互补性弱，但这绝不意味着中国与它们没有合作的空间。这些有成效的合作都是非常具体的，是同某一国家在某一方面的合作，数量和规模相对来说也都有限。由于巴尔干国家的多样性和复杂性，以及中国同它们的巨大的差异性和较弱的互补性，中国与它们的经贸合作也必然是多样性、多层性的。另外，考虑到中国对外经贸关系和巴尔干地区对外经贸的各自的格局和重点，应恰当地评估中国与巴尔干地区经贸合作的价值和意义，既不可小觑但也不能高估。在恰当、全面评估的基础之上，中国的不同地区、不同行业的不同企业分别有针对性地同它们开展点对点、面对面的合作，积小、积少成多，为"一带一路"倡议的实施，为中国与巴尔干国家的关系发展提供坚实的物质支撑。

俄罗斯在西巴尔干的经济存在及政治影响

朱晓中

内容提要 近代以降，巴尔干地区一直是列强争夺和博弈的场所。南斯拉夫联邦解体之后，特别是科索沃战争以来，欧盟、美国、俄罗斯等组织和国家竞相介入巴尔干地区内部事务，对这一地区国家的政治、经济和对外关系产生了不同程度的影响。在巴尔干地区国家整体向欧盟靠拢的同时，俄罗斯以能源和其他经济手段不断介入该地区，并试图借此增加对巴尔干国家的影响。虽然俄罗斯介入巴尔干地区的深度与欧盟不可同日而语，但欧美国家认为，俄罗斯扩大在巴尔干的存在的努力会危及欧洲一体化进程，欧美国家须予以警惕，并做出适当反应。

关 键 词 巴尔干 前南地区 俄罗斯 欧盟 地缘政治

作者简介 朱晓中，中国社会科学院俄罗斯东欧中亚研究所研究员

巴尔干半岛地处欧亚大陆的战略要冲，身处地中海和黑海之间，自古以来便是文明碰撞、宗教分裂、种族对峙以及大国或大国集团割据的角斗场，在漫长的历史进程中留给人们诸多以血腥为底色的斑斓画面。自近代以来，特别是19世纪以来，巴尔干一直是大国竞争的焦点。

1991年南斯拉夫联邦解体之后，巴尔干地区国家（前南地区国家）经历了一系列重大政治和社会变动。在巴尔干地区发生的每一次重大事件中，都可以看到国际组织和一些大国的身影，它们试图从中斡旋和化解危机。大国和国际组织涉足巴尔干事务，对寻找解决危机的出路、稳定地区局势具有积极意义；同时，这也是大国在巴尔干地区寻求并捍卫自身利益与其他利益攸关方进

行博弈的过程。2000年以来，巴尔干地区存在两个明显的趋势：一方面，欧盟和北约不断推动巴尔干国家加入跨大西洋框架，① 巴尔干地区的亲欧洲（西方）情绪日益浓厚；另一方面，俄罗斯通过经济手段不断在巴尔干地区渗透，努力扩大在这一地区的影响力，使之成为俄罗斯与西方进行地缘政治博弈的一个重要角斗场。

当前俄罗斯在巴尔干半岛的利益源于南斯拉夫的解体及其后果，它们从根本上改变了俄罗斯对巴尔干半岛利益的看法。虽然由于国力衰弱，俄罗斯无力向包括巴尔干在内的中东欧地区投射更多影响力，但随着近10年来俄罗斯与西方关系持续紧张，特别是2014年因克里米亚归属发生重大变化导致西方与俄罗斯关系急转直下，俄罗斯对巴尔干地区的政策被纳入俄罗斯与西方关系这一更大框架中来。俄罗斯在努力确保其在巴尔干的核心利益的同时，利用其在巴尔干事务中相当可观的影响力，在与西方就其他核心利益问题（如格鲁吉亚或乌克兰问题）的谈判中作为讨价还价的筹码。

基于俄罗斯的国家利益，俄罗斯对西巴尔干地区至少有四点战略考虑。

第一，避免西巴尔干地区发生战乱，保障俄罗斯西南部安全。因为，历史上每一场巴尔干战争都对俄罗斯产生了负面影响，损害了俄罗斯的长远利益。

第二，保障俄罗斯的主权和领土完整。俄罗斯批判西方干涉他国内政观念，无论是基于人道主义还是其他哲学原则，避免这种观念成为"普遍接受的原则"，从而助长车臣分裂主义。同时，限制西方民主思想，以避免可能会破坏俄罗斯的国家观念和东正教教会的角色。

第三，寻求和扩大俄罗斯的经济和能源利益。俄罗斯是巴尔干国家的主要投资者，能源是俄罗斯在巴尔干半岛的主要利益以及它所拥有的主要经济武器。普京强调，俄罗斯外交政策的当务之急是反映俄罗斯企业的需求。

第四，基于泛欧亚地缘政治概念，利用人口和欧亚大陆战略潜力形成一个反对西方的大陆集团。莫斯科期望，巴尔干国家不加入北约；如果不得不加入其中，希望他们发挥"破坏大西洋安全领域的解决方案"的作用。

基于上述几点，近年来，俄罗斯强化其在巴尔干的经济和政治存在，希冀实现俄罗斯的战略目标。

---

① 目前，巴尔干地区国家处于欧洲一体化的不同阶段：2004年和2013年，斯洛文尼亚和克罗地亚先后加入欧盟。黑山和塞尔维亚已开始入盟谈判。北马其顿因与希腊存在国名之争导致入盟谈判迟迟不能启动，阿尔巴尼亚和波黑已递交入盟申请。

一、俄罗斯在巴尔干的政治杠杆

俄罗斯认为，巴尔干的历史是俄国历史和俄国民族意识不可分割的一部分，是俄罗斯利益的一个组成部分。这当中既有地缘政治的驱动，也有纯粹经济利益的考量，还与维持国家威望有关。冷战结束以后，俄罗斯对巴尔干政策的目的有两个：限制美国和北约在巴尔干的影响，扩大和提升俄罗斯的存在感。虽然在经济实力和政治影响力方面不能与跨大西洋框架比肩，但它试图利用巴尔干危机和不稳定来影响这一地区。

俄罗斯对巴尔干地区的主要政治杠杆大致有四种：尽可能利用巴尔干地区的危机；根据与俄罗斯关系程度将西巴尔干地区国家划分为三种关系类型，制定相应的政策分而治之；推崇与巴尔干国家的宗教和历史文化联系；利用欧盟合法性的缺陷。

（一）利用巴尔干地区的危机

20世纪90年代以来，俄罗斯充分利用了南斯拉夫联邦解体引发的各种危机，试图干扰西方国家在南斯拉夫危机中实施有效政策，削弱欧美解决巴尔干冲突的能力，以提高俄罗斯的威信。

在利用危机方面，波黑战争结束后，俄罗斯曾呼吁在巴尔干建立不依托于北约的新的"集体安全体系"，旨在绕过北约，将尚未同北约建立联系的塞尔维亚包括进来，并以此维持巴尔干国家的现有边界，防止黑山和科索沃独立。从联合国决定启动科索沃最终地位的相关谈判（2005年11月）到科索沃单方面宣布独立（2008年2月17日）这段时间里，俄罗斯一直对以美国为首的西方国家在科索沃问题上的立场持强硬的批评态度，并称科索沃单方面宣布独立不仅损害了塞尔维亚共和国主权，也违背了联合国宪章和联合国安理会第1244号决议的原则和精神，并可能引发巴尔干地区的新一轮冲突，使这一地区的紧张和种族暴力升级。俄罗斯驻北约代表罗戈津还强硬表示，如果北约军队在科索沃的行动超出联合国授权的范围，俄罗斯不排除"武力解决科索沃问题"。虽然俄罗斯的强烈反应未能阻挡住科索沃独立（而且人们也很难想象俄罗斯会因此采取具有实际意义的行动），但俄罗斯在科索沃问题上的立场却博得了塞尔维亚的心，使之成为今天俄罗斯在巴尔干最坚定的盟友。

(二）据国家间关系亲疏程度分类

俄罗斯将西巴尔干地区国家分为三种关系类型：即传统伙伴关系：塞尔维亚和黑山（均同俄罗斯有"历史关系"）；有前景的伙伴关系：波黑（特别是波黑塞族共和国）和北马其顿；潜在的伙伴关系：克罗地亚和斯洛文尼亚。

(三）推崇宗教和历史文化联系

在同巴尔干国家打交道时，俄罗斯政治家经常提及两者之间文化和文明的相似性，这对巴尔干国家的民众有较大的象征意义。尽管对巴尔干社会中存在的一些决定性因素——是否为奥斯曼帝国的遗产，或它是否具有东正教和伊斯兰（及加尔文教）的共同特征——存在争议，但在巴尔干地区，某些精妙的类似"神话"的东西在国际关系中的确发挥着特定作用。比如，流传着东正教徒之间是兄弟，东正教国家需要团结一致的说法；经常将信奉东正教国家的社会现实（人们积极、友善）同西方的政治（不是社会）现实进行比较；在塞尔维亚首都贝尔格莱德竖立着俄国沙皇尼古拉二世的纪念碑，象征着俄塞的历史友好关系。在外交实践中，俄罗斯也时常以文明或民族划界。例如，在波黑塞族共和国向联邦机构争夺自治权时，俄罗斯支持前者的主张；在科索沃问题上俄罗斯向塞尔维亚提供支持。俄罗斯使用的另一个工具是泛斯拉夫主义，这在与塞尔维亚（和希腊）打交道时更有效（对其他东正教国家的效用稍差）。

(四）利用欧盟合法性的缺陷

俄罗斯利用欧元区金融和经济危机和欧洲经济一体化的某些缺陷来为自己的战略寻找突破口。迄今为止，欧洲一体化没有给所有成员国（特别是许多中东欧新成员国）带来预期的成果。2004年以来的三次欧盟东扩，扩大了欧洲福利和繁荣的地区，但许多中东欧国家依然保持着边缘的特征，由此提出了欧盟新成员国转型是否成功的问题。国家的边缘化也导致有关社会中的边缘化。也就是说，国家的宏观经济指标对冲了因社会不满导致的日益恶化的社会形势的微观指标。在这种社会中，政治精英异化，脱离社会和社会经济现实。无疑，较穷的中东欧国家需要几个十年才能赶上老成员国的发展，这期间不能有准确的预期和计划性。经济增长没有带来一种社会中较好的和更有效的收入再分配，也没有降低失业率，这可能导致事实上的低工资和社会支持的大幅下降。

成功的自由市场转型的代价一直由社会支付，只给少数人带来福利。[①] 无疑，波兰在衰退的海洋中作为一个"绿岛"是例外的，它不代表转型的全部场景。对社会的大多数人来说，他们付出了更多的成本，他们是输家，他们处于不利的位置。塞尔维亚人或北马其顿人没有看到邻国克罗地亚、保加利亚或匈牙利发生迅速的变化。希腊的金融危机进一步给欧洲一体化蒙上了一层阴影。欧盟的合法性（主导性）正在褪去。因此，这给了俄罗斯以可乘之机，特别是在那些与俄罗斯具有某些共同文化价值的国家。

二、俄罗斯在西巴尔干的经济存在

虽然冷战后俄罗斯在巴尔干的战略目标是限制美国和北约在巴尔干的影响，但在欧洲一体化在巴尔干愈演愈烈的大背景下，俄罗斯意识到，它在巴尔干的当务之急并非一味地口头上遏制欧美国家势力的扩张，而是要努力提升俄罗斯的影响力，通过扩大在巴尔干的经济存在，以便同西方国家进行竞争。为此，针对巴尔干国家不同程度的能源需求，俄罗斯充分利用其能源渠道，扩大其在巴尔干的经济影响力。迄今为止，俄罗斯在西巴尔干地区的经济合作主要集中在能源和投资两大领域。

（一）能源领域合作

在前南地区国家中，塞尔维亚是俄罗斯进行能源合作的重点国家之一。2003年8月26日，俄罗斯卢克石油公司（Lukoil）出资1.17亿美元，获得塞尔维亚第二大石油产品的国营储存和零售公司Beopetrol 70%的股份，建立了卢克—Beopetrol公司（2011年3月5日更名为"卢克—塞尔维亚公司"，卢克公司拥有98%的股份）。该公司控制着塞尔维亚20%的石油产品市场，拥有塞尔维亚境内的180座加油站。在这期间，卢克—塞尔维亚公司改造了塞尔维亚境内的74家加油站，对70家加油站进行了升级，新建了5家加油站。公司还从事石油产品的批发贸易，以及出售卢克石油公司在俄罗斯和罗马尼亚生产的机

[①] Jan Muś, "Peripheral Position of the Balkans and its Future Relations with Russia," in *Rocznik Instytutu Europy Środkowo-Wschodniej Rok*, 13（2015），p. 116, http：//www.iesw.lublin.pl/rocznik/pliki/Rocznik_2015-226.pdf.

油。卢克—塞尔维亚公司的目标是做地区老大。为此,公司计划增加塞尔维亚的石油加工量,将公司的市场份额提高到25%—30%,并向其他巴尔干国家市场进军。

俄塞两国最大的能源合作项目是俄罗斯天然气工业石油公司〔俄罗斯天然气工业股份公司(俄气)的子公司〕参股塞尔维亚国家石油公司(NIS)。2008年1月25日,双方签署了关于石油和天然气领域合作政府间协议(期限为30年,每5年延长一次)及其后若干协定。该协议确定双方在能源领域进行一系列合作。第一,塞尔维亚参加"南溪"天然气管道项目,在塞尔维亚境内修建400公里天然气过境管线;① 第二,俄罗斯天然气工业石油公司控股塞尔维亚石油工业公司,由此控制了塞尔维亚大量能源资产,包括在塞尔维亚、安哥拉、波黑开采碳氢化合物(相当于150万吨原油,其中包括100万吨石油);在潘切沃和诺维萨德的两家炼油厂(年生产能力为730万吨,占塞尔维亚年需求量的85%②);一家液化天然气工厂;控制了塞尔维亚70%的零售市场,包括480座自动加油站和油罐区;向欧盟国家和乌克兰出口汽车燃料、苯、甲苯、道路和工业沥青;③ 第三,两国共同合资成立建设天然气地下储气库("巴纳特院子")公司。④ 同俄罗斯进行能源合作将使塞尔维亚成为欧洲的天然气过境和大型储气中心,以及知名的石油产品生产商。

根据2015年的数据,塞尔维亚国家石油公司拥有325家加油站(占塞尔维亚所有加油站总数的24%),卢克石油公司有148家(占10%),他们成为塞尔维亚最大的两家石油零售商。此外,塞尔维亚的石油和天然气公司供应其他竞争性零售加油站销售总量的78%的燃料。这组数据表明,俄罗斯拥有的公司几乎完全控制和垄断了塞尔维亚燃料市场的批发,超过1/3的零售市场,全上游生产,以及绝大多数批发仓储设施。2014年,国际原油价格下跌超过一半,零售汽油和柴油价格只分别下跌了4.4%至10.4%,俄罗斯公司从中获利巨大。

波黑所需的天然气完全依赖从俄罗斯进口。2015年,天然气仅占波黑能源

---

① 2013年11月24日,"南溪"项目塞尔维亚段输气管线工程正式开工。
② 俄罗斯的石油通过"友谊"石油管线运到塞尔维亚东部城市尼什的炼油厂。
③ 西方把俄塞之间石油天然气协议称为"政治交易",怀疑塞尔维亚政府没有通过招标便将战略资产卖给了俄罗斯天然气工业公司,以换取俄罗斯对其在科索沃问题上的支持。
④ 俄方拥有该公司51%的股份。2011年11月21日,"巴纳特院子"开始运营,它是东南欧最大的地下天然气存储库,实际规模为4.5亿立方米,最大生产能力为一昼夜500万立方米,而且有进一步扩大的潜力。该储气库使俄罗斯可以同时向塞尔维亚、匈牙利和波黑出口天然气。该项目实际上也是"南溪"项目的第一个工程。

终端消费总量的4%左右，以绝对数字计算，每年不超过2.2亿立方米。出于地缘政治的考虑，俄罗斯在与波黑进行经济合作过程中对波黑联邦和波黑塞族共和国采取了不同的策略，给予波黑塞族共和国部分优惠待遇，试图利用天然气价格差来影响波黑联邦和波黑塞族共和国之间的关系，进而影响波黑与欧盟和北约的关系。2014年9月，俄气和波黑塞族共和国签署一项合同，俄气从2015年7月1日至2016年12月31日向波黑塞族共和国提供1.06亿立方米天然气。2016年2月，波黑塞族共和国天然气公司和俄气又签署一项新的协议，后者绕过波黑联邦的天然气供应商以优惠的价格向波黑塞族共和国直接供气。在解决波黑欠俄罗斯天然气债务问题上，俄罗斯也有意施惠于波黑塞族共和国。根据波黑塞族共和国与俄罗斯签署的协议规定，该共和国天然气公司不必参与偿还在1992—1995年战争期间波斯尼亚所欠俄罗斯的9800万美元的天然气债务，债务只由波黑联邦的天然气公司负责偿还。

目前，波黑塞族共和国控制着波黑天然气总需求的一半左右。波黑联邦担心，由于塞族共和国与俄气关系密切，在必要时，波黑塞族共和国可以听命于俄罗斯，利用其掌握的天然气管道，减少天然气供应，使波黑联邦天然气供应面临巨大风险。

在波黑，俄罗斯国外石油公司（Zarubezhneft）通过参与企业私有化进入波黑塞族共和国的能源市场。俄罗斯国外石油公司以1.258亿欧元的价格赢得了波黑两家石油公司（Rafinerija Nafte Brod 和 Modrica）的私有化招标，该价格远低于2005年2.85亿欧元的初始标的。2011年，波黑塞族共和国给予俄罗斯国外石油公司28年的排他性特许权，准许该公司在塞族共和国境内开采石油和天然气。俄罗斯收购的波黑炼油厂成为俄罗斯所有的Optima集团的核心资产。2011年，该集团大致控制了波黑60%燃料批发市场（2017年为35%），为当年波黑GDP贡献了19%。俄罗斯国外石油公司现占有波黑最大的连锁加油站Nestro Petrol 80%的股份。

俄罗斯卢克石油公司目前在东南欧每个国家控制着大约10%的燃料销售终端，但在影响价格制定方面不如其在邻近保加利亚成功。在保加利亚，卢克石油公司拥有欧洲东南部最大的炼油厂，其一半以上的产品出口到北马其顿、希腊、土耳其、塞尔维亚和黑山。在北马其顿和黑山，俄罗斯卢克石油公司是这两国中第二大燃料零售供应商。北马其顿石油公司（Makpetrol）是该国最大的石油产品经销商，拥有全国一半的加油站。2012年前，北马其顿进口大部分原油来自俄罗斯。目前，北马其顿完全依赖从希腊塞萨洛尼卡港进口原油，通过一条管道到斯科普里附近的 OKTA 炼油厂。为了偿还其对国际债权人的部分债务，希腊政府先前提出出售其在希腊石油中的国家股份。卢克石油公司和俄罗斯天然气工业股份公司都表示购买的兴趣。如果希腊公司被俄罗斯公司控制，这将进一步增加俄罗斯在北马其顿和黑山石油部门企业的存在。

（二）投资合作

近年来，俄罗斯加大了在西巴尔干地区的活动力度。俄罗斯看重该地区的地缘政治和经济价值，视这一地区为抵御西方影响、恢复其大国影响力的主要地区。这里也是俄罗斯向欧洲国家提供天然气和石油的重要交通要道和基础设施枢纽。在西巴尔干地区，俄罗斯将塞尔维亚和波黑（特别是波黑塞族共和国）视为盟友和主要合作伙伴。

由于各种原因，俄罗斯在巴尔干地区的经济存在一直被低估，导致对其影响的真实程度认识不足。首先，人们在评估俄罗斯在巴尔干地区的投资时一直同欧盟在这一地区的直接投资总量进行比较，没有考虑到欧盟不是一个单一的实体。一个欧盟国家的外国直接投资不一定反映欧盟共同的经济政策；其次，俄罗斯的外国直接投资很多是通过离岸区和像塞浦路斯这样的"避风港"进行，隐蔽性强，导致资本接收国不能及时了解和应对俄罗斯隐性投资可能产生的影响；再次，俄罗斯利用外国直接投资作为外交政策工具的能力一直被忽视，没有一个欧盟成员国在对企业法人的控制速度和范围上可与俄罗斯竞争；最后，俄罗斯的公司在西巴尔干地区主要集中在战略领域，如能源、燃料加工、银行业。通过直接投资和并购，俄罗斯控制了西巴尔干国家的若干资产。

在西巴尔干地区，俄罗斯在黑山的经济存在最为明显。黑山的主要外国直接投资来自俄罗斯。根据黑山共和国企业注册中心的统计，2016 年，黑山 1/3 的外国公司（1723 家）的所有者为俄罗斯国籍,[①] 约 40% 的不动产为俄罗斯人所有，甚至有的村庄不动产百分之百归俄罗斯人所有。[②] 俄罗斯在黑山的投资有两个特点。第一，完全是私人投资。主要原因是黑山缺乏大企业，且远离交通要道，而且俄罗斯有在此投资失败的前例。第二，投资规模小，不动产、旅馆、咖啡馆和饭店是投资的主要对象。黑山对俄罗斯人的吸引力在于其宜人的

---

① Александра Вагнер，Российскийследв Черногории，08.04.2013，http：//www.svoboda.org/content/article/24950844.html.

② Paul Bradbury，"Half of Montenegro's property bought by Russians，claims paper"，Jan. 8，2012，http：//www.digitaljournal.com/article/317523.

气候、当地民众的友好态度、类似的文化和便宜的食宿和不动产。同时，黑山所得税税率（9%）在欧洲最低，法律环境较好。2014年5月，黑山加入欧盟对俄罗斯制裁的队伍，希望以此加快其加入北约和欧盟的速度。① 2015年8月，俄罗斯将黑山纳入反制裁国家名单。② 制裁和反制裁给在未来俄罗斯对黑山的投资蒙上了阴影。

目前俄罗斯在塞尔维亚的直接投资总额大约为11亿美元，占外国直接投资存量的4%。由于俄罗斯对塞尔维亚的大部分投资来自在欧盟成员国（如奥地利和荷兰）注册的俄罗斯公司，因此，俄罗斯在塞尔维亚的直接投资的总值显然被低估了。因为，仅俄罗斯对塞尔维亚国家石油公司就投资近10亿美元，③ 用于改造其在潘切沃的炼油厂。此外，俄罗斯卢克石油公司在塞尔维亚燃油批发市场投资2.5亿美元。因此，俄罗斯对塞尔维亚直接投资的总额（包括间接投资）更现实的估计应该是20亿美元，占塞尔维亚GDP的6%。

通过投资，俄罗斯国有和私营石油和天然气公司拥有塞尔维亚几乎国内所有的石油和天然气储量，控制了50%以上的批发和零售燃料市场，并间接影响着塞尔维亚国有燃气供应商塞尔维亚天然气公司的财政管理和公司治理，以及供应商的主要工业客户。俄罗斯公司直接雇用的职工大约占塞尔维亚全国劳动力人口的2%；间接雇用劳动力约7万人，约占塞尔维亚劳动力总人口的5%。

俄罗斯也通过政府间贷款来扩大其在塞尔维亚经济中的影响力。在2012—2013年，塞尔维亚遭遇财政危机，塞尔维亚请求莫斯科提供贷款，以避免因向国际货币基金组织请求援助而不得不进行结构性改革。俄罗斯同意向塞尔维亚提供5亿美元贷款，并立即支付3亿美元以帮助塞尔维亚维持经济运转。

俄罗斯还投资参与塞尔维亚的铁路建设。2013年1月11日，俄罗斯向塞尔维亚提供8亿美元贷款（年利率4.1%）。④ 该笔贷款用于塞尔维亚政府向俄罗斯铁路国际公司［2012年12月成立的俄罗斯铁路公司（俄铁）的子公司］支付建设塞尔维亚铁路系统的费用。该工程于2014年3月26日开工。俄铁国

---

① "Montenegro supports Russia sanctions in order to hasten EU accession", 22 May, 2014; https://www.rt.com/news/160776-montenegro-eu-sanctions-russia/

② Dusica Tomovic, "Russia Extends Sanctions to Include Montenegro", 14 Aug. 2015, http://www.balkaninsight.com/en/article/montenegro-gets-revenge-for-sanctions-agains-russia-08-14-2015.

③ 2008年，俄气收购了该公司。

④ 俄罗斯贷款的年利率（4.1%）不仅高于欧洲复兴开发银行和欧洲投资银行的贷款利率，而且使俄罗斯公司在塞尔维亚基础设施现代化项目中获得了优势地位。

际公司计划将塞尔维亚350公里铁路现代化（并提供火车头），包括200公里贝尔格莱德到黑山巴尔的线路。这是俄罗斯在巴尔干第一个非能源大项目，也是俄铁在欧洲经营的第一个项目。2017年4月，俄铁国际完成了塞尔维亚境内维那奇至卓尔捷沃段的施工，这是泛欧10号走廊6段铁路线中的最后一段。① 它不仅标志着俄铁国际完成了其中标的所有工程，也成为俄铁同其他巴尔干国家进行基础设施改造合作的范本。

俄罗斯是波黑塞族共和国的第四大投资国。② 2008年经济危机以来，俄罗斯在波黑的直接投资从2.35亿美元增加到2016年的5.47亿美元，占波黑外资存量的8.1%（和GDP的3.3%）。俄罗斯的大部分投资集中在波黑塞族共和国境内的石油加工、燃料和天然气分配和金融服务领域。俄罗斯在波黑的更大一笔投资是2007年俄罗斯国外石油公司购买波黑布罗德和莫德里奇炼油厂。③ 随着俄罗斯对炼油厂改造的不断投资，使一个萧条城市的炼油厂起死回生。该炼油厂带来的收益可以稳定塞族共和国的政治形势，也有助该实体从波黑中央政府和国际社会驻波黑高级代表那里获得更多的经济自主权。在2006—2015年，俄罗斯公司在波黑的经济存在增长超过了一倍。2016年，俄罗斯企业在波黑的营业额约为10亿欧元，俄罗斯公司在波黑塞族共和国经济中的份额占该实体经济的8%以上。除能源以外，俄罗斯私人投资者对波黑塞族共和国境内的乌格列维克热电站和煤炭开采进行投资，总价值10亿欧元。

表面上看，在2009年之前，俄罗斯在北马其顿几乎没有直接投资，2015年时也只有区区3000万美元。俄罗斯直接投资只占北马其顿GDP的1%左右。但对俄罗斯在该国的存在进行详细研究后则发现，俄罗斯企业利用塞浦路斯、伯利兹和荷兰等离岸国进行隐身投资。俄罗斯在北马其顿最大的公司是卢克石油公司。分析显示，在北马其顿注册的78家外国公司中至少25%是俄罗斯所有。在北马其顿运营的俄罗斯公司的收入从2006年的6300万欧元增加到2015年超过2.12亿欧元。

---

① Tatiana Kanunnikova, "Russian Railways complete reconstruction of railroads in Serbia", 19 April 2017, http：//russianconstruction.com/news-1/27257-russian-railways-complete-reconstruction-of-railroads-in-serbia.html.

② "Bosnian serbs woo investors from Russia", April 1, 2016, http：//www.balkaninsight.com/en/article/russia-republika-srpska-seek-stronger-economic-ties-03-31-2016.

③ "Neftegazinkor to invest 150 mln euros in Bosnia's oil refinery Brod next year", Dec. 24th 2010, http：//www.fondsk.ru/news/2014/02/14/bosnijskaja-vesna-i-serbskij-zakat-25728.html.

值得关注的是，俄罗斯在西巴尔干国家能源领域的投资具有明显的排他性，通过锁定天然气供应来强化自己的地位，同时也推动这些国家与俄罗斯的相互依存。虽然塞尔维亚和波黑两国与俄气签署的天然气长期合同的价格一直高于多数欧洲国家，但这两国没有试图重新谈判这些协议以获得更大的灵活性，也没有采取措施来寻求天然气供应多样化。相反，两国的决策者公开力挺俄罗斯主导的大型天然气基础项目（如"南溪"和"特斯拉"）。有关这些项目的政府间协定完全保密，没有进行成本效益分析。《2017年欧盟能源共同体报告》指出，塞尔维亚和波黑两国的天然气市场高度集中，且基本上是封闭的。目前，俄波两国双边合作存在诸多问题。俄罗斯和波黑尚未签署双边投资保护和避免双重征税协定，没有双边贸易协定，两国之间没有直航。此外，波黑的政治形势也尚未最终稳定下来。这些都不利于双方开展进一步经贸合作。

三、俄罗斯在西巴尔干的政治影响

自2008年以来，俄罗斯积极利用其资源型经济力量，与业已存在的安全网络结合起来，使用传统软实力，在整个西巴尔干地区开发和扩大战略突破口。

当下，俄罗斯已在塞尔维亚实现某种突破。在与塞尔维亚进行经贸合作的同时，俄罗斯在其他领域多管齐下，着力在文化、传媒与信息、科学研究等多领域与塞尔维亚建立和扩大双边合作，培养亲近感。2005年以来，"俄罗斯世界"基金会①的分支机构和国际东正教统一基金会②的代表处已经在诺维萨德和贝尔格莱德设立并运营。2013年后，俄罗斯与塞尔维亚在非经贸领域中的合作水平进一步提升。俄罗斯战略研究所（RISI）③在贝尔格莱德建立了分支机构，这是该机构在西巴尔干地区唯一的分支机构。此外，戈尔恰科夫公共外交基金会、战略文化基金会、国家荣誉中心、圣安德鲁基金会等也先后在塞尔维亚落户。这些机构通过资助塞尔维亚科研项目，组织召开有关俄罗斯问题的各

---

① 2007年创立的由俄政府提供财政支持的非营利性机构，旨在世界各地推动俄语发展和推广俄罗斯文化。
② 俄罗斯民间友好团体，1995年成立。
③ 战略研究所是一个应俄罗斯总统要求建立的战略、科研和分析中心。主要目标是向总统和其他国家提供信息。

种会议，在塞尔维亚学术机构建立俄罗斯中心等方式促进双边合作，寻求并扩大俄罗斯的利益。

俄罗斯主要媒体也纷纷在塞尔维亚设立分支机构，用当地语言全面介绍俄罗斯的政治、经济和外交事务。2012年以来，俄罗斯一些新闻门户网站在塞尔维亚落户，其中包括：Novi Standard（www.standard.rs）、Srbin.info（www.srbin.info）、Vaseljenska（www.vaseljenska.com）、Gazeta（www.vesti-gazeta.com）、Fakti（www.fakti.org）、Kremlin（www.kremlin.rs）和Glas Moskve（www.glasmoskve.rs）等。俄罗斯官方的卫星通讯社（Sputnik）于2015年在贝尔格莱德开设了一个地区编辑部，通过塞尔维亚的门户网站和电台发送节目，并向当地电台提供免费节目。塞尔维亚最著名的每日小报（如《塞尔维亚电讯报》和《信使报》）也刊登有关俄罗斯的新闻。

俄罗斯大企业也参与塞尔维亚的社会文化建设。俄气在向塞尔维亚能源领域不断进军的同时，也积极在社会文化领域施展影响力。该公司的石油分公司的塞尔维亚东正教会捐赠500万美元，用来修复贝尔格莱德的圣萨瓦教堂的马赛克穹顶。这个项目是俄气关于文化和保护塞尔维亚历史遗产项目的综合计划的一部分。[①] 2018年2月22日，世界第二大东正教教堂圣萨瓦教堂穹顶圣象揭幕。[②]

俄罗斯在塞尔维亚的各种机构和组织及其塞尔维亚媒体同行的活动主要集中在如下几个领域。首先，宣传俄罗斯对国际事务的看法。[③] 用俄罗斯视角，从支持俄罗斯—塞尔维亚长期联盟的角度诠释巴尔干历史和双边关系史，强调塞尔维亚和俄罗斯历史的共同方面，特别是在两次世界大战中并肩作战的传统。其次，诋毁北约和欧盟。称北约对全球的和平和稳定构成威胁，称欧盟支持伏伊伏丁那的分离分子，与塞尔维亚的利益背道而驰。再次，宣称俄罗斯是塞尔维亚最亲密的盟友，一直致力于维护塞尔维亚人的利益；同时批评塞尔维亚的亲欧行为，暗讽塞尔维亚不断受到欧盟和美国羞辱但仍"执迷不悟"申请

---

① CSD, Assessing Russia's economic Footprint in the Western Balkans, 2018, p.53, www.csd.bg/fileSrc.php?id=23366.

② "Ceremony of Unveiling Mosaic in Church of Saint Sava Held in Belgrade", 22 February 2018, https：//www.nis.eu/en/presscenter/ceremony-of-unveiling-mosaic-in-church-of-saint-sava-held-in-belgrade.

③ 例如，2017年有媒体称，由于美国的介入，乌克兰目前的危机将会更加戏剧性。Sputnik, "Recent news, allegedly, about US military activities in Ukraine", December 26, 2017, htps：//rs.sputniknews.com/rusija/201712261113945545-karasin-ukrajina-isporuka-oruzjedonbas/.

加入欧盟，此举分裂了塞尔维亚社会。最后，俄罗斯媒体不断地提及历史上塞尔维亚和巴尔干邻国之间的争端和冲突，旨在使巴尔干国家之间的和解进程增加变数。

作为俄塞双边关系的一种高级形式，俄罗斯也同塞尔维亚展开军事合作。2017年，俄罗斯决定向塞尔维亚捐赠6架二手米格-29战斗机，[①] 并承诺将提供30辆T-72坦克和30辆装甲运兵车。[②] 塞方还希望俄方能够提供两个营的S-300防空导弹和一个团的指挥所装备，以及6架多功能米格-17直升机。此外，塞尔维亚还对俄制中程导弹BUK-2和中短程导弹Panzir表现出兴趣。[③]

近年来，北马其顿同俄罗斯一直保持着较好的国家关系。2014年，北马其顿政府拒绝加入西方国家发起的对俄罗斯的制裁。[④] 2015—2016年，北马其顿爆发10多年来最严重的政治危机，大规模抗议示威不断。俄罗斯不失时机地利用了这场危机。期间，俄罗斯外交部定期发表声明，称抗议活动系为外部操纵所致，北马其顿是极端主义的受害者，外部势力正利用阿尔巴尼亚族人问题分裂北马其顿社会，企图将"颜色革命"的剧本在北马其顿重演。[⑤]

在谴责外部势力干预北马其顿内部事务的同时，俄罗斯不断扩大其在北马其顿各领域的影响力。根据2013年俄罗斯与北马其顿签署的政府间协议，2016年俄罗斯联邦独联体国家、侨居国外同胞和国际人道主义合作事务署在北马其顿设点，在北马其顿建立若干俄罗斯文化和科学中心。在斯科普里建立了一个俄罗斯文化中心，在奥赫里德和比托拉开设了两个领事馆。俄罗斯直接资助北马其顿媒体，包括那些为阿尔巴尼亚少数民族服务的媒体，使之纳入俄罗斯的信息发布渠道。除此之外，俄罗斯的情报机构、俄罗斯塔斯社和俄罗斯国家安全局的代表甚至参与北马其顿政府官员的招聘工作。

俄罗斯最明显的政治干预表现在黑山。在黑山政府宣布其加入的目标并与

[①] 这6架战斗机价值1.85亿欧元。但其检修和设备升级大约需要2亿欧元。2017年10月3日，两架米格-29交付塞尔维亚空军。Associated Press, "Russia starts delivery of MiG-29 fighter jets to Serbia", October 3rd, 2017, http://www.foxnews.com/world/2017/10/02/russia-starts-delivery-mig-29-fighter-jets-to-serbia.html.

[②] Djordjevic, "Six Russian MiG-29 are coming".

[③] Snezana Bjelotomic, "Vucic to meet with Putin in Moscow today", 19 December 2017, https://www.serbianmonitor.com/en/vucic-to-meet-with-putin-moscow-today/.

[④] "Macedonia, Serbia not to join EU's sanction against Russia", Sep. 16, 2014, http://zeenews.india.com/news/world/macedonia-serbia-not-to-join-eus-sanction-against-russia_1470523.html.

[⑤] "Russia says West stirring 'color revolution' in Macedonia", 18 May 2015, https://www.demdigest.org/russia-says-west-stirring-color-revolution-macedonia.

西方国家一道因克里米亚归属问题而制裁俄罗斯后,俄罗斯政府对黑山的政策出现转折。俄罗斯通过支持黑山的种族民族主义团体,试图阻止该国加入北约。2015 年和 2016 年黑山反北约领导人与俄罗斯领导人举行了几次会面。2016 年 6 月,在统一俄罗斯党代表大会期间,反对党代表参加了在莫斯科举行的西巴尔干国家反北约政党集会。这些政党签署了一项声明,主张在巴尔干建立军事中立地区。同样是在 2016 年,黑山政府指责俄罗斯干涉前者的议会选举,称黑山最大的反对党联盟民主阵线(DF)在接受俄罗斯离岸公司的竞选贿金,并试图以暴力推翻政府。

在波黑塞族共和国,俄罗斯通过多种方式支持亲俄的政客。2014 年 3 月,为支持塞族共和国总统多迪克的竞选活动,俄罗斯国际东正教人民统一基金会向他颁发奖状。随后,俄罗斯为多迪克的竞选活动进行政治捐款。此外,俄罗斯投资铺设通往波黑塞族共和国的天然气管道,并保证天然气供应、提供政府贷款等。俄罗斯还在 2016 年支持塞族共和国进行关于国庆日的公投。通过这些措施,俄罗斯确保对波黑塞族共和国施加影响,拖慢波黑融入欧洲—大西洋共同体的步伐。俄罗斯如愿以偿。首先,波黑塞族共和国迟迟没有执行欧盟要求的对俄罗斯的制裁;其次,2017 年 10 月,塞族共和国议会通过了一项决议,反对该国加入北约,支持波黑军事中立。①

四、结语

进入 21 世纪之后,随着俄罗斯外交政策日益强势、欧元区主权债务危机爆发,加之美国的战略重心转向(中)东欧和亚太地区,巴尔干俨然已经成为俄罗斯和西方利益对抗的绝佳地点。

俄罗斯针对巴尔干国家的不同国情采取了差异性政策,在经济、政治甚至军事领域同具有不同需求的西巴尔干国家发展不同层级的关系。在一定程度

---

① 2016 年 6 月,为阻止北约不断向西巴尔干地区扩大,统一俄罗斯党同来自塞尔维亚、黑山、北马其顿、保加利亚和波黑的部分反北约的政党代表签署了"在巴尔干建立军事中立区"的合作宣言。BIRN Team, "Putin's Party Signs 'Military Neutrality' Agreements with Balkan Parties", Jun. 29, 2016, https://medium.com/@ balkaninsight/putins-party-signs-military-neutrality-agreements-with-balkan-parties-8f2bbad4c23; "Bosnian Serb Lawmakers Pass Resolution On 'Military Neutrality'", RFE/RL, October 18, 2017, https://www.rferl.org/a/bosnia-serbs-pass-resolution-military-neutrality/28801992.htm.

上,俄罗斯已经取得了某种预期成果。当然,俄罗斯与欧盟在巴尔干的影响不可同日而语。虽然俄罗斯同巴尔干国家的经贸联系不断增多,但同西方国家相比,俄罗斯介入巴尔干的程度有限。它不可能取代欧盟,也不能发挥吸引巴尔干国家经济注意力的作用。① 另外,由于西方的制裁、卢布持续贬值、外国直接投资减少,俄罗斯经济形势不断恶化,也极大限制了它在巴尔干地区多领域的影响。

面对俄罗斯在巴尔干地区影响不断增加局面,西方的政治家认为,应该采取措施抵制甚至消除俄罗斯在巴尔干地区日益增长的影响力。欧盟认为,推动巴尔干地区融入欧洲一体化,是阻止普京可能利用巴尔干的不稳定来达到其目标的最重要途径。② 为此,欧盟在继续推进"柏林进程",巩固西巴尔干国家的欧洲观念,保持其向欧盟不断接近的同时,决定向西巴尔干国家提供明确的欧洲愿景。欧盟在2018年2月公布了西巴尔干地区扩大的新战略,称只要塞尔维亚和黑山政治经济转型不出轨,塞尔维亚能够妥善解决与科索沃关系问题,两国有望在2025年加入欧盟。

俄罗斯是前南地区的重要外部因素,它同这一地区的主要国家塞尔维亚签署了政治、经济和军事等领域的合作协定。从巴尔干地缘政治和民族政治的角度看,塞尔维亚占有核心地位。客观地说,没有稳定的塞尔维亚就不会有科索沃问题的妥善解决,也不会有整个西巴尔干地区的长期稳定。基于这种逻辑关系,将俄罗斯完全排除在巴尔干之外,该地区国家的国内和国际关系的正常化有可能产生困难。因此,西巴尔干国家如何在大国势力之间求发展,外部势力的博弈如何影响西巴尔干地区的未来发展,这些依然是未决的问题。

---

① Balcer, "Matushka Rossiya and the Balkans", *Aspen Review Central Europe*, 2015, no. 2, p. 68.
② Henrik von Homeyer, "Don't leave Serbia to Russia and China", 27 Mar. 2015, https://euobserver.com/opinion/128157.

Policing the Peace after Yugoslavia: Police Reform between External Imposition and Domestic Reform*

[卢森堡] 弗洛里安·比伯

内容提要 20年代90年代中期以来,许多国际组织参与了前南斯拉夫各地的警务改革。本文从克罗地亚、波斯尼亚和黑塞哥维那、塞尔维亚、科索沃和北马其顿的经验出发,讨论了冲突后干预的四种形式:国际行动者的警务行动、实施警务改革、冲突后警务援助以及条件性的警务工作改善。通过比较分析,本文认为,尽管付出了广泛的努力,但收效甚微。由于缺乏明确的国际或欧洲标准,警务改革受到不平衡和不断变化的期望以及相互矛盾的要求的影响。

关键词 前南斯拉夫 警务改革 战后重建 国际干预

作者简介 弗洛里安·比伯(Florian Bieber),卢森堡政治学家、历史学家,奥地利格拉茨大学东南欧研究中心教授

Abstract: Since the mid-1990s, a plethora of international organizations have been involved in police reform across former Yugoslavia. This article discusses four forms of post-conflict intervention: policing by international actors, imposing police reform, post-conflict police assistance and change to

---

* Research for this article has been supported by a British Academy Grant for the Project "From Peace to State Building: An Assessment of NATO and EU Conditionality in Bosnia and Herzegovina" with Gülnur Aybet.

policing through conditionality, drawing on the record from Croatia, Bosnia and Herzegovina, Serbia, Kosovo and North Macedonia. Through this comparative analysis, the article will argue that despite extensive efforts, the results have been modest. Lacking clear international or European standards, police reform has been subject to uneven and changing expectations and contradictory demands.

Keywords: Former Yugoslavia, Police Reform, Post-war Reconstruction, International Intervention

I . Introduction

Police Forces across Central and Southeastern Europe have experienced a fundamental transformation since the fall of Communism. The transition to multiparty democracy necessitated a profound change: enforcing the rule of law, protecting human rights and not viewing citizens as potential threats and subordinates (Mawby, 2001). Additional new challenges arose, such as organized crime (often linked to power centers), discrimination of minorities (esp. Roma), and political violence. This plethora of needs has been compounded by the large scale violence in the process of the wars of Yugoslav succession.

Police forces during the conflicts were often the main source of violence, discrimination and "ethnic cleansing". They ceased to embody the "monopoly of the legitimate use of force by the state". The police in Serbia was the most prominent example for the politicization of police forces in the region. The police force was controlled by President Slobodan Milošević until his fall and served as his praetorian guard (Bavic, 2003).

The reform of the police has been understood to be a central pillar of post-conflict reconstruction from Northern Ireland to Sudan (Stanley and Call, 2008, pp. 305 – 307). The reforms which are initiated in the post-conflict period had to meet six particular challenges. First, they need to penalize and remove police officers who have been involved in serious breaches of human rights during the conflict. Second, former combatants need to transition to civilian jobs and police forces are often the obvious employers. Third, police forces need to be made more representative of the larger population composition, which in most cases entails increasing the share of minority members. Fourth, police reform is necessary in order to allow for the return of minorities and to provide a secure environment in which democratic elections can take place. Fifth, police reform is inherently political and often controversial as the structure of the police reinforces the political structures after the war. Finally, the policing practice needs to be professionalized and reformed. While all aspects seek to transform police forces from a cause of conflict to a legitimate representative of an inclusive state to maintain peace, the different priorities often pull the reform efforts in opposite directions.

International intervention in the form of assistance, advice, policing, mentoring, training, enforcement and coercion shaped the evolution of post-conflict policing in former Yugoslavia. These different forms of international intervention are the focus of this article. First, international policing, where international organizations exercised executive policing functions and re-built police forces from scratch, will be examined. Second, externally imposed police reforms are explored. These two first forms of external intervention are particular to the (semi-) protectorates in Kosovo and Bosnia and Herzegovina. Third, a discussion on short-term post-conflict assistance which includes measures that have assisted governments to reform police forces in response to a conflict, as has been the case in southern Serbia and North Macedonia, will be examined. Finally, the article will explore how conditionality of membership of the European Union has sought to facilitate the reform of police forces, taking the example of Bosnia.

In addition to the European Union, most international intervention in the context of policing has been carried out by the Organization for Security and Cooperation in Europe (OSCE) and the United Nations. Bilateral donors have also shaped the police reform agenda, as has the North Atlantic Treaty Organization (NATO), which through a lead role in peacekeeping has often held executive police competences, in particular through the Kosovo Force (KFOR) in Kosovo.

The record of this experience has been mixed. While conflicts have ended, bloated militarized police forces have become more professional and inclusive, political influence remains strong. Furthermore, external intervention has been struggling to convince local authorities to "buy into" the reform processes. As such, police reform has shared greater similarities with other aspects of public administration reform, rather than defense reform which has generally been more successful due to clearer standards of armed forces and the lead role of NATO in the process (Bieber and Aybet, 2011, pp. 1911–1937).

II. International Policing

International policing constitutes the highest degree of external imposition. It encompasses both an executive role for international police officers, including the power to arrest citizens, and the complete reconstruction of a new local police force. Despite extensive external involvement in policing, international police officers have only actively conducted policing in Kosovo and in eastern Slavonia. Such extensive external involvement rarely occurs, since states are unlikely to relinquish one of its core functions. International actors are generally ill-prepared to provide executive policing—due to reasons ranging from linguistic and cultural obstacles, the lack of familiarity with local laws and procedures and the large number of international police officers required. In Kosovo, external policing became a necessity, since all Yugoslav and Serbian security personnel withdrew from the province following the ceasefire agreement (Military-Technical Agreement 1999). In this environment, policing was first carried out by military personnel in their capacity as peacekeepers with little experience in regular police duties. KFOR soldiers competed against the Kosovo Liberation Army which also sought to fill the vacuum created by the Serbian state withdrawal (Judah, 2009, p. 93). They were unable to prevent large scale revenge attacks against Serbs and other minorities by radical Albanians (Caplan, 2005, pp. 46, 49).

Eastern Slavonia was the eastern most region of Croatia, bordering Serbia, and the only part of the self-declared mini-state of the Republic of Serbian Krajina (RSK) left in the Fall of 1995. The region came under temporary international administration through the Erdut Agreement signed between Serbia and Croatia in November 1995.

The UN mission established the Transitional Authority Police Force (TAPF), a multiethnic police that was formed with the assistances from the Croat state institutions and the local Serb authorities with rough parity of Serbs and Croats (Kutnjak Ivković, 2004, p. 206). The police was a part of the United Nations Transitional Administration in Eastern Slavonia, Baranja and Western Sirmium (UNTAES) which governed the region for a transitional period prior to the full reintegration into Croatia. The TAPF eventually consisted of 811 Serb officers, 815 Croats and 52 from other ethnic groups. The force was trained by the UN who also maintained observers in all local police stations. In addition, a 50 person special international police unit existed in parallel with the local police, established under UN mandate (Kutnjak Ivković, 2004, p. 58). The international police unit was in eastern Slavonia and was able to make some high-profile arrests during the UN mandate, but never played more than an auxiliary role to the reforms of the local police force. By December 1997 responsibility over the police was transferred to the Croatian government after the government promised to maintain the ethnic composition (Caplan, 2005, p. 58).

In Kosovo, the UN Mission in Kosovo (UNMIK) built up the international civilian police gradually after the entry of KFOR. The two main policing structures were the internationally staffed civilian police force (CIVPOL) and the Kosovo Police Service (KPS), which was recruited locally, but remained under UN control until 2005 (Wilson, 2006, p. 153). Local political institutions were only established in Kosovo in 2001, following the promulgation of the UN imposed Constitutional Framework for Provisional Self-Government in Kosovo that established the "Provisional Institutions of Self-Government" (PISG) and general elections. The UN was reluctant to relinquish policing competences to the new authorities due to the sensitivity of policing, in particular when it came to retaining minority members among its ranks and protecting Serbs and minorities (especially Roma) from attacks.

The CIVPOL was the first civilian police force to take over from KFOR in the months following the end of the war. However, it was unable to deploy swiftly and it took CIVPOL around a year to reach its planned strength. The CIVPOL force was first established by a transfer staff of the International Police Task Force (IPTF) in Bosnia to Kosovo. In late 1999 it counted only 1,800 police officers. By 2000, its number had more than doubled to 4,450, at which level it approximately remained until 2004

(Wilson, 2006, p. 158). Among the international police officers, approximately two-thirds formed part of the CIVPOL, while the remainder constituted special police units and the border police (Human Rights Watch, 2004, p. 14). The reasons for the slow build-up are in part specific to Kosovo and in part representative of a broader problem of international missions. UNMIK gained the mandate to administer the international police force only at the beginning of international deployment and was thus unable to plan for such a mission aspect ahead of time (Wilson, 2006, p. 159). The "deployment gap" often is more pronounced in regard to civilian international staff, who cannot simply be "called up" as military personnel. Qualified professionals are often not readily available. This problem is even more pronounced for policing as few countries can spare large numbers of qualified police officers who are serving in their communities. This gap has often led to low standards among the international police. It has been frequently reported that police officers in Kosovo and Bosnia were at times unable to speak English or even to drive (both formal requirements for UN police deployment), or came from backgrounds that raised legitimate doubts over the good policing practices they were meant to be bringing to the countries (Donais, 2006, p. 186; The Scotsman, 2005; Jansson, 2005). In Kosovo, some 46 countries contributed to CIVPOL in March 2004. The largest contributors were the USA, India, Germany, and Jordan, but there were also police officers from countries with a highly problematic policing record, such as Zimbabwe.

In addition, the international police force had the goal to prepare the transition to the Kosovo Police Service (KPS) that would take over from CIVPOL. The first recruits of the KPS were trained in 1999 and the ratio of KPS to CIVPOL police officers increased steadily, with KPS overtaking the number of international police officers by 2002. KPS officers were recruited by the UN and trained by the OSCE in a program that was similar to later training programs in North Macedonia and southern Serbia, discussed below, involving 20 weeks training at a police academy, followed by 15 weeks field training (Wilson, 2006, p. 160). The number of KPS police officers reached 5,700 in March 2004, more than twice the number of international police officers (Human Rights Watch, 2004, p. 14).

In terms of recruitment, UNMIK paid particular attention to secure the adequate representation of minorities. By 2003, 84% of its members were Albanians, 9% Serbs and 7% from other communities, slightly over representing minorities. ①This careful distribution, however, should not be mistaken for a multiethnic police force. As Serbs and Albanians live in segregated areas, the police tended to reflect the local demographics and contained few members of non-dominant groups in any given region (Human Rights Watch, 2004, p. 14).

Despite this success in terms of minority recruitment, the KPS, together with CIVPOL and KFOR, took a serious blow in March 2004. After three days of rioting by extremist Albanians, resulting in the torching of Serb Orthodox churches and houses of Kosovo Serbs, and the displacement of several thousand Serbs, the international security efforts were severely discredited. The international presence itself became a target of the mob violence with around 60 members from each KFOR, CIVPOL and KPS injured. The violence and the inability of KPS to effectively stem the attacks revealed a number of structural weaknesses of the international police effort. Coordination within KFOR and between KFOR, the UN police and KPS was minimal, and lines of authorities were confused. None of the security providers appeared to be equipped and trained for large-scale crowd control and civil disturbances (Human Rights Watch, 2004, pp. 15, 25). The officers pay and morale were low. The support that the UN and KFOR had enjoyed in 1999 had dissipated by March 2004 (Caplan, 2005, p. 51). This crisis led to the process which paved the way to Kosovo's independence in February 2008. ②

After the riots, the KPS gained autonomy from the UN, and came under control of Kosovo authorities in 2005. Shortly before independence, the KPS had 7,124 police officers: 6,082 Albanians, 746 Serbs and 414 from other communities (Judah, 2009, p. 95). This distribution meant that Serbs remained part of this institution and were well represented. In response to the Kosovo declaration of independence in 2008, however, most Serb officers in the KPS walked out of their jobs, coinciding with a general Serb boycott of Kosovo institutions (Džihić, Kramer, 2009, p. 6).

---

① No reliable census has been held in Kosovo since 1981, but it is generally assumed that the share of Albanians population is close to 90%.

② In response to the crisis, the UN commissioned a report from the Norwegian diplomat Kai Eide. Upon his recommendation, the UN launched the final status talks in 2005. See, Weller, "The Vienna Negotiations on the Final Status of Kosovo," *International Affairs*, 84 (4), 2008, pp. 659–681.

This boycott turned out to be only temporary and by July 2009 most Serb officers returned to work for KPS (Beqiri, 2009). After the declaration of independence, the EU rule of law mission EULEX took over from most policing activities from the UN (see next section) and the international civilian police was gradually phased out (UN Secretary-General, 2009, p. 17).

III. Internationally Imposed Police Reform

Short of taking over executive police functions or forming a police force from scratch, international actors have most commonly shaped the police in post-conflict states of through a combination of advice and imposition of police reform. International organizations have exercised strong control over the police in Bosnia and in Kosovo after independence, albeit without a full executive mandate. This approach combines an international presence with limited executive and oversight competences with a functional local administration. This hybrid creates inherent tensions between national and local authorities and international actors imposing or "suggesting" particular reforms to the police force.

The focus is not on establishing public safety and security, but to transform the existing police structures. These reforms are often focused on making the police more representative of minority groups, ensuring that the police protects minorities (in particular refugees) returning to their homes, and reducing direct political influence and police abuse.

The most substantial international effort in the region took place in Bosnia. Initially, the UN-lead International Police Task Force (IPTF) was only equipped with a weak mandate to advise, monitor and observe the local police in the 1995 Dayton Peace Accord (Annex 11). At its peak 1,800 international police officers staffed the mission, whose task it initially was to monitor the work of the different local police forces, to participate in joint patrols, provide training and advise authorities (Palmer, 2004, pp. 171-172). The IPTF was caught between conflicting visions of the USA and the West European countries involved in defining its mission, leaving it "weak by a mixture of accident and design" (Caplan, 2005, p. 48). The limitations of its mandate became apparent in 1996 when the hand-over of Serb-held suburbs of Sarajevo to the Bosniak-Croat dominated Federation led to most Serbs being forced out by their own authorities, and large numbers of buildings being burnt down under the passive eye of the international presence, including the fledgling IPTF (Sell, 2000).

Although the military presence had a more robust mandate and quickly established itself, the peacekeeping force IFOR, succeeded by SFOR in 1996, initially refrained from taking over any policing rule beyond conventional peacekeeping tasks, unlike KFOR in Kosovo. Initially they were even unwilling to arrest suspected war criminals indicted by the International Criminal Tribunal for the former Yugoslavia (ICTY).

Just as the mandate of the Office of the High Representative (OHR) was enhanced by the so-called Bonn Powers, the IPTF received additional powers from UN Security Council Resolution 1088 in 1996. The resolution allowed the IPTF to vet police officers and to bar police officers for human rights abuses (Palmer, 2004, p. 178). Subsequently, IPTF officers were co-located in local police stations, which enhanced the international supervision of policing practices. A large vetting program was initiated by two bilateral agreements, first with the Federation in 1996, then with the Republika Srpska (RS) in 1998. The vetting process was aimed at eliminating officers that had either breached human rights in service or otherwise had made grave misrepresentations during the vetting processes to the UN. This process included a test for existing police officers, and confirmation that they were not publically indicted by the ICTY, or did not have a known criminal record (Palmer, 2004, p. 178). During this process, which was completed hurriedly in 2002, the number of police officers was reduced from 44,750 in 1995 (32,750 in the Federation and 12,000 in the RS) to 11,500 in the Federation and 8,500 in the RS (Palmer, 2004, p. 177).

In parallel with this process, the different police forces were also required to include members from non-dominant communities.[①] The IPTF sought to recruit new minority officers by offering refresher courses for former police officers among IDPs and refugees, redeploying police officers to region of origin, and seeking new recruits

---

[①] There were 12 territorial police forces (one for each of ten cantons of the Federation, one for the RS and one in the district of Brčko).

(Palmer, 2004, p. 180). Despite concerted efforts by the IPTF, the numbers remained well below the targets. The first non-Serbs only joined the RS police in 1999 and the number had not exceeded 5% by 2002. In the Federation, less than 1.5% of police officers were neither Croats or Bosniaks in 1999, the number only rising to 15.5% by 2002 (Bieber, 2006, pp. 82–83).

In Bosnia, experiences in Brčko and Mostar stand out (Bieber, 2005a). In Mostar, a small police contingent (up to 182 international officers) of the West European Union (WEU) assisted the EU effort to unify the city between July 1994 and October 1996. The goal of the WEU mission was to provide security and to forge a unified police out of the two ethnically divided police forces. Little had been achieved when the EU and WEU left in 1996 (van Eekelen, Blockmans, 2008, pp. 47–48).

Brčko came under full international protectorate in 1997 and an international arbitration transformed it into a separate district by 1999. Although the structures—the IPTF in combination with the OHR—were formally the same as elsewhere in Bosnia, the intervention was considerably greater than any other region in Bosnia. In Brčko alone, 250 international police officers were deployed. The international supervisor succeeded in establishing a multiethnic police force, based on preexisting police officers, but with a new structure (Perry, 2006, pp. 172–173). The combination of direct international intervention and higher levels of salary made the police in Brčko more professional (Parish, 2010, pp. 80–81).

After the UN declared its mission in Bosina (UNMIBH) successfully completed, the EU Police Mission (EUPM) took over (Donais, 2006; Penksa, 2006; Mace, 2003). Overall, the record of both the IPTF and the EUPM remains modest. While the number of police officers has been drastically reduced and some human rights offenders were weeded out, the number of minority police officers remained disappointingly low and many serious human rights violators remained beyond the reach of the IPTF. Decertified police officers could be employed by the Ministry of Interiors in non-policing roles, and remained part of the internal security apparatus (Palmer, 2004, p. 179). The IPTF only slowly reached its operating staffing quota (reaching its assigned capacity only in 1997) and its members have been criticized for low policing standards and involvement in prostitution (Donais, 2006, p. 186; Caplan, 2005, p. 55; Lindvall, pp. 70–71).

Some of these challenges have been replicated by the EULEX mission in Kosovo which formally took over rule of law related competences from the UN in late 2008. While the mission was formally set up shortly before Kosovo's declaration of independence, it remained passive and inactive for months as different EU member states took conflicting positions on Kosovo's independence and a UN Security Council Resolution to authorize the mission failed to materialize primarily due to Russian objections. Only a six-point plan by UN Secretary General with Serbia in late 2008 paved the way to the mission's deployment (UN Secretary General, 2008). In exchange, it had to remain status-neutral, instead of supporting Kosovo's independence as originally intended. In addition, Serb enclaves remained beyond the reach of Kosovo institutions that were linked only to the EU and UNMIK. The compromise with Belgrade undermined the legitimacy of EULEX in the eyes of many Albanians. EULEX reached its full operation strength of 2,569 (1,651 international and 918 local staff) by April 2009. The mission holds greater executive powers than the IPTF (Council of the European Union, 2008). Furthermore, the limited sovereignty of Kosovo grants international actors significant informal powers (Džihić, Kramer, 2009, p. 15). Its primary executive role is to act as a second line of defence in case of serious incidents, i.e. if the KPS is unable to resolve the incident and before KFOR becomes involved. Another particularity of EULEX in comparison to other police missions is its broader mission which includes police, justice and customs. In particular, the link between support for police, prosecutors and judges marks a more comprehensive understanding of police reform than other regional efforts (EULEX, 2009).

IV. Short-term Post-Conflict Police Reform

A less intrusive form of international assistance is a set of measures to address the ethnic composition of the police. Police forces tend to be unrepresentative of the wider population in the immediate aftermath of conflict. Minorities, especially if they were party to the conflict, are usually reduced to a few token representatives, if at all. A particular challenge of increasing the number of police officers from minority communities is the tension with some long-term reform goals. The quick increase of minority members in the police force often does not facilitate the professionalism of the police, but might crucially enhance the legitimacy of the police which takes priority in an environment of low trust after conflict.

Southern Serbia and North Macedonia experienced two low-scale ethnic insurgencies in 2001. Two interlinked Albanian rebel movements, the National Liberation Army (UÇK) and the Liberation Army of Preševo, Medveđa and Bujanovac (UÇPMB), launched attacks against North Macedonian and Serbian security forces in 2001 and 2000 respectively. Unlike the wars in Bosnia, Croatia and Kosovo, these conflicts did not escalate and the number of victims remained small. The settlement in both cases included an important component of police reform which sought to improve the participation of minorities in the police force.

The conflict in southern Serbia was settled as the democratic government that had replaced the Milošević regime in October 2000, was more open to a peaceful resolution and crucially the Albanian insurgents, unlike in Kosovo a few years earlier, could not count on international support. In the aforementioned Military-Technical Agreement between Yugoslavia and NATO, Yugoslavia had to demilitarize a five kilometer zone around Kosovo, covering a large part of the three Albanian populated municipalities, which became staging ground for the UÇPMB. In March 2001, NATO allowed the Yugoslav security forces to gradually take control of this region (ICG 2001, pp. 4-8). A condition for the reentry of the security forces was a viable peace plan to address the grievances of the Albanian population. The new Serbian government proposed such a "Programme and Plan for the Resolution of the Crisis in the Municipalities of Bujanovac, Preševo and Medveđa" drafted by deputy Prime Minister Nebojša Čović, and was passed by the Federal Yugoslav Government in February 2001 (Koordinacionotelo, 2001). Police reform was one of four core aspects of the strategy to end the conflict, together with economic development, increasing the employment of Albanians in public administration and publically owned enterprises.

In the initial phases in both North Macedonia and Serbia, the lead international organization for police reform was the OSCE. In Serbia, the OSCE trained police officers in a three-stage model. During the first two stages the OSCE offered a five day and a five week courses aimed at former police officers, including Albanians who had been dismissed or had resigned during the Milošević era. The more sustained third pillar focused on the establishment of a new multiethnic local police force. The training was directed at former UÇPMB fighters without criminal records and civilians, in particular Albanians. In addition, current police officers also received training. Of the 375 persons trained in the first year, nearly two thirds were Albanians (239), the remainder were Serbs except for two Romas (OSCE Mission in FRY 2002). By late 2003, Albanians constituted a similar proportion of (270 of 430) police officers in the three municipalities.

As a short term post-conflict program, it did not result in a permanent mechanism to recruit, promote and retain Albanian police officers. More than two years after the of the conflict, the number of Albanians in the police still remained well below the population share, in particular in Preševo where Albanians constitute an overwhelming majority of 89.1% (Trivunovic, 2004, p. 174).

The local police units were often overshadowed by the special police unit Žandarmerija—a militarized police unit based on the model of the Italian Carabinieri. The militarized appearance of the unit in the region has been a source of contention between the Serbian state and the Albanian minority ever since 2001 (International Crisis Group, 2003, pp. 18–19; MacDonald, 2006). Police officers who had served in Kosovo during the conflict in 1998/9 had retained their posts in the region, which has heightened tensions (Downes, 2004, p. 71).

In North Macedonia, international organizations had been present since the early 1990s. The OSCE Spillover Monitor Mission was established in 1992 as an instrument of conflict prevention together with a small UN peacekeeping deployment (UNPROFOR, later UNPREDEP). Limited efforts to reform the police began during the Kosovo war when North Macedonia was overwhelmed with more than 300,000 refugees. Police reform began in earnest in 2001 following the signing of the Ohrid Framework Agreement. The Agreement aimed to transform North Macedonia into a multinational state with a greater stake in the public administration and parliament for Albanians (Bieber, 2005b). The challenge in North Macedonia was to reintroduce the police to the areas of conflict—predominantly Albanian populated villages in northwestern North Macedonia. In 2001, only around 2.5 percent of the employees in the Ministry of Interior were Albanian (Ristovski, 2003). The OSCE trained 1,000 non-North Macedonian police officers by July 2003 and supported efforts by the government to make the police force representative of the population composition by 2004 (Lesja, 2004, p. 187; Framework Agreement, Annex C, 5.3.). By 2006, the number of Albanians in the police force had increased to 16% (from 2% prior to the conflict), a dramatic increase in a short period of time, but still well below the population share (Cvetkovska, 2006). In particular in the higher ranks of the police hierarchy, few non-Macedonians were represented.① In a first step, the OSCE organized 12 week training courses, followed by six months field training for new, mostly Albanian, police officers to boost the number of non-North Macedonian police officers by 500 in the first year after the end of the conflict. The OSCE also dispatched police advisors and confidence building monitors to "crisis areas" to assist with restoring trust between the police and estranged Albanian communities. Many Albanians saw Western officials as implicitly supportive of their grievances, giving the Western officials unique chance to contribute to building trust between police and citizens (Lesja, 2004, pp. 187, 189-190).

Between late 2003 and late 2005, the EU replaced the OSCE as the lead agency in police reform through Proxima mission. It aimed at promoting a "depolitized, decentralized, multiethnic police" (Ioannides, 2006, p. 72). Unlike the IPTF, it lacked any ability to dismiss police officials and was mostly focused on monitoring police officers, being initially colocated with North Macedonian police units in the regions populated by the Albanian population and providing advice and support to the government reform agenda. Proxima was forced to close down in 2005 due to government reservations about the impact of the mission on country's chance of EU accession. Upon closing its mission, the EU handed issue of police reform back to the OSCE. A key flaw of the Proxima missionwas the extensive infighting between the mission and other EU institutions in North Macedonia (i.e. the EC delegation, the EUSR) and other international actors (OSCE, bilateral donors) (Ioannides, 2006, pp. 80-81). The transformation of the police has been slow and cumbersome. Not

---

① By 2006, 14.56% of all police officers were Albanians, but only 10.2% of top posts. See, Ramadani, "Power Sharing and Internal Security," *Power Sharing and the Implementation of the Ohrid Framework Agreement*, Skopje: Friedrich Ebert Stiftung, 2008, pp. 120-121.

only did the minority representation in the police not reach the share in the general population, but other aspects continued to lag behind. A new police law that would allow the election of police chiefs by local authorities was only passed in 2006, but not according to the so-called Badinter voting rule that was introduced in North Macedonia in the Ohrid Framework Agreement, requiring a double majority of all MPs and among minority community MPs. Furthermore, the law was not implemented for well over a year (Mehmeti, 2008, p. 81).

In both Serbia and North Macedonia, the interethnic conflict triggered first a localized and minority-focused police reform, but the international engagement led to broader scope reform initiatives (Trivunovic, 2004, p. 174; Lesja, 2004, p. 188). While this could be considered a form of "mission creep", it more accurately reflects two deeper-rooted problems. First, without structural changes to the police, including a broad reform agenda to emphasize community policing, modern policing methods and human rights, the inclusion of minority members in the police force is unlikely to shift the overall relationship between the state and its citizens. Second, expanding the remit of reform has been an effective strategy particularly in North Macedonia to secure broad popular support, as measures only focused on improving interethnic relations are often viewed by citizens from minority communities as privileging minorities over majorities.

V. Police Reform through Conditionality

The latest form of international intervention in policing has been through the policy of conditionality of the European Union membership. The EU had acted as a donor for numerous police reform initiatives in the region, in particular through the assistance programs such as PHARE and later CARDS. However, it only became a key player in its own right in 2002/3. The EU first took over the UN police mission in Bosnia, followed by the mission in North Macedonia. These missions followed the established pattern of post-conflict assistance and the particular nature of the European Union and its offer of possible membership initially had little impact. However, in Bosnia, the thrust of police reform after 2003 was driven not by the EU Police Mission, but by political conditionality of membership of the EU, supplemented by pressure of the Office of the High Representative.

As neither the IPTF nor the EUPM were able to impose a structural reform of the police sector and no such reform was foreseen in the Dayton Peace Agreement, any further reforms had to take a different point of departure. The structural reforms were deemed necessary by both the OHR and the EU due to the high administrative cost of policing, the lack of coordination between the different police authorities, and the close links to ethno-nationalist power structures (European Commission, 2003). EU accession provided a starting point for further reform: The rule of law constitutes an integral aspect of the enlargement process and both human rights and a functional democracy became a core requirement for all future EU member states at the Copenhagen summit in 1993. The Stabilization and Association Process (SAP) and the subsequent Stabilization and Association Agreement (SAA) with countries of the region did not initially entail any particular direction such reforms should take. However, in the case of Bosnia, the tool of the SAA would become a key engine for police reform. Police reform became part of the international effort to reduce the vast competences of the entities to promote a viable central state. In parallel, the armies of the two Bosnian entities (the Army of the Federation of Bosnia and Herzegovina and the Army of the Republika Srpska), the security services and the border controls were gradually reduced and eventually replaced by state level institutions. Paddy Ashdown, High Representative from 2002 to 2006, encouraged the European Commission to set police reform as a requirement for signing an SAA. In parallel the OHR established a Police Restructuring Commission to draft a plan for police reform under the chairmanship of the former Belgian Prime Minister Winfried Martens. The commission was under pressure to propose a police reorganization where financial and legislative oversight would rest solely with the state and police regions would cut across the entity boundaries. The Commission's works was rejected by the Serb Republic which jealously guarded its autonomy. This conflict resulted in the failure of consensual proposal by the Commission and led to a protracted conflict between the OHR and EU on one side and the Serb Republic on the other hand.

As the European Union set three criteria in regard to police reform as conditions for signing the SAP, police reform continued to dominate debates in Bosnia until 2008. The EU insisted in its conditionality that (ⅰ) all legislative and budgetary competencies for all police matters must be vested at the state level, (ii) no political interference with operational policing, and (iii) functional local police areas must be determined by technically policing criteria where operational command is exercised at the local level (European Commission, 2005b).

Conceptually, conditionality offers a strong incentive for reform, not just in the domain of policing: support for EU membership runs high in the western Balkans and conditionality has been used effectively by the EU to induce reform in the first two rounds of enlargement towards central and eastern Europe. However, there was one large difference concerning police reform which set them apart from other forms of conditionality for administrative structures. The EU lacks an *acquiscommunitaire* for police matters as these remain firmly within the remit of member states. As a result, the EU could not draw on specific requirements, in particularly not in regard to the structure of the police. In its informal guidelines for future member states on the administrative structures required to implement the acquis, the police is scarcely mentioned. The requirement is for an "accountable, reliable and effective police organization, which cooperates fully internally, is essential for adequate implementation of the acquis related to cooperation in the field of justice, freedom and security, and in particular for the fight against organized crime and new types of crime" (European Commission, 2005a).

Repeated efforts by three High Representatives were unable to usher the police reform through. While Bosnian elites repeatedly reaffirmed their broad commitment to police reform, all concrete efforts came to naught. In April 2008, the Bosnian parliament passed two police reform laws, but they effectively retained the decentralized police structures and only created additional weak supervisory institutions at the state level. The laws even link all further police reforms to the constitutional changes. The watered down version of police reformed allowed Bosnia to sign the SAA with the EU in June 2008. Essentially, the EU had backed down from its initial conditions. This failure was a consequence of the lack of clear EU standards which could have been legitimately upheld in Bosnia, and the lack of commitment to the standards the EU had set earlier in conjunction with the OHR (Lindvall, pp. 230-239; Bieber, Aybet, 2011, pp. 1925-1926). The "carrot" of EU accession was not large enough for Bosnian elites in light of the distance towards EU membership and the importance of policing for their own power base. This does not mean that police reform through EU membership conditionality is altogether impossible, but the experience suggests that ill-defined and too-specific requirements might backfire.

VI. Conclusion

Post-conflict regions of former Yugoslavia saw more than ten distinct international efforts to reform the police over the past twenty years. These efforts have lasted from a few months to over a decade, and continue in Bosnia, Kosovo and North Macedonia. The comparison of the international police assistance in post-conflict settings in southeastern Europe allow for some conclusions to be drawn. The challenges underpinning the efforts are common to most aspects of post-conflict peace and state building.

First, reforms cannot be successfully pursued against the will of local domestic political elites. Even when international actors engage in policing directly, local elites have power, and can influence the outcome of such a policing effort. Long term reforms cannot be imposed externally: laws might be imposed, but their implementation inherently has to result from the political commitment of domestic actor. Without the commitment of domestic political elites to reforms, changes are unlikely to occur or will remain superficial.

Second, international organizations frequently display structural weaknesses in effectively engaging in civilian peace-building missions. The deployment gap has been particularly noticeable in the case of the different police missions. The delay in building up missions is not only time wasted, it also results in international organizations missing the "golden hour".

Third, the often intrusive approach of external actors in domestic security provision can certainly be benign in intent, but can also undermine citizen trust in the state which is instead placed in external security providers. It creates new power-relations which links citizens to external actors (Merlingen, Ostrauskaite, 2005). The agenda of international police mission may be driven by agenda set by their own security concerns and perceptions, which are not shared by the local communities.

The rule of law and Western fear of terrorism might clash, as they did in Bosnia when the government was pressured by the USA in early 2002 to surrender six Algerian-born Bosnian citizens to the US without due process (ISN, 2008).

Fourth, "there is no agreement on what the standards of a democratic police system are" (Szikinger, 2001, p. 15). As such, police reform is rather about hitting a moving target. International efforts have pushed countries in the region in very different directions: North Macedonia had to decentralize the police after 2001, granting more power to municipalities, while Bosnia has been pressured to centralize and reduce the powers of sub-state units. These trends are not necessarily a contradiction: North Macedonia's police force before 2001 was highly centralized while Bosnia's police was arguably too decentralized. The absence of clear standards has, however, undermined the EU's conditionality over police reform in Bosnia and also expresses itself in a variety of approaches chosen by different countries.

Fifth, reform of the police by international actors poses competing and at times contradictory demands on domestic actors. In both North Macedonia and Bosnia, reforms sought to reduce the overall number of police officers to bring the proportion to the population in line with European standards. At the same time, both countries had to increase the number of minority members in the police force. The push for rapid recruitment of minority members may stand in conflict with the goal of a professionalization of the police as the short term training programs hardly provides for a sufficient education for a police officer.

Sixth, the limited time horizon of the international intervention restrains the ability to engage in long-term structural reforms. The missions thus only focused on addressing short-term and immediate goals. While there have been also donor funded police reform initiatives in former Yugoslavia, they received less assistance and international support than the shorter post-conflict engagements. As a consequence, international engagement has often been oriented towards short-term goals, such as providing quick training to recruit new police officers and to rapidly increase the representation of minorities in the police. The quick rise in minority recruitment and the non-reoccurrence of conflict might prove this strategy at least partially right. However, the quota-focused recruitment strategies have often not been replaced by more sustainable policies and became an instrument of political patronage (SIGMA,

2009, p. 9).

Finally, the regional comparison suggests that a strong executive intervention is only possible in the immediate aftermath of a violent conflict when the state or a legitimate state-like structure has disappeared. Such a situation calls for large scale international policing. But practical and structural obstacles and doubts about legitimacy of policing in a post-conflict setting restrain an international executive police mission with a broad mandate. As a result, large scale international intervention rarely occurs, and the international organizations settle down for smaller scale reform missions. On the other hand, reform efforts—be they with the ability to impose decision or purely advisory efforts—have often been torn between the perceived need for immediate results and structural change. Superficial reforms have been easier to accomplish due to limited long term interest of international organizations and limited commitment of governments. As a result, international intervention has often been successful in providing basic services or helping to undo the more egregious flaws in the structure, but has been unable to fundamentally transform the police.

These observations are consistent with the broader experience of international state building in Southeastern Europe and raise questions about the inherent flaws and limitations of international state-building interventions more broadly.

References:

Basic Agreement on the Region of Eastern Slavonia, Baranja and Western Sirmium, 12 November 1995, http://www.usip.org/files/file/resources/collections/peace_agreements/croatia_erdut_11121995.pdf, 1 August 2018.

Beqiri, B. (2009), "Kosovo Serb officers end boycott," *SEE Times*, 3 July.

Bieber, F. (2005a), "Local Institutional Engineering: A Tale of Two Cities, Mostar and Brčko," *International Peacekeeping*, 12 (3), 420-433.

Bieber, F. (2005b), "Partial Implementation, Partial Success: The Case of Macedonia," Rusell, D., O'Flynn, I. (eds.), *Power Sharing: New Challenges for Divided Societies*, London: Pluto, 107-122.

Bieber, F. (2006), *Post-War Bosnia*, Basingstoke: Palgrave.

Bieber, F., Aybet, G. (2011), "From Dayton to Brussels: The Impact of EU and NATO Conditionality on State Building in Bosnia and Herzegovina," *Europe-Asia Studies*, 63 (10), no. 10, 1911-1937.

Caplan, R. (2005), *International Governance of War-Torn Territories: Rule and Reconstruction*, Oxford: Oxford University Press.

Council of the European Union (2008), Council Joint Action of 4 February 2008 on the European Union Rule of

Law Mission in Kosovo, EULEX Kosovo, 2008/124/CFSP, 16 February.

Cvetkovska, F. (2006), "Row frustrates Albanian equality efforts," *Institute on War and Peace Reporting Report*, 23 August.

Donais, T. (2006), "The Limits of Post-Conflict Police Reform," Innes, M. (eds.), *Bosnian Security after Dayton: New Perspectives*, London and New York: Routledge.

Downes, M. (2004), Police Reform in Serbia, Towards the Creation of a Modern and Accountable Police Service, Law Enforcement Department, OSCE Mission in Serbia and Montenegro, January.

Džihić, V., Kramer, H. (2009), "Kosovo after Independence: Is the EU's EULEX Mission Delivering on its Promises?" *International Police Analysis*, Friedrich-Ebert-Stiftung, July.

EULEX report to the UN (17 March 2009), Available from: http://www.eulex-kosovo.eu/?id=8&n=81, 1 August 2018.

European Commission (2003), Report from the Commission to the Council on the preparedness of Bosnia and Herzegovina to negotiate a Stabilisation and Association Agreement with the European Union, COM/2003/0692 final, November.

European Commission (2005a), Guide to the Main Administrative Structures Required for Implementing the Acquis, Informal Working Document, May.

European Commission (2005b), Communication from the Commission to the Council on the progress achieved by Bosnia and Herzegovina in implementing the priorities identified in the "Feasibility Study on the preparedness of Bosnia and Herzegovina to negotiate a Stabilisation and Association Agreement with the European Union" (COM (2003) 692 final), COM (2005) 529 final, 21 October.

ISN (19 December 2008), Guantanamo Algerians back in Bosnia ISN, Available from: http://www.isn.ethz.ch/isn/Current-Affairs/Security-Watch/Detail/?lng=en&id=94887, 1 August 2018.

Human Rights Watch (2004), Failure to Protect, Anti-Minority Violence in Kosovo, March 2004, 16 (6), July.

International Crisis Group (10 August 2001), Peace in Presevo, Quick Fix or Long Term Solution? http://www.crisisgroup.org/en/regions/europe/balkans/serbia/116-peace-in-presevo-quick-fix-or-long-term-solution.aspx, 1 August 2018.

International Crisis Group (9 December 2003), Southern Serbia's Fragile Peace, European Report, 152, http://www.crisisgroup.org/en/regions/europe/balkans/serbia/152-southern-serbias-fragile-peace.aspx, 1 August 2018.

Ioannides, I. (2006), "The EU Police Mission Proxima: Testing the 'European' Approach to Building Peace," Nowak, A. (eds.), *Civilian Crisis Management: The EU Way*, Chaillot Paper 90, June 2006, 69-86.

Jansson, E. (2005), "Kosovo raises concern over UN staff role," *Financial Times*, 16 September.

Judah, T. (2009), *Kosovo: What Everyone Needs to Know*, Oxford: Oxford University Press.

Koordinacionotelo zaopštine Preševo, Bujnaovac i Medveđa (2001), *Program i plan rešavanjakrize u opštinama Preševo, Bujanovac i Medveđa*, 8 February.

Kutnjak Ivković, S. (2004), "Distinct and Different: The transformation of the Croatian Police," Caparini, M., Mareni, O. (eds.), *Transforming Police in Central and Eastern Europe: Process and Progress*, Geneva and Münster: Geneva Center for the Democratic Control of Armed Forces and Lit Verlag, 194-219.

Lesja, D. (2004), "Community based policing in the Former Yugoslav Republic of Macedonia," *Helsinki Monitor*, 14 (3), 187-192.

Lindvall, D. (2009), *The Limits of the European Vision in Bosnia and Herzegovina: An Analysis of the Police Reform Negotiations*, Published Doctoral Thesis, Stockholm University.

MacDonald, N. (2006), "Shootings highlight fragility in south Serbia," *Financial Times*, 9 July.

Mace, C. (2003), "ESDP Goes Live: The EU Police Mission in Bosnia and Herzegovina," *European Security Review*, 16 February, 4-6.

Mawby, R. I. (2001), "The Impact of Transition: A Comparison of Post-Communist Societies with Earlier 'Societies in Transition'," Kádár, A. (eds.), *Police in Transition*, Budapest: Central European University Press, 19-35.

Mehmeti, E. (2008), "Implementation of the Ohrid Framework Agreement," *Power Sharing and the Implementation of the Ohrid Framework* Agreement, Skopje: Friedrich Ebert Stiftung, 67-88.

Merlingen, M., Ostrauskaite, R. (2005), "Power/Knowledge in International Peacebuilding: The Case of the EU Police Mission in Bosnia," *Alternatives*, 30, 297-323.

Military-Technical Agreement (9 June 1999), http://www.nato.int/kosovo/docu/a990609a.htm, 1 August 2018.

OSCE Mission to FRY (2002), Assisting Police Reform in FRY, Ensuring a Coordinated Approach, Vienna, http://www.osce.org/documents/fry/2002/10/111_en.pdf, 1 August 2018.

Palmer, L. K. (2004), "Police Reforms in Bosnia-Herzegovina: External Pressure and Internal Resistance," Caparini, M., Mareni, O. (eds.), *Transforming Police in Central and Eastern Europe: Process and Progress*, Geneva and Münster: Geneva Center for the Democratic Control of Armed Forces and Lit Verlag, 169-193.

Penksa S. (2006), Policing Bosnia and Herzegovina 2003-2005, Issues of Mandates and Management in ESDP Missions, 2006, CEPS Working Document No. 255.

Perry, V. (2006), *Democratic Ends and Democratic Means. Peace Implementation Strategies and International Intervention Options in Bosnia and Herzegovina*, unpublished Ph.D. Dissertation, George Mason University.

Ramadani, S. (2008), "Power Sharing and Internal Security," *Power Sharing and the Implementation of the Ohrid Framework* Agreement, Skopje: Friedrich Ebert Stiftung, 109-130.

Ristovski, L. (2003), Head, Unit for Coordination of the Implementation of the Framework Agreement, Government of Macedonia. Interview, 22 July.

Sell, L. (2000), "The Serb Flight from Sarajevo: Dayton's First Failure," *East European Politics and Society*, 14 (1), 179-202.

SIGMA (2009), Former Yugoslav Republic of Macedonia Public Service Assessment May 2009, http://www.oecd.org/dataoecd/32/28/43913255.pdf, 1 August 2018.

Stanley, W. D., Call, C. T. (2008), "Military and Police Reform after Civil Wars, 300-312," Darby, J., Mac Ginty, R. (eds.), *Contemporary Peacemaking: Conflict, Peace Processes and Post-war Reconstruction*, 2nd Edition, Basingstoke: Palgrave Macmillan.

Szikinger, I. (2001), "The Question of Transition," A. Kádár (eds.), *Police in Transition*, Budapest: Central European University Press, 15-18.

The Scotsman (2005), "UN Sex Abuse Enquiry in Kosovo," *The Scotsman*, 6 June.

Trivunovic, M. (2004), "Status of Police Reform after Four Years of Democratic Transition in Serbia," *Helsinki Monitor*, 14, 3, 172-186.

UN Secretary-General (2008), Report of the Secretary-General on the United Nations Interim Administration Mission in Kosovo, UN Security Council, 24 November, S/2008/692, http://daccess-ods.un.org/access.nsf/Get?Open&DS=S/2008/692&Lang=E&Area=UNDOC, 1 August 2018.

UN Secretary-General (2009), Report of the Secretary-General on the United Nations Interim Administration Mission in Kosovo, UN Security Council, 30 September, S/2009/497, http://www.unmikonline.org/UNMIKONLINE2009/misc/docs/sc-reports/S-2009-497.pdf, 1 August 2018.

UN Security Council (1996), UN Security Council Resolution 1088 (1996), 12 December.

Van Eekelen, W. F., Blockmans, S. (2008), European crisis management avant la letter," S. Blockmans (eds.), *The European Union and Crisis Management. Policy and Legal Aspects*, The Hague: TMC Asser Press, 37-52.

Weller, M. (2008), "The Vienna Negotiations on the Final Status of Kosovo," *International Affairs*, 84 (4), 659-681.

Wilson, J. M. (2006), "Reconstruction of Kosovo's Police and Justice Systems," *The Annals of the American Academy of Political and Social Science*, 605, 152-177.

Slovenes between the Balkans and Central Europe

[斯洛文尼亚] 博佐·雷佩

内容提要 在这篇文章中,作者讨论了中欧和巴尔干半岛的一体化,并使用了一个共同的术语——东南欧。作者总结了巴尔干、中欧、东南欧和其他涉及这一地区的术语的定义,分析了20世纪中叶至今的各种整合(联邦和联盟)的计划和尝试。在这方面,作者特别注意斯洛文尼亚人的角色及其对这个问题的态度。他认为,在集团解体后的时期,欧洲正在被重新塑造,斯洛文尼亚(同其他较小的国家一样)得到了加强其区域(中欧)一体化和与所谓的西巴尔干(前南斯拉夫地区未加入欧盟的部分)一体化的机会。

关 键 词 中欧 巴尔干 东南欧 斯洛文尼亚

作者简介 博佐·雷佩(Božo Repe),斯洛文尼亚卢布尔雅那大学哲学院历史系教授

Abstract: In the article the author discusses integrations in Central Europe and the Balkans, for which he uses the common term Southeastern Europe. He sums up the definitions of the terms the Balkans, Mitteleuropa, Central Europe, Southeastern Europe and others referring to this area. He analyses the plans and attempts at various integrations (federations and confederations) from the mid-20th century to the present day. In this context, he devotes special attention to Slovenes and their attitude towards this issue.

He believes that in the post Bloc period, when Europe was being reshaped, Slovenia (similarly as other smaller nations) was given a chance to strengthen its regional (Central European) integrations and integrations with the so-called Western Balkans (the part of the former Yugoslavia that had failed to join the EU).

Keywords: Central Europe, Balkans, Southeastern Europe, Slovenia

I

The term "Central Europe" first appeared In the 19th century, as did the various political concepts connected with the area supposedly covered by Central Europe.[①] As regards what Central Europe is or what it should be in the political, geographical and cultural sense, many different theories have been and still are being posed. There are basically two concepts: in the broad sense, it refers to the so-called *Centralna Evropa* that is said to cover the entire territory between Scandinavia (or the Baltic Sea) and Greece (including it), and between Russia and France. When the term Eastern Europe was formed in the 18th century and after the fall of the Holy Roman Empire, when the question arose regarding the layout of German territory, they also started debating Central Europe (after the Congress of Vienna in 1815).[②]

In the narrow sense, it refers to the territory covered by the former Austria-Hungary (even though its territory extended to the Balkans—Vojvodina and Bosnia and Herzegovina after annexation in 1908). That is the so-called *Mitteleuropa*. In the Anglo-Saxon and Francophone world there is only one term for both (Central Europe, *L' Europe Centrale*).

Designations for the territory covered by Central Europe had already appeared in the 19th century, as had the origins of the later Central European political concepts;

---

① For more on the topic, see *Srednja Evropa* (*zbornik*), Mladins kaknjiga, Ljubljana, 1991, p. 87 (hereinafter: *Srednja Evropa*).

② Peter Vodopivec, "Srednja Evropa," *Enciklopedija Slovenije*, 12 zvezek, Mladinska knjiga, Ljubljana, 1988, pp. 247-248.

however, at that time Central Europe was "not at all used as a self-evident and universally accepted geographical and political term".① The first to define Central Europe more precisely was Friedrich Naumann in 1915 with his famous work *Mitteleuropa*. Naumann's book reflected the plans of Greater Germany before and during World War I for geopolitical control over Eastern and Central Europe and the Balkans, and through them the establishment of a connection with the Middle East (as expressed in the slogan *Drangnach Osten*).② Following the initial success at the onset of World War I, the Germans also counted on a portion of French territory (especially on the Port of Calais), and, of course, on Belgium, the Netherlands and Luxembourg. In his book, Naumann advocated the formation of a large confederation, which would be based on a connection between Germany and Austria-Hungary, and would extend from France and Italy on one side to Russia on the other. In this entity, the author—as opposed to later concepts of Greater Germany—nevertheless acknowledged non-Germanic nations the right to live—hence, Germans should not strive towards forced political, linguistic and national unification, and the community should not have a German nature, but a supranational one (this idea later appeared in modified form among Austrian Social Democrats). German nationalists greatly opposed this notion, even though, like them, Naumann primarily wished to consolidate the position of Germany between the European East and West; the only difference being that he assessed it could not be realised without reaching an agreement with the Central European nations.③ In addition to the aforementioned territories in the West and Switzerland, Naumann's concept of *Mitteleuropa* also encompassed the territory of Scandinavian countries (except for Finland) in the north, and Romania and the Balkan countries (Serbia, Bulgaria, Greece and Albania) in the south. According to his calculations, which were based on a census of 1910, that territory was inhabited by 166.4 million people; a total of 116.3 million in Austria-Hungary alone.④ (These

---

① Peter Vodopivec, "Srednja Evropa je, Srednje Evrope ni," *Srednja Evropa*, p. 5.
② If this plan were realised, it would have turned Germany into a world power; it also served as the basis for subsequent Nazi plans of conquest, as has been clearly proved by the German historian Fritz Fischer in his book *Griff nach der Weltmacht*.
③ Peter Vodopivec, "Srednja Evropa je, Srednje Evrope ni," *Srednja Evropa*, p. 6.
④ Friedrich Naumann, *Mitteleuropa*, Berlin: Georg Reimer, 1915, pp. 265, 281.

figures are important because at the time of imperialist expansion, it was estimated that a country with less than forty million people—including colonies and certain other factors, in particular a large territory and natural riches—was unable to exist independently). During the war, Naumann's plan was the most widely discussed, however, it was not the only one; plans for the postwar organisation of the world, especially in the interwar period, included plans for a Greater Germany and other proposals for various federations and confederations, which also included the nations and countries of Central Europe. Broadly speaking, some of these ideas—especially in the case of non-Germanic nations in the Austria-Hungarian Monarchy—were influenced towards the end of the war by the Fourteen Points on international relations written by the U. S. President Woodrow Wilson, particularly Point 10 on the freest opportunity to autonomous development for these nations (and consequently establishing voluntary connections with other nations); the leftwing political parties were also somewhat influenced by the anticipation of a universal revolution in European countries (it was believed that a social revolution would also eliminate any national conflicts).

Another concept of political integration, in addition to Naumann's, is the concept of the integration of Central European nations on an equal footing. Such plans were already being prepared during Austria-Hungary (the Czech historian, F. Palacky, and others wrote about them); the basic idea was to divide Austria-Hungary by nationalities (the federalistic concept). One such plan was "our" trialistic concept, which appeared at the turn of the century and proposed the division of Austria-Hungary into three equal parts (a German, Hungarian and South Slavic one).

In addition to the term Central Europe, people were beginning to use the term Southeastern Europe, which is geographically and politically just as undefined, and which encompasses different territories in various combinations: in addition to Central Europe in the narrower sense and the Balkans, also a few territories or countries further east. The term Southeastern Europe is most often used by the Germans and Austrians to define the common Central European and Balkan area, for they have been showing great political, geostrategic and economic interest in this territory for decades. After the war in the Balkans in the early 1990s, this term became established in international diplomacy, however, with different notions of what Southeastern Europe encompasses, politically speaking. Even without the topical political note, it is difficult to reach a "pure" demarcation between Central Europe and the Balkans, even though there is so much literature on both topics that it has become practically uncontrollable. Depending on the political situation and the writer's views, various publications, and political plans even more so, "move" entire territories from one sphere to the other and vice versa, whereas affiliation with one sphere or the other has a specific ideological and political meaning.

II

In Slovenia the question of (self-)placement into the first or second area was one of the most pressing issues after the attainment of independence; it concerned the domestic policy (the reorganisation of society or a "new social structure"[1]) and Slovenia's position in the emerging new Europe. According to one definition, it is a matter of whether Slovenia "is capable of legitimately leaving the Periphery, integrating with the countries of Central Europe, and defending itself against Balkanism"; the realisation of this intention will allegedly trigger new polarisation in the Slovene political sphere: "In the near future, Slovene parties will be divided based on the border between the 'North' and 'South', between the developed and underdeveloped, between Europeanism and Balkanism".[2]

On the one hand, such projections were a reflection of the belief that Slovenia had not yet fully shaken its Yugoslav heritage, and, on the other hand, of the far from stable domestic scene; of course, the geographical position of Slovenia also plays a part—because of it Slovenia will most likely continue to border on a conflict and turbulent zone for a long time to come.

Unlike Slovenia, certain Central European countries (especially those without unstable conditions in their vicinity and those that are more successful in their European integrations) in their post-socialist rush towards "Europe" began to lose

---

[1] France Bučar: "Nova družbena zgradba," *Slovenci in prihodnost*, Nova revija, Ljubljana, 1993, pp. 33-43.
[2] Dimitrij Rupel, "Nedokončano osamosvajanje Slovenije ali meditacija o razočaranju," *Slovenci in prihodnost*, Nova revija, Ljubljana, 1993, p. 82.

their enthusiasm for the narrower Central European identity over the last decade and a half; politicians have even let people know that in their eyes Central European integrations are of secondary importance. When the refugee crisis began, nationalism escalated in these countries and they started uniting into a sort of "unprincipled coalition" against the European immigration policy (the so-called Visegrád Group, which includes Poland, Hungary, the Czech Republic, Slovakia and the Baltic countries).

Before joining the EU in 2004, Slovenia—unlike the countries for which the label Central European was self-evident—had to fight to be recognized such status. Politicians were truly shocked in the beginning of 1994 when Madeleine Korbel Albright, a special envoy of the U. S. President Bill Clinton, who came to Slovenia to explain the Partnership for Peace initiative, ranked Slovenia among "Balkan democracies", alongside Romania, Bulgaria and even Albania. The U. S. Ambassador to the United Nations (the later United States Secretary of State and a devout advocate of the opinion that the international recognition of Slovenia and Croatia in 1992 was "premature"[①]) afterwards corrected herself that the adjective "Balkan" had not been meant in a cultural, historical or spiritual sense, but in a geographical one. She tried to mitigate the proverbial American weak knowledge of geography by stating that whether Slovenia geographically belongs to the Balkans or not should be debated by geographers.[②] Soon afterwards, Slovenes were given a Band-Aid on our wounded self-importance when the Council of Europe decided not to categorise Slovenia, at least on a symbolic level, among Mediterranean countries (under which Yugoslavia had been categorised according to one criterion prior to its disintegration), but move it instead to the group of Central and Eastern European countries; and moreover by being offered to join the Partnership for Peace surprisingly quickly—with it European and American diplomacy attempted to undo the previous assessment of Slovenia—and by concluding an association agreement with the European Union. In 1997, a new grievance resulted from the decision that Slovenia would not be included

---

① "Brez nas ne gre", interview with Madeleine Albright in *Der Spiegel*, reprint: *Delo, sobotna priloga* 31 July 1999, p. 33.

② "Clintonova odposlanka Albrightova v Sloveniji," *Delo*, 15 January 1994.

in the first round of NATO candidates, in which Poland, the Czech Republic and Hungary had been placed (and later accepted); instead, it was stuck in the uncertain second round together with Romania (originally, Slovenia and Romania were candidates for the first round, in addition to the three aforementioned countries, mostly because of Romania, which was greatly promoted by a few influential countries that did not have any arguments for rejecting the higher-ranking Slovenia). On the other hand, in the 1990s Slovenia strove very hard to become a non-permanent member of the UN Security Council (which it achieved, beating Hungary to it), even though it meant that it would in a way represent Balkan countries or the countries of Southeastern Europe. This ambivalence is continuously reflected in Slovene foreign policy: on the one hand, it still shows great interest in the Balkans (especially in the former Yugoslav republics that have become states) for economic and other reasons; on the other hand, ever since it has founded an independent state it has been trying to distance itself from any solid links with this region, into which it was being forced by the European Community member states and by the USA within the framework of the so-called Stability Pact that had been created after the war in Kosovo and after NATO's air raids on Serbia in the spring of 1999. [1]

III

Slovenes are not the only ones that do not wish to be placed in the Balkans. As early as 1915, the most famous Western observer of the Russian revolution, John Reed (*Ten Days that Shook the World*), wrote as a war correspondent that the easiest way to anger a Romanian (who is, of course, Latin and not a "wild" Greek or Slav) is by telling him or her that Romania is a Balkan state. [2]

---

[1] According to plans, the Stability Pact was to be joined by seven countries (Hungary, Slovenia, Croatia, Romania, Bosnia and Herzegovina, Bulgaria, Macedonia and Albania; as regards the regions of the Federal Republic of Yugoslavia—until the replacement of Milošević's regime—it was to include or give aid to Kosovo and Montenegro ("Paktstabilnostiza JV Evropo," *Delo*, 30 July 1999, p. 7). This pact did not carry greater political weight.

[2] John Reed, *War in Eastern Europe: Travels Through The Balkans in 1915*, Orion Books, 1994.

This orientation towards Central Europe was strong in Slovenia also during the socialist Yugoslavia, though, due to the division into blocs, it was expressed in the specific Alps-Adriatic integration, which was in a way also taken up by the central government. The idea of Central Europe became especially strong in the Eighties, when the intellectual opposition used it to highlight the differences from other (Balkan) parts of the state (back then, Central Europeanism was also very popular among the intellectuals of other socialist countries). An expression of this orientation was the establishment of the Vilenica literary award, which the Slovene PEN Centre awarded to authors from Central Europe. Their enthusiasm was occasionally thrown a cold shower; one of the worst ones was the statement by writer Peter Handke, much esteemed in Slovenia (and the winner of the Central European Vilenica award for literature), that to him Central Europe is nothing more than a meteorological term. ①

Of course in a historical context, the term Central Europe was not always unambiguously positive for Slovenes, rather the other way around, as has been established by Slovene writers. ②

While under Austria-Hungary, the advocates of "Greater Germany" turned a deaf ear to Slovenes, because they were living in the territory that was blocking the way to the Adriatic Sea and Trieste for the Germans. Yet even the plans of the political powers that were sympathetic to resolving the national issue of non-Germanic nations in the Austro-Hungarian Monarchy did not extend beyond the reorganisation of the Austrian Empire, which would allow nations only cultural autonomy (the so-called Austro-Marxism). Consequently, the Austrian state that had in fact united Central European nations and had spread its territory to the Balkans (occupation of Bosnia and Herzegovina in 1878 and its annexation in 1908), dissolved because of its failure to comply with the demands of non-Germanic, particularly Yugoslav nations. Hence the question remains open as to the extent to which this state would have been able to democratise itself or which level of observance of national demands (as the statehood of certain nations—for example the Czechs—would finally mature) would have

---

① Drago Jančar, "Srednja Evropa med metereologijo in utopijo," *Srednja Evropa*, p. 87.
② See especially the article by Bogo Grafenauer: "Srednja Evropa? Zakaj ne preprosto Evropa," pp. 15-26 and by France Bučar: "Srednja Evropa-mit ali stvarnost?" *Srednja Evropa*, pp. 55-65.

satisfied the non-Germanic nations in Austria-Hungary on the one hand and the demands of the Entente Powers on the other. In the case of Slovenes—regardless of whether they were personally in favour of a Yugoslav state within Austria-Hungary (and consequently the predominantly Central European option) or in favour of national integration outside of it (and consequently the predominantly Balkan option) as the circumstances dictated—they did not have much sway over global events that concerned their existence as a nation. The famous "statesmanlike" words of the then Slovene political leader Dr. Anton Korošec to the Austrian Emperor and King of Hungary Charles, who attempted to save the monarchy in the last minute ("it is too late, Your Majesty"), and his attempt to convince him that Slovenes would not commit suicide for anyone, somewhat pale in comparison to the words spoken earlier by the Russian Minister of Foreign Affairs Sazonov that Russia would not fight even half a day longer for Slovenes to get their satisfaction (at that time Russian Slavophilism reached only as far as Bulgaria and partly Serbia); even more so in comparison to the many statements made by the then most important Entente politicians about how Austria-Hungary would survive only if it withdrew from the war. Another question that remains open is what would have happened had the trialistic concept been realised (namely, the demand of Slovenes and other South Slavs in Austria-Hungary to divide the state into three parts: an Austrian, Hungarian and South Slavic part), if by some miracle German politicians had been persuaded. Even if that had been the case, we would surely have been divided among Italy, Austria, Hungary and the newly formed Kingdom of Serbs, Croats and Slovenes (the Kingdom of Yugoslavia) after World War I, and almost as surely would not have avoided the constant internal tension within a Baltic-Central European substate, likely based in Zagreb or perhaps even in Sarajevo, had Austria-Hungary survived. The existential resistance against German pressure (which surely would not have vanished) and the dilemmas whether to survive as a nation or drown in Croatianism or Yugoslavism, would have been joined by the permanent aspirations of Austro-Hungarian Serbs for unification with Serbia; a new element would have been introduced in the political sphere by the aspirations of Muslims for emancipation, etc. The political and cultural ambience of such a community would probably not have differed much from the one in the Kingdom of Yugoslavia, despite the fact that the final arbitrator would be located in the Central European Vienna and not in the Balkan Belgrade. At any rate: speculations are one thing but reality is another, and Slovenia—as a part of the short-lived (one-month) and internationally unrecognized state community of Austro-Hungarian Yugoslavs, that is, the State of Slovenes, Croats and Serbs which had been formed as a transitional formation upon the dissolution of Austria-Hungary—joined the newly formed state of the Kingdom of Serbs, Croats and Slovenes (called the Kingdom of Yugoslavia after 1929) and within this new political (national) framework became a part of the Balkans for more than seventy years.

In the inter-war period, both notions of Central Europe were encountered: on the one hand, under the hypothesis on the right to the expansion of living space (the so-called *Lebensraum*), we encounter the hypothesis on a German Central Europe, which was further strengthened after 1933 by Nazi racial ideology (more than half of Slovenia was declared the so-called German cultural territory); and on the other hand, the nostalgic search for a Central European identity which had disappeared with the disintegration of Austria-Hungary. In this period, the demarcation and use of this term were again not very precise. A few writers (in Slovenia, the writer Edvard Kocbek who was a great advocate of the idea of Central Europe) occasionally used the term Central Europe (even though they actually meant *Mitteleuropa*), whereas others wrote about *Mitteleuropa*, but were actually describing Central Europe.① (Thus, for example, the famous Austrian writer Joseph Roth entitled his lyrical description of a

---

① In this case, I view the demarcation between *Mitteleuropa* and Central Europe in the same way as Tine Hribar: "The borders of *Mitteleuropa* as a cultural and political term greatly overlap with the borders of Austria-Hungary prior to World War I. However, the centre of *Mitteleuropa* has been moved far to the West. Whereas the geographical centre of Austria-Hungary is occupied by Hungary, the central political and cultural area is taken up by (present-day) Austria. The capital of *Mitteleuropa*, and not just of Austria-Hungary, is Vienna. If in Austria-Hungary second place belongs to Budapest, in *Mitteleuropa* it belongs to Prague. Belgrade and Bucharest are located outside of Austria-Hungary and of *Mitteleuropa* too. Of course, Trieste belongs to Austria-Hungary and to *Mitteleuropa*. Gravitating towards the centre of *Mitteleuropa*, formed by Vienna as the capital of Austria-Hungary, are the parts of Poland and Romania that had been incorporated into Austria-Hungary, which also applies to Bosnia and Vojvodina. If we take a look at *Mitteleuropa* from the four cardinal points, we see that it takes up the southern part of the European territory that lies in the middle between the East and West. Before the war, the northern part belonged to the German Empire and thus, even if it is situated in the middle of Europe, it in no way belongs to *Mitteleuropa*... On the contrary, this northern part between Eastern and Western Europe goes by the name Central Europe. The capital of Central Europe is not Vienna but Berlin." (Tine Hribar, "Podoba Srednje Evrope," *Srednja Evropa*, p. 23).

Sunday in Berlin in 1920 "Sonntag in Mitteleuropa").①

One of the more interesting projects for integrating Central Europe and the Balkans in the inter-war period is the idea of the so-called Sudoba that was being developed by one of the most prominent Communist theoreticians of the time, Dragotin Gustinčič.②Gustinčič was convinced that the situation in the Balkans (to which he added Romania) prevented people from carrying out a revolution because of poverty and a lack of the industrial proletariat. Even if a revolution had occurred, they would not have been able to defend a socialist federation on their own, hence they would need help from Central European countries (from their industrial proletariat). Together, they were to have established a Danubian-Balkan (Sudobian) economic unit comprising the territory between the Krkonoše and Carpathian mountains and the Black, Aegean and Adriatic Sea. "Some have called this territory Central Europe, others call it the Danubian-Balkan Federation, whereas I call it 'Sudoba' (*Sudetes-Danube-Balkans*) for short. In the end, it does not matter what we call it, as long as we do not understand Central Europe as the concept created during the war by the famous German imperialist, Naumann, and that we correctly imagine it as a single workers' and peasants' state, comprising the present-day Czechoslovakia, Austria, Hungary, Yugoslavia, Romania, Bulgaria, Greece and Albania, the Greek islands in the Aegean Sea, and perhaps later on also Istanbul."③

At the time of the great ideologies in the inter-war period, not only were the chances for a democratic regime decreasing, but so were the chances for the survival of the relatively small states which had been formed after World War I ended and which had been let down by the new world order with the powerless League of Nations. From the national perspective, many have failed to resolve the national issue, or have resolved it only partially. Despite the formation of new states or precisely because of that, tens of millions of people were stranded outside of their

---

① Joseph Roth, *Werke 2 (Das journalistische Werk 1924–1928)*, Koln: Kipenheuer in Witsch, 1990, pp. 371–372.

② *Razprava o nacionalnem vprašanju v KPJ leta 1923*, collected, edited and commented by Jurij Perovšek in cooperation with prof. dr. Janko Prunk and prof. dr. Janko Pleterski, introductory study written by dr. Latinka Perović, Partizanska Knjiga, Ljubljana 1990, p. 72 (hereinafter: *Razprava o nacionalnem vprašanju*).

③ *Razprava o nacionalnem vprašanju v KPJ leta 1923*, p. 78.

mother country and many of them could not even obtain minority status. The Slovene nation went from one national framework to as many as four of them, in the process losing a few important cultural centres (Trieste above all); due to the political situation, the cultural, economic and other ties between the motherland and the newly created minorities were being established slowly and painfully and were virtually non-existent in many places (Raba Valley), or were weak and even illegal (Italy after the rise of Fascism, and Austria after the Anschluss).

Alliances and integrations between the newly formed states were also weak and most often subordinate to the interests of the Great Powers, as well as ideologically conditioned (the creation of the so-called *cordon sanitaire* towards the Soviet Union, which in many ways influenced the decision of the Great Powers to, for instance, agree at all to the formation of the Kingdom of SCS). In the new political reorganisation, the Central European – Danubian – Balkan integrations between Czechoslovakia, Poland, Romania, Greece and Yugoslavia were to have ensured peace.[①] Some of these integrations were created from the aspirations for defence against other Central European and Balkan countries, which had not been satisfied by the peace treaties after World War I (Hungary, Bulgaria) and which had indirectly or directly expressed territorial claims to their neighbouring countries in the inter-war period. One such integration was the Little Entente between Czechoslovakia, Romania and the Kingdom of SCS from 1920 and 1921, which had been intended for defence against Hungary. According to some, this union at first contradicted French policy (France namely supported Hungary and promised it territorial concessions in relation to the neighbouring Soviet Union), but after the signing of the Treaty of Alliance and Friendship between France and Czechoslovakia in 1924, it became a factor in the French policy of protecting the "Versaille system". The French Foreign Minister Tardieu was especially endeavouring to establish Central European and Balkan integrations. The so-called Tardieu Plan was to realise a "French regime" in Central Europe and in the Balkans, and integrate the Danubian countries (Austria, Hungary

---

① Milan Skakun, *Balkan i velike sile* KTRZ Arion, GRO D, Davidović, Smederevo, 1986, p. 61 (hereinafter: *Balkan i velike sile*).

and members of the Little Entente) into an economic (and partly political) community. ① France allegedly "never" had any ambitions to expand its territory to the Balkans (as was written in the 1920s by the writer of the popular book on the Balkans, Jacques Ancel), but only cultural and economic ambitions. ②

Under Nazi pressure at the end of the Thirties (at the time of the Anschluss, the Sudeten crisis, the occupation of the Czech Republic and Moravia, and the aggressive penetration of Italy into the Balkans), the French Balkan policy failed completely.

IV

In the years prior to World War II, the term "Intermediate Europe" (*Zwischeneuropa*) appeared, which denoted the area between the borders of the German and Russian territory. Reflections on this area were, as the Slovene writer Dr. Bogo Grafenauer had written, "distinctly geographical and political, and aimed towards a new European community, which we idealistically hoped would be created after the end of the storm that was so obviously coming."③ The possibility of establishing a union of countries "from the Baltic to the Aegean Sea" in various combinations and "sub-combinations" (one version was e. g. a union of northeastern countries—that is, Poland and the Baltic countries of Finland, Latvia, Estonia and Lithuania, which was also advocated by the Polish president of Lithuanian descent, Pilsudski) was discussed at several peace conferences and other conferences in the inter-war period. ④After Nazis assumed power, a few of these proposals were aimed towards excluding Germany from such integrations and create a sort of line of defence against it or prevent closer integration between Germany and Austria, which had originated in the desire to establish a customs union between both countries.

---

① Joachim Kühl, *Föderationspläne im Donauraum und in Ostmitteleuropa*, Untersuchungen zur Gegenwartskunde Südosteuropas, herausgeben vom Südost-Institut München II, R. Oldenbourg, München, 1958, pp. 43-54 (hereinafter: Kühl, *Föderationspläne*).
② Jacques Ancel, *Peuples et nations des Balkans*, Paris: Collection Armand Colin, 1926, pp. 200-201.
③ Bogo Grafenauer, "Srednja Evropa? Zakaj ne preprosto Evropa?" *Srednja Evropa*, p. 20.
④ Kühl, *Föderationspläne*, pp. 57-60.

In the inter-war period, Slovene intellectuals of various political orientations contemplated the smallness and dividedness of the Slovene nation. The majority of Slovene cultural magazines and newspapers were engrossed in the national issue; views on "the contents of Slovenism" and on Slovene fate differed and often gave rise to "grave political dissension."[①]

Alongside the growing ideological polarisation and mutual opposition, not just between the Great Powers but also between the countries formed after World War I, the "search" for Central Europe or broader integrations among the small nations in the intermediate area between Eastern and Western Europe, from Greece to the Scandinavian countries, was primarily the domain of journalists; even when it grew into more tangible political programmes, these were no less utopian than the views of individual writers.

World War II completely shattered any illusion of a multicultural and equal community of nations in the Central European area and the concept of Greater Germany was realised in its most brutal (Nazi) version. Even those Central European countries which had preserved their own statehood in limited form (Hungary) or even acquired it in a twisted, marionette form (Slovakia, Croatia), were completely subordinate to the German policy of creating "a new European order". In Slovenia, which had been carved up among four occupying forces, the most important inter-war political programme, supported by the real military and political power (the Liberation Front programme), was aimed towards liberation and towards the rebuilding of Yugoslavia, but on an equal (federal) footing. The leading bourgeois programme (the so-called London Programme) also advocated the rebuilding of Yugoslavia up until the end of the war (also demanding a federation, but under the Karadjordjević dynasty). Bourgeois politicians collaborated with both the Italian and the German occupiers; the Catholic Church was even more active. Even before the attack on Yugoslavia, the leading Slovene Catholic politicians had forsaken Yugoslavia and secretly tried to get the Nazis to award Slovenia protectorate status after the anticipated attack, as they had

---

① Peter Vodopivec, "Slovenci v tridesetih letih," *Socialni realizem v slovenskem jeziku, književnosti in kulturi*, Univerza Edvarda Kardelja v Ljubljani, Znanstveni inštitut, Oddelek za slovanske jezike in književnost, Ljubljana, 1987, p. 599.

awarded Croatia. ①At the start of the war, certain bourgeois politicians proposed to the Germans that they occupy all of Slovenia and award it a similar status as they had awarded the Independent State of Croatia and Slovakia. Among less important political groups, programmes emerged that envisaged Slovenia under an Italian Empire (a part of the territory, the so-called Province of Ljubljana, was indeed annexed to Italy), or autonomous Carniola under the reign of the German Reich, and various types of federations and confederations. Some of these ideas are reminiscent of the pre-war thoughts on integrations in the middle and central European area (a Danubian federation, a federation of all nations between the German and Russian world, a Catholic, corporatist Central European federation, etc.). These programmes were merely the expression of the writers' powerlessness under the existing circumstances, the search for an alternative (that would not require any direct involvement) to a successful liberation programme; in their essence, they were far from an idea for a genuine democratic community in the area in question and had practically no influence over events in Slovenia during the war. The most perfected plan was that of the extreme Catholic theologian dr. Lambert Ehrlich. Ehrlich saw the future of Slovenia in a Central European-Balkan union, which would comprise Poland, Ukraine, the Czech Republic, Slovakia, Slovenia, Croatia, Serbia, Bulgaria, Hungary, Romania, Greece and Albania. Ehrlich considered Slovenia "a nation in the centre of Europe", on whose territory "a European railway station" had developed during contemporary history; after the war and the victory of the Allies, United Slovenia with Trieste would be a sort of "Adriatic Switzerland" and become either a sovereign state or an equal state—a member of a contractual confederation of Yugoslav nations or a member of a broader European union of countries. ②

The plans of Western Allies, in particular that of Winston Churchill, were more realistic. Both Balkan coasts—the Adriatic and the Aegean Sea—were crucial in the imperial policy of Great Britain and Churchill tried to secure that influence for the post-war times by proposing that the Allies land on the Adriatic coast and a "fifty-

---

① Bojan Godeša, *Čas odločitev*, Mladinska knjiga, Ljubljana, 2011.

② Ciril Žebot, *Slovenija včeraj, danes, jutri*, 2. knjiga samozaložba 1969, pp. 46–47 (see also the revised reprint of the book entitled *Neminljiva Slovenija*).

fifty" agreement. His efforts include contemplating the forming of a Central European Federation (Churchill often regretted the fall of the Habsburg Monarchy), which would presumably include Slovenia, Croatia, Vojvodina, Bosnia and Herzegovina, Austria, the Czech Republic, Slovakia, Hungary and Bavaria. A similar thought was his proposal at the Tehran Conference in late November 1943 that after the war Prussia should be excluded from Germany, and that the southern part of the German state and Austria would be transformed into a sort of Danubian state. This state was to become an antipode to the emerging Balkan federation or confederation, which was also being contemplated at that time on several levels. According to some writers, a Catholic Central Europe, headed by Otto von Habsburg, was mainly the post-war objective of the Vatican, which was trying to save "the remains of the quisling state of Cardinal Tiso in Slovakia, Horty in Hungary and Pavelić in Croatia". [1] In that regard, the Vatican's and Churchill's aims overlapped (paralysing the revolutionary movements and the influence of the Soviet Union, strengthening or preserving the role of the catholic Church, restoration of the Habsburg dynasty, the weakening of Germany), while their aftermath would have been, among other things, the sacrificing of Yugoslavia in its pre-war size. Due to the situation at the end of the war and after it (the penetration of the Soviet Union, the autonomy of the Yugoslav resistance movement and other reasons), but mostly because of the division into blocs, such efforts died away or were redirected to two, mutually exclusive circles.

"Substitute" versions of Central European integration, which started coming to life in the second half of the 1970s after the Helsinki Conference on Security and Cooperation in 1975 (the Alps-Adriatic integration, various other forms of economic and cultural cooperation), were replaced after 1990 by specific economic agreements (CEFTA) and the attempts of certain statesmen to nevertheless identify and concretise a common interest of Central European countries. Yet all of these efforts were limited on the one hand by the primary goal of the former Communist countries to directly join the European Union and NATO as soon as possible, while, on the other hand, potential tighter integration highlighted the issue of Central European countries. Several calculations emerged (again in connection with the definition of Central

---

[1] Sava N. Kosanović, *Jugoslavija je bila osuđena na smrt*, Zagreb: Globus, 1985, p. 132.

Europe), from Prague (which showed no particular interest in this role in political circles—with the exception of the then, now late President Vaclav Havel) to Vienna (which has been doing that quite successfully all this time, at least in the cultural sense connected with the area of the former Austria-Hungary).

After the so-called big bang, i. e. the expansion of the EU in 2004, the interest in Central European integration declined. Thus, not much has remained but a "meteorological term", a few common features imprinted by history, and politically encouraged cultural cooperation. Last but not least, the French and the English were not particularly excited about the revival of ideas of Central Europe (that was supposedly one of the reasons why they wanted to preserve Yugoslavia at any cost), for in their eyes the return of Central Europe also meant the return of German imperialism, as the French philosopher Alain Finkielkraut (and not only him!) had claimed years ago. [1] So far, Finkielkraut's fear has not been proved justified, because the local Central European nationalisms are the ones that have vampirised.

In the Nineties, ideas (not the imperialist "Naumann's" but the nostalgic "Danubian" ones) were revived among certain French intellectuals, who rekindled interest in Central Europe after the end of Communism and the "return" of Central Europe, even by founding a new journal named after *l'Europe Centrale*, which had been published in Prague in 1926. [2]

V

Similarly as has been said for Central Europe, after World War II and the Cominform conflict, the previously strong ideas and concrete plans for Balkan integration, which had been emerging from the mid – 19th century to the first post-

---

[1] Alain Finkielkraut, "Hrvatska ne smije biti građanska država," *Nedjelnja Dalmacija* št. 1216, Split 19 August 1994, p. 5.

[2] Jean Paul Bled, *Avant-Propos Revue d'Europe Centrale*, Tome I, Numero I, 1er Semestre 1993, p. 2.

World War II years, died away. ① Initiatives for reviving cooperation reemerged in the early Fifties (the Balkan Pact of 1954 which did not stick).

In the post-war decades, the Balkan countries enjoyed different statuses; as regards international relations, they were categorised into three groups: Bulgaria and Romania were in the Eastern Bloc, and Greece and Turkey in the Western Bloc, while Yugoslavia and Albania were not associated with either (after its conflict with Yugoslavia, Albania began to establish ties with the Soviet Union and China, and eventually became completely isolated, whereas Yugoslavia opted for a non-aligned foreign policy).

Disintegration processes, the war in Yugoslavia and the altered geostrategic image at the end of the 20th century reintroduced the reputation the Balkans had earned at the end of the 19th century and which journalists and reporters usually labelled with expressions such as "a powder keg", "the Balkans cauldron" and the like. Once again, various ideas for integrating Balkan and Central European countries were revived. They are (were) based on the desire to ensure peace and stability, and to assert old "special interests". One of the more earnest initiatives, in which Slovenia was also involved, was SECI (Southeast European Initiative). Eleven Eastern European countries (Albania, Bosnia and Herzegovina, Bulgaria, Greece, Croatia, Hungary, Macedonia, Moldavia, Romania, Slovenia and Turkey) were to have collaborated on various economic projects. ②The initiative was given by the USA in January 1997; the former Austrian Vice-Chancellor Dr. Gerhard Busek, otherwise a

---

① See also the following (selected) literature on this topic: Jacques Ancel, *Peuples et nations des Balkans*, Paris: Collection Armand Colin, 1926; Nevill Forbes, Arnold J. Toynbee, D. Mitrany, D. G. Hogarth, *The Balkans: A History of Bulgaria, Serbia, Greece, Rumania, Turkey*, Oxford: Clarendon Press, 1915; Georges Castellan, *Histoire des balkans*, Paris: Fayard, 1991; Mladen Gavrilović, "Balkanska politika Grčke, Balkan krajem osamdesetih godina" (znanstveni posvet), Centar za marksizam univerziteta, 1987; Hans Hartl, *Der "einige" und "unabhängige" Balkan*, München: R. Oldenbourg verlag, 1977; Barbara Jelavich, *History of the Balkans, Twentieth Century*, Cambridge University Press, 1983; Joachim Kühl, *Föderationspläne im Donauraum und in Ostmitteleuropa, Untersuchungen zur Gegenwartskunde Südosteuropas*, herausgeben vom Südost-Institut München II, München: R. Oldenbourg, 1958; Branko Petranović, *Balkanska federacija 1943–1948*, Šabac: IKP Zaslon, 1991; Janko Pleterski, "Narodi, Jugoslavija, revolucija," Komunist, Ljubljana, 1986; Milan Skakun, *Balkan i velike sile* KTRZ Arion, GRO D. Davidović, Smederevo, 1986 p. 61; Lev Trocki, *Kosovsko vprašanje*, DZS, Ljubljana, 1989, p. 10.

② SECI: "Draft methods of work", kept by the author of the article.

strong advocate of integration in Southeastern Europe, was appointed project coordinator. This initiative, as many similar though less perfected ones, was not particularly successful. ① After the war in Kosovo, it was replaced by the Stability Pact for Southeastern Europe, which was solemnly declared by a multitude of leaders, including the U. S. President Bill Clinton, at the end of July 1999 in a semi-rebuilt Sarajevo, who promised million dollar sums for it. Slovenia accepted the proposal hesitantly (as did Hungary), for it saw it as a means of indirectly "shoving" Slovenia back to the Balkans and thus slowing down its entry into the European Union.

Did the national and political integrations with Central Europe end for Slovenes with World War I, whereas integrations with the Balkans ended after the disintegration of Yugoslavia? How did they benefit from them and what would have happened had they not been involved in them? There is no final answer to that question. The end of World War I did not bring them what they had wanted: they were carved up among four countries, and in the Kingdom of Yugoslavia they barely attained an informal cultural autonomy and never a political one. Economically speaking, when Austria-Hungary disintegrated, Slovenes lost a large economic space. Even though the monarchy was economically lagging behind the developed European Great Powers, it enabled Slovenes to gradually strengthen their economic power—while competing with German capital; the economic lag of Austria-Hungary also enabled small nations to shape their own national identity, which the liberalist and centralist pressure of a modern state would have slowed down or even deterred. It also enabled them a relatively high level of education; after all, Austria-Hungary taught them political thinking and political culture; they established parties and became accustomed to parliamentarism (many nations lost that in the inter-war period and later on for several decades). Probably the greatest loss for Slovenes and other Central European nations

---

① At the time of the Dayton Agreement (the agreement on Bosnia and Herzegovina) in 1995, a proposal emerged on the initiative of France and under (subsequent) auspices of the European Union for the so-called sub-regional integrations, which were to promote mutual cooperation in the Balkans and help to stabilise the situation. The project with the working title Royaumon Initiative was to include the former Yugoslav republics, Hungary, Romania, Bulgaria, Albania, Greece and Turkey, and EU member states, the USA and Russia. Panajotis Rumeliotis was appointed coordinator. The initiative did not have solid financial support and fell through. ("Načrti, ki so ostali na papirju," *Delo*, 30 July 1999, p. 7).

is the common culture which they had shaped within the Danubian monarchy. The latter was being given its characteristic mark from the end of the 19th century until the onset of World War I, drawing on the tradition of the West and East, intertwining and enriching itself. It was coshaped by many poets, writers, composers, painters, philosophers and other intellectuals of Slavic, Romance, Hungarian, German and Jewish descent. Even though it was a conglomerate of languages and styles, of different hopes and fears, desires, love and hatred, it carried within it enough recognisable common characteristics to be labelled a specifically Central European culture. Without a doubt, we can still draw on its tradition today, and look for points of reference for future integrations.

For Slovenes, Yugoslavia as a Balkan state denoted a great change in the cultural space, which they had difficulty understanding and with which, despite the efforts of the central authorities and a segment of the Slovene political powers, they were never able to fully integrate. Nevertheless, the first (royal) Yugoslavia enabled Slovenes to obtain all of the main cultural and educational institutions, which the Central European Austria-Hungary had refused to provide. In the second (socialist) Yugoslavia, they developed statehood (the status of a federal republic) and grew from a people into a nation, even though they did not receive an independent state until the chaotic circumstances resulting from the end of bipolarity, the fall of Communism, and the dissolution of the Soviet Union and of Yugoslavia. In the transitional, post-Bloc period, when Europe and the balance of power in it and in the world were being reshaped, Slovenia's main goal was the European Union, which it managed to achieve in 2004. Merely fifteen years later, it is once again facing the question of what will happen in the future to the third supranational formation in Slovene history.

References:

Barbara Jelavich, *History of the Balkans, Twentieth Century*, Cambridge University Press, 1983.

Branko Petranović, *Balkanska federacija 1943–1948*, Šabac: IKP Zaslon, 1991.

Ciril Žebot, *Slovenija včeraj, danes, jutri*, samozaložba, 1969 (see also the revised reprint of the book entitled *Neminljiva Slovenija*).

Friedrich Naumann, *Mitteleuropa*, Berlin: Georg Reimer, 1915.

Georges Castellan, *Histoire des balkans*, Paris: Fayard, 1991.

Hans Hartl, *Der "einige" und "unabhängige" Balkan*, München: R. Oldenbourg verlag, 1977.

Jacques Ancel, *Peupleset nations des Balkans*, Paris: Collection Armand Colin, 1926.

Janko Pleterski, *Narodi, Jugoslavija, revolucija*, Komunist, Ljubljana, 1986.

Joachim Kühl, *Föderationspläne im Donauraum und in Ostmitteleuropa, Untersuchungen zur Gegenwartskunde Südosteuropas*, herausgeben vom Südost-Institut München II, München: R. Oldenbourg, 1958.

Joseph Roth, *Werke 2 (Das Journalistiche Werk 1924-1928)*, Koln: Kipenheuer in Witsch, 1990.

John Reed, *War in Eastern Europe: Travels Through The Balkans in 1915*, Orion Books, 1994.

Lev Trocki, *Kosovsko vprašanje*, DZS, Ljubljana, 1989.

Milan Skakun, *Balkan i velike sile* KTRZ Arion, GRO D. Davidović, Smederevo 1986.

Mladen Gavrilović, "Balkanska politika Grčke, Balkan krajem osamdesetih godina" (znanstveni posvet), Centar za marksizam univerziteta, 1987.

Nevill Forbes, Arnold J. Toynbee, D. Mitrany, D. G. Hogarth, *The Balkans: A History of Bulgaria, Serbia, Greece, Rumania, Turkey*, Oxford: Clarendon Press, 1915.

Razprava o nacionalnem vprašanju v KPJ leta 1923, zbral in uredil ter opombe napisal Jurij Perovšek v sodelovanju s prof. dr. Jankom Prunkom in prof. dr. Jankom Pleterskim, uvodno študijo napisala dr. Latinka Perović, Partizanska Knjiga, Ljubljana, 1990.

Sava N. Kosanović, *Jugoslavija: bila je osuđena na smrt*, Zagreb: Globus, 1985.

Slovenci in prihodnost (zbornik), Nova revija, Ljubljana, 1993.

Srednja Evropa (zbornik), Mladinska knjiga, Ljubljana, 1991.

Montenegro's Foreign Policy between the EU and Russia

[克罗地亚] 白伊维

内容提要 本文涉及黑山外交政策的重要特点,并对其形成过程进行了评述。本文脱离了黑山外交政策的概念化中形成特定二元论的政治和社会语境,并提出了黑山外交政策的两种特征或矛盾,即对加入欧盟前景的日益正常化和通过坚韧的政治精英所体现的隐性主权主义。

关 键 词 黑山 外交政策 北约 欧盟

作者简介 白伊维(Ivica Bakota),首都师范大学历史学院世界史专业副教授

Abstract: This paper deals with important traits in Montenegro's foreign policy and gives account on the recent changes in its formation. It departs from political and social context which formed specific dualism in Montenegro's foreign policy conceptualization. The paper proposes two characteristic traits or contradictions in Montenegro's foreign policy, i.e. increased normativism regarding the EU accession perspective and recessive sovereignism reflected through the resilient political elite.

Keywords: Montenegro, Foreign Policy, NATO, EU

I . Introduction

Despite geographical size, the political elite in Montenegro has regarded Montenegrin FP (Foreign Policy) capacity in a small-power narrative.[①] Within regional power relations Montenegro had resources and leverage to be in position to influence power relations and (re) create regional political layout. In this sense, until 2012 when Montenegro started with accession negotiations with the EU, DPS (The Democratic Party of Socialists of Montengro) foreign policy manifested in accommodation of European and Russian influence while maintaining sovereignist tendencies against normative engagements from the former and subversive influence from the latter (and its regional proxy, Serbia). Even after the start of "cold-warlesque" tensions between the EU and Russia, DPS led government has continued to uphold "small-power" FP goals that defied the size of Montenegro and successfully "adapt-adopted" asymmetric constellation between regional and global powers in the Western Balkans. This means that Montenegro's government adapted to the position where a big power (the EU) is more concerned to pressure its neighbours (Republic of Serbia, the RS) to steer off Russian influence and basically adopted these steering strategies to, on the one hand, demonstrate the commitment to Brussels and, on the other, to show that pro-Serb (ian) influence is as dangerous as the Russian influence.

This small-power narrative for the last few years generated certain impression that Montenegro, despite of its strategic goals (the EU and NATO accession), could be an unpredictable "swing state" in yielding support for hedging Russian subversive activities in the Europe's "soft underbelly". Unveiling of the coup plot and Russian increased hostility towards Montenegro's resoluteness in pursuing NATO integration moved Montenegro decisively closer to the West and significantly deteriorated its relations with Russia. However, it still didn't "burn all the bridges" with Russia.

---

① See: Christopher Hill, "Small powers and small nations", ENC, No. 6, 2008.

II. Montenegro's Foreign Policy before NATO Accession

1. Political background

Montenegro's many FP predicaments outweigh and predate the existence of the country itself. In pre-independence period (before 2006), the main political cleavage was between pro-European independentists and pro-Serb unionists. The legacy of this period remained politically acute to this day and is mainly reflected in a stark cleavage between Euro-Atlantic FP goals of the ruling political party (DPS) and Eurosceptic, Russia & Serbia friendly aspirations of the unruly opposition. Ruling DPS party, in the previous report epitomized as a "state apparatus pretending to be a political party",[1] uses its almost total political clout over the state institutions, media and academia to reinvigorate the existing cleavage and hyphen its liberal and democratic progressivism against "Oriental despotism'[2] behind the opposition's agenda. Another legacy of the pre-independence period is rather unusual level of ethnic tolerance between majoritarian Montenegrins and Serbs, and Albanian, Bosniak and Croat minorities which could be regarded as one of the most tangible achievements of the DPS regime in pre-independence period. However, since a long-standing (almost 30 years) DPS regime needs strong cleavages to hold a power, a great deal of the political processes in the country is devoted to hedge the risk of Serbs (or pro-Serb forces) outnumbering Montenegrins and accommodating the demands of the minorities to maintain their loyalty.

To put it more recently, Montenegrin political and quasi-ethnic cleavage has been fermenting from 2013. The government led by Machiavellian DPS and its leader Milo Djukanovic has been plagued by serious accusations of the connections with organized crime, masterminding systematic corruption that involved not only embezzlement, but also electoral frauds, grand-scale cronyism, influencing the media and the

---

[1] See: Ivica Bakota, "Montenegro—FP developments", China-CEE Think Tank, February 2017.
[2] Word used by some of DPS politicians and party mouthpieces.

intimidation of political opponents. A series of protests organized by "civil", yet weak opposition parties and political groups with pro-Serb inclinations started over dramatic accusations against brutal politics and corruption of ruling DPS. From 2014 oppositional groups gathered around DF (The Democratic Front) took the streets in not so much massive but rather continuous protests which in conjunction with the elections in October 2015 heated up to a large-scale protest. In the parliamentary elections in October 2016, notwithstanding the boycott and fraud accusations from some of the opposition parties, DPS managed to secure a margin for the next 4-year term. However, in the aftermath of the elections, Montenegrin security forces prevented the murder attempt on the incumbent PM (prime minister) Djukanovic and Montenegro in the last moment avoided *coup d'état* that was allegedly organized by some Serbian and Russian citizens. After months of investigations, Montenegrin Attorney General finger pointed to Russian security apparatus to stand behind the coup attempt. Coup attempt trials gave a new impetus to DPS government led by Djukanovic close aide Markovic to step up NATO integration policy and enjoying the strong support of the West (US and the EU) to refute the opposition as conspiring the "Russian candidate" or denigrating democratic institutions and procedures while continuing with the boycott in parliament.

2. Persistent dualism in the FP formation

Over the years a cross-party consensus has emerged that Montenegro's strategic goal is to join the EU. On the other hand, the DPS led FP project, i. e. NATO integration has met a strong resentment not only from the political opposition, but also from some moderate political forces. NATO accession policy was, as PM Djukanovic argued, indispensable path Montenegro should take to preserve internal stability and regional security. Yet, pro-Serb political forces have seen the NATO accession as an irreversible declension from Serbian non-aligned security policy and *propter hoc* Serbia itself. Over a time, Montenegro's politics became a black-and-white game that soon spread in the media and created either pro-NATO or anti-NATO opinions that circulated in the public space. A paradoxical situation occurred when DPS fearing unfavourable outcome rejected the referendum on NATO accession, instead offered the vote in the parliament which triggered public outcry and raised some critiques from

NGO sector.

The start of the EU accession negotiations and, moreover, the restitution of the Cold War between the EU and Russia, moved Montenegrin FP more towards the EU, while resolute stance towards the NATO integration brought into light stark political and social divisions and temporarily created "cordon sanitaire" in Montenegrin political relations with Russia. On the other hand, this estrangement in political relations with Russia entrusted some political parties on the side of Montenegrin weak opposition to set a broad range of revisionist policies that seek rapprochement with Russia and more balancing attitude towards the EU and NATO. So far, there is no clear vision as to what is the alternative to Montenegrin Euro-Atlantic integration, and much of the promises of the opposition parties are framed in abstract and inconclusive ways that have no tenable platform in the short and medium term.

In this sense, clear-cut dualism between Euro-Atlantic integrations and sustainable balancing between the West and the East are two opposite ideals that make no concessions among their proponents in political arena and can only amount to a clash in some public discussions between one dominant and two or more alternative ideological narratives: usually involving particular set of values and beliefs that try to counter dominant ideology of neoliberalism and Western style democracy with more traditionalist and conservative Orthodox brotherhood theories, or populist promise on cross-party consensus regarding the goals in Montenegro's FP. Therefore, dualism in conceptualizing Montenegro's FP is in fact a weak dualism—unlike Serbia's dominant "playing two pianos" policy—it has no diplomatic or political infrastructure to support sustainable balancing attitude between the EU and Russia, nor there is any down to earth discussion what will happen if Montenegro downsizes commitment for the EU or NATO integration.

Another source of such dualist thinking on Montenegro's FP is the zero-sum discourse employed by the West (US and the EU) in treating Montenegro's accession to NATO and "successful track of record in the EU negotiations"[1] as a particular "victory" of progressive and reform-minded political forces against the manipulative and subversive behaviour of the Russian state-proxy actors. On a foreign policy level,

---

[1] See: Bakota, February 2018.

this has led to self-indulging behaviour in which the speed and dynamics of the reforms and EU accession negotiations have often been regarded as proportionate to the level of political same-mindedness with the Brussels. Therefore, it boosted the expectations that Montenegro somehow should have priority in joining the EU and should not be put in slot with the other country-candidates in the Western Balkans.① On the domestic level, unprecedented level of support by the West, paradoxically, created so called stabilocracy,② a condition where a nominal support for pro-European FP is followed by more lax conditionality from the EU regarding the reformist agenda, hence regressive tendencies in democratic transition, surge of illiberalism in society and resilient clientelism in economy.

III. Post-accession Developments

1. Broad implications

NATO accession gave a strong impetus to Montenegrin government for furthering the EU negotiations. Until May – June 2017, Montenegro opened Chapter 1 (Free Movement of Goods), Chapter 22 (Regional Policy) and closed important chapter on External Relations (Chapter 30).③ At the same time, Montenegrin government started to prepare for hosting NATO sponsored Adriatic Chapter summit in August, with the US Vice President Pence as the highest guest, which gave the government high grounds to boost Montenegro's international standing for domestic audience. US Vice President, several State Department officials send "a strong message" that the US and the EU has unison stance regarding the uncooperative boycott from the opposition and further silenced their demands for new elections.

NATO accession had slightly negative repercussions on Montenegro's relations with Serbia. The assertive role of the former towards pro-Serb opposition in

---

① Particularly strong resentments are heard in media against joint accession with Serbia.
② Bieber, 2017.
③ The Strategy for the Western Balkans: The European Commission report, August 2018, Brusells.

Montenegro had cooling effects between Belgrade and Podgorica, and had negative effects on the domestic development. The relations with Croatia, Slovenia and Albania improved over the time which many ascribed to the security cooperation enhanced with the NATO accession.

Slight disappointment occurred in August, when the EU Commission submitted "The strategy for the Western Balkans", announcing a year 2025 as the earliest possible date for the next "joint enlargement".[①] Ruling DPS was dissatisfied with the date and the joint enlargement, while the opposition raised their doubts on the Euro-enthusiasm lasting for the next five years and depicted the remaining interim period as a "window of opportunity" for the opposition to assume power and lead Montenegro into the EU.

Among regional countries with rather unstable EU integration trajectories, Montenegro figured as a role model in completing the reforms and following the instructions of the Enlargement Commissioner. Montenegro has also responded to the EU initiatives that seek to integrate the WB (Western Balkans) region, such as the Berlin Process. Yet, Montenegrin diplomats have several times on semi-official occasions raised concern that the Berlin Process is a mere substitute for the postponed promise on the EU accession. It is, therefore, band-wagoning with the initiative—attended the Trieste Summit and signed the MoU (Memorandum of Understanding) between 3 EU and 6 WB countries[②]—but is the least committed to become more economically or politically integrated with the other WB countries. The new government is facing difficult task to trade in its excellent track of record in accession negotiation process for a more earlier accession date or the perspective of individual accession.

2. The "regatta principle" and normative traits in Montenegro's FP

After "The Strategy" left some space for ambiguities regarding the accession order. In the last two years, Montenegrin politicians have voiced self-indulging

---

① Ibid, pp. 3–16.

② Details, see: Florent Marciacq, "The EU and the Western Balkans after the Berlin Process Reflecting on the EU Enlargement in Times of Uncertainty", FES, Sarajevo, 2017.

statements on Montenegro as a "regional leader in the EU integration", last two months, this narrative gained more tangible features in the country's foreign policy and has been reflected in a new buzzword introduced into Montenegro's diplomatic circle: the "regatta principle". FM (Foreign Minister) Darmanovic has been quoted several times using this term with the EU dignitaries and some diplomats stood very confidently in the media with a more detailed account on what the "regatta principle" should mean—all of which, in turn, signaling not only a careful diplomatic consideration, but a new diplomatic strategy behind the Montenegro's accession policy.

The "regatta principle", applied to pre-accession situation of the WB countries, means respecting individual differences in regard to their EU accession negotiations accomplishments and awarding accordingly those who based on individual merit completed the negotiations first, to enter the EU first. Or in simple terms, advocating "first come, first served" approach. In this sense, if Montenegro so far keeps the best record track in the negotiation process (and if it continues to so) it should be given the opportunity to access the European community earlier than the rest of the WB countries.

For Montenegro, the main question left undecided is therefore should the "regatta principle" be a part of the normative approach itself and how strict should it be respected. "The Strategy" has a good point of departure in setting up a purely normative approach to the order of accession of candidate-countries, dismissing any concessions for intransigent political problems and leaves no space for selective approach. However, the paper is typically not precise enough in regards to "who and when" and "who with who". After the Juncker's Balkan tour in February, the impression was that the EU, although generally not objecting the "regatta principle", envisages the accession of the WB countries in three-stepped "package" process: Montenegro and Serbia taking the lead, Albania and Macedonia coming in the following round and Bosnia and Herzegovina with Kosovo coming at the latest.

Montenegro's diplomats openly acknowledged that they would not prefer anything short of an individual accession, because in case of "package" accession, Montenegro will most likely be put in stand-by arrangement waiting other country-candidate (s) or its accession negotiations could "artificially" procrastinate over a time with obvious symbolic, social and opportunity costs. Therefore, PM Markovic in his joint press conference with Juncker, probably in order to preempt stand-by fears, somewhat hastily announced that 2025—a year that "EU's Strategy for the Western Balkans" marked as the next earliest possible enlargement—would in fact be the year of Montenegro's accession. FM Darmanovic statements have also showed concerns with possible relativization of "regatta principle" and "accepting other evaluation principles at the expense of the individual merit".

Additionally, even if Montenegro relents to "package principle", there are several objections that arise with Serbia, its expected pair for the accession. Immediate reaction of the Montenegro's top officials following the Juncker's visit nuanced the unease and discomfort with the fact that Montenegro might expect the same accession slot with Serbia. At the first glance, there is a relative time lag in Serbian EU accession negotiations and, if no unexpected delays are accounted, Serbia still has approximately a year-two period to catch up with Montenegro's negotiation pace. By February 2018, Serbia opened 12 (out of 35) and closed 2 chapters, while Montenegro opened 30 and closed 3 chapters. Beside disagreements with a possible stand-by scenario, wordings of Montenegrin politicians tend to emphasize a "qualitative step ahead" instead of a mere quantitative advantage Montenegro's negotiation process has obtained. This is primarily related to the Chapter 35 which is not expected to be "closed" by Serbia any time soon as it involves the normalization of relations between Belgrade and Pristina.

There are also considerable domestic concerns that the joint accession with Serbia might highlight. The Euro-Atlantic project under the ruling government has been "advertised" as a project more competitive than complementary to the country's foreign relations with Serbia (think of NATO accession and rapprochement with regional NATO members Croatia and Albania) and for domestic audience was usually contrasted with the "anti-European" undertones stemming from "pro-Serb(ian)" political parties. Therefore, a joint accession with Serbia could backlash on the idea of competing commitments, literally and symbolically "return" Montenegro on the same track with Serbia. This backlash might not revive Eurosceptic or Euro-balancing voices from the opposition but could surely impact on the electoral results of the ruling DPS.

3. Recessive sovereignism

With the unveiling of the coup plot and Russian increased hostility towards Montenegro's resoluteness in pursuing NATO integration—escalating in minor diplomatic scandal in June 2017①—many of the formerly moderate figures within Montenegrin political elite became increasingly alienated from the idea to "balance back" Russian support either through maintaining low-profile in NATO activities or active engagement in maintaining stable economic and people-to-people relations. At some point, the overall bilateral relations were rumoured to reach "point of no return" and that Montenegro should not count any more on Russian investors, tourists and businessmen; however, no negative domino effect followed in bilateral exchanges and PM Markovic himself emphasized in public interviews that the NATO accession does not change Montenegro's stance regarding the bilateral relations with Russia.

However, in April 2018 political and diplomatic relations with Russia started slowly to resume previous level of communication. It can be said that the opposition was partially right regarding the backchannel diplomacy the government maintained with Russia. Indicative to pre-arranged and carefully planned mutual rapprochement was specific timing of the thaw (immediately after Djukanovic was elected as a president) and specific vocabulary that the both presidents used, both "coinciding" on the traditional friendly relations and avoiding focus on the recent issues. From the Russian perspective, the fact that purports this claim could be seen in dismissive attitude the United Russia had towards the opposition parties, especially in the fact that the first signals came even before the elections. The impression is that despite declaratively pro-Russian stance Russia never quite counted on pro-Serb opposition. Additionally, unlike with the other European countries, Russian hybrid war against Montenegro never had economic backdrops.

Nevertheless, only few opinions put the odds of Montenegro fully recovering the previous level of political relations with Russia. The record of tumbling deterioration in

---

① The scandal occurred in June when Montenegrin MP (member of parliament) was denied transfer on Minsk bound flight and due to "newly updated immigration regulations" had to return from Moscow's airport to Podgorica.

the last 2 years is full of red flags to expect that bilateral relations could overnight be back to past levels. Despite somewhat exaggerated concerns from the opposition, no one expects from the arch-pragmatist politician like Djukanovic to lead the country from the doorstep of the EU back to a "bear's den".

There are few sticking points in the Russo-Montenegrin political relationship that could be easier to ignore than to tackle. A big hot potato is Russian involvement in the coup attempt and possible judicial cooperation regarding the coup trials. No one thinks that Russia could extradite its citizens Sismakov and Popov, tried in absentia by Podgorica Court; but there are several question marks over the Russian "official" cooperation in providing relevant insights that could help to explain some loose ends in the investigations over the coup preparations. Concerns about the revising the coup attempt might have implications on the Montenegrin-American relations, especially because it was M. Pence that condemned the "involvement of the Russian state structures" in the coup attempt. Therefore, any sliding from the doxa will bring unnecessary attention of Washington, let alone renewed scrutiny surrounding the coup investigations. Of course, Montenegro should also explain its behavior to Brussels, where the rumors on Montenegro's rapprochement with Russia already incited some articles to call the thaw as a move "behind the back" and "under the radar of the EU".

However, in order to give more accurate account on the significance the possible rapprochement with Russia, there are two additional points that have to be made. First, despite relatively strong Euro-Atlantic appeal, Montenegro actually never abandoned sovereignist tendencies in its foreign policy. Balancing between the commitments to the West (the EU, US) and accommodation of the influences arriving from "the East" (primarily Russia, but also Turkey, UAE) were wrapped up in a small-power narrative that stems from Montenegro's pre-independence foreign policy thought and conceptualization.

It can be said that in the last years this narrative hibernated or has been temporarily "outsourced" to the opposition, but resilience of the ruling political elite and continuity of the same political actors that generated the narrative made sure it could not just die out in couple of years. As a matter of fact, a coincidence of the Russian thaw with Djukanovic's presidency urged some opinions to conjure convalescent tendency towards sovereignism as a reaction to increasingly assertive European conditionality and relatively strong appeal it has obtained in Montenegro's government.

Second, the fear of so called "silent chapter" (departure of the long-standing political elite within the ruling DPS party) in the accession negotiations with the EU also drives current political elite back to sovereignist positions. Contrary to FP convergences with the EU, Montenegro's success in implementing internal reforms, according to the opinion of S. Muk, director of the leading NGO in Montenegro, clearly shows disparity between its role as "a regional leader" and "reform simulator".[①] The last EU report for Montenegro stated in April that Montenegro is still due a considerable effort in tackling the rule of law, media freedom and independent judiciary, while four main NGO's (CGO, CEMI, CRNVO, Alternative) sent to the EU Commission a document highly critical of government's commitment in making any progress on these issues, even calling for temporary suspension of negotiations.

To pre-empt European conditionality regarding the internal matters, but also to maintain his informal power over state structures, fulfill his descending political career and protect his ailing business empire, President Djukanovic made several statements indicating refusal to align with government's preemptive obedience to the EU.

As a matter of fact, President Djukanovic positioned himself as the patron of sovereignism. In expounding this position to FP matters, it is likely that Montenegro will assume "two-headed foreign policy": the government will continue pursuing Euro-Atlantic integrations while the president will "check and balance" relations with the EU by keeping Russia and other non-Western powers in backup. Bifurcation of Montenegro's foreign policy could thus essentially follow the trajectory of the other regional countries whose presidents intended to add some personal flavor to their national foreign policy. However, it can assume more assertive sovereignist tendencies should European normative appeal become too strong within the government circles.

---

① CRNVO, *Otvoreno pismo Europskoj komisiji*, Vijesti, April, 2018.

Ⅳ. Concluding Remarks

As for the future of Montenegro's foreign policy formation and conceptualization, recent changes have several implications. First, dualism in Montenegro's foreign policy formation instead of being a weak dualism with the government (and ruling political elite) and pro-Serb opposition as the main contending actors, might assume trajectory of a strong dualism, where political elite gathered around President Djukanovic could counter-balance increasing normativity stemming from the EU and supported by (some circles within) the government. Second, the success in advocating normative approach vis-à-vis the accession negotiation with the EU will also largely depend on redefining a "small-power" narrative as the one not balancing the EU conditionality. So far, as the country particularly interested to transcend the frameworks based on the cooperative engagements within the "immediate region", Montenegro should have relatively high propensity to continue to be an active supporter of the norm-based approach toward the EU accession. Lastly, reconciling sovereignist and normative traits in its FP conceptualization is the main challenge Montenegro will face in furthering EU integration processes while maintaining the current political elite.

References:

Christopher Hill, *Small powers and small nations*, ENC, No. 6, 2008.

Ivica Bakota, "Montenegro—FP developments", China-CEE Think Tank, February 2017.

The Strategy for the Western Balkans: The European Commission report, August 2018, Brusells.

Florent Marciacq, "The EU and the Western Balkans after the Berlin Process Reflecting on the EU Enlargement in Times of Uncertainty", FES, Sarajevo, 2017.

CRNVO, *Otvoreno pismo Europskoj komisiji*, Vijesti, April, 2018.

BRI—Potential for Economic Cooperation between China and the Western Balkans: The Case of The Republic of North Macedonia

[北马其顿] 安娜·布拉热斯卡

内容提要 巴尔干在中欧关系中具有地缘战略地位，是"一带一路"倡议的核心地区之一。从尽可能广泛的意义考察巴尔干国家的话，从政治上来看西巴尔干可以被挑出来作为次区域——西巴尔干国家不是欧盟成员国；但从经济上看，它们与其他国家（希腊、克罗地亚、斯洛文尼亚、保加利亚和罗马尼亚）相比，是比较贫穷的国家，人均国内生产总值只有欧盟平均水平的1/3。本文旨在分析"一带一路"背景下中国与西巴尔干国家经济合作的前景，重点分析北马其顿的情况。本文将分析北马其顿对经济合作的最初预期、合作的现状和未来的可能发展，并回答"一带一路"建设是否实现了北马其顿经济合作的预期。

本文的额外价值在于，运用理性选择理论对以下假设进行验证或证伪：尽管"一带一路"倡议和"17+1"合作启动以来，中国和北马其顿的经济合作有所加强，但其仍存巨大潜力尚未开发。根据理性选择理论，利益优先于价值，"个体在约束下采取行动以最大化其预期效用"。（Pollack，M. 2006）

本文着重分析了中国和北马其顿共和国在"一带一路"框架内开展合作的主要动因。文章认为，在国内政治、国内经济规模和结构以及欧盟成员国身份等诸多制约因素的影响下，北马其顿国内两党间存在着利益不匹配。因此,任何一方都不能使其利益最大化,从而导致幻想破灭和合作动机的减少。文章分析了造成这一局面的根本原因,并以主要调查结果和结论为基础,对中国和北马其顿两国重振合作、增进互利提出了几点建议。

关键词 中国 巴尔干 欧盟 一带一路 北马其顿

作者简介 安娜·布拉热斯卡(Ana Blazheska),北马其顿政策制定和研究中心项目主管

Abstract: The Balkans, with its geostrategic position on the EU-China pathway, is one of the core regions in the design of the One Belt One Road Initiative (BRI). Within the Balkan countries, considered in the broadest possible sense, the Western Balkans (WB) can be singled out as a subregion from a political point of view—Western Balkan countries are not EU member states, but also from an economic point of view—they are generally poorer countries when compared to the others (Greece, Croatia, Slovenia, Bulgaria and Romania), with an average GDP per capita amounting to only 1/3 from the EU's average. This paper aims to analyze the prospects for economic cooperation between China and the Western Balkans in the context of the BRI, focusing particularly on the case of the Republic of North Macedonia. It will analyze the initial expectations for economic cooperation, the current state of play and possible future developments in order to provide an answer to the question: has the BRI fulfilled the expectations of the Republic of North Macedonia in terms of economic cooperation?

The added value of this paper is the application of the rational choice theory to verify or falsify the following hypothesis: although the economic cooperation between China and the Republic of North Macedonia improved since the launch of the BRI and 17+1 forum, there is significant potential that remains untapped. According to the rational choice theory, interests take precedence over values and "individuals act to maximize their expected utility subject to constraints" (Pollack, M. 2006).

This article focuses on the specific economic interests of China and the Republic of North Macedonia as main drivers behind the rationale for their cooperation within the framework of the BRI. It argues that under the influence of several constraints, namely domestic politics, size and structure of the domestic economy and EU membership, there is a mismatch between the interests of the two parties. Thus, neither side can maximize their benefit, which in turn leads to disenchantment and reduced incentives for cooperation. The paper examines the underlying reasons for this situation and, using the main findings and conclusions as basis, it proposes several recommendations for both China and the Republic of North Macedonia to reinvigorate their cooperation and increase mutual benefit.

Keywords: China, Balkans, EU, BRI, the Republic of North Macedonia

I. Introduction

The Balkan Region, with its geostrategic position on the EU-China pathway, is one of the core regions in the design of the One Belt One Road Initiative. Within the Balkan countries, considered in the broadest possible sense, the Western Balkans can be singled out as a sub-region from a political, as well as economic point of view. They are the only group of countries which aspire EU membership, but are not yet Member States and still do not fully meet the accession criteria. They are also generally poorer when compared to the other European and Balkan countries (Greece, Croatia, Slovenia, Bulgaria and Romania), with an average GDP per capita amounting to only 1/3 from the EU's average and catching-up process which has significantly slowed down since the European economic and financial crisis.[1] In addition, the average infrastructure development for the region is 50% lower than the EU's average, which inhibits the countries to reap the possible economies of scale, integrate European supply chains and attract FDI.[2] A reduction of this index by 1%

---

[1] Atoyan, R., Benedek, D., "Public Infrastructure in the Western Balkans: Opportunities and Challenges", April 17, 2018, p. 14, http://www.imf.org/en/Publications/Departmental-Papers-Policy-Papers/Issues/2018/02/07/Public-Infrastructure-in-the-Western-Balkans-Opportunities-and-Challenges-45547.

[2] Ibid., p. 14.

could lead to an increase in the real GDP of 0.1%.[1] Economic development and growth is a strategic priority of any government that comes into power in these countries and efforts are made to promote exports, attract foreign direct investments (FDI) and build infrastructure to facilitate transport, communications, tourism and energy supply.

This paper aims to analyze the prospects for economic cooperation between China and the Western Balkans in the context of the BRI, focusing particularly on the case of the Republic of North Macedonia. It strives to provide an answer to the question: has the BRI fulfilled the expectations of the Republic of North Macedonia in terms of economic cooperation? The first part analyzes the initial expectations for economic cooperation and the general interests of both China and North Macedonia; the second part examines the current state of play and the constraints which impact the cooperation, namely: on the North Macedonian side—size and structure of the domestic economy, domestic politics and the prospects for EU membership; on both sides—image, perceptions and intercultural differences; the third part draws conclusions and propose several recommendations for both China and the Republic of North Macedonia to reinvigorate their cooperation and increase mutual benefit. For the purpose of the paper, the economic cooperation is analyzed through 3 different lenses: trade, investment and infrastructure.

II. Analytical Framework

The rational choice theory is applied to verify or falsify the following hypothesis: although the economic cooperation between China and the Republic of North Macedonia improved since the launch of the BRI and 17+1 forum, there is significant potential that remains untapped. According to the rational choice theory, individuals

---

[1] Atoyan, R., Benedek, D., "Public Infrastructure in the Western Balkans: Opportunities and Challenges", April 17, 2018, p.14, http://www.imf.org/en/Publications/Departmental-Papers-Policy-Papers/Issues/2018/02/07/Public-Infrastructure-in-the-Western-Balkans-Opportunities-and-Challenges-45547.

"act to maximize their expected utility subject to constraints".[1] They engage in rational cost-benefit analysis of alternative courses of actions and choose the one that is likely to maximize their interests.[2] Their interests are exogenously given, determined by the objective situation they find themselves in and mainly related to economic issues.[3] When making their choices, actors are usually under constraints which stem from various formal and informal institutions, such as the "rules of the game",[4] inter-actor relations and policy impacts.[5]

This paper argues that under the influence of several constraints, namely domestic politics, size and structure of the domestic economy and EU membership, there is a mismatch between the interests of the two parties. Cultural differences and perceptions further increase the gap and reduce the prospects for cooperation. Therefore, neither side can maximize their benefit, which in turn leads to disenchantment, reduced incentives for future cooperation and untapped potential.

III. BRI in the Western Balkans

The launch of the 17+1 cooperation in 2012 and the BRI one year later marked an important turn in the relationship between China and the Western Balkans. The Balkan countries suddenly appeared on the Chinese agenda as potential partners in concrete projects and beneficiaries of funds intended for infrastructure development. The essence of the BRI is to create favorable conditions for economic cooperation by tackling several fronts at once—infrastructure, logistics, trade facilitation, investment promotion, tourism etc. Although the multi-trillion dollar initiative is mainly financed by China, one of the guiding principles is the notion of mutual benefit. This naturally

---

[1] Pollack, M. A., "Rational Choice and EU Politics," in Jorgensen, Knud E., Pollack, M. A., Rosamond, B., *Handbook of European Union Politics*, London: Sage Publications, 2006, pp. 31-56, p. 32.
[2] Ibid.
[3] Nugent, N., *The Government and Politics of the European Union*, Basingstoke: Palgrave Macmillan, 2010 (7th ed.), p. 438.
[4] Riker, W., Shepsle, K., quoted in Pollack, Marc A., "International Relations Theory and European Integration," *Journal of Common Market Studies*, Vol. 39, No. 2, 2001, pp. 221-244, p. 227.
[5] Nugent, loc. cit.

raised the expectations in all the Western Balkan countries who anticipated tangible benefits from their participation in the initiative, such as an increase in their exports to China, an important rise in Chinese FDI to the region and cheap loans to build the much-needed infrastructure projects, especially in transport and energy.

From today's perspective, exports to China have started to increase, but so have Chinese exports to the region, leaving the trade deficit rate relatively unchanged. Chinese investments in these countries (both infrastructural and FDI), amount to less than 3% of the overall Chinese FDI in Central and Eastern Europe.① Many infrastructure projects have been announced and initiated, but their implementation is oftentimes sluggish, problematic and accompanied with negative publicity, for different reasons. All this has certain impact on the future and intensity of the cooperation and makes both sides reconsider their efforts and expected utility.

Ⅳ. Chinese-North Macedonian Bilateral Cooperation

The Republic of North Macedonia has so far implemented several projects with Chinese funding through grants or loans. The first major Chinese project in the energy sector in North Macedonia and generally the broader region was Kozjak hydropower plant, built by the China Water Electric company on the river Treska in 2004 with a US $ 413 million from the China Development Bank. The first complete construction project financed with Chinese aid funds was the primary school Rajko Zhinzifov in Drachevo, Skopje, which was built by the Chinese company IPPR, following Chinese standards. Chinese development cooperation funds in the amount of US $ 7 million were also used to implement a project called e-Education, aiming to connect all the education institutions in the country. The Chinese company Huawei was chosen to be the implementing party following a public tender. The capital, the City of Skopje, purchased 202 Zhengzhou Yutong buses in the amount of US $ 38.5 million to replace

---

① Liu, Z. quoted in Kratz, A., Stanzel, A., "China's investment in influence: the future of 16 + 1 cooperation", December 14, 2016, http://www.ecfr.eu/publications/summary/chinas_investment_in_influence_the_future_of_161_cooperation7204.

the fleet of the Public Transport Company.① The North Macedonian National Railway Company bought electric trains and locomotives from China Railway Rolling Stock Corporation to modernize the rail transport using a loan from the EBRD in the amount of US $ 29.5 million.②

In addition, North Macedonia was the first country in Central and Eastern Europe to make use of the US $ 10 billion put at the disposal of the CEE countries through Chinese state-owned banksfor infrastructure projects in the framework of the 17 + 1 cooperation. Using a concessional loan from the Export-Import Bank of China in the amount of US $ 677.3 million (to be paid back over 20 years, with 2% interest rate and 5 years grace period), the North Macedonian government started the construction of a section of the highway linking the cities of Kichevo and Ohrid (57km) and the construction of a section of the highway linking the capital, Skopje, to the city of Shtip (50km).

V. Expectations and Interests

1. China

It is important to understand that BRI has so far been a Chinese-led initiative. It aims to respond to Chinese domestic economic concerns, such as the excess capacity in some sectors (ex. construction, steel and cement industries) or the elimination of trade barriers to facilitate the flow of Chinese exports to Europe. More broadly, China uses the multi-trillion foreign currency reserves in its possession to strengthen its role of important regional and global player.③ In that context, BRI is driven predominantly by Chinese interests and aims to maximize China's benefits. Nonetheless, Chinese

---

① Unnamed author, "The double-deckers will be produced by the Chinese Yutong," *Vecher Newspaper*, March 26, 2010. https://vecer.mk/skopska/dvokatnite-avtobusi-kje-gi-proizveduva-kineski-jutong.

② Unnamed author, "The last train in the MNRC fleet arrived—an investment worth 25 million euros", Channel 5 TV, February 8, 2017, http://build.mk/pristignaa-sheste-kineski-vozovi-za-makedonski-zheleznitsi/.

③ Interview with Mr. Nikola Poposki, North Macedonian Member of Parliament and former Minister of Foreign Affairs, Skopje, May 18. 2018.

foreign policy, through its basic principles of harmonious development and mutual benefit, indirectly acknowledges that any bilateral initiative is condemned to fail unless it is grounded in win-win cooperation. Thus, the BRI develops in a loose and flexible way in order to integrate different countries and stakeholders that find common areas of interest with China and Chinese partners.

China used the European financial, sovereign debt and economic crisis to promote its companies and enter sectors where otherwise it would have probably not been allowed to invest. The strategy of Chinese companies was focused not on immediate profit, but on long-term success. Therefore, they preferred to engage in mergers and acquisitions and to buy "discounted" European companies which provided them with technology transfer, advanced management and brands—all of which takes time to build and provides significant competitive edge. Before the crisis, the Chinese economy which was mostly based on low value products and exports was approaching a standstill in terms of growth. Chinese smart investment policy allowed its companies to reform the structure of the exports, increase the value of their share in export products and climb up the supply chains. This in turn led to further economic development and stable growth rates and promoted China into a more sophisticated global economic force. In line with the rational choice theory, China used the European crisis to lead its economy to a new level and thus maximize its benefits. The same objectives continue to guide the rationale behind Chinese foreign investments today.

Given its ambitions, the size of its economy overall, as well as individual companies, China usually seeks to implement large-scale projects using funding from its outward-oriented state-owned banks (China Development Bank or China Export-Import Bank) with very favorable conditions-approximately 1% annual interest rate, grace period etc.

2. North Macedonia

The Republic of North Macedonia is a milestone country on the pathway leading from Athens to Budapest in Central Europe and further to Western and Northern Europe, and one of the locations with central geographic importance when it comes to the implementation of BRI. The country was among the first ones in CEE to embrace the BRI and 17+1 cooperation, hoping to increase its visibility in China, especially among Chinese policy makers and big companies, in order to create new avenues for economic cooperation and speed up its economic development. A memorandum for cooperation within the framework of BRI was signed between the two countries in March 2015 which contains broad and general wording that the two parties commit to develop their mutual cooperation within the framework of the BRI.

In the past decade, the efforts of North Macedonian national institutions were mostly oriented towards the domestic economy, seeking for ways to create growth and jobs. Following numerous shady and failed deals to privatize public and national companies in the 1990s, 2006 marked record-high unemployment rate of 38.6%. The newly elected government in 2006 considered that the best way to reduce unemployment and generate growth was to attract greenfield or alternatively brownfield investments, mainly from foreign companies, that would open new factories or restart the old ones. Many reforms were implemented aimed to improve the business environment, including fiscal policy reforms (introduction of low and flat tax rates, no tax on re-invested profit), creation of special zones for foreign investors with more favorable rules and regulations in comparison with investments outside the zones, (partial) exemption from certain public duties and charges, subsidies for construction of production plants and other production-related expenses, like machinery, creation of state agency tasked with attracting FDI and providing post-investment support and services, etc. These efforts led to North Macedonia ranking 11th worldwide according to the World Bank's Doing Business report in 2017.[①]

China's economic assent, its outward expansion and the big investments in different European countries during and after the economic crisis fueled North Macedonian expectations from the bilateral cooperation to avery high extent. The previous government (2006-2017) had made a plan to create special "free zones" for Chinese companies only, with even more favorable conditions. This proposal was put forth at every 17+1 summit in the first several years of the cooperation. Yet, not a single big Chinese company came to invest and stay in North Macedonia and the

---

① World Bank, *Doing Business Report*, 2018, http://www.doingbusiness.org/data/exploreeconomies/macedonia-fyr.

overall level of Chinese investments remains below 0.1% of the total FDI inflows.

When it comes to trade, North Macedonian imports from China in 2016 amounted to US $ 421 million, while exports to China accounted for US $ 47.8 million (6.3% and 1% from North Macedonian trade respectively).① The trade balance is strongly in favor of China, although it does not rank among North Macedonia's top trade partners who include Germany, United Kingdom, Serbia, Bulgaria, Greece and Italy.②

In terms of infrastructure, North Macedonia, as well as the rest of the Western Balkan countries, lags behind the EU average in terms of modern and functional transport, energy, telecommunications and social infrastructure. Given that Western Balkan countries are not EU members, the access to funding for these purposes is quite limited compared to the amounts available for member states within the framework of the EU's structural funds. The European Commission, through the Western Balkans Investment Framework (WBIF), allocated US $ 1.18 billion of grants for 7 years (2014 – 2020) for the entire region, but the estimated amount needed to catch up and close the infrastructure gap only in North Macedonia amounts to approximately US $ 6 billion (for the sectors transport, energy and social infrastructure).③ That is why North Macedonia often looks up to China as a possible source of funding for the much needed infrastructure projects.

VI. Constraints

1. Size and structure of the domestic economy

Unlike big European countries which provide significant market potential and investment opportunities, North Macedonia has a population of only 2 million. It offers

---

① Observatory of Economic Complexity, Massachusetts Institute of Technology, 2016 data, https://atlas.media.mit.edu/en/profile/country/mkd/#Destinations.

② China would rank 3rd for imports and 5th for exports if EU Member States are considered as a block—EU.

③ Calculation made by the author based on the Single Project Pipeline approved by the National Investment Committee of the Republic of North Macedonia in 2016.

solid conditions for doing business, especially in the free zones, FTAs which offer tax-free exports to a market of 500 million consumers, but the size of its market, along with its organization, or lack thereof, acts as impediment to big investments.

First, despite the high unemployment rate, investors often face problems to hire staff with the skills they need because of a big mismatch between the labor supply and demand. The education is mostly focused on theoretic and academic disciplines, while vocational training is often considered second-class, underestimated and thus unattractive for young people. A notable example is the investment of Weibo Group in a textile factory which was supposed to hire 5000 people. Following several years of unsuccessful efforts to recruit textile workers, they decided to scale down and relocate their investment to Serbia.

Second, it has few companies and limited resources for shipping and logistics and there are no services to support exports that are standardized in terms of quality, availability and price.

Third, the limited production output is not sufficient to satisfy the needs of bigger markets and ensure permanent supply.

Fourth, most of the potential investment opportunities do not offer any technological or innovation advantages, nor brands, and rank low in the supply chain.[1] Thus, they do not match the interests of Chinese investors and the priorities of the Chinese outward investment policy.

Fifth, Chinese ideas for infrastructure projects are usually too grandiose for the small Balkan states. In the case of North Macedonia, the public debt level has reached 45.8% of GDP,[2] which means that it is approaching the limit of 60% imposed by the EU and cannot provide bank guarantees for new large-scale projects. That is why some of the projects that the government has initially agreed to implement would need to be postponed—indefinitely, maybe even cancelled.

2. EU membership

As a prospective EU member and EU candidate country for 14 years, North

---

[1] Interview Poposki, op. cit.

[2] Ministry of Finance of the Republic of North Macedonia, *Economic Reform Program 2018-2020*, p. 39, https://www.finance.gov.mk/files/Macedonia_ERP_2018.pdf.

Macedonia has been working on the alignment of its legislation with the EU acquis and the implementation of EU standards and best practices. It is bound to follow EU's guidance and rules in all areas, including trade, investments, environment, social standards, public procurements etc. and is strongly encouraged to cooperate with European banks, like EIB, EBRD and KfW in the implementation of infrastructure projects within the Western Balkans Investment Framework (WBIF).

In addition, following the efforts to enhance Western Balkans regional cooperation within the framework of the Berlin Process and especially at the last EU-Western Balkans summit which took place in Trieste, Italy in 2017, the countries from the Western Balkans region decided to engage in the creation of a Regional Economic Area. This initiative aims to foster reconciliation and regional cooperation in order to improve regional connectivity, remove trade barriers and create a level-playing field in the area of investment policy. The underlying reason is the fact that despite the geographic proximity, the level of trade relations between the countries is very low, mostly because of bad connectivity and historical and political issues. Moreover, the region has started to build an image as an investment destination with cheap and high-skilled labor producing low-value goods, which essentially leads to a "race to the bottom" in terms of social and environmental standards. The long-term result should be greater convergence with EU policies and standards which will eventually prepare the countries for EU membership. Given that the initiative is still in an initial phase, the impact on the economic cooperation with third countries, like China, is yet to be evaluated.

3. Domestic political, legislative and institutional situation

The past 4 years have been politically very turbulent for the Republic of North Macedonia. Following a wire-tapping scandal in 2015, a series of corruption allegations have surfaced against high representatives from the former government which led to a prolonged political crisis, early elections in December 2016 and a new government in June 2017. This had serious impact on the economy, plunging the country in recession and putting the activity of foreign investors on hold. Although the crisis is over and notwithstanding the good official scores for doing business, the economic conditions have not substantially improved and meaningful reforms need to be implemented for the economy to gain impetus and achieve sustainable growth. The country report published by the European Commission in April 2018 reveals profound challenges that have a negative impact on attracting FDI: mismatch between the skills that are needed and offered on the labor market; political and economic instability; frequently changing legal framework and ambiguous legislation; corruption; efficiency of the judiciary; red-tape and inefficient public administration.①

Chinese business people, like any other, need and expect stable political atmosphere and support from the institutions to invest and conduct their operations. An atmosphere of uncertainty, along with frequent elections and changes of the highest decision-making level do not serve the purpose of attracting FDI, nor implementing infrastructure or other projects. For example, the construction of the highways (which was also mentioned in the wiretaps within the context of a corruption affair) has been prolonged for several years.

Political changes are sometimes coupled with changes in strategic priorities, which is particularly harmful to the country's long-term development. Despite a multitude of strategic papers formally adopted in various areas, the country does not have a long-term vision of its development which would be based on a broad political and societal consensus and would be pursued for the benefit of the country regardless of the political party in power. That is why some projects which need to be conceived and implemented beyond the narrow 4-year political cycle, which require political vision and long-term commitments are still uncertain. An illustration would be the Chinese idea to create a navigable channel that will connect the rivers of Vardar, Morava and Danube and enable cheap transport of goods from the Port of Piraeus to Germany.②

Moreover, despite the big number of administrative servants in the public institutions, there is a lack of capacity—both human and technical to support the implementation of large-scale projects.

---

① European Commission, *2018 Report on the Republic of North Macedonia*, April 17, 2018, https://ec. europa. eu/neighbourhood-enlargement/sites/near/files/20180417-the-former-yugoslav-republic-of-macedonia-report. pdf.

② Interview with Ambassador Ilija Isajlovski, former North Macedonian Ambassador to China and currently foreign policy advisor to the President of the Republic of North Macedonia, Skopje, May 7, 2018.

4. Image and reputation

The issues of image and reputation can be analyzed in both directions.

Chinese consumers tend to buy brands and products from countries they know and they associate with quality in that particular area. But, North Macedonia is completely unknown to the average Chinese, with no reputation in any area or product.[①] This situation is further deteriorated by the lack of understanding that North Macedonian companies have about the Chinese market and the lack of effort to increase their visibility and credibility. A solid indicator would be the very limited interest that North Macedonian companies show in participating at the first China International Import Expo that is planned to take place in November 2018, despite the intensive lobbying by Chinese diplomats and officials.[②]

It has to be mentioned that under the influence of big Chinese companies present in North Macedonia and in the region, especially in the area of technology (Huawei, ZTE, Xiaomi, Haier, etc.), the perceptions are gradually improving. But broader efforts are needed to make a meaningful impact in terms of image and reputation and the development of the Chinese PR strategy targeting Europe is lagging behind the improvements of Chinese technology and quality.[③]

Furthermore, the corruption affair regarding the construction of the highways with Chinese funds has enormous influence on the perceptions on both sides, as well as on the image of Chinese investments in Europe more broadly. Even before the court publishes a verdict and the accusations are proven, the affair is seen through extremely negative eyes: speaking of ordinary people, North Macedonians associate Chinese projects with corruption and shady deals, which also in their eyes impacts the quality of the works. Chinese see North Macedonia as a country where corruption flourishes and companies should beware when concluding business deals. EU think-tanks and media used the corruption affair to make a point against Chinese development and infrastructure projects in the region, underlining their negative

---

① Interview with Mr. Huang Jun, Huawei Country Director for the Republic of Macedonia, Skopje, May 10, 2018.
② Interview with an anonymous Chinese diplomat, Skopje, May 9, 2018.
③ Interview Poposki, op. cit.

impact on the rule of law and the democratic reforms supported by the West.[①]

5. Language and cultural barriers

Stereotypes and cultural differences are another obstacle to a more intensive economic cooperation. English is usually the common language that both North Macedonian and Chinese counterparts speak in the mutual communication. Given that it is not the mother tongue of any party and neither side is perfectly proficient, miscommunication and/or incomplete understanding are common. Several steps have been undertaken on both sides to remedy this situation. Confucius institute has been opened in Skopje in 2013 which offers free language classes for different interested parties (schools, companies, ordinary citizens) and occasionally organizes cultural events. It is important to mention that in cooperation with the Government, free classes have been organized in the public institutions since 2015 and at the moment around 60 civil servants are learning Chinese. On the other side, Beijing Foreign Studies University has set up the Macedonian major since 2015. In time, these efforts will certainly yield positive results in bridging the inter-cultural differences and improve mutual understanding as a precondition for further cooperation in any area, including the economy.

VII. Conclusions and recommendations

The mismatch between the expectations and interests from the economic cooperation on both sides is evident. The BRI allows China to support its own economic development by investing in infrastructure that will facilitate Chinese exports and by promoting Chinese companies on the global market. It also creates a framework for win-win cooperation with all the countries along the Belt and Road, providing that their interests and abilities align with what China and its companies need. In the case

---

[①] Gjorgioska, A., Vangeli, A., "A Battle of Perceptions: The social representations of the BRI and the '16+1' in Macedonia", China-CEE Institute Working Paper Series, December 11, 2017, https://china-cee.eu/wp-content/uploads/2018/02/Work_paper201701.pdf.

of North Macedonia, the country is willing, but unable to offer many attractive areas for cooperation and business deals because of several constraints: the size of its economy which offers relatively small production output and small market in terms of labor, consumers, services and products; lack of investment opportunities which would offer technology transfer, brands or other assets of interest for Chinese companies; political instability, legal uncertainty and lack of vision and institutional capacity; strategic orientation to join the EU, which implies abiding by EU rules and favoring cooperation with European partners—banks and companies; lack of visibility for North Macedonian products in China and possible bad image following the corruption affair with the highways; negative perception and stereotypes for China in North Macedonia, although sometimes without any foundation in reality; inter-cultural differences.

All these constraints negatively impact the cooperation between North Macedonia and China and reduce the prospects for both sides to maximize their interests. Several recommendations for overcoming this situation are provided below.

1. Regional cooperation

Given the size of the North Macedonian economy, as well as the other countries in the Western Balkans, enhanced regional cooperation would be highly useful to promote and increase the visibility of the entire region as an attractive business destination for Chinese companies and to allow them to use the economies of scale. In terms of investments, despite the efforts in the past decade, many reforms remain to be implemented and many of the implemented ones need to be reconsidered because of the lack of results achieved. Notwithstanding the fact that the economies in the region act as competitors in attracting foreign investments and promoting their exports, there are joint challenges that could be best tackled and joint benefits to be reaped if they cooperated and defined joint measures to be undertaken.

2. Smart specialization

Given the small production capacities in most areas which are insufficient to make a sustainable entry on the Chinese market, North Macedonia and other Balkan countries should focus on their "niche" advantages and develop smart specialization in certain areas. Bearing in mind the size and diversity of the Chinese market, specific consumer population should be selected and targeted. This would also help at the same time to optimize the use of (scarce) resources. For example, given the quality, ecologic origin and competitive price of most North Macedonian farming products, they could be further developed as smart specialization and used as an avenue for North Macedonian products to become popular on the Chinese market for a portion of the middle class which pursues a healthy life style.

3. Innovative visibility strategies

North Macedonian companies need to pay more attention to their marketing in China and building a positive image and reputation. It does not have to be through the mainstream media (TV/newspapers) which usually have high prices and will not be rentable for companies with small production output, like the North Macedonian ones. Alternative channels should be used like live streaming (直播) and Chinese social media to promote specific products.[①] In addition, North Macedonian companies should be encouraged and assisted by the national authorities to promote themselves at different events in China, like expos, fairs, business forums etc.

Chinese stakeholders, especially companies need to focus on increasing and improving their visibility and credibility as well. Particular attention needs to be invested in the application of high (European) standards in terms of social protection, environment, corporate social responsibility, as well as the inclusion of local (North Macedonian) companies in the supply chains as suppliers or subcontractors. This would have direct impact on the local development and the positive reputation of China and Chinese companies. Successfully implemented projects in North Macedonia and the Balkan region in general would be a good reference for them when they want to apply for bigger contracts in Europe because they would demonstrate know-how and experience in the implementation of European standards and values.

---

① Interview Huang, op. cit.

References:

Atoyan, R., Benedek D., "Public Infrastructure in the Western Balkans: Opportunities and Challenges", 17.04.2018, retrieved from http://www.imf.org/en/Publications/Departmental-Papers-Policy-Papers/Issues/2018/02/07/Public-Infrastructure-in-the-Western-Balkans-Opportunities- and-Challenges-45547.

European Commission, *2018 Report on the Republic of Macedonia*, 17.04.2018, retrieved from https://ec.europa.eu/neighbourhood-enlargement/sites/near/files/20180417-the-former-yugoslav-republic-of-macedonia-report.pdf.

Gjorgioska, A., Vangeli, A., "A Battle of Perceptions: The social representations of the BRI and the '16+1' in Macedonia", China-CEE Institute Working Paper Series, 11.12.2017, retrieved from https://china-cee.eu/wp-content/uploads/2018/02/Work_paper201701.pdf.

Interview with Ambassador Ilija Isajlovski, former Macedonian Ambassador to China and currently foreign policy advisor to the President of the Republic of Macedonia, Skopje, 07.05.2018.

Interview with an anonymous Chinese diplomat, Skopje, 09.05.2018.

Interview with Mr. Huang Jun, Huawei Country Director for the Republic of Macedonia, Skopje, 10.05.2018.

Interview with Mr. Nikola Poposki, Macedonian Member of Parliament and former Minister of Foreign Affairs, Skopje, 18.05.2018.

Kratz, A., Stanzel, A., "China's investment in influence: the future of 16+1 cooperation", 14.12.2016, retrieved from http://www.ecfr.eu/publications/summary/chinas_investment_in_influence_the_future_of_161_cooperation7204.

Ministry of Finance of the Republic of Macedonia, *Economic Reform Program 2018-2020*, retrieved from https://www.finance.gov.mk/files/Macedonia_ERP_2018.pdf.

Nugent, Neill, *The Government and Politics of the European Union* (7th ed.), Basingstoke: Palgrave Macmillan, 2010.

Observatory of Economic Complexity, Massachusetts Institute of Technology, 2016 data, retrieved from https://atlas.media.mit.edu/en/profile/country/mkd/#Destinations.

Pollack, M. A., "Rational Choice and EU Politics," in Jorgensen, Knud, E., Pollack, M. A., Rosamond, B., *Handbook of European Union Politics*, London: Sage Publications, 2006, pp. 31-56.

Riker, W., Shepsle, K., quoted in Pollack, Marc A., "International Relations Theory and European Integration," *Journal of Common Market Studies*, Vol. 39, No. 2, 2001, pp. 221-244.

Unnamed author, "The double-deckers will be produced by the Chinese Yutong," *Vecher Newspaper*, 26.03.2010, retrieved from https://vecer.mk/skopska/dvokatnite-avtobusi-kje-gi-proizveduva-kineski-jutong.

Unnamed author, "The last train in the MNRC fleet arrived—an investment worth 25 million euros", Channel 5 TV, 08.02.2017, retrieved from http://build.mk/pristignaa-sheste-kineski-vozovi-za-makedonski-zheleznitsi/.

World Bank, *Doing Business Report*, 2018, retrieved from http://www.doingbusiness.org/data/exploreeconomies/macedonia-fyr.

No Escape from Balkan?:
The "Balkans" in the Contemporary Croatian Scientific Thought

[克罗地亚] 左立明、
[克罗地亚] 高山·久尔杰维奇

内容提要 在本文中，作者希望呈现和批判性地评价20世纪90年代到2017年克罗地亚科学文献中对"巴尔干"的不同展现。学者们从政治、媒体、历史、教育（课本）、文学、音乐、电影等多方面研究巴尔干与克罗地亚之间的关系，常得出对立的、有时是混淆的结论和观点。由此，本文的作者得出这样的结论：克罗地亚学者的普遍看法主要是基于玛莉亚·托多洛娃所确定的方法，即"巴尔干"——自"克罗地亚以东"起的区域以这两种面貌之一呈现：外来的、野蛮又略带积极意义的，或原始的、粗鲁的、未开化的、消极的、"他者"的形象。不过，作者也通过赫姆·尊德豪森的方法，得出从克罗地亚清除"巴尔干"远没有看上去那么容易或必要的结论。

关 键 词 克罗地亚 巴尔干 刻板印象 东南欧 西巴尔干 中欧 地中海

作者简介 左立明（Zvonimir Stopić），首都师范大学历史学院世界史专业讲师；高山·久尔杰维奇（Goran Đurđević），首都师范大学历史学院考古学专业博士研究生

Abstract: With this paper, the authors wish to present and critically assess the different representations of the Balkans in the Croatian scientific literature from the 1990s to 2017. Following the various, often opposing and sometimes confusing conclusions and viewpoints of the scholars who researched the connection between the Balkans and Croatia from the various perspectives of politics, media, history, education (textbooks), literature, music and movies, the authors of this paper conclude that the general Croatian view is mostly based on the approach identified by Maria Todorova, by which the "Balkans" —the area which starts "east of Croatia" is presented in one of two views: exotic, wild with slightly positive meaning or primitive, rude, uncivilized, negative, image of the "Other". However, the authors also conclude, by using Holm Sundhausen's approach, that eliminating "Balkan" from Croatia is far from as easy or necessary as it seems.

Keywords: Croatia, the Balkans, Stereotype, Southeastern Europe, Western Balkans, Central Europe, Mediterranean

I. What Do the Croatian's Write About When They Write About the Balkans?

Generally speaking, Croatians rarely write and talk about the "Balkans"[①]. When brought up in media, political talk or general public discussions in Croatia, the

---

[①] The phrase "Balkan" is quite complex and consists of a mixture of geographical, political, historical, cultural and anthropological meanings. Literature about Balkans' different meaning is huge and it is still growing. For the basic ideas and different approaches see: Bakić-Hayden (2006), Bjelić (2011), Bjelić and Savić (2003), Čolović (2008), Goldsworthy (1998), Jezernik (2007), Jezernik (2010), Luketić (2008), Luketić (2013), Matešić and Slapšak (2017), Matošević and Škokić (2014), Mishkova (2006), Mishkova (2009), Moranjak-Bamburać (2004), Petrović (2009), Skopetea (1991), Sundhausen (1997), and Todorova (2008). General histories of Balkans are written by many scholars around world. For understanding contemporary history of this area see: Glenny (2000), Jelavich (1983), Mazower (2003), Pavlović (2004), and Stoianovich (1995).

phrase itself usually invokes negative connotations Croatians would rather, and automatically, project to others than link with themselves in any way.① However, when Croatians do write about it, whether it is to negate the Balkan elements or to rationalize them, they usually write about issues the "Balkans" create about the "Croatian identity". The "Balkans", whether it is an unspecified geographical region of Europe, or a phrase which encompass mostly negative connotations, is something which all the Croatian political circles have no desire to identify with, but, due to the complex cultural, historic, social, linguistic, and ethnic connections Croatian lands have with its southeastern neighboring countries, have a difficult time getting away from. Thus, the attempts of the Croatian politicians to shrug this phrase off Croatia, deflect it into the direction of their neighbors, and escape from it into the safety of the phrases such as the "Central Europe", the "Mediterranean" or the "Bridge between Europe and the Balkans", not only that becomes difficult to defend when they are confronted with the various moments from Croatia's past and present realities, but also keep Croatia itself tied to the same Balkan stereotypes political discourse wishes to project into others. The main goal of this article is not to provide yet another overview of what "Balkans" is, what it means, or to explain where Croatia lies in it. This article wishes to present, analyze and confront the colorful and sometimes contradictory viewpoints about the Balkan which emanate from the Croatian politics, art culture, public opinions and researchers, and offer a rough sketch of the answer to the questions of (1) why the Balkan stereotypes continue to live inside of Croatia, despite of its continuous focus on Europe, and (2) why the idea of "Balkans" creates

---

① In public discourse during the past twenty years, the phrase "Balkans" is usually being tied to Serbia and Yugoslavia, and refers to to a negative stereotype. See: Luketić, *Balkan: od geografije do fantazije* (The Balkans: From Geography to Fantasy), Zagreb: K. Algoritam, 2013, pp. 183-186.

issues for the defining the Croatians identity. ①Although this article is written upon the foundations of the wider discussions about the Balkans, namely upon the work of notable authors such as Maria Todorova, Holm Sunhaussen, Milica Bakić-Hayden, Mark Mazower, Stevan Pavlović, Katarina Luketić, Božidar Jezernik, Svetlana Slapšak, Marina Matišić, Larry Wolf and many others, the paper will focus more on the work of Croatian authors written in the past two decades who in many ways attempted to deal with this wider discussion. ②

II. Perceptions of the Problem in the Croatian Eyes

The aversion Croatians have toward the phrase "Balkans", as well as toward all the phrases that can be derived from it, comes more or less from the same stereotypes

---

① Croatian identity is usually described as a combination of Mediterranean, Southeastern and Central European identities, in which there is not any room the "Balkan" one. This "official" interpretation has been implemented in the education system through textbooks and has completely eliminated event the phrase "Balkans". On differences and similarities of the "imagined" Mediterranean, Central and Southeastern Europe and Balkans, See, Luketić, *Balkan: od geografije do fantazije*, pp. 224 – 228. For understanding concepts of the "Central Europe", See, Cipek, "Mitteleuropa: prilog povijesti germanskih ideja Srednje Europe do 1919," (Mitteleuropa: A Contribution to the History of Germanic Ideas of Central Europe until 1919) *Politička Misao*, 35 (1), 1997, pp. 154–166; B. Matan, eds., *Srednja Europa: izbortekstova* (Central Europe: Selected Texts), Gordogan, 1987, pp. 17–18; Matan (1987a), Rider (1997), and see Roksandić, "Postoji li jošuvijek Srednja Europa?" (Does Central Europe still exist?) *Historijski zbornik*, 65 (1), 2012, pp. 187 – 202. Different views of the "Mediterranean" concept are presented by: D. Roksandić, P. Strpić, eds., "Mediteran: izbortekstova," (Mediterranean: Selected Texts) *Naše Teme*, 33 (5), 1989, pp. 979–1095. Concept of "Southeast Europe" is analyzed in by: Kolozova, "Identitet (jedinstva) u izgradnji O smrti 'Balkana' i 'rođenju' Jugoistočne Evrope," (On the Death of the Name of the "Balkans" and the "Birth" of Southeast Europe) in D. Bjelic, O. Savić, eds., *Balkans as Metaphor*, Belgrade, Serbia: Beogradskikrug, 2003, pp. 295–306.

② In this paper, the authors analyze scientific papers published in the Croatian academic journals from 1991 to 2017. We didn't analyze popular or art papers as well as the writings about the Balkans in daily and weekly magazines. Daily and weekly magazines are analyzed by: Razsa, M., Lindstrom, "Balkan is Beautiful: Balkanism in the Political Discourse of Tudman's Croatia," *East European Politics and Societies*, 18 (4), 2004, pp. 628–650. Rihtman-Auguštin, *Ulice moga grada* (The Streets of My City), Belgrade, Serbia: XXvek, 2000, pp. 211–236. And Luketić, *Balkan: od geografije do fantazije* (The Balkans: from geography to fantasy), pp. 220–224.

Maria Todorova pointed out in her book *Imagining the Balkans*.①For most Croatians, especially in the political and diplomatic circles, the phrase "Balkans" has almost exclusively negative connotations, and refers not only to the not-to-well defined geographic place,② but also to a certain mentality which has the traits of being uncivilized, wild, rude, violent, and, what's most important, "non-European".③ Generally speaking, it does seem that at the first glance the Croatians, often without realizing it, fully accept the Todorova's thesis that the Balkans are a construct of the West, and, due to their overzealous attempts to avoid being referred to as "Balkanian", that the Balkans are also an imagination of the Balkanians themselves. Croatians' sensitiveness to any discourse that puts them into the same context with the phrase "Balkan", which can be observed most clearly in the political discourse, as well as their aversion to any of the instances which tend to "re-create" the differences

---

① The explanations of the negative connotation of the phrase "Balkans", as well as the logic behind the Balkan area being the European "Other" is well described by Todorova in her book *Imagining the Balkans* (2008). Similar approach also developed by Božidar Jezernikin in his book *Wild Europe: The Balkans in the Gaze of Western Travelers*. The book *Gender and Balkan* by Marina Matešić and Svetlana Slapšak is refers to gender issues and women travelers, but also concentrates on the representations of Balkans in feministic and postcolonial approach. While approaching to the topic of Balkans, it is also quite informative to see the work of Holm Sundhaussen, who takes a different approach to the issue and contests Todorova's "imaginations" of Balkan with a possibility that there actually exists quite enough of real and specific characteristics of the area which fuels and shapes our perception of it the way it does.

② An informative analysis of the problems of defining the borders of Balkan peninsula, given from the geographical perspective, is provided by Mirela Slukan Altić (2009). This question of border is quite important for Croatians (and Slovenes), because depending on the approach, both countries have a geographic chance of being placed outside of the detested peninsula. As Slukan Altić explains, from the geographical point of view, it is quite difficult to justify the old definitions of the Balkan "peninsula", which places this part of the Europe below the Trieste-Odessa line, and between the Adriatic, Ionian, Aegean and Black Seas. The problem lies in the fact that the land border of 1,635 km is the longest one, opposing the 1,285 and 1,350 km long sea borders, which contradicts to the geographical definition of "peninsula" by which the land borders is supposed to be the shortest ones. As the solution to this issue, Slukan Altić proposes the complete abandonment of the "Balkan peninsula" designation, and recommends the acceptance of the Croatian geographer Josip Roglić's idea of introducing the Greece-Albanian peninsula, since only that part of the today's Balkan area fulfills the geographical definition of the "peninsula". See: Slukan Altić (2015), pp. 402–405.

③ The genealogy of such meaning is provided by: Todorova, *Imagining the Balkans*, New York: Oxford University Press, 2008, pp. 33–37.

between the European East and West in which they belong to the "East",① fits them into Todorova's theory almost perfectly. In fact, several papers in the last decade written by the Croatian authors about the perceptions the West has on Croatia and Balkan indicate that Croatians do notice and are still bothered by the "old Western stereotypes about the Balkan". Focusing on the representations of Croatia, Ivona Grgurinović in 2008 still found the need to point out the problem of the Rebecca West's travel book about Yugoslavia "Black Lamb, Grey Falcon", which was originally published in 1941. Although she had no reservations when using a few stereotypes about the "imperial other" herself, if we may notice, Grgurinović did conclude that West's book is a typical example of how a traveler coming from an "imperial tradition whose superiority is symbolically and literally established through centuries of history" creates and sets stereotypes and constructions of the "other".② Another, more contemporary example, is provided by Zlatan Krajina (2009) with his article about the BBC's news. After detailed analysis of the news reports, Krajina concluded that the reporters which made the news about Croatia continued to fall into the traps of stereotypisation, so that as a result the Croatia was at the time in the BBC News still being presented as the Europe's "Other".③ In analyzing the Italian news reports on the War in Croatia, Ivana Škevin and Iva Grgić (2016) noted that the Italian perceptions were filled with "several types of polarized representations, for example, the one between the good (Italy/Europe/West) and the bad (Croatia/the Balkans-associated with "primitive" nationalism and chaos)."④ In the Italian case, the Trieste was recognized as a demarcation point between west and east, good and

---

① Dividing Europe on the West and East is an 18th century idea which gradually replaced the traditional division of the Europe (and the world) on its northern and southern part. The creation of the "Eastern Europe" is tightly connected with the Enlightenment movement. On "Eastern Europe" and the meaning this phrase has in the Western World see: Wolf, *Inventing Eastern Europe: The Map of Civilization on the Mind of the Enlightenment*, Stanford: Stanford University Press, 1994.

② See: Grgurinović, "Constructing the Other in Rebecca West's 'Black Lamb, Grey Falcon'," *Etnološka istraživanja* (Ethnological Researches), 12/13, 2008, pp. 159-169.

③ See: Krajina, " 'Mapping' the 'Other' in Television News on International Affairs: BBC's 'Pre-Accession' Coverage of EU Membership Candidate Croatia," *Politička Misao*, 46 (5), 2009, pp. 140-170.

④ See: Ivana Škevin, Iva Grgić Maroević, "The Balkans as European Otherness: On Shaping Italian Public Opinion about the War in Croatia," *Sic: Časopis za književnost, kulturu i književno prevođenje*, 6 (2), 2016, p. 9.

bad, peace and war, civilization and chaos.[1] Yet another example of Croatian "noticing" the stereotypisation coming from the West, comes from Zrinka Borovečki and Martina Poljak (2013), who pointed out to the reestablishment of the Balkan stereotypes in connection to Croatia in the two recent Austrian novels, namely the *Das Handewerk des Tötens* and *Die gefrorene Zeit*, written by Norbert Gstrein and Anne Kim, respectively.

As we can see, Croatians do notice the stereotypes "others" have toward them. Although all these papers are focused on Croatia, the basic idea they all carry is that the discourse about the Balkan is not something Europe should continue to develop, because it does bring out the feeling of uneasiness into all those Europe designates as it's "Other". However, as we will soon show, the issue does not lie only in the Europe's understanding of what Balkan and/or Croatia are. Further in the text we will show how this awareness of the stereotypes gets misused, sustained, over-emphasized, and how in reality, on many different levels, the stereotypes of Balkan pulse out from Croatia in much greater force than they would ever be forced upon Croatia form the outside.

III. Politics, Media, Textbooks and Mentality: More We Look, Blurriest the Line Becomes Between Croatia and Balkan

If we were to pick through the political discourse in the post-1991 Croatia which includes the phrase "Balkan", it is possible to roughly discern two phases, one before and one after the parliamentary and presidential elections in 2000.[2] As Nataša

---

[1] See: Ivana Škevin, Iva Grgić Maroević, "The Balkans as European Otherness: On Shaping Italian Public Opinion about the War in Croatia," *Sic: Časopis za književnost, kulturu i književno prevođenje*, 6 (2), 2016, p. 17.

[2] The Croatian parliamentary and presidential elections, held in January and February 2000, respectively, at least for a while, managed to change the political face of Croatia. In the parliament, the decade long rule of the conservative center-right Croatian Democratic Union (Hrvatska Demokratska Zajednica, HDZ) was overturned by the coalition of parties led by the center-left Social Democratic Party of Croatia (Socijaldemokratska Partija Hrvatske, SDP), while in the presidential elections victory was won by an independent candidate Stjepan Mesić. See: Zambelli (2011), p. 60.

Zambelli (2010) presented, the newly elected political leadership after the mentioned elections began shaping the discourse concerning Balkan and Croatia in a brand new way. Although during the nineties Croatia never did label itself as a Balkan country, and although it was never truly necessary to explain to the Croatians themselves that Croatia does not belong to the Balkans, but only in Europe, the post-2000 political discourse was still taken to a completely new level, hoping that the Croatia's road to the European Union could be made easier if Croatia provides an additional proof to the European countries that Croatia is was always one of them. So what were the changes and how was this done? Zambelli noticed that the new political leadership at that time gave their best to present the new, post-2000 Croatia as a country that not only has nothing to do with the Balkans mentality (or geography), but also as a country that wishes to distance itself from all of the negative moments which occurred in its recent history, moments which were nothing but forced upon it. The two most important elements of such discourse stand up: (1) the process of so called "de-Tuđmanization", during which the SDP's leaders began presenting the first Croatian president Franjo Tuđman, who was also the paramount leader of their opposing political option HDZ, as a typical representative of the Balkan mentality, which shouldn't be a part of European Croatia;[①] and (2) the process of "pushing Balkan to the East", clearly demarking Croatia's border with Serbia as the actual line after which true Balkan begins.[②] Croatian leading politicians, as Zambelli emphasized, were at the time trying to reconstruct Croatia's image as the undeniably true European country, and a country which has the will to take the burden of connecting the Europe with the (uncivilized) East.[③] As far as stereotypes go, the new developments in the political discourse were not steered into the direction of negation, but quite the contrary, into direction of making them more tangible. By placing Croatia on the European side of the imaginary border Croatian politicians tried recently tried to adjust, the political discourse which they carried out as a direct result actually accepted and highlighted the European-Balkan divisions, strengthening the visibility of the line between the civilized Europe and the

---

① See: Zambelli (2011), p. 56.
② Ibid., p. 60.
③ See the statements of Ivica Račan, Tonino Picula and Stjepan Mesić made in early 2000, in: Zambelli (2011), pp. 62-63, 66, 71.

uncivilized, violent Balkan which exists east of Croatia. In this discourse, the foundations of Croatian identity, of course, were firmly anchored exclusively in Europe.①

This same shift in the political discourse was also noticed by Filip Jurić (2013), who analyzed the Croatian high school history textbooks and tried to find in what volume and in what manner did its authors used the phrase "Balkans". Jurić's analysis revealed two important findings. First, it is quite clear that the usage of the phrase Balkan never overlaps with the the phrase "Croatia" in any way. There are virtually no occurrences in which Croatia is situated on the Balkan, or in which Croatia is referred to as "Balkanian". Croatian lands, no matter which historical period is reviewed, are always set next to the Balkan, but they themselves never belong to it. When necessary, Croatia is always presented as it belongs to the Southeast Europe.②The other interesting find is that after the year 2000, the meaning contained in the phrase "Balkan" either completely evaporated from the history textbooks, or was thoroughly being substituted with the phrases such as the "Southeast Europe".③ Although the authors of the high school history textbooks did not go as far as politicians in deliberately and directly projecting the image of Balkan to Croatia's neighbors, and by avoiding the phrase generally did in a way made the attempt to neutralize the stereotipisation of the Balkan, they also, as Jurić notices, focused mostly on the "European" in the Croatian identity, generally disregarding all else.④

---

① See: Zambelli (2011), pp. 65, 71, 74.

② See: Jurić, "Balkan u hrvatskim udžbenicima povijesti za osnovnu školu," (The Balkans in Croatian History Textbooks for Elementary School) *Povijest u nastavi*, 21 (1), 2013, pp. 39-40.

③ Ibid., pp. 36-37.

④ History as school course is in Croatia taught in two levels. The first level belongs to primary school where history taught from 5th to 8th grade two hours per week (70 hours per year in every grade), while the second level belongs to the secondary (high) school where, depending on whether the school a grammar school (also called gymnasiums) or a vocational school, the history is thought 70 hours per year from the 1st to the 4th grade or 70 hours only one year, respectively. The curricula for the history course is designed so that students chronologically learn about the world (mostly European) and Croatian history from the Paleolithic to the contemporary times. History textbooks are written by various teachers and university professors and published by different publishing houses, but the whole process is controlled from the state. The topics, titles as well as the major chronology of events are suggested by the National Curricula, the Ministry of Education and Science provides anonymous peer reviewers and must give its approval to each of the textbooks that wishes to enter the market. On average between two and four history textbooks are approved for each grade. History teachers are allowed to freely choose textbook they wish to use, but teachers from a single school should agree to use the same history textbook.

Despite of the differences in the development of the political discourse before and after the year 2000, there is a clear consensus that Balkan is something that clearly belongs to the east of Croatia. However, as Sandi Blagonić (2016) and Jure Perišić (2016) warns us about, the solution for Croatian "Balkans" problem, because of how Croatia functions on the inside, is reality quite difficult to find in such a simplistic way. Blagonić analyzed the construction of identity of the Croatia's Istria peninsula and reached the conclusion that in the case of Istrian identity, the Balkan discourse was being used in many ways as similarly as it has been used in the attempts to construct the Croatian identity. As it seems, in the mind of Istria's politicians at least, Serbia belongs to the Balkans from the perspective of the Croatians in the same way the rest of the Croatia belongs to the Balkan from the perspective of Istria.① Even if the shiny political discourse is omitted, as Blagonić points out, for Istrian people the Balkan begins right after the mountain range Učka, which separates the peninsula form the rest of the Croatia. In the minds of many Istrians, Istria is a "land of good people", which lies in opposition to the "Other" Croatians who live right across the Učka mountain.② Adding more confusion to the discussion, Jure Perišić points out to the unavoidable emergence of certain contradictions when it comes to confronting the most representative and most noticeable of all Croatian mentalities, the one which has a tendency to establish itself as the "proper" Croatian mentality, with the attempts to set up Croatia as a strictly "non-Balkan" country. Purposely constructing it in the opposition to the "communist mentality" by several political forces in many ways, the prominent "Dinarian mentality", named after the mountain of Dinara which lies on the border of Croatia and Bosnia and Herzegovina, render itself in a form of brave and hospitable warrior who values the patriarchal social structure, draws strength from friendship, brotherly unity and strong leaders; a man who is also cunning, resourceful, deceitful, has a knack for trade and lacks altruism sentiment, revolution

---

① See: Blagonić, "Istrijanski regere fines: Tradicijska kultura i Balkan u diskurzivnoj konstrukciji identitcta (Istrianregere fines: Traditional Culture and the Balkans in Discursive Identity Construction) *Problemi sjevernog Jadrana*, 15, (2016), pp. 124-125.

② Ibid., pp. 123, 128.

spirit, willingness for a change and has an aversion toward the state-building initiatives. ① A man belonging to the "Dinarian mentality" also values mythology, is fascinated by the heroic songs, especially those of "hajduks", ② and owns emphasized ethical values, such as the condemnation of any insult made to the human physical or moral person, family or homeland. ③Perišić argues that all these "Dinarian mentality" traits are actually the same ones which belong to the "Balkan mentality" stereotypes, which steadily kindle equally in the West and in Croatia. Paradoxically, as it seems, Croatia on one hand wishes to remove itself from the Balkan area and from all the negative connotations glued to it, but on the other, it gives a bit too much freedom to the development of one particular mentality which creates an idea of what a "Croatian man" should look like, never realizing how much it corresponds with the general idea of a "Balkan men". To make things worse, the Catholic Church, which exercises a huge influence over the social developments in Croatia, as Perišić points out, continues to play an important "godfather" role in singling out and breeding this particular Croatian mentality, which in praxis only further supplements the general notion of slow development of democracy and constitution based rule of law in Croatians society, and creates a distance between Croatia and the ideas of European values. ④

These examples show that Croatians themselves, for various of reasons, tend to keep the Balkan stereotypes alive. Whether these stereotypes are just a tool of one

---

① See: Perišić, "Balkansko u dinarskom mentalitetu: teološko viđenje dinarskog utjecaja u konstituiranju suvrjemen hrvatske države," (The Balkan Element in the Dinaric Mentality: A Theological View of the Dinaric Influence on the Creation of the Modern Croatian State) *Obnovljeni život*, 71 (1), 2016, pp. 107–108.

② Today, a word "Hajduk" invokes an idea of a, as Mirosłav Dymarski (2016) explains, "heroic guerrilla defying unjust laws and fighting against the Ottoman (and Habsburg) authorities for the people's political and religious freedom." Dymarski also brings out the observation of a Serbian linguist Vuk Karadžić, who pointed out at the hajduk's various criminal activity. Interestingly, "Hajduk" is also a name of one of the most successful Croatian football clubs. See: Dymarski (2016), p. 85. Also see: http://hajduk.hr/eng/.

③ See: Perišić, "Balkansko u dinarskom mentalitetu: teološko viđenje dinarskog utjecaja u konstituiranju suvrjemen hrvatske države," (The Balkan Element in the Dinaric Mentality: A Theological View of the Dinaric Influence on the Creation of the Modern Croatian State) *Obnovljeni život*, 71 (1), 2016, pp. 107–108.

④ See: Perišić, "Balkansko u dinarskom mentalitetu: teološko viđenje dinarskog utjecaja u konstituiranju suvrjemen hrvatske države," (The Balkan Element in the Dinaric Mentality: A Theological View of the Dinaric Influence on the Creation of the Modern Croatian State) *Obnovljeni život*, 71 (1), 2016, pp. 114–117.

political option against the other, the political projection of Balkan stigma to Croatia's immediate political "Other" —Serbia, the tools of politics inside of Croatia, or the strange manifestations of the certain Croatian mentality, they continue to be a part of Croatia's reality. As we will see in continuation of this paper, politicians cannot all be blamed for keeping these Balkan stereotypes alive. The idea of Balkan, negative as well as the positive, continues to emerge from many other aspects of the Croatian society.

Ⅳ. Balkan Wolf in European Skin: Movies, Literature, and Music

Despite of all the attempts to misuse, manipulate and project the Balkan phraseology to their Eastern "other", and despite of all of the contradictions mentioned so far, the Croatian politicians generally do all agree that "Balkans" is not something either of them wishes to associate with, and that Europe is the only proper setting for modern Croatia today. However, as we already have hinted above, if we change the perspective and begin searching for "Balkans" in Croatia's insides, one can be quite surprised, overwhelmed even, just by how many "Balkan" elements it is possible to find. Research the Croatian scholars made about Croatian film, literature, art, music and the general feeling of identity, all steer us in that realization.

Andrea Matošević (2011), who compared the three movies, *Prije Kiše* [Before Rain] (1994), *Podzemlje* [Underground] (1995), and *Kino Lika* [The Lika Cinema] (2007), which came from three different Balkan authors, the Macedonian Milča Mančevski, Serbian Emir Kusturica and Croatian director Dalibor Matanić, respectively, indicated to the existence of many similarities between them regarding the representation of Balkan. In these three movies, Matošević managed to detect many, in her words, "constitutional elements of the discourse on the untamed, wild, pre-modern Balkan, the Id of Europe",① and showed us quite directly that the examples of the "auto-exotisation" of the Balkan does not only belong to the areas "east" of Croatia, but to Croatia itself. We may add that Matanić's movie, which Matošević used for his analysis, was obviously not chosen as a unique occurrence, but more because it can stand as a representative example of how (many) Croatian movies look like in general. Truly, the Croatian directors quite often use exactly those kinds of settings and iconography for the telling of their stories which can be characterized as "balkanian" with ease. The backward, distant, unusual, wild, traditional and in many other ways Balkan-stereotyped nature of the social structures and characters they portray, as well as the over-emphasized sharp distinction between the "Croatia-Balkan" and the "European" area/mentality/society elements, is something which is difficult not to notice. To name only a few, Ognjen Sviličić's *Oprostiza Kung Fu* [Sorry for Kung Fu] (2004), Branko Schimdt's *Put Lubenica* [The Melon Route], Vinko Brešan's *Svećenikovadjeca* [The Pries's Children] (2013), as well as one of the latest Matanić's movies *Zvizdan* [The High Sun] (2015), all are movies in which we find abundance of those elements. The question is why? Is it because all those directors fell into a Todorova's imagination trap and deliberately chose such settings because Europe wants it, or it is because they simply want to artistically and critically inspect the certain elements which are weaved into the fabric of the Croatian society? The answer lies probably somewhere in the middle between the two extremes.

Similar phenomenon, as far as the research results allow us, can also be observed in literature. As Miranda Levanat-Peričić (2016) points out, when it comes to "metastasing of the Balkan stereotypes" the two Croatian names shine out, standing right next to the Slovenian authors Aleš Debeljak and Goran Vojnović. ②Critically acclaimed authors, especially outside of Croatia's literary scene, Dubravka Ugrešić

---

① See: Matošević, "(Auto) egzotizacija Balkana i etnografija nositelja značenja u tri primjera sedme umjetnosti," [(Auto) Exotisation of the Balkans and the Ethnography of the Bearer of Meaning in Three Examples of "The Seventh Art"] *Narodna umjetnost*, 48 (2), 2011, p. 33.

② See: Levanat-Peričić, "Kako se gnijezdio Balkan na 'jugoslavenskoj Atlantidi' (Četiri pogleda na reprodukciju orijenatlizma u postjugoslavenskoj književnosti)," [How the Balkans nested on the "Yugoslav Atlantis" (Four views on the reproduction of orientalism in post-Yugoslav literature)] *Sic*: *Časopis za književnost, kulturu i književnoprevo denje*, 6 (2), 2016, p. 3.

and Slavenka Drakulić often invoke Balkan's negative connotations in their writing: violence, primitivism, backwardness and hate. Slavenka Drakulić, as Levant-Perišić notices, uses the phrase Balkan so that she could designate the universal or particular evil. [1] Similarly, Dubravka Ugrešić uses the phrase "Balkan" to explain the political violence tied to the territories of ex-Yugoslavia, and draws a distinctive line between the "Balkanized" Croatia and Europe, which should take on the task of upbringing of the people that live in that backward place. [2] Even though the examples of Dubravka Ugrešić and Slavenka Drakulić, due to their stigma of "exile narration", [3] cannot be used to represent the entire Croatian literature, they are still are far too influential to be disregarded. Besides, other prominent Croatian writers, such as Ante Tomić, Miljenko Jergović, Boris Dežulović, Kristijan Novak, Igor Mandić, Ivan Aralica and others, all in various ways play with the "Balkan" elements in their work. [4]

Besides movies and literature, music is yet another interesting indicative media in which the "Balkan" factor can be found living quite comfortably. [5] In it's short, but informative internet article, Barbara Matijević (2016) listed four popular musicians/groups, namely, Elena Georghe, Rambo Amadeus, Neda Ukraden, Dubioza Kolektiv, and Maja Šuput, coming from Romania, Montenegro, Serbia, Bosnia and Herzegovina and Croatia, respectively, all of who use the Balkan stereotypes in their songs. Although violence is not mentioned in these songs, the typical Balkan person is still wild, hedonistic, belongs to a patriarchal social system, loves to drink Balkan drinks and eat Balkan food, and, for Rambo Amadeus at least, has questionable

---

[1] See: Levanat-Peričić, "Kako se gnijezdio Balkan na 'jugoslavenskoj Atlantidi' (Četiri pogleda na reprodukciju orijenatlizma u postjugoslavenskoj književnosti)," [How the Balkans nested on the "Yugoslav Atlantis" (Four views on the reproduction of orientalism in post-Yugoslav literature)] Sic: Časopis za književnost, kulturu i književnoprevođenje, 6 (2), 2016, p. 6.

[2] Ibid., pp. 6, 17-18.

[3] During the early 1990s, both Dubravka Ugrešić and Slavenka Drakulić left Croatia because of political reasons and pressures.

[4] For more on the "Balkans" in the Croatian literature in the first part of 20th century see: Rihtman Auguštin (2000), pp. 222-234. On the "Balkans" in the Croatian contemporary literature see: Luketić (2013), pp. 198-199, 224, 225, 239.

[5] On Croatian popular music and "Balkans", see: Luketić, Balkan: od geografije do fantazije (The Balkans: from geography to fantasy), pp. 399-428.

hygiene habits.① As we can see, the Croatian popular music scene is not exempt from this phenomena. Quite the contrary, it is the content of the Croatian singer's songs which actually implies on the existence of the commonly understood connection Balkan people share, no matter from which Balkan country they are coming from.② Another author, Marin Cvitanović (2009) analyzed the connection between music and Balkan elements more thoroughly, and reached several interesting conclusions. First of all, as he noticed, the "Balkan" motif is commonly used in popular songs, and when compared with other phrases of similar type, the frequency of its usage is surpassed only by more precise terminology which includes names of the states and nations.③ Altogether he found 110 songs made in the two decades prior to time the article was published and sang in Serbian and Croatian language which in one way or another use the phrase "Balkan" or some of its derivatives. Out of this number, 45 of them used the phrase only as a geographical designation, while 75 of them contain "coded messages, metaphors, or directly try to evoke and explain either the atmosphere of war, misery, conflict, division, passion, or the one of beauty, love and pride."④ Out of those 75 songs, most belong to the Bosnia and Herzegovina and Serbia, while only 9 came from Croatia. Still, Croatian songs blend perfectly with the other ones in their usage of the Balkan motifs. In those songs, as Cvitanović points out, "Balkan" phraseology was used usually in four different ways, mostly to denote (1) area of war and conflict, (2) area of hedonism, passion and fatalism, (3) dichotomy between the primitive and aggressive male and beautiful, proud and persistent female

---

① Songs Matijević mentions are: *Balkan Girls* (Elena Gheorghe, 2009), *Balkan Boy* (Rambo Amadeus, 1989), *Na Balkanu* [On the Balkan] (Neda Ukraden, 2012), and *Hej, Balkano* [Hey, Balkan] (Maja Šuput, 2015). See: Matijević, B. (2016), *Balkanizam* [Balcanism], Retrieved from (1 May 2018): http://cultstud.ffri.hr/kultura-u-akciji/osvrti/564-balkanizam-barbara-matijevic, 7 April 2016. Matijević also mentions Dubioza Kolektiv's *Balkan Funk* (2010). However, it is worth mentioning that Dubioza Kolektiv's opus which deals with the "Balkan elements" or the dichotomy between Balkan/Bosnia and the West is not limited just to this one song. Among others, as examples of their work, also see and listen *U.S.A.* (2013), *Kažu* [They say] (2013), *Volio BiH* [I would like] (2013), and especially *No Escape* (*from Balkan*) (2014). Many of their songs are sang in English, which makes their messages understandable to wider audience.

② See: Ibid.

③ See: Cvitanović, "(Re) konstrukcija balkanskih identiteta kroz popularnu glazbu," [(Re) construction of the Balkan Identities through Popular Music] *Migracijske i etničketeme*, 25 (4), 2009, p. 320.

④ Ibid., p. 321.

factor, and (4) area which belongs to the European "other". ①

At the end of the analysis of Balkan-themed songs, Cvitanović notices that the "negative stereotypes about Balkan in the songs are actually never questioned, but taken for granted and often reaffirmed as a part of one's identity, and then criticized, accepted, turned into auto-parody, or used as a undeniable and unavoidable fact which is present in various aspects of life."② As we have seen above, this last part of Cvitanović's observations can easily be extended to the spheres of film, literature and personal identity. As it seems, the idea of "Balkan" does actually live within the people of Croatia in the similar way it does in "other" Balkan countries. We cannot really say that, apart from the attempts from the state and certain politicians, who also use the phraseology to achieve their particular agendas, a widespread social or cultural revolt against the Balkan elements exists in Croatian society.③ In fact, out of the numerous articles we consulted during the writing of this paper, we could only find one which covered instances of direct revolt against the invoking of the Balkan stereotypes. So besides the works of Serbian film director Dušan Makavejev, Croatian and Serbian/Canadian illustrators and cartoonists Irena Jukić Pranjić and Nina

---

① See: Cvitanović, "(Re) konstrukcija balkanskih identiteta kroz popularnu glazbu," [(Re) construction of the Balkan Identities through Popular Music], p. 317.

② Ibid. , p. 332.

③ Politicians continue to hold their ground. Just recently, for example, Croatian President Kolinda Grabar Kitarović spoke about the "Balkans" in negative manner several times. In June 2018, during the panel in Bruxelles, organized in honor of the Croatia's five-year EU membership, she argued against the phrases "Balkans" and "Western Balkans" and suggest the use of the phrase "Southeast Europe" when needed for Croatia. Quite interesting is the phrasing she used, for example: "I don't want Balkan in my home, but it is not true that I don't want it for neighbors." What is also quite interesting is that, on several occasions when she mentioned talked about the Croatian connections with the Central Europe and the identities in the Central Europe (during the UN General Assembly in New York in July 2016, at the Diplomatic academy in Zagreb in June 2017, during the Initiative of Three Seas summit in Warszaw in July 2017, at the Corvinus University in Budapest in September 2017), President Grabar Kitarović always avoided making any connections with the "Balkans" and focused on (re) establishing Croatian links with Central Europe (more) or Southeastern Europe (less). See: http://hr. n1info. com/a309707/Vijesti/Termin-Balkan-ne-zelim-u-svojoj-kuci. html, https://www. vecernji. hr/vijesti/hrvatska-predsjednica-na-korvinovu-sveucilistu-o-vaznosti-srednje-europe-1194044, https://direktno. hr/direkt/trump-ova-regija-mi-je-vazna-grabar-kitarovic-mi-smo-srednja-europa-91086/, https://www. tportal. hr/vijesti/clanak/predsjednica-nezadovoljna-imidzem-hrvatske-u-svijetu-20170605, https://dnevnik. hr/vijesti/hrvatska/kolinda-grabar-kitarovic-zavrsava-posjet-poljskoj---424769. html, https://www. jutarnji. hr/vijesti/hrvatska/sve-tajne-kolindine-uspravnice-kako-sefica-drzave-stvara-novu-regiju/4491053/, 1 September 2018.

Bunjevac, respectively, and Serbian painter and writer Mileta Prodanović, who, as Tomislav Oroz (2016) noticed, "disassemble or ironically perpetuate the imposed visions of Balkan, leading them to the absurdity,"① and probably a few others no one bothered to notice and scientifically process, the rest, no matter being aware or not of the theoretical implications, generally accept the Balkan stereotypisation. In the end, as it seems, still way too many writers, directors, musicians, and others do just that purposely, mostly because they see it, or some parts of it at least, as true.

V. What Do Croatians Think About Where Their County Lies?

As we have seen so far, Balkan stereotypes and discourse are quite present in movies, literature and music, similarly in Croatia as much as in other "Balkan" countries. However, the most vivid indication that part of Croatian identity might in fact lurk somewhere on the inside of the Balkan idea, or at least a glimpse of understanding of why the Balkan stereotypes continue to vibrate in Croatia, all appear when we began conducting research on how the new, young, and presumably modern generations see themselves and understand what Balkan means and is. This kind of research was done by Laura Šakaja (2001), who investigated the extent of Balkan stereotypes of young people from Zagreb, Ksenija Klasnić and Izvor Rukavina (2011), who tried to see what Croatians themselves think influences the Croatian image abroad, and Alistair Ross, Saša Puzić and Karin Doolan (2017), who made the attempt to inspect the identities of young people in Croatia in terms of "place identifications".

After interviewing 395 high school students from Zagreb in 2001, Šakaja concluded that in the minds of the young students the phrase "Balkan" was at the time usually oversimplified and generalized, encompassing the negative meaning, such as

---

① See: Oroz, " 'Mislim da sam vidio Micu Macu': animalna naličja Balkana i popularna kultura," ["I Tawt I Taw a Puddy Tat": Reverse Faces the Balkans and Popular Culture] *Narodna umjetnost*, 53 (2), 2016, p. 30.

aggression, barbarism and destruction. ①As the students explained, the Balkan peninsula, excluding Greece, was their least desirable place to live, a sentiment which probably did not change much since then, and a place which begins just east of Croatia. ②Out of all of the Balkan countries, many of which they did not know much about, except again for Greece, the country which they understood to be the most closely related to the most negative connotations of the phrase "Balkan" at the time was, as expected, Serbia—a country "which always creates wars, but loses all the time."③ For the students, the phrase "Balkan" was a synonym for all of those who do not belong to the West, and a phrase which is the opposite form the phrases such as "culture" and "civilization". The students themselves, when confronted with the Balkan-Serbia-violence idea, always answered that they belong to the West, of course. ④Ten years after Šakaja's paper was published, Klasnić and Rukavina took upon themselves to investigate not the perceptions others have of Croatia, but the Croatians' own understanding of what influences the perceptions of others over them. As it turned out, at the time Croatia was getting close to enter the European Union, Croatians still felt that the two basic images influenced the outside perception of Croatia the most: the image of tourism and the image Balkan. ⑤Finally, just recently, Ross, Puzić and Doolan made a new research which showed that the young Croatians today not only do not have such a strong aversion toward Balkan idea, but also that "the Balkan" is actually is recognized and acknowledged as an important part of their identity. As the authors conclude, "the young people showed a sense of aspiring to be European, of feeling almost European, of being not-quite-yet European, of being

---

① See: Šakaja, "Stereotipi mladih agrepčana o Balkanu: Prilog proučavanju imaginativne geografije," (Stereotypes Among Zagreb Youth Regarding the Balkans: A Contribution to the Study of Imaginative Geography) *Revijaza Sociologiju*, 32 (1-2), 2001, pp. 27, 31.
② Ibid., p. 28.
③ Ibid., pp. 31-32.
④ Ibid., p. 32.
⑤ As the authors explain, the Croatians felt that the Balkan image was influenced by the indictments from The Hague International Criminal Tribunal, corruption, organized crime, the violent behavior of sport club and national teams supporters, and the communist heritage. See: Klasnić, Rukavina (2011), pp. 138, 145.

"Balkan".① In the minds of the interviewed young people, Croatia was understood as being on a "threshold, though still leaning towards the Balkan side: underdeveloped, with littered streets and quarrelsome people."② "Europe was, as an entity on its own, seen primarily as political—it was over there, offering financial mutual support, travel opportunities and education."③

Each one of these three analysis show that the stereotypes about the "Balkans" are continuously excepted by the generations of young people in Croatia. What these three studies also show, as is also indicated by the studies of Croatian movies, literature and music, is that as the time moved forward from 2001, the Balkan stereotypes not only did not evaporate, but also managed to infiltrate into, or re-emerge from, the Croatian identity. There is one important difference, however, in the meaning of the phrase Balkan has today and had twenty years ago, which can be noticed and should be further investigated. The research done by Šakaja, Klasnić and Rukavina, and Ross, Puzić and Doolan, does indicate that although not completely gone, violence, as the prime association with the Balkan phrase has been substituted with the underdevelopment and backwardness.

Ⅵ. Balkan as an Area of Freedom? The Past and the Present...

So far we have shown that the Balkan stereotypes continue to exit in Croatia today, and that they are even latently accepted by the Croatians as part of their own identity, despite the fact that, generally speaking, country officially do wish to "escape" form Balkan and hide itself in Europe. The question which yet remains unanswered is why? Perhaps history can aid us in understanding this phenomenon. The politicians, when the "Balkans issue" appear, as we have shown, usually hold

---

① See: Alistair Ross, Saša Puzić, Karin Doolan, "Balkan and European? Place Identifications of Young People in Croatia," *Revijaza Sociologiju*, 47 (2), 2017, p. 125.
② Ibid., p. 143.
③ Ibid., p. 144.

their ground, often reaching for the irrefutable (and superficial) historical facts which are to prove that Croatian lands were always a part of the civilization circle belonging to the western Europe. After all, all of the Croatian history textbooks teach us that when Croatians arrived to their lands centuries ago they did not settle on the Balkan, but on the former Roman provinces and the Adriatic coast.①For most of the history which followed, Croatian lands were always a part of European kingdoms and empires, and were never effectively ruled by the Ottoman empire, as the other Balkan countries, excluding the Slovenia, were. Also, not only that Croatia (and Slovenia) do not share the Oriental heritage from which a large part of the "Balkan" characteristics emerge from, Croatia itself has always proudly been the only Balkan country which belonged to the heritage of the Western Christianity—Catholicism. Further more, as Igor Despot (2012) notices, the "Western Croatia" did not perceive the Balkan wars as it's own affair,② and was submerged in the Balkan affairs only after the political "mistakes" were made during the aftermath of the First World War. However, what is usually not mentioned by politicians and all the others who jump into this complex discussions without a wish to see or understand the bigger picture is: (1) the entire Balkan area, and not only Adriatic coast were a part of the Roman Empire at least at one point in history and Croatia is not an exception; (2) at the moment Croatians "arrived" to their final settling place, Roman provinces did not exist for more than three centuries; (3) it is true that the Croatian lands were never a part of the Ottoman Empire, but it is also true that for many centuries, the European empires did not exercise an effective rule over the large part of today's Croatia, thus allowing ethnic, religious and cultural mixture; (4) the lack of interest in the Balkan Wars by one part of Croatia was mirrored, as Despot also notes, by the substantial interest of some other parts.

As far as the "political miscalculations", made in the final years of the First World War which took Croatia away from Europe and tied it with the first Yugoslavia, are concerned, two important things are often conveniently forgotten. Firstly, these

---

① See: Jurić, "Balkan u hrvatskim udžbenicima povijesti za osnovnu školu," (The Balkans in Croatian history textbooks for elementary school), p. 39.

② See: Despot, "Sjeverozapadna hrvatska u vrijeme Balkanskih ratova," (Northwest Croatia during the time of the Balkan Wars) *Podravina*, 11 (22), 2012, p. 80.

"miscalculations" were far from being momentary lapse of judgment, since they've been for the large part influenced by the ideas envisioned of many prominent and influential Croatians in the 19th and the beginning of the 20th century.① And secondly, those decisions, despite of being painful to look at by some, especially when still recent memory of the violent end of Yugoslavia are taken under consideration, not only that managed to encompass all of the Croatia's territory under one jurisdiction for the first time, but also, since Croatia was actually on the losing side of the First World War, also managed to save the Croatian lands from being permanently dismembered by more powerful European forces.②

Looking from such perspective, we could say that at the beginning of the 20th century, Croatian politicians saw the Balkans not as the place Croatia needs to escape from, but as an area of freedom and security in which Croatia could achieve its full independence. Not from the Ottomans, but from all of those European empires and kingdoms, which are so much valued today. Indication that the political decisions made in history were not the only demonstration of Croatia's aversion to Europe can be shown with the case of the central figure of Croatian 20th century literature—Miroslav Krleža. Vastly influential "Croatia's greatest writer" and encyclopedist, Krleža spent his entire life creating, discovering and mapping the unique Croatian cultural identity,

---

① As Neven Budak pointed out, in the Croatian territories prior to the 19th century it is possible to distinguish more ten different identities, depending on their ethnical or territorial affiliation: Slavonians, Dalmatians, Slavicness, Illyrians, Slavics, Unionist, and Austroslavics, to name only some. An attempt to unify this diversity was made in during the 19th century when the Illyrian movement (named after the southeastern part of Habsburg Empire; other name used much today is Croatian National Revival) and its leader Ljudevit Gaj pushed for the idea of a linguistic, cultural and ethnic unity. This idea under the Illyrian name was not successful, however, but it did give a significant push to the creation of idea of separate South Slavic nations such as ones of Slovenia or Croatia. In the second half of the 19th and the beginning of the 20th century, the continuation of this movement eventually led to the creation of a modern Croatian nation. However, it is important to note that aside from the idea of the unity under the Illyrian name and later Croatian name, in the 19th century Croatian lands there were other ideas of national unity, at certain moments equally strong and influential, out of which the most prominent were "Panslavism" and "Yugoslavism". See: Budak, "Hrvatski identitet između prošlosti i moderniteta," (Croatian identity between past and modernity) in Budak, N., Katunarić, V. (eds.), *Hrvatski nacionalni identitet u globalizirajućem svijetu* (Croatian national identity in globalized world), Zagreb, Croatia: Center for democracy Miko Tripalo, 2010, pp. 3-12. Luketić, *Balkan: od geografije do fantazije* (The Balkans: from geography to fantasy), p. 293. Roksandić, "Yugoslavism before Creation of Yugoslavia," Biserko, S. (eds.), *Yugoslavia in Historical Perspective*, Belgrade, Serbia: Serbian Helsinki Committee, 2017, pp. 29-61.

② See: Jakovina, *Trenutci Kararze* (Moments of Catharsis), Zagreb, Croatia: Fraktura, 2013, p. 28.

basing it equally on the distinctions toward the West, as well as from the East. ①

The feeling of reservations toward Europe do exist even today, and was observed by Branko Caratan (2008) during the time Croatia was struggling to enter to the European Union. As Caratan noticed, the Croatian "euroscepticism" was not based on the same reasoning Switzerland or Norway shared over entering the European Union, or the United Kingdom's, Sweden's or Denmark's reservations toward their inclusion to the Eurozone. Croatians were not bothered by the political issues brought by the federalization ideas of the EU, fears of non-transparent non-national structure of the European Union or by the loss of jobs due to the influx of the cheaper workforce. Croatian reasons for saying no to Europe were exhausted mostly in the the fears of losing sovereignty and selected parts of the "traditional" Croatian identity. Listening to the whispers of the ghosts of the past, the largest Croatian fear was still the one that Croatia will once again be politically or economically "ruled" or dominated by the greater powers, or even manipulated (again) into the new Yugoslavia-type political or economical entity. ②Because of such attitudes, it is not so surprising to understand why many Croatians on some level do feel a connection with the idea of "Balkans", as well as with the stereotypes this idea invokes. In a way, despite all of its misgivings, when necessary, Balkan does from time to time emerge as an imaginary geographical and political area of freedom, a place in which Croatia "can be itself", and area in which there might be even an opportunity for Croatia to play a role of a (regional) leader, something it could never become in Europe.

VII. Conclusions: Balkan, European, Mediterranean, Southeast European or a Bridge Between the East and West?

Seems like the task of where and how to place Croatia on the geographical,

---

① See: Roksandić (2012), pp. 187-188. On Krleža's positioning concerning the project of Encyclopedia of Yugoslavia see: Roksandić (2015).

② See: Caratan, "Hrvatska u regionalnom kontekstu," (Croatia in Regional Context) *Anali Hrvatskog politološkog društva*, 4 (1), 2008, p. 63.

political, cultural and even historical map of Europe is not an easy one. However, in reality, the task would not be that difficult if the Croatians themselves wouldn't have such a problem in confronting and coming to terms with their own past and present realities. All we have presented in this paper indicates that the unique manifestation of the "Balkan" element in Croatia's identity is the one that continuously stirs up the Balkan stereotypes, and not the other way around. If we look closely, it is obvious that it is quite difficult to explain the persistent existence of the Balkan stereotypes in Croatia only through the imaginings of the West. After all we have stated above, we could conclude that Croatians do actually believe in the existence of the Balkan, in the similar manner Sundhaussen (1997) would imply, and that many believe that the stereotypes they invoke aren't just stereotypes, but actual characteristics of the area.① Whether this is just a case of "nesting Orientalism", as Milica Bakić-Hayden would describe, or not, its is hard to say. ② But the one thing is clear: Croatians do not negate the existence of the Balkan or it's stereotypes, but only their own direct connection to it.

One of the popular solutions of how to overcome the problem of Croatia's connections with Balkan is to proclaim that although it did belong to the European cultural circles for most of its history, because of their circumstantial proximity to the Balkan, Croatia always played a specific and important historic role of the "bridge or borderland" between West and the East, between Europe and Europe's "Other".③ Such explanations are quite convenient because they at the same time do allow Croatia to be in contact with the "eastern" element, but also, by placing Croatia safely on the "better" European side, allow it to maintain the Balkan stereotypes in general. These types of explanations, however, fail to provide an answer to the question of why much to often the Croatians themselves feel that their country belongs to the Balkans,

---

① Holm Sundhaussen questioned Todorova's approach, confronting her directly with the several unique characteristics which do make the Balkan area as the recognizable subject of history. See: Sundhaussen, "Europa balcanica: Der Balkan als historischer raum europas," (Europa Balcanica: The Balkans as a historical space of Europe) *Geschichte und Gesellschaft*, 25 (4), 1997, pp. 638-651. Also see: Luketić, *Balkan: od geografije do fantazije* (The Balkans: from geography to fantasy), p. 115.

② See: Bakić-Hayden (1995), pp. 917-931 and Bakić-Hayden (2006), p. 54.

③ For an overview of such interpretation see: Mirjana Kasapović's (2007) paper "Area Studies and Eastern Europe: How Eastern Europe Collapsed".

despite of their apparent European heritage and current European Union membership. Deeper analysis, as usual, gives complex results. Looking from a wider historical context, Drago Roksandić (2012) will say that although since 16th century Croatia is a country which belong to the "Central Europe", the "important questions of it's (Croatia's) preservation in 19th and 20th century belonged always to the Mediterranean/Adriatic (area), while the process of Croatian national integration in the same period is impossible to absolve outside of the Balkan context."[1] By superimposing the ideas of Balkan, Mediterranean and Danube concepts, evaluation the definitions of "family types, and looking at the origins of Croatian literature, Dunja Rihtman-Auguštin (1999), Jasna Čapo-Žmegač (1996), Maja Bošković-Stulli (2000), respectively, further questioned the attempts to define the traits of Croatian identity in a narrow one-dimensional way, without including the wider regional context. These authors give the impression that not only Croatia was not strictly tied to Europe, but that the whole Croatia-border between Europe and its own imagined theory of the East is not viable when a wider context is considered. Croatia is not a border of anything, but, as Jasna Čapo-Žmegač eloquently stated, "multicultural *area*, crossroad of different cultural and historical influences and ecologic zones".[2] When we confront these and many other indications of Croatia's multiculturality and its undeniable connections to the Balkans with the simplified political discourse one cannot neglect, in which, as we have seen, the idea of Balkans is often purposely demonized and misused, sharp contradictions and confusion are immediately born. So while on one side, the attempts to provide a bigger picture of Croatia's placement in past and current realities do show that it is understandable that Croatians on many levels, as we have seen, do feel connected with their Balkan neighbors, the blind misuse of the Balkan stereotypes in political and public discourse, in the attempts to place Croatia on the East-West colored map of Europe, on the other, not only create the severe case of the "split personality" of Croatian identity, in which the Balkan is

---

[1] See: Roksandić, "Postoji li jošuvijek Srednja Europa?" (Does Central Europe still exist?) *Historijski zbornik*, 65 (1), 2012, p. 191.

[2] See: Čapo-Žmegač, "Konstrukcija modela obitelji u Europi i povijest obitelji u Hrvatskoj," (The Construction of Family Models in Europe and Family History in Croatia) *Narodna umjetnost: hrvatski časopis za etnologiju i folkloristiku*, 33 (2), 1996, p. 191.

often treated as an "abject", as Julia Kristeva, would put it, but also continues to keep the Balkan stereotypes alive and well.① Further more, as Ross, Puzić and Doolan's research have indicated, the short-sightedness of the negative projections and misuse of the Balkan phrase backfired in a way, and are now, probably due to the recent and continuous political, economic and social failures, being reflected back to Croatia by it's own population. Vastly disappointed by the current economic, social and political situation, the Croatians today find it hard not to place Croatia anywhere else except on the Balkans, despite of the fact that their country has been a member of the European Union for the past five years. After all, in the minds of many Croatians, if it is not communism, it is war. If it is not war, then it is economic and social depression. If it is not depression, then it is corruption. If not corruption, then it is institutional inefficiency. If not institutional inefficiency, then it is clientelistic and self-serving politics. If not politics, then it is the ideological distortion of reality. If not for nationalism, communism or other ideologies, then it is the overtaxed state, the non-function healthcare system, the unadjusted education system, the Catholic Church's meddling into public and political life, or the hordes of young people fleeing the country in the search for a better life. In the end, if not all which is mentioned, then it is the mentality and the general feeling of resignation and fatalism, which eliminates prospect of any kind of progress. Many would say, it is simply "Balkan".

So, when and how can Croatia actually "leave" the Balkan and free itself from the Balkan stereotypes? First, once the country stops projecting the image of the Balkan away from itself to the it's neighbors, and use the negative stereotypes to

---

① Julia Kristeva introduced a phrase "abject" as something between the subject and object in a patriarchal culture which denies/rejects/disturbs and represents taboo elements in a social order. Social elements which fall under abject are often loathed by the dominant currents of the society, despite the fact that they are an undeniable part of it. If we were to use this approach to the case of Croatian issue of the Balkans, we could conclude that some of the politicians, journalists and scholars do treat (loathe) the Balkans as it were an abject of Croatia. Some authors began exploring the discussion in this direction. See for example Dunja Rihtman Auguštin's paper "Why and when are we terrified of the Balkans?" on the Croatian discourse of the Balkans in the 1990s and Ivan Čolović's paper "Why are we proud of the Balkans?" on the Serbian discourse of the Balkans. Also see Bjelić's critical assessment of the Julia Kristeva's approach. See: Kristeva, *Powers of Horror. An Essay of Abjection*, New York: Columbia University Press, 1982, pp. 1–2. Rihtman-Auguštin, *Ulice moga grada* (The Streets of My City), pp. 211–236. Čolović (2010), pp. 113–118, and Bjelić (2011).

devalue its neighbors. ①Secondly, once the the whole area of Balkan enters the European Union, and, what is more important, actually begins to act like it wants to be part of European processes of democratization. ②Thirdly, once the conditions are made for the creation of a system in which the healthy economic prosperity will neutralize the continuous economic and social depression, and a widespread feelings disparity, resignation and self-pity. ③Finally, Croatia will escape the Balkan once it begins politically and publicly confront its historic, current and future positions in the wider regional, European and world contexts, and realizes that there is actually no need to do so in the first place.

References:

Bakić-Hayden, M. (1995), "Nesting Orientalisms: The Case of Former Yugoslavia," *Slavic Review*, 54, 917-931.

Bakić-Hayden, M. (2006), *Varijacije na temu "Balkan"* (Variations on the Theme "Balkans"), Belgrade, Serbia: Filip Višnjić.

Bjelić, D. (2011), *Normalizing the Balkans: Geopolitics of Psychoanalysis and Psychiatry*, Farnham, Burlington, VT: Ashgate Publishing Limited.

Bjelić, D., Savić, O. (eds.) (2003), *Balkan kao metafora: između globalizacije i fragmentacije* (Balkan as Metaphor: Between Globalisation and Fragmentation), Belgrade, Serbia: Beogradskikrug.

Blagonić, S. (2016), "Istrijanski regere fines: Tradicijska kultura i Balkan u diskurzivnoj konstrukciji identiteta," (Istrian Regere Fines: Traditional Culture and the Balkans in Discursive Identity Construction) *Problemi sjevernog Jadrana* 15, 113-132.

Borovečki, Z., Poljak, M. (2013), "Zamrznuti Balkan—Narativne trauma i litraumatiziranje narativa u suvremenom književnom diskurzu?" (Frozen Balkan—Narrating trauma or Traumatizing of the Narration in the Contemporary Literary Discourse?) *Jat: Časopis studenata kroatistike*, 1, 134-159.

Bošković-Stulli, M. (2000), "Regional necrte usmene hrvatske književnosti," (Regional Features of the Croatian Oral Literature), *Narodna umjetnost*, 37 (2), 151-162.

Budak, N. (2010), "Hrvatski identitet između prošlosti i moderniteta," (Croatian identity between past and modernity) in Budak, N., Katunarić, V. (eds.), *Hrvatski nacionalni identitet u globalizirajućem svijetu* (Croatian national identity in globalized world), Zagreb, Croatia: Center for democracy Miko Tripalo, 3-12.

---

① Similar ideas to approach Balkans are presented in: Luketić (2013), Balkan: od geografije do fantazije (The Balkans: from geography to fantasy).

② Close to Skopetea (1991). Different political discourses from European Union to (Western) Balkans are analyzed in: Petrović (2009).

③ Similar in: M. Mazower, *Balkan: kratkapovijest* (The Balkans: A Short History), Zagreb, Croata: Srednja Europa, 2003.

Caratan, B. (2008), "Hrvatska u regionalnom kontekstu," (Croatia in Regional Context) *Anali Hrvatskog politološkog društva*, 4 (1), 61-72.

Cipek, T. (1997), "Mitteleuropa: prilog povijesti germanskih ideja Srednje Europe do 1919," (Mitteleuropa: A Contribution to the History of Germanic Ideas of Central Europe until 1919) *Politička Misao*, 35 (1), 154-166.

Cvitanović, M. (2009), "(Re) konstrukcija balkanskih identiteta kroz popularnu glazbu," [(Re) construction of the Balkan Identities through Popular Music] *Migracijske i etničke teme*, 25 (4), 317-335.

Čapo-Žmegač, J. (1996), "Konstrukcija modela obitelji u Europi i povijest obitelji u Hrvatskoj," (The Construction of Family Models in Europe and Family History in Croatia) *Narodna umjetnost: hrvatski časopis za etnologiju i folkloristiku*, 33 (2), 179-196.

Čolović, I. (2008), *Balkan: terorkulture* (The Balkans: Terror of Culture), Belgrade, Serbia: XXvek.

Despot, I. (2012), "Sjeverozapadna hrvatska u vrijeme Balkanskih ratova," (Northwest Croatia during the time of the Balkan Wars) *Podravina*, 11 (22), 72-81.

Dymarski, M. (2016), "The Ottoman Tradition as the Model of the Culture of Power in the Balkans in the 19th-20th c.," *Historijski zbornik*, 59 (1), 71-90.

Glenny, M. (2000), *The Balkans 1804-1999: Nationalism, War and the Great Powers*, London: Granta books.

Goldsworthy, V. (1998), *Inventing Ruritania: The Imperialism of the Imagination*, New Haven: Yale University Press.

Grgurinović, I. (2008), "Constructing the Other in Rebecca West's 'Black Lamb, Grey Falcon'," *Etnološka istraživanja* (Ethnological Researches) 12/13, 159-169.

Jakovina, T. (2013), *Trenutci Kararze* (Moments of Catharsis), Zagreb, Croatia: Fraktura.

Jelavich, B. (1983), *History of the Balkans* (two volumes), Cambridge: Cambridge University Press.

Jezernik, B. (2007), *Divlja Evropa* (Wild Europe: The Balkans in the Gaze of the Western Travellers), Belgrade, Serbia: XXvek.

Jezernik, B. (eds.) (2010), *Imaginarni Turčin* (Imagining The Turk), Belgrade, Serbia: XXvek.

Jurić, F. (2013), "Balkan u hrvatskim udžbenicima povijesti za osnovnu školu," (The Balkans in Croatian history textbooks for elementary school) *Povijest u nastavi*, 21 (1), 23-44.

Kasapović, M. (2007), "Regionalna komparatistika i Istočna Europa: Kako se raspala Istočna Europa," (Area Studies and Eastern Europe: How Eastern Europe Collapsed) *Anali Hrvatskog politološkog društva*, 4 (1), 73-96.

Klasnić, K., Rukavina, I. (2011), "Što utječe na Sliku hrvatske u inozemstvu?" (What Affects the Image of Croatia Abroad) *Socijalna ekologija*, 20 (2), 131-145.

Kolozova, K. (2003), "Identitet (jedinstva) u izgradnji. O smrti 'Balkana' i 'rođenju' Jugoistočne Evrope," (On the Death of the Name of the "Balkans" and the "Birth" of Southeast Europe) in Bjelic, D., Savić, O. (eds.), *Balkans as Metaphor*, Belgrade, Serbia: Beogradskikrug, 295-306.

Krajina, Z. (2009), "'Mapping' the 'Other' in Television News on International Affairs: BBC's 'Pre-Accession' Coverage of EU Membership Candidate Croatia," *Politička Misao*, 46 (5), 140-170.

Kristeva, J. (1982), *Powers of Horror: An Essay of Abjection*, New York: Columbia University Press.

Levanat-Peričić, M. (2016), "Kako se gnijezdio Balkan na 'jugoslavenskoj Atlantidi' (Četiri pogleda na reprodukciju orijenatlizma u postjugoslavenskoj književnosti)," [How the Balkans nested on the "Yugoslav Atlantis" (Four views on the reproduction of orientalism in post-Yugoslav literature)] *Sic: Časopis za književnost, kulturu i književno prevođenje*, 6 (2).

Luketić, K. (ed.) (2008), "Balkan: imaginariji, mitovi, stvarnost," (The Balkans: imagining, myths, reality), *Zarez*, 224.

Luketić, K. (2013), *Balkan: od geografije do fantazije* (The Balkans: from geography to fantasy). Zagreb, Croatia: Algoritam.

Matan, B. (eds.) (1987), "Srednja Europa: izbor tekstova," (Central Europe: selected texts). *Gordogan*, 17-18, 23-24.

Matešić, M., Slapšak, S. (2017), *Rod i Balkan* (Gender and Balkans), Durieux, Zagreb: Croatia.

Matijević, B. (2016), Balkanizam (Balcanism), http://cultstud.ffri.hr/kultura-u-akciji/osvrti/564-balkanizam-barbara-matijevic, 7 April 2016.

Matošević, A. (2011), "(Auto) egzotizacija Balkana i etnografija nositelja značenja u tri primjera sedme umjetnosti," [(Auto) Exotisation of the Balkans and the Ethnography of the Bearer of Meaning in Three Examples of "The Seventh Art"] *Narodna umjetnost*, 48 (2), 31-49.

Matošević, A., Škokić, T. (2014), *Polutani dugog trajanja: Balkanistički diskursi* (Bastards of long duration: Balkanist discourses), Zagreb, Croatia: Institut za etnologiju i folkloristiku.

Mazower, M. (2003), *Balkan: kratka povijest* (The Balkans: A Short History), Zagreb, Croata: Srednja Europa.

Mishkova, D. (2006), "In Quest of Balkan Occidentalism," *Tokovi istorije*, 1-2, 29-62.

Mishkova, D. (2008), "Symbolic Geographies and Visions of Identity: A Balkan Perspective," *European Journal of Social Theory*, 11 (2), 237-256.

Moranjak-Bamburać, N. (2004), "Političke i epistemologijske implikacije postkolonijalne teorije," (Political and epistemological implications of postcolonial theory) *Sarajevske sveske*, 6-7, 87-101.

Oroz, T. (2016), "'Mislim da sam vidio Micu Macu': animalna na ličja Balkana i popularna kultura," ("I Tawt I Taw a Puddy Tat": Reverse Faces of the Balkans and Popular Culture) *Narodna umjetnost*, 53 (2), 9-34.

Pavlović, S. (2004), *Istorija Balkana 1804-1945* (A History of the Balkans: 1804-1945), Belgrade, Serbia: Clio.

Perišić, J. (2016), "Balkansko u dinarskom ementalitetu: teološko viđenje dinarskog utjecaja u konstituiranju suvrjemen hrvatske države," (The Balkan Element in the Dinaric Mentality: A Theological View of the Dinaric Influence on the Creation of the Modern Croatian State) *Obnovljeni život*, 71 (1), 103-118.

Petrović, T. (2009), *A Long Way Home: Representation of the Western Balkans in Political and Media Discourses*, Ljubljana: Mirovni inštitut.

Razsa, M., Lindstrom, N. (2004), "Balkan is Beautiful: Balkanism in the Political Discourse of Tudman's

Croatia," *East European Politics and Societies*, 18 (4), 628-650.

Le Rider, J. (1997), *Mitteleuropa* (The Central Europe), Zagreb, Croatia: Barbat.

Rihtman-Auguštin, D. (2000), *Ulice moga grada* (The Streets of My City), Belgrade, Serbia: XXvek.

Rihtman-Auguštin, D. (1999), "A Croatian Controversy: Mediterranean-Danube-Balkans," *Narodna umjetnost*, 36 (1), 103-119.

Roksandić, D., Strpić, P. (eds.) (1989), *Mediteran: izbor tekstova* (Mediterranean: selected texts), *Naše Teme*, 33 (5), 979-1095.

Roksandić, D. (2012), "Postoji li još uvijek Srednja Europa?" (Does Central Europe still exist?) *Historijski zbornik*, 65 (1), 187-202.

Roksandić, D. (2015), "Krležina Enciklopedija Jugoslavije između euroskepticizma i euronormativizma: prilog poznavanju početaka Krležina projekta Enciklopedije Jugoslavije," (Krleža's Encyclopedia of Yugoslvia Between Euroscepticism and Euronormativism: Contribution to the Understanding of the Origins of Krleža's Encyclopaedia of Yugoslavia Project] *Studia Lexicographica*, 8 (2), 5-22.

Roksandić, D. (2017), "Yugoslavism before Creation of Yugoslavia," Biserko, S. (eds.), *Yugoslavia in Historical Perspective*, Belgrade, Serbia: Serbian Helsinki Committee, 29-61.

Ross, A., Puzić, S., Doolan, K. (2017), "Balkan and European? Place Identifications of Young People in Croatia," *Revijaza Sociologiju*, 47 (2), 125-150.

Skopetea, E. (1991), "Orijentalizam i Balkan," (Orientalism and Balkans) *Istorijski časopis*, 38, 131-143.

Slukan Altić, M. (2015), "Hrvatska kao zapadni Balkan—Geografska stvarnost ili nametnuti identitet?" (Croatia as a Part of the Western Balkans—Geographical Reality or Enforced Identity?) *Društvena Istraživanja*, 20 (2), 401-413.

Stoianovich, T. (1995), *Between East and West: The Balkan and the Mediterranean Worlds: Material Culture and Mentalities: Land, Sea and Destiny*, New Rochelle: A. D. Caratzas.

Sundhaussen, H. (1997), "Europa balcanica: Der Balkan als historischer raum europas," (Europa Balcanica: The Balkans as a historical space of Europe) *Geschichte und Gesellschaft*, 25 (4), 626-653.

Šakaja, L. (2001), "Stereotipi mladih Zagrepčana o Balkanu: Prilog proučavanju imaginativne geografije," (Stereotypes Among Zagreb Youth Regarding the Balkans: A Contribution to the Study of Imaginative Geography) *Revijaza Sociologiju*, 32 (1-2), 27-37.

Škevin, I., Grgić Maroević, I. (2016), "The Balkans as European Otherness: On Shaping Italian Public Opinion about the War in Croatia," *Sic: Časopis za književnost, kulturu i književno prevođenje*, 6 (2).

Todorova, M. (2008), *Imagining the Balkans*, New York: Oxford University Press.

Wolff, L. (1994), *Inventing Eastern Europe: The Map of civilization on the Mind of the Enlightenment*, Stanford: Stanford University Press.

Zambelli, N. (2010), "Između Balkana i Zapada: problem hrvatskog identiteta nakon Tuđmana i diskurzivna rekonstrukcija regije," (Between the Balkans and the West: A problem of Croatian Identity in the Post-Tuđman Period and a Discursive Reconstruction of the Region) *Politička Misao*, 47 (1), 55-76.

历史研究

Bosnia and Herzegovina in the First World War, 1914–1918

[波黑] 兹雅德·塞西奇

内容提要 根据相关文献和档案资料,作者认为波黑历史上的一个重要时期在南斯拉夫史学中被边缘化,并被意识形态的要求所界定。文章着重于第一次世界大战的战时情况及其对波黑政治、经济和人口变化的影响,并特别注意到背景的情况、前线部队的状况以及影响奥匈帝国军队解体的其他因素。文章通过对现有文献的批判性评价和对新档案来源的研究,以获得来源多样化的资料,希望在经过核实的事实基础上得出令人信服的结论。作者试图消除与第一次世界大战期间波黑人在哈布斯堡王朝军事组织中所起作用有关的史学上的刻板印象,这些刻板印象是出于政治需要而产生的,或者出于同样的原因而被忽视或边缘化。

关 键 词 欧洲危机 萨拉热窝事件 波黑 战线 统计数据

作者简介 兹雅德·塞西奇(Zijad Šehić),波黑萨拉热窝大学哲学院教授

Abstract: Based on relevant literature and archival sources, the author considers an important period of Bosnian and Herzegovinian history that was marginalized in Yugoslav historiography and defined by ideological requirements. The paper focuses on wartime circumstances and their influence on political, economic and demographic changes in Bosnia and Herzegovina. Special attention is dedicated to the conditions in the background, the state of the army at the front as well as other elements which impacted the break-up of the Austro-Hungarian army. It was possible to reach convincing conclusions founded on verified facts through critical evaluation of the existing literature and research of new archival sources, with the aim of obtaining documentation of diverse provenance. The author has attempted to remove historiographic stereotypes related to roles of Bosnians and Herzegovinians in the military organizations of the Habsburg Monarchy during the First World War which were created out of political needs or were for the same reason ignored or marginalized.

Keywords: European Crisis, Assassination of Sarajevo, Bosnia and Herzegovina, Fronts, Statistics

The international disagreements caused deep crises in the relations between the blocs of great powers, leading to the direct military conflict in 1914. The assassination in Sarajevo on 28 June 1914 seemed to the competent military and political circles in Vienna and Berlin as a cause for a confrontation with Serbia, so a request in the form of an ultimatum was sent to her. When a part of the request had been rejected, the pathway towards the First World War was opened.

The crisis that broke out in the autumn of 1908 when Austria-Hungary annexed Bosnia and Herzegovina represents a turning point in international political life. Its course and results actively influenced the European political scene until the breakout of the First World War, primarily taking into account the differences between Vienna and Belgrade, the multi-layered South-Slav complex and the difficulties which it caused for the Habsburg Monarchy. The outcome of the annexation crisis hastened the intention of the Balkan states to resolve the issue of the Ottoman Empire.

After long lasting diplomatic negotiations, a secret final agreement was reached and approved by Russia and France in the spring of 1912. Soon after that, Italy expressed her readiness to support the Balkan states. A foremost agreement was reached on 13 March 1912 between Serbia and Bulgaria according to which it was necessary to go on the offensive against the Ottoman army in the south and be on the defensive against Austria-Hungary in the north. The interested parties also agreed on the territorial division of Macedonia. The disputable zone was confirmed and the Russian Tsar Nikolai II was named the arbitrator. Serbia, Bulgaria, Greece and the Ottoman Empire declared general mobilization on 30 September 1912. Montenegro declared war against the Ottoman Empire on 8 October and started with the attack on Scutari. The vicinity of the battlefield and the strength of forces engaged in military operations caused unease among the relevant circles of the Monarchy. ① The events of the Balkan Wars had great impact on political relations in Bosnia and Herzegovina, deepening the gap between Serb and Muslim policy that was based on agrarian relations. Muslims followed war developments with the fear of the agrarian question being resolved in the same way it was done in Serbia and Montenegro—expecting the same fate in the case of defeat and withdrawal of the Monarchy from Bosnia and Herzegovina only highlighted the connections of the Muslims with the Monarchy which they considered as their only protector. ② Serbia's political and military victories in the Balkan Wars intensified national enthusiasm while at the same time attracting support of the Orthodox Christians from the Habsburg Monarchy. Measures undertaken by the Monarchy forced the Montenegrin King Nikola to concede out of fear of her action and he soon ordered partial mobilization in Montenegro. The instruction of the Provincial Government for Bosnia and Herzegovina called of the emergency measures from 15 May. ③

The evaluation conducted by political authorities of the Monarchy revealed the strengthening of Serbo-Croatian nationalism in Croatia which had a tendency to transform into irredentism, especially among the young population. Even though certain support for the Yugoslav programme existed, the official aim of Serbian policy was the expansion and extension of the Serbian state. ④ A part of Serbia's aspirations were realized with the Balkan Wars—Serbia gained the desired part of the Ottoman

---

① Wilchelm Deutschmann, *Die militärischen Massnahmen in Oesterreich-Ungarn während der Balkankriege 1912/13*, Disertation, Universität Wien, 1965, p. 20.

② Weinwurm, 1964, p. 357.

③ Dževad Juzbašić, Zijad Šehić (ur.), *Lične zabilješke generala Oskara Potioreka o unutrašnjopolitičkoj situaciji u Bosni i Hercegovini*, Akademija nauka i umjetnosti Bosne i Hercegovine, Građa, Knjiga XXX, Centar za balkanološka ispitivanja, Knjiga 1, Sarajevo, 2015, pp. 33-34. Deutschmann Wilchelm, 1965, pp. 213-214.

④ Charles Jelavich, *Južnoslavenski nacionalizmi: Jugoslavensko ujedinjenje i udžbenici prije 1914*, Zagreb, 1992, p. 47.

Empire, but the intentions concerning the Monarchy could not have been achieved. Because of that, Serbs referred to Croats, Slovenes and Serbs in the Monarchy as *unfree brothers* and the success in the Balkan Wars was considered as the realization of one part of the plan, whereas it was believed that Bosnia and Herzegovina, as a Serbian land, belonged to Serbia. ①

At the beginning of 1914, the military industry in Serbia gained momentum which was a sign for an upcoming continuation of the Balkan Wars. The capital of the Austrian Bank helped a lot, the Vienna based *Bodencreditanstalt* participated with 20% in Serbian loans for arms. French weapon factories could not make the deadline of arms delivery to Serbia, so that in spring 1914 Austrian and German weapons factories took their place: 200,000 of the most modern rifles were sent to Belgrade during the spring. ② During April of 1914 the Provincial governor of Bosnia and Herzegovina, General Oskar Potiorek met up with a Serb who was in close relation with the military circles in Belgrade. He delivered the message that Serbia planned to create Yugoslavia which would encompass the whole Balkan Peninsula—Bosnia, Herzegovina, Croatia, Slavonia, a part of Hungary, Carniola, Carinthia and Styria. The division would be done in the way that three exclusively Serb districts would be formed, one Croatian and one Slovene. The districts would be divided in accordance with confessions and the transfer of population would be done in the way that 400,000 Catholics from Bosnia and Herzegovina should be relocated to Croatia, whereas Serbs from Lika and Slavonia (around 20%) should be moved to Bosnia and Herzegovina. This offer was followed with a message that it was better to reach an agreement before the Serbs appear with guns near Zagreb, and this was soon to happen, since all the preparations for this had been undertaken. The Balkan League aimed to perform this task. Russia would help by mobilizing the Serbs and forcing Austria-Hungary to send 500,000 soldiers on the borders which should enable the Allies to fight successfully. This actually happened in 1914 and Serbia fulfilled the vow given to Russia. ③ In this plan Potiorek saw the realization of the idea of Greater Serbia which in return

---

① Šehić, 2015, p. 103.

② Wilhelm J. Wagner, *Der Grosse Bildatlas zur Geschichte Österreich*, Wien: Verlag Kremayr & Scherian, 1995, p. 176.

③ Šehić, 2015, p. 24.

influenced the shaping of his plan about the division of Bosnia and Herzegovina between Austria and Hungary, which he exposed in December of 1914. ①

After the manoeuvres of 26 and 27 June near Tarčin in which the troops from the Sarajevan 15th and the Ragusan 16th corps took part, the Archduke Franz Ferdinand arrived for the official visit in Sarajevo on the Orthodox feast of St. Vitus Day. He was expected not only by the officials, but also by the assassinators, and the Archduke's personal security had not been well organized. The bomb, thrown by Nedeljko Čabrinović did not hit the target, but the first bullet fired by Gavrilo Princip was deadly and shot Archduke Franz Ferdinand. The other one, intended for the Provincial Governor General Potiorek, killed the Archduke's wife Sophia, the Duchess of Hohenberg. ② In the trial, held at a later date, the accused Gavrilo Princip, who had left the gymnasium in Tuzla four years previously and relocated to a gymnasium in Belgrade, stated that he "did not repent for what he did, that he was not a criminal because he only wanted to remove the evil". In the company he kept Princip became known as a veritable Serb nationalist. He hated Austria because he believed that it "only caused evil to the South Slavs". He considered Archduke Franz Ferdinand "the greatest danger for the idea of union of Serbs and generally of South Slavs under the Serb leadership". In his opinion, "Serbia had the mission to tear off Bosnia and Herzegovina from Austria". This thought encouraged him to commit the assassination. ③ Immediately after the killing of Franz Ferdinand, Bosnia and Herzegovina faced real wartime circumstances. The assassination caused uproar among the Muslim and Catholic population. Already in the evening hours of 28 June 1914, first demonstrations were held in Sarajevo and the officers took part in them. On the following day, a real small war began. Out of bitterness, Muslims and Catholics started destroying Serbian shops and houses. Police, gendarmerie and even military

---

① About the plan on division of Bosnia and Herzegovina in December 1914, see more in: Šehić Zijad, *Lajos Thallóczy über die Ereignisse in Bosnien-Herzegowina nach dem Atentat von Sarajevo am 28. Juni 1914*, u: *Lajos Thallóczy der Historiker und Politiker*, Akademie der Wissenschaften und Künste von Bosnien-Herzegowina, Ungarische Akademie der Wissenschaften, Institut für Geschichte, Sarajevo, Staats Archiv Wien, 2010, pp. 168-169.

② Petar Tomac, *Ratovi i armije XIX veka*, Beograd, 1968, p. 11.

③ From the discussion about the high treason, Sarajevskilist, No. 247, 14 October 1914, p. 2.

forces were not capable to stop the demonstrations. Demonstrators concentrated on Serbophile citizens and institutions, and the first ones to be attacked and devastated by the raiders were the newspapers "Prosvjeta", "Narod" and "Srpskariječ", Serbian schools, the hotel "Europe" and many objects that belonged to "Narod" and the group gathered around "Otadžbina". Because of robbery, 58 persons were imprisoned. ① Peace in the town was restored again only after the introduction of the court-martial. Regardless of political orientation, Serbs were bitter, requesting complete compensation for the damage, according to the example of Zagreb. General Potiorek ordered that the persons whose property was damaged be reimbursed from the support funds. ② After the unrest and prosecution of Serb population, the Grand Mufti Hajji Mehmed Džemaludin Čaušević sent an epistle to Muslims in which he called for *order and peace and the preservation of goods of their fellow citizens.* ③

The Provincial Government for Bosnia and Herzegovina announced the establishment of court-martial for the territory of Sarajevo municipality and Sarajevo district on 29 June 1914, suggesting death sentences for 12 kinds of crime. ④ After Sarajevo, demonstrations also spread to other places: Doboj, Vareš, Zenica, Županjac, Žepče, Bugojno, Visoko, Maglaj, Mostar, Travnik, Tuzla, Stolac, Konjic, Čapljina, Ljubuški, Livno, Šamac, Brčko. ⑤ As a result of devastation of Serb property, courts-martial were established in Tuzla and Maglaj counties. ⑥The common Minster of Finances, Leon Bilinski, believed that ideas about shutting down

---

① Božo Madžar, *Izvještaj vladinog komesara za glavni grad Bosne i Hercegovine Sarajevo o političkoj i privrednoj situaciji u Sarajevu od sarajevskog atentata do kraja januara 1915. godine*, Glasnik arhiva i Društva arhivskih radnika BiH, 26, Sarajevo 1986, p. 208.

② Ibid., p. 209. The damage caused during demonstrations amounted to about 500,000 crones; 150 persons were injured who were compensated with 37,787 crones.

③ Sarajevski list, No. 137, 4 July 1914, p. 3.

④ Sarajevski list, No. 131, 29 June 1914, p. 1. The punishment was anticipated for the Crime of high treason, Crime against military power, Crime against disturbance of public order, Crime against uprisings, Crime against revolts, Crime of public violence for certain cases, Crime of assassination, Crime of murder, Crime of severe body injury, Crime of arson, Crime of robbery, Crime of providing help for some of the mentioned examples.

⑤ Slijepčević, 1929, p. 222.

⑥ ABH, ZMF, Präs. BH 1914, 781. *Verhängung des Standesrechtesüber die Beßirke Tuzla u. Maglaj*, The Provincial Government of Bosnia and Herzegovina to the Common Ministry of Finances, Sarajevo, 2 July 1914.

the Bosnian and Herzegovinian Parliament should be suppressed since such a measure was contradictory for a favourable situation. He was convinced that once the Parliament began working again it would not only save the existing condition but would also act pleasingly on the general situation. In a telegram sent to Potiorek, Bilinski exposed the agenda of administration in Bosnia and Herzegovina after the assassination and the disorder. Interpreting the attitude of Monarch Franz Joseph who received him for the audience on 29 June, listened to his reports and completely expressed his satisfaction with the measures undertaken by Potiorek, Bilinski insisted on further work of the Bosnian Parliament and arrangement of the condition. He stated that the Emperor had expressed his opinion that for the crimes of individuals and dropouts of enraged groups of population the whole country should not be punished. The majority of population was loyal to the Emperor and for them the breach of political and economic interests would mean a lot. The former political course was still in force according to which it was necessary to work together on the constitutional system with the majority of people in the country. Emergency measures in Bosnia and Herzegovina were introduced foremost with the Legal Decree of the Provincial Government from 26 July 1914, suspending certain provisions of the Provincial statute, which represented the legal foundation for the introduction of emergency measures based on the Law on Emergency Measures from 5 March 1910. These were proclaimed in numerous orders by the Provincial Government. On the day of the announcement, it was stated that weapon certificates had lost their validity for the whole country and that weapon owners were obliged to submit their arms to authorities within 8 days. Those owners who were in possession of explosive were obliged to submit it within 24 hours to political authorities. For the disregard of these provisions, the fine of 2,000 crones was determined and the initiation of proceedings at court-martial.

After the decree in Bosnia and Herzegovina was in force, individuals who were involved in illegal affairs, cooperated or were in touch with the enemy, broke the oath about military service or who did not respond to the call for service, committed therewith a criminal deed for which they were surrendered to court-martial which were in charge for such deeds so that other punishments were not taken into consideration. Emergency measures were announced in a number of orders of the Provincial Government such as the Order on restriction of travel documents, reporting, organizing and gathering, Order on prohibition against fleeing of conscripts over the border, Order on restrictions for possession and selling of arms, Order on subjection of civilians to military power, Order on strengthening of criminal proceeding for Bosnia and Herzegovina and abolishment of jurors at courts, Order on the introduction of censure on post and the supervision and control over telegraph communication. [1]

After the decisions of the Ministry Council, Vienna and Berlin worked on a Memorandum which was kept in secrecy. On 24 July, diplomats of the Monarchy informed the governments in Petersburg, Paris, London, Rome and Istanbul about the undertaken actions and the content of the ultimatum. Shortly after the president of the Serbian Ministry council, Nikola Pašić, submitted a note stating that the Serbian government refuses to investigate the assassination on her territorry, the Austro-Hungarian representative in Belgrade indicated that the content of this message was not pleasing and that the delegation would leave Belgrade the same day. By the end of ulitimatum, Serbia started mobilization since it was expected that war declaration would follow in a few hours. [2] A day before the war outbreak, the High Command of the Balkan military forces was appointed. Its commander was entitled to independently lead operations on the Balkans. With a forthcoming offensive against Serbia, it was decided to submit the civil and military administration to military commanders of the Balkan armed forces in the case of crossing over to enemy's territory. [3] An omen of an upcoming war was also the fact that the families of officers were transported from Bileća and Trebinje. [4] When it became certain that the breakout of the war was inevitable, on 31 July, Emperor Franz Joseph issued authoritisation for the High command that all fortified places in Bosnia and Herzegovina and Dalmatia and the fortification Petrovaradin were to be set up for warfare. [5] Mobilization included not only armed forces but also economy, industry, agriculture, traffic and media which

---

[1] Sarajevski list, No. 155, 26 July 1914, p. 1.
[2] Klaus Dorst, Wolfgang Wünsche, *Der ersten Weltkrieg. Erscheinung und Wesen*, Berlin, 1989, pp. 44–45.
[3] Ö. St. A. – Österreichische Staats Archiv, Kriegsministerium, Armeeoberkomando, Operations Abteilung, Nr 5, k. u. k. Ministry of War to the Military command in Sarajevo, 27 July 1914.
[4] Ibid., Op. Nr 43, k. u. k. Ministry of War to the Military command in Sarajevo, 27 July 1914.
[5] Ibid., Op. Nr 95, k. u. k. Ministry of War to the Military command in Sarajevo, 31 July 1914.

gained the main role in creation of public opinion. An act for general mobilization was signed by Emperor Franz Joseph on 31 July, but 2 August was defined as alert day whereas 4 August was the first day for mobilization. A part of *B-echelon* which had not begun with transport towards Serbia, was detained in places of mobilization from where it was sent directly to Galicia. Mobilization in the Monarchy was done correctly and lasted 3 days for the cavalry and 7 days for infantry and artillery.

In all parts of the Monarchy the situation was almost the same. Among one million people who were enthusiastic about future victories, rarely anybody saw a battlefield in front of them. Religious dignitaries blessed the soldiers who left for the war without a clear goal, and military marches were a marker for their way into the unknown. In the night of 4 August when the British ultimatum expired and the World War started, Sir Edward Grey, standing at the window of his room in the Foreign Office, told his friend: "The lamps are going out all over Europe. We shall not see them lit again in our life-time".①

At the beginning of August 1914 three fronts were formed in Europe and maintained their primary significance until the end of the war. From December 1914, the Western front spread from North Sea to Switzerland, 700 kilometres in length. On this front the German army opposed the British-French and Belgian armies. The Eastern or Russian front spread from the Baltic Sea to Romania where the Austro-Hungarian and German armies were opposed to the Russian army. Along the rivers Sava and Danube, the Balkan front was formed where Austro-Hungarian army confronted Serbia. After the declaration of war for the reinforcement of the border towards Serbia and Montenegro, beside gendarmerie and the Veteran corps (1,600 soldiers), among the loyal local population the Protection corps were engaged with 11,000 people and they were attached to gendarmerie. In this way, at the beginning of mobilization, the beating heart of the country was established—a narrow gauge railway and the border zone towards Serbia and Montenegro.②

At the beginning of mobilization in Bosnia and Herzegovina, by the order of the army inspector Potiorek, i. e. the commander of the 6th army, "Schutzkorps"

---

① Josip Horvat, *Prvi svjetski rat*: *Panorama zbivanja*, Zagreb, 1967, p. 152.
② Österreich-Ungarns letztes Krieges 1914-1918., Bd 1, 1914, p. 92.

("Protection corps") was established by gendarmerie and they were composed of Bosnian and Herzegovinian Muslims and Catholics. The "Schutzkorps" was formed and filled by people who were not subject to military duty and from the composition of the second and third reserve that were not scheduled for war. Their purpose was to provide instructions and support for gendarmerie in preserving peace and order in the country. They were also used against gangs and to lead "small wars" against the broken opponents. The formation and establishment of Schutzcorps was exclusively in military authority and the Provincial Government of Bosnia and Herzegovina did not have any influence on it. The "Schutzkorps" functioned according to the principle of territorial defence, providing instructions on mobilization and protecting military objects, military devices, railway, post and telegraphy...① Beside this, a voluntary "Protection corps" ("Freiwilige Schutzkorps") was formed. The decision about its formation was assigned to the command of the gendarmerie corps for Bosnia and Herzegovina. A contingent of 1,000 infantrymen and 22 horsemen was formed for Bosnia and for Herzegovina. ②On the front, the members of the "Schutzkorps" moved together with their military units. Bosnian and Herzegovinian Serbs, who had joined Serbian and Montenegrin forces at the time of their breach into Bosnia and Herzegovina and caught at the time of duration of court-martial, were punished with a death penalty. The executors of these penalties were members of "Schutzkorps" and were largely Bosnian and Herzegovinian Muslims. In historical memory of Bosnian and Herzegovinian Serbs this fact was later used as an instrument for genocide policy towards Muslims. During the service in "Schutzkorps" there were violations of duty for which its members were charged and prosecuted. One such lawsuit, where several persons were convicted, was led by the end of April 1916. ③ By the order of general Potiorek, many kinds of military formations were established along with the regular army. For the purpose of defence of Sarajevo and its surroundings a concrete plan for

---

① ABH, ZMF, 1914, 14.498, *Schutzkorpsmanschaft*, *Versorgung*. The Provincial Government of Bosnia and Herzegovina to the Common Ministry of Finances, Sarajevo 3, November 1914.
② Ö. St. A., KA-W, N. P, K. 6, Geh. Nr 68 b, Sarajevo, 12 September 1914.
③ *Prozesgegen Schutzkorps Leute*, Sarajevoer Tageblatt, 30 April 1915, p. 5.

the creation of *Scharfschutzkorps* was made during the September of 1914. ① This military organized body was to patrol, gather intelligence and ensure safety and command. Special attention was dedicated to weapon handling and fostering of sharpshooting among the younger people, as was the custom in Alpine countries of the Monarchy. For performing of tasks, a command of "Scharfschutzkorps" was established with three permanent inspectors at the front who should change shifts every 8 hours. Twenty members of "Scharfschutzkorps" were distributed per each barrack, fully prepared for war, dressed in brown-grey clothes, with breeches, long stockings or puttees. ② "Bürgerwehr" was also formed, as civil protection to administer public order and peace in the country and was not subject to the regulations of military discipline. The Provincial Government decided on the formation of these units on the 11th August 1914. They should have been formed according to gendarmerie regions with the task to patrol unarmed even if their commander was armed. For the formation, it was necessary to recruit four times more people than the number of rifles they possessed. This "civil army" functioned as civil guard and on the battlefield and it was subordinated to gendarmerie. ③ Apart from this, the "Schutzwehr" —small-armed units along the gendarmerie stations, were also set up. In the country, watch guards were organized in the areas which included 6 or 12 villages. All these formations were officially called "Bürgerwehr" and their goal was to support police since police officers had left for the regular army. They were supposed to carry out police patrols, keep watch in front of administration buildings, posts, next to telephone and railway lines and prominent places along river banks and to reinforce financial watches. ④

After war broke out and mobilization was proclaimed, a significant role was attributed to religious leaders in Bosnia and Herzegovina—the Grand Mufti Čaušević, Archbishop and Metropolitan Evgenije Letica, and the Bishop of Mostar Mišić, who

---

① ABH, ZV BH, 1914, 12. 020, *Formierungeines Scharfschutzkorps*, The fort command Sarajevo to the The Provincial Government of Bosnia and Herzegovina, Sarajevo, 22 September 1914.

② ABH, ZV BH, Präs, 1914, 11. 721. *Entwurffür die Aktivierung des Sarajevoer Scharf-Schutzkorps*, *Military Command Sarajevo*, 3 September 1914.

③ Milorad Ekmečić, *Ratni ciljevi Srbije 1914*, Beograd, 1974, p. 474, nap. 89.

④ Ibid. , p. 173.

took care that mobilization was done in peace and order, thereby using the opportunity to spread patriotism and emphasize the connection with the Monarchy. ①

In the first year of war, the impact of military "soul carers", chaplains, imams and rabbis on military conscripts was especially strong. The emphasis in their activities was placed on atonement in case of breaching the oath given to the Emperor and the King which had crucial significance for their conduct on the front and endurance of superhuman efforts. ②General Potiorek was especially interested in using the enthusiasm of the Muslim population for the war goals of the Monarchy, insisting to manifest it in every possible moment. When the war started, prayers were held for the victory of Central Powers in all mosques in Bosnia and Herzegovina. When Great Britain entered the war on 15 August, after the prayer for the Emperor in the Emperor's mosque, in agreement with General Potiorek, the Grand Mufti and the Waqf director Šerif Arnautović organized a prayer against Britain. Grand Mufti Čaušević, dressed as mullah of Mekka and Medina, delivered a solemn speech from a specially decorated podium. This act was photographed; postcards were made with the text of his speech and addressed to Muslim soldiers at the Russian front and Muslim countries all over to India. ③

After the war declaration, General Conrad ordered that the *B-echelon*, along with units of the Minimal group Balkans, should also be concentrated towards Serbia. It was very active during the following days in South-Eastern Bosnia. The Serb and Montenegrin operation plan against Austria-Hungary, which was presented on 6 August 1914 by Ratomir Putnik, suggested to engage the strong Austro-Hungarian forces and to weaken therewith the attack in direction of Russia. The basis for the offensive operation plan which suggested the combined operations of the Serbian and Montenegrin army was the engagement of Serbian army from Užice which was to

---

① Sarajevski list, No. 183, 13 August 1914, 2; No. 184, 14 August 2; No. 191, 19 August 2.

② While on the Italian front, captain Pero Blašković met a Muslim who was hungry and thirsty, and was pulling a gun onto a far-away hill, crying and saying that "trodding as a goat he was constantly praying to Allah to be shot down by artillery, because this is not life". These words portray the attitude towards the military service: the oath to God and the Emperor, because one includes the other, was the motive which moved the soldiers to endure superhuman efforts. See: Pero Blašković, *Sa Bošnjacima u svetskom ratu*, Beograd, 1939, p. 368.

③ Ö. St. A., KA-W, Nachlass Potiorek, Karton 5, No. 136, Sarajevo, 15 August 1914.

operate on the direction Višegrad-Sarajevo and the Montenegrin army in the direction Pljevlja-Goražde-Sarajevo. ① The offensive toward Sarajevo was founded in the strategic concepts of Serbian general staff but its success was limited to connecting and marking of Austro-Hungarian forces. The tasks of Chetnik units show offensive character. ② Raising revolts in Bosnia and Herzegovina was included in the plans of military circles of Serbia. After the outbreak of war, Colonel Dragutin Dimitrijević-Apis composed an instruction for the conduction of Chetniks' activities in the war against Austro-Hungarian military forces. This document foresaw that in the case of offensive, Chetnik troops should cross over on territory of Bosnia and Herzegovina and serve there as a nucleus for instigating revolts in areas inhabited by Orthodox Christians. The High Command of the Serbian army entrusted Chetnik units with the execution of specific military tasks, mainly guerrilla warfare. During offensive operations Chetniks should have been engaged as precursors and patrols of regular Serbian army with the task to intrude on territory controlled by the Austro-Hungarian army, to attack them from behind, also to attack in hinterland, destroy communications and large mobile institutions, gather intelligence etc. Their basic goal was to force the enemy to take apart its forces and to weaken its attacking abilities. During the withdrawal of the Serbian army, Chetniks were supposed to remain on the occupied territory behind the back of their enemy's army, to attack and destroy bridges, passages, telegraph and telephone lines, the chamber etc. Troops were also to be formed from the remaining population. Through specially organized intelligence channels, Chetniks established connections with the regular Serbian army. ③ The place and role of Chetnik units during First World War was confirmed by a special directive of High command. All Chetnik formations were sent to the River Drina on 9 August. ④ Some units were engaged during 1914 on the territory of Bosnia, i. e. the area of Vlasenica, Olovo,

---

① Hrabak, 1964, p. 5.

② About the role of Chetniks, see: Nusret Šehić, *Četništvo u Bosni i Hercegovini (1918-1941)*, Sarajevo, 1971, pp. 13-39.

③ About the role of chetniks, see: Nusret Šehić, *Četništvo u Bosni i Hercegovini (1918-1941)*, Sarajevo, 1971, p. 40.

④ Zijad Šehić, *U smrt za cara i domovinu: Bosanci i Hercegovci u vojnoj organizaciji Habsburške monarhije 1878-1918*, Sarajevo Publishing, Sarajevo, 2007, p. 92.

and also towards Srebrenica, Han Pijesak and Pale and even arrived in the direct vicinity of Sarajevo. In the places where Serbian and Montenegrin forces penetrated, Chetniks were joined by local population who voluntarily entered their troops. The attempt to provoke an uprising through the actions of Chetnik units did not succeed since the population who were not allowed to carry weapons was either interned in the inner parts of the Monarchy or were mobilized or assigned to work units. This is why Chetnik orders in the area where they operated, found mainly older people, women and children. ①During their military operations, the captured committees were shot or hanged. In the county of Mostar 154 people were killed, in Duvno 19, whereas in both counties 36 people were killed in battles. In the county of Trebinje 78 people were hanged, 30 were killed in battles, whereas in the Bileća county 6 people were shot dead and six were hanged. ②

Breach of Serbian and Montenegrin military forces into the territory from Višegrad to Foča caused massive flight of the Muslim population from the counties of Višegrad, Rogatica, Čajniče and Foča whereas the Orthodox Christians welcomed them as liberators, cooperating and joining them. This attitude of the local Serbian population served as a motive to implement the harshest repressive measures. After the Montenegrin army had withdrawn from Čelebići near Foča, in the middle of August 1914, 180 Serbs were arrested and 71 shot dead in Foča on the basis of the court-martial decision, whereas 24 were sent to the camp Arad. ③

In the morning of 17 September a part of the Sandžak army entered Rogatica. The county administration of Rogatica informed the Provincial Government what had been going on after the offensive of Austro-Hungarian forces by the end of October 1914. Pillaging started immediately after Sarajevo. On both sides of the road, houses were burnt down, mainly desolated and plundered. All Serbs from Sokolac and Podromanija withdrew with the Serbian and Montenegrin troops. Montenegrins arrived at Rogatica in the afternoon of 17 September. Local Serbs welcomed them with applause, flags and flowers. The town administration was in their hands. One third of the Muslim

---

① Nusret Šehić, 1971, p. 41, nap. 97.
② Slijepčević, 1929, p. 396.
③ ABH, ZMF, Präs. BH 1914, 1.715. County office in Foča to the Provincial Government of Bosnia and Herzegovina, Sarajevo, 23 September 1914.

population, who had not escaped on time, remained in the town and was exposed to the terror of Montenegrins. One café owner and one-day labourer were killed, whereas Muderis Muhamed Effendi Škaljić, 8 imams, respected citizens—Bećirbeg Šahinpašić, Uzeiraga Daidžić, hafiz-Effendi Muftić, Ibrahim Teskeredžić and 70 other persons from the county were taken as hostages. Muslims were stopped on the streets and were deprived of their money and watches. Montenegrins burnt down 20 houses with side buildings, 20 shops and a mosque in a neighbourhood. Serbs and Montenegrins plundered and took everything possible—supplies, clothes, precious things and equipment. They even robbed the local Orthodox Christians with the excuse that Austro-Hungarian money was not valid any longer and should be exchanged. They extorted the money and collected in this way around 4,000 crones. Due to the penetration Austro-Hungarian troops, 80% of Orthodox Christians joined Serbian and Montenegrin forces which were withdrawing, to a great extent voluntarily but partially also because they were forced to do so.① For instance, the complete population of Trnovo fled. Montenegrins, dressed in uniforms of the Austro-Hungarian army, burnt properties and plundered everything, even Serbian women so that the population had to escape. The return of Serbian population was not an option since it was assumed that they would join the enemy.② By the end of October 1914 the county branch of Trnovo was completely cleansed from Serbian and Montenegrin troops, so that the traffic on the route Sarajevo-Trnovo-Kalinovik was established and after it the postal service as well. Muslim families from Trnovo started returning home. One small part of Orthodox Christians remained whereas a greater part of them had fled and joined the Serbian and Montenegrin units. After the reoccupation of the places, many inhabitants made the statements at the stage headquarter about the events in the county of Vlasenica during the invasion of Serbian and Montenegrin forces. When Serbians marched into the villages Pomol and Štedra for a second time, many residents were massacred. Serbian patrols besieged Muslim houses requesting food and cattle which was given to them without any resistance and after which they requested money. In

---

① ABH, ZMF, Präs. 1914, 1.740. County office in Rogatica to the Provincial Government of Bosnia and Herzegovina, Sarajevo, 20 October 1914, transcript.

② Ö. St. A., KA-W, N. P, K. 6, 86 ad c, Rapport, 27 September 1914.

these villages, soldiers also raped women. ① After the offensive of Serbian and Montenegrin units, around 50,000 people from East-Bosnian counties of Kladanj, Srebrenica, Vlasenica, Rogatica, Višegrad and Zvornik left, partially voluntarily and partially because they were forced to do so since military circles spread the news that "Swabians were killing everyone on their way". Apart from this, fear was present among them after the solemn welcome of Serbian and Montenegrin units and involvement in plunders. Army gathered refugees and directed them towards Serbia. ②

Having expelled Užice and Sandžak armies from South-Eastern Bosnia, General Potiorek resolved the question of securing the hinterland on this space, after which he had to decide about the third offensive against Serbia. ③ In the governing circles in Sarajevo it was considered that a fast pacification of the Orthodox Christians should not be expected if the Austro-Hungarian forces did not act decisively on the prevention of an uprising. From 28 June to 15 August at Central Courts in Bosnia and Herzegovina criminal lawsuits were raised against 637 persons. After finding the material from Loznica, several hundred people were taken to the prison in Sarajevo either from the group of hostages or trough new arrests. ④ It was surprising to see to what extent the Serbian idea became popular not only among the intelligentsia but also among the rural population. ⑤Military authorities in Trebinje used penal measures so that on the 12th August, Gujo Gudelj from Pokrajčići, who sent signals to Montenegrin troops was hanged and Vid Parežanin from Lastva-Korjenić taken hostage because Serbs from Lastva joined Montenegrins during the attack on Trebinje. ⑥Such scenes and examples

---

① *Zlodjela Srba u Bosni*, Sarajevski list, No. 114, 24 April 1915, p. 3.

② Ö. St. A., KA-W, N. P, K. 5, 109 b, Kladanj 17 October 1914. M. Ekmečić denoted the flight of Orthodox Christian population from eastern Bosnia as "ethnic cleansing of its subjects by Austro-Hungary" (Ekmečić, 1974, p. 180).

③ Zelenika, 1962, p. 638.

④ Zijad Šehić, 2007, p. 97.

⑤ Hauptmann-Prasch, 1981, p. 430. It is known of the case of a Serb peasant who, before his hanging, shouted three times "Long live King Peter". He was then massacred by the soldiers, and while he was dying he mentioned his name again.

⑥ ABH, ZMF, Präs. BH 1914, 1.410, The trancscript of report No. 320 from 13/8 1914, A branch of command in Trebinje to the gendarmarie command. While he was standing on the scaffold with a rope around his neck, priest Parežanin shouted: "Long live Serbia, Serbian army, Serbian people and Great Russia."

of fanaticism strengthened the conviction that they could only be fought by force. The committees were not always fought consistently. At first they could not be differentiated from the regular troops and many of them were captured. Only after some time, they began not to be treated as soldiers. They themselves did not know what they were fighting for, only that they were pushed forward by their officers. ① The Austro-Hungarian administration considered that such examples indicated that Bosnian Serbs were long preparing in secrecy in terms of high treason for the events which followed. "They were raised in that way, because logically, it is difficult to assume that an ordinary uneducated peasant or even old women could have offered such military services without previously being prepared for it", concluded the court counsellor Grasl, suggesting that the "administration has the main goal to educate people that it governs in the spirit of loyalty towards the throne and respect of law regardless of personality and to show in all administrative procedures good intentions and consistent firmness." He believed that it was important to eliminate any kind of militaristic spirit and thereby the harmful protection which obstructed the work i. e. giving recognition for merits to each individual. "If this was done", he concluded, "It could not happen that among Serb intellectuals, there are many of those who are deep in their hearts on the side of the enemy". ② Investigation against participants of assassination carried out in Sarajevo showed the entire severity of the crisis in education and school system in the country and the proportions of the youth movement which negated Austro-Hungarian rule. Authorities investigated, arrested suspicious high school students and prepared lawsuits against them. According to the Austro-Hungarian central authorities, high schools in Bosnia and Herzegovina faced a crisis, discipline problems and conflicts among students. ③ As the number of excesses of high school students increased with years, for the suppression of this phenomenon and its causes, the emergency measures proved to be unsustainable. It was established that the excesses were motivated by elements who systematically and frequently acted and

---

① Ferdinand Hauptmann, Anton Prasch, *Dr. Ludwig Thallóczy: Tagebücher*, Graz, 1981, p. 430.

② Galib Šljivo, *Raspoloženje naroda Bosne i Hercegovine prema austrougarskoj politici i austrougarske političke protivmjere*, u: Zbornik radova s međunarodnog skupa: Veleizdajnički proces u Banjaluci 1915–1916, održanog 25–27. septembra 1986. godine u Banjoj Luci, Institut za istoriju, Banjaluka, 1987, p. 138.

③ Kapidžić, 1965, p. 398.

agitated against loyal elements in school bodies. As result of this, regulations of the second main body, of the third section of the Criminal code for Bosnia and Herzegovina were supplemented. Those who were convicted could expect imprisonment from one to six months. If the convicts were not citizens of Bosnia and Herzegovina, they were expelled from the Monarchy. ① Military command from Mostar estimated that Serbophile propaganda which had earlier been eliminated by the example of draconic measures was fully continued after mobilization. Proof of such convictions was the sending of signals to the Serbian and Montenegrin army as well as the mood of the Orthodox Christians who openly demonstrated joy after the slightest sign of failure of Austro-Hungarian army which was followed with rumours. Due to this, military command required more effective measures for prevention. Primarily, all enemies were to be expelled from the country and emigration of population from the Balkan countries was to be prohibited. All those who were hostile towards the country should be confiscated their property.

Fifteen days before he was dismissed, the Provincial governor Potiorek, in a report addressed to the Common ministry of finances, had justified the harsh measures in Bosnia and Herzegovina after the assassination in Sarajevo. In the report he argued that after gathering information during the previous months, the majority of the Orthodox Christians successfully acknowledged the state idea. Moreover, facts in all areas of administration indicated that the subversive spirit and disloyalty were not only present among some exalted politicians but were also deeply rooted in all strata of society to an unimaginable extent. A great part of clergy, teachers in religious schools and other educated people of free vocations, as well as town landlords were infected with this spirit. It was even spread among provincial clerks and officials of all categories despite their oath to serve. The conservative and loyal population was seduced by the irredentist movement, completely joining the Serbian army near borderline. According to Potiorek's opinion, the trial showed the assassinators that Serbia had fanned national passions among the Serbs in Bosnia and Herzegovina and

---

① ABH, ZMF, Präs. BH 1914, 1.078. *Entwurfeines Gesetzeswomit die Bestimmungen des zweiten Hauptstückes des dritten Teiles des Strafgesetzesergänztwerden.* The Provincial Government of Bosnia and Herzegovina to the Common Ministry of Finances, Sarajevo, 26 July 1914.

inspired their megalomaniac aspirations. Potiorek cited complaisance of the administration towards the requests of Serbs as the main reason for strengthening of Serb nationalism, especially after the movement for church and school autonomy had finished. Giving Statute to church and school autonomy was considered to have been a fatal mistake of the administration. It established a national church and school and created such a conscience among Serbs that they did not feel any longer as Bosnians of Orthodox Christian faith or members of Monarchy but as a special privileged element which considered that they had the right to separatist aspirations and created a proper platform for subversive activities. ① Immediately after the announcement of mobilization in Bosnia and Herzegovina, military authorities started taking hostages. This measure was supposed to guarantee peace in the country and in this way the activities of committee troops were limited. Hostages vouched with their lives for the damage that could have happened in the country to the army, military objects, transport, public transport means and everything that was important to the army. They were positioned on those places which could have been in danger from guerrilla warfare. ②

A note from the Provincial Government for Bosnia and Herzegovina addressed to county offices and branch offices in the country from 28 July 1914 contained instructions on introduction of the institution of hostage. The most influential and most respected persons of Orthodox faith who politically belonged to "Narod", "Otadžbina" and "Srpskariječ" should be taken as hostages and serve as pawns for the loyal behaviour of their members and supporters. It was emphasized that it was of special importance to take hostages who were their closest relatives in order to achieve calming effects on the population. Political authorities should teach the population about the significance of taking hostages, arguing that it is not punishment but an instrument for protection of state and respect their treatment. Hostages vouched with their lives for objects of military significance and every incident had as consequence their execution. ③For deliberate damage of railways, bridges, roads, telegraph and

---

① ABH, ZMF, BH Präs. 1914, 1994. The report of the chief of the Provincial Government of Bosnia and Herzegovina to the Common Ministry of Finances, Sarajevo, 15 December 1914.

② Galib Šljivo, 1987, p. 91.

③ ABH, ZV BH, Präs. 1914, 7. 493. Aushebung von Geiseln und Behandlungderselbe. The Provincial Government of Bosnia and Herzegovina to all county offices and county branches, Sarajevo, 28 July 1914.

telephone lines the penalty was hanging. Every municipality that suffered such destroying was exposed to high penalties or other difficult contributions which needed to be initiated immediately. Military commands for insurance of railways and bridges and commands of military transports were authorised to take hostages and could dispose them at the department for protection and military trains. In attacks on railways or bridges, hostages should be shot on the spot. ① In all municipalities, especially in those near railways, posters were to be put on prominent places. ②In the inner parts of the Monarchy politically suspicious hostages were taken first. ③ From 380 Orthodox priests in country, 163 of them were captured or taken as hostages. ④ In regard to repressive measures against the Serbian population which participated in battles of the Serbian and Montenegrin army against Austro-Hungarian troops, the Ministry of foreign affairs of Monarchy approved the undertaken measures. It principally agreed to deprive them of their citizenship and to confiscate their property remarking the principle of its implementation of distribution of property to loyal neighbours. Reason for such an attitude was fear that division of confiscated property would serve as a motive for Russia to do the same in regions of east Galicia, occupied by Russian troops. These measures could have had long lasting negative consequences for the Monarchy in a political sense. Because of this, it was believed that the right for confiscated land should be given to the Provincial Government for Bosnia and Herzegovina. ⑤

After the deportation of Serbian and Montenegrin forces from East-Bosnian counties and establishment of Austro-Hungarian administration, the question of settlement in border areas became current again. In the end, the opinion was accepted to expatriate the Orthodox Christians and to confiscate their property. Since they turned away from the Monarchy, their property was to be taken by other, mixed

---

① ABH, ZV BH, Präs. 1914, 8.352, The decree of the command of the 15th corps.
② ABH, ZV BH, Präs. 1914, 7.441. *Beschedigung von Komunikationsmitteln*, The Provincial Government of Bosnia and Herzegovina to all county offices and county branches, as well as to the government's commissary for the capital Sarajevo, 27 July 1914.
③ Ö. St. A., KA-W, N. P. K. 6, Geh. Nr 61 b.
④ Ferdinand Hauptmann, Anton Prasch, 1981, p. 444.
⑤ ABH, ZMF, BH Präs. 1915, 980. Ministry of Foreign Affairs to the k. u. k. Ministry of War, 15th June 1915.

population, primarily Muslims and Catholics from different parts of Bosnia and Herzegovina, war victims, veteran soldiers, corporals, gendarmes and financial guards. ①

After the end of the Balkan Wars, the Ottoman Empire was in a difficult situation because of the loss of the greatest part on the European continent and immediate threat to Istanbul from Bulgaria and Greece and their aspiration to its territory. After the assassination in Sarajevo the government in Istanbul was convinced that it could not escape entry to war. Even though the Minister of War, Enver Pasha, was the most influential politician and personally fond of Germans, the Porte initially attempted to approach the Entente forces. Germany used this immediately and on 2 August concluded an agreement about participation of the Ottoman Empire in the war on the side of Central Powers. Germany hoped that this arrangement would positively influence Bulgaria, Romania, Persia, and Afghanistan to join it. Germany expected a lot from the Sultan's reputation as a religious leader of the whole Muslim world of around 300 million people. It hoped that the announcement of holy war (jihad) would show that their place in this war was on the side of Central Powers. ② The entry of the Ottoman Empire into the war on 1 November 1914 had a significant impact on events in the South-Eastern Europe. Foremost, for the proclamation of holy war, the Sheikh ul-Islam's needed to proclaim a holy fatwa so that the Sultan might proclaim the war on its basis. In Istanbul, on 14 November 1914, after the noon prayer in Fatih's mosque, a representative of Sheikh ul-Islam presented the fatwa which proclaimed the holy war. A crowd of people moved to the Ministry of War, in front of the Porte where a prayer was held for the victory of army and navy. ③ The Government sent the media the proclamation of holy war, bearing the date 21 November 1914, and the Sultan ordered the proclamation to be sent to all Muslim countries. It was signed by the current and former Sheikh ul-Islam, as well as by 24 great Muslim scholars. All Muslims were invited to take part in the war on the side of Central Powers. Hence, to Muslims in the Balkans, it was clearly shown that their place was on the side of the Monarchy. ④

---

① ABH, ZMF, BH Präs. 1915, 1. 377. "Pro domo".
② Petar Tomac, *Ratovi i armije XIX veka*, Beograd, 1968, pp. 152-153.
③ Sarajevski list, No. 278, 17 November 1914, p. 1.
④ Ibid. , No. 290, 26 November 1914, 1; Cf. Bihl, 1982, p. 35.

According to Sharia all Muslims were obliged to participate in the war. Children, women, slaves, the blind and disabled people did not have to fight. If the enemy was defeated the war could end, but if it was the other way around and the enemy won, then a wife could go to war without asking her husband, a slave without asking his master. Mutilation of the enemy was forbidden. All Muslims were obliged to participate in the war against those who were marked as enemies of Islam. [1]

General Potiorek did not hesitate to order the reading of Sheikh ul-Islam's fatwa with the command about the holy war-jihad, in all mosques in the country and to all soldiers at the front as a welcome tool for psychological and ideological war fighting. In order to direct their religious enthusiasm towards a voluntary joining of the army, General Potiorek sought to influence the Grand Mufti as soon as possible so that the fatwa of the Sheikh ul-Islam would be published in all the mosques in the land, proclaiming jihad against the British, French and Russians. [2] At the same time he told Palavichini, the Austro-Hungarian ambassador in Istanbul, to ask the Sheikh ul-Islam for an explanation as to whether the Muslims can fight under the imperial flag. Bearing in mind that jihad was a legal institution of Islam, he wanted to know whether it had to be waged under Muslim command. [3] After he officially received the fatwa and the epistle from Sheikh ul-Islam, the Grand Mufti Čaušević invited all the muftis and dignitaries to Sarajevo, at the same time issuing an epistle to all muftis, imams, and sharia judges to begin collecting contributions for the army. [4] In the courtyard of the Gazi Husrev-bey's mosque on 11 December 1914, before noon, the Muslim population began gathering in order to hear the speech of the Grand Mufti. The mosque and the courtyard were full and it is estimated that more than 3,000 individuals were present at the time. In the mosque all of the most prominent representatives of the Muslim people came together. After the Friday noon prayer, the imam of the Bey's mosque, hafiz Esad effendi Sabrihafizović, delivered a khutba and later extracts from the Koran

---

[1] Sarajevski list, No. 282, 18 November 1914, p. 2.

[2] Manfried Rauchensteiner, *Der Tod des Doppeladlers: Österreich-Ungarn und der Erste Weltkrieg*, Wien, 1991, p. 183.

[3] ABH, ZMF, BH Präs. 1914, 1815. *Heilige Krieg*, Tuzla, 15–16 November 1914.

[4] ABH, Präs. BH, 1914, 1913, *Heilige Krieg*, The Provincial Government of Bosnia and Herzegovina to the Common Ministry of Finances, Sarajevo, 2 December 1914.

were read from the surah on the victory. After the reading was finished, the Grand Mufti climbed to the pulpit, turning to the gathered populace, stressing that the Ottoman Empire had entered the World War as an ally of the Monarchy and Germany. ①

  The war destruction on the area of military operations, mobilization, migrations, evacuations and interning of people caused a great disturbance in the economy of the country. In the majority of industrial companies and mines the production did not reach the pre-war level, and in many cases it was halved or completely stopped. Due to the lack of working power during the war the agricultural production was organized on the principle of compulsory public works. The agrarian produce declined swiftly so that during 1916 they were twice smaller than in 1914. The war contributions and the lack of food conditioned the excessive slaughtering of cattle and the quick regression of livestock farming. The war especially hit the poorer layers of the society. With the engaging of labour capable population for the war effort, the economy was left without workforce so that the militarized companies resorted to employing women and children, and during 1915 and 1916 they also employed prisoners of war and militarized workers who filled work places in mining, metallurgy, and wood cutting. ②With its production Bosnia and Herzegovina could not satisfy the necessities for cereals even in peacetime, so that it had to import large quantities. The knowledge that the war would last for a longer period of time forced the authorities to undertake numerous measures for the rational spending of existing supplies and ensuring the provisioning of the population. Special attention was given to the spring sowing in 1915 which had to include all the security organs in the state—gendarmerie, Schutzkorps, veterans, foresters, and all municipal officers. Also, the refugees were to be involved in the sowing since they received help from the state resources. ③ For the conducting of the spring sowing, an especially important role was given to the gendarmerie which was given the instructions

---

  ① Sarajevski list, No. 306, 12 December 1914, pp. 2-3.
  ② Hadžibegović, 1990, p. 70.
  ③ ABH, ZMF, 1915, 8.820. *Wirtschaftliche Massnahmen der Landesregierungfür Bosnien und Hercegovinawährend des Krieges (bis Mai 1915). Im Auftrage der Landesregierungverfasst von Dr Stephan Fodor, Regierungssekretär*, The Provincial Government of Bosnia and Herzegovina to the Common Ministry of Finances, 16 August 1915, p. 83.

for its implementation. The ploughing and sowing was to be conducted via public works, so in each settlement all labour capable male and female workforces were required to help. In these works refugees were also supposed to be involved, whereas only the necessary female workforce was allowed to remain home. Under no circumstance was it allowed to take the working cattle to graze before the sowing was completed. On the agricultural units where the male individuals were mobilized, not one single part was supposed to remain uncultivated. This land was supposed to be worked on by the whole population, in the final instance even if some of them had to be forced to do it. Each settlement needed to provide all of the labour capable men, women and children, with the available cattle and equipment in the service of the state, so that from the early morning hours until very late in the evening they would be engaged in sowing until the job was completed in a certain region. If a surplus of workforce was to appear, it was to be sent out to aid the neighbouring areas. ① In the lack of agricultural workforce for the sowing even prisoners were engaged and they were organized by the authorities from the county and regional courts. Beside that, it was allowed to involve school children in the performing of easier agricultural tasks, and the supervision and control of these measures was entrusted to the teaching staff. Also, it was favourable to engage females among the Muslim refugee women and girls in the conducting of field works. The lower organs were especially reminded not to intensively engage these categories of refugees, but that this should be done in an appropriate way, since this was the first instance of activity of Muslim females in public life. These provisions were met by complete understanding from the Grand Mufti and he supported them strongly. ② In order to prevent the chaos in the provisioning of the population in Bosnia and Herzegovina, the Government passed on 3 August 1914 the Law on the rational provisioning with necessary life supplies. All food supplies were required, and export from Bosnia and Herzegovina was forbidden

---

① ABH, ZMF, 1915, 8.820. *Wirtschaftliche Massnahmen der Landesregierungfür Bosnien und Hercegovinawährend des Krieges (bis Mai 1915). Im Auftrage der Landesregierungverfasst von Dr Stephan Fodor, Regierungssekretär*, The Provincial Government of Bosnia and Herzegovina to the Common Ministry of Finances, 16 August 1915, pp. 84-86.

② Ibid., p. 91.

without a special permission of the authorities.① For the more effective control of prices and supplying of population, the Provincial Government was authorized by the law of 7 December 1914 to undertake special measures in the field of economy due to the outstanding circumstances caused by war. ②The law of 29 March 1915 arranged the trade of wheat and grist for the mill. It established the monthly-allowed ration per capita of 7.2 kg of flour or 9 kg of wheat, which amounted to 250 grams of flour or 300 grams of wheat per person per day. ③ Since the supplying of the population was in constant decline, the Provincial Government, dissatisfied with the work of the Office for the trade of wheat, formed by the end of 1915 the Institute for the trade of life supplies which was united with the Office. Its task was to find supplies of life victuals and to distribute them equally on the territory of Bosnia and Herzegovina. ④

After the southern and eastern areas of the country became the direct zone of war operations, a great part of the population was forced to flee their homes, whereas on the other side a large number had to be evacuated militarily. In that way the problem of refugees became prominent immediately after the outbreak of the war. Considering the small receiving capabilities in the country, as well as the specific social, confessional and economic relations, the solution of this issue was more problematic than in Austria and Hungary. The movement of refugees began in the end of August of 1914 when the Austro-Hungarian units retreated from Sandžak, and when 9,000 Muslims joined them with women and children. When the wave of refugees began moving from Sandžak, General Potiorek thought that the best solution would be to include all capable males into military units. ⑤ He believed that their return by force

---

① Law that regulates provisions on procurement of population with basic supplies while emergency circumstances are in force caused by war, *Glasnik Zakona i naredbiza BiH*, 1914, No. 76, 3 August 1914, p. 363. Hereafter: *Glasnik Zakona i naredbi*...

② Law that authorises the Provincial government, due to war circumstances to order what to do on the field of economy, *Glasnik Zakona i naredbi*... No. 167, 7 December 1914, p. 589.

③ Law that regulates the transport of wheat and grist, *Glasnik Zakona i naredbi*... No. 32, 29 March 1915, p. 81.

④ Order of the Provincial government according to which the Institute of the Provincial government for Bosnia and Herzegovina for the transport of life provisions was founded, *Glasnik Zakona i naredbi*... No. 128, 3 December 1915, p. 291.

⑤ Ö. St. A. KA-W, N. P, K. 5, 48. *Dienstzettel*, 10 August 1914.

was out of the question due to the consideration towards the Muslims of Bosnia and Herzegovina. Since they could not remain on the border due to military reasons, and since inland accommodation was excluded because the possibilities and the authorities could not bear it, their passage to Ustiprača was approved, and after that they were to be directly transported towards Bosanski Brod. At the same time the k. u. k. Ministry of War required the refugees to be settled outside of the country. ① After they reached Brod, the refugees were dispersed to Banja Luka, Kotor Varoš, Kozarac, Derventa and Teslić, while the refugees from Foča and Čajniče were taken to Vareš, Fojnica and Busovača. ② The Muslim population from Sandžak fled en masse with their cattle towards Bosnia in order to save themselves from the Montenegrin attacks. The k. u. k. Ministry of War ordered that the refugees are to be treated in the same way as they were in 1912. ③ The Office for the supervision of war thought that the refugees from Sandžak should be allocated in the interior, along with the conduction of strict sanitary measures so that the outbreak of any infections would be prevented. ④ Under the leadership of the Grand Mufti Čušević an action was initiated for the gathering of aid for the refugees, and it brought funds in the amount of 61,687 crones and 84 hellers. Franz Joseph and minister Leon Bilinski gave larger contributions, 10,000 crones each, while the other donations were mostly the result of the Grand Mufti's work. Since the refugees were supplied from the provincial budget, the income of the fond was used for the improvement of their position, for the buying of food, clothes and footwear, Nestlé flour for the feeding of children... These necessary supplies were bought by the Refugee Office of the Provincial Government and the regional offices on whose areas the refugees were settled. ⑤

The Muslim population which did not succeed to flee because they were surprised by the enemy, remained on the occupied territory. On 20 September 1914 the regional representative Hrasnica submitted a report to the president of the Provincial Government about the violence to which they were exposed: "As soon as the conflict

---

① Ibid., K. 6, 51 ad Potiorek to Bilinski, Sarajevo, 29 August 1914.
② Ibid., 52, *Dienstzettel*, Sarajevo, 30 August 1914.
③ Ibid., 52 d, 30 August 1914.
④ Ibid., 52 f, 1 September 1914.
⑤ *Sabiranjezamuhadžire*, Sarajevski list, No. 39, 28 Februar 1917, p. 2.

began on the border, and when the border troops began retreating together with the gendarmerie, finances and members of Defensive Council, and when the Serb army began encroaching into the Višegrad region, the elders of the Orthodox Christians ceased to perform the entrusted tasks and all to a man joined the enemy along with the population, while the Muslims retreated with the army". They told Hrasnica that they were forced to flee and that they did not have the time to take their cattle in fear that they would remain on the left bank of the river Lim and thus fall into the hands of the enemy. Those who were left behind suffered horrible atrocities: "They were being murdered, enslaved, flayed alive, and from one hajji they took 10,000 crones and then they killed him".① The suppression of the Serb and Montenegrin units was followed by the return of refugees to Rogatica so that by the end of November 1914 their number decreased to 26,448 persons. However, soon a new attack followed and Rogatica had to be completely evacuated again. Due to that, the number of refugees from the eastern areas rose so that in mid-January 1915 the number of refugees was 46,000 individuals, of which around 20,000 were children and 16,000 women. ②

In the summer of 1915 a total number of 104,000 persons were displaced. This situation lasted until the autumn of 1915 when the successful offensive in Serbia made it possible for them to return. In the spring and summer of 1915 refugees, among which were women and children, found an additional source of income in agricultural work. On the initiative of the Grand Mufti funds were gathered throughout the land for the care of refugees, which brought an amount of 35,000 crones. Despite the difficulties, adapting to the circumstances in the land, the refugees were also provided with shelter and care during the winter. The successful operations in Serbia and Montenegro in the end of 1915 made it seem likely that all the refugees would return home, so preparations were made for such an outcome. In the end of November 1915 a great number of evacuees from the fortified places were able to return homes, in the cases where no additional conditions had to be met. There were 5,000 inhabitable and 10,000 uninhabitable destroyed or damaged houses and economic buildings. By the end of 1916 the number of destroyed buildings was still great: 3,221 houses were

---

① Galib Šljivo, 1987, pp. 134-135.
② Bericht, 1914-16, p. 141.

completely destroyed, 7,075 economic buildings, 1,644 severely damaged houses and 2,099 severely damaged economic buildings. ①

During 1915, a series of political trials were held in Bosnia and Herzegovina and they were mostly aimed against the high-school youth. That same year four big student trials were organized: in Banja Luka with 27 accused, in Mostar, but which was held in Sarajevo against 10 accused, in Sarajevo, tried in Travnik with 65 accused, and in Tuzla, which was held in Bihać against 40 accused students. In these trials a number of professors were also accused. In the student trials most of the accused were Orthodox Christians, while a lesser number of Muslims and Catholics was tried too. Apart from many small-scale proceedings, there were a few bigger trials such as the one against Damjan Đurica with 36 people and Savo Ljubibratić with another 30 individuals, Nikola Kašiković and his family, as well as against Gligorije Jeftanović and his son Dušan. ② During the First World War in Bosnia and Herzegovina 17 individual and group lawsuits were organized. After the intelligence archives of the Serb officer Kosta Todorović were found in Loznica and in some other places on the occasion of the entrance of the army into Serbia in August of 1914, the authorities began arresting all those whose names were found on the lists of the confidants. The greatest high treason trial was held in Banja Luka against 156 Serbs, who were public, cultural and political workers from the whole of Bosnia and Herzegovina. It lasted from 3 November 1915 to 22 April 1916. According to the statistical data, 19 clergymen, 14 teachers, 5 professors, 2 doctors, 8 state officials, 32 merchants, 26 peasants and 12 students were brought to trial. The key role for the decision of the court was attributed to the specialist report of the intelligence expert, Georg Sertić, intelligence officer of the Command of the 15th Corps. In the conclusion of his report he stated that in Bosnia and Herzegovina from 1911 to 1914, and also during the first year of the war, an expansive, well organized and functional spy network was created, whose leadership was in the hands of the Serb intelligence officers and the "regional inspector" in Loznica, Captain, and later Major Kosta Todorović. The intelligence

---

① Bericht, 1914-16, pp. 146-147.
② Komandierende General in BHD, *Hochverat und Spionage-processe in BH*, Wien, 1917, 3 Manuscript in the Library of ABH.

service was conceived for the times of peace and war. The damaging consequences of these high treason activities for the operations of the k. u. k. army had become evident in the first year of the war. The expansive intelligence gathering activities were supported, and furthermore even carried out by the People's defence and other Serb organizations. For the accused in the trial the last point of the report was of crucial significance. "Considering that and the circumstances, that the intelligence confidents were engaged in peace-time specially for the case of war and that the intelligence service organized by Todorović during the times of outstanding military measures in 1912 and 1913, and that it functioned during this war against Serbia, Sertić concluded that the confidents who were organized by Todorović, if they had not been interned immediately in the beginning of the war, were taken as hostages or invited into the army so that they could perform the same tasks in war-time".① By the court verdict which was reached on 22 April 1916, 16 persons were condemned to death by hanging, and other to prison sentences lasting from 3 to 20 years. With the interventions from the outside, the death penalties were reduced to life imprisonment. ② Beside that, the convicts were ordered to pay 14,644,769 crones to the budget of Bosnia and Herzegovina as a compensation for the expenses incurred for the domestic refugees from border counties and as a compensation for the upkeep of the poor family members of mobilized soldiers. ③

In the First World War Bosnia and Herzegovina gave many fighting units whose military value became almost legendary on all battlefronts. On the fronts of Austria, Isonzo, Tyrol, in Russia, Serbia, Montenegro and Albania, they were always among the first ones, the bravest of the brave, representing an example of the ideal soldier. After the mobilization of 1914, the military conscripts from Bosnia and Herzegovina were arranged into the formation of the 4th BH (Bosnian-Herzegovinian) regiment and one BH hunting battalion. In November of 1914 the command of the Balkan military forces used the surplus of individuals who were mobilized in Bosnia and Herzegovina in order to form fort infantry battalions No. 1 and 2. In March of 1915 the mobilized

---

① Horst Haselsteiner, Prozess Banja Luka 1916. Militärgutachten, Zbornik radova s međunarodnog skupa Veleizdajnički proces u Banjaluci 1915-1916, Institut za istoriju, Banjaluka, 1987, pp. 151-152.
② Kapidžić, 1959, p. 17.
③ Slijepčević, 1929, p. 239.

conscripts were used to create fort infantry battalions Nos. 3-7, whereas in March of 1916 two more formed (Nos. 8 and 9).① In August of 1915 on the South-Western front two reserve BH regiments were used to create BH hunting battalions Nos. 2 and 3, with four war units and one firearms department with two guns. In each unit 33% of absolutely reliable Orthodox Christians were to be deployed, and up to 67% of soldiers of other confessions. Each of the hunting battalions were to be given by the k. u. k. Ministry of War a number of 1,100 repetition rifles. B-H hunting battalions 2 and 3, as well as the 5th battalion of the 1st-4th BH regiments, were supposed to receive an additional war unit per month. In February of 1916 another five BH hunting battalions were formed. The BH battalion No. 4 was created from the fort infantry battalion No. 4, and hunting battalions No. 5, 6, 7 and 8 were formed from the 5th battalion of BH infantry regiments No. 1, 2, 3, and 4.② The High Military Command of the Austro-Hungarian army immediately undertook preventive measures with the BH units. Each BH regiment could form only two war battalions made up of reliable persons, whereby the battalions were usually made up from an average of 26% Catholics, 41% Orthodox Christians and 32% Muslims, which also matched the confessional structure of the population. Beside that, the High Military Command ordered that 4 reserve BH battalions be formed, 1st, 2nd and 4th in Budapest and the 3rd in Vienna. From the remaining conscripts unarmed working units were to be formed.③

In the first war year the BH units were arranged in various divisions, fighting on the Balkan front, engaging in battle against the Serb forces on the territory of Serbia and Eastern Bosnia, as well as on the Eastern front (on the battlefields of Galicia, Poland and the Carpathians). In the military operations on the Balkan front the 3rd battalion of BH regiments was involved and it was within the 48th infantry division. In the fight near the beech for the hill 552 on 25 November, an esteemed role was played by the commander of the artillery division of the 3rd battalion, 2nd BH regiment, first

---

① Franek, 1933, p. 22.
② ABH, ZMF, Präs. BH 1916, 108. *Aufstellung der bosnisch-herzegowinischen Feldjägerbaone Nr 4 bis 8*, k. u. k. Ministry of War to the Common Ministry of Finances, Vienna, 31 January 1916.
③ Ö. St. A., KA-W, KM, AOK, Op. Nr 13.784, k. u. k. Ministry of War to the Common Ministry of Finances, Vienna, 5 August 1915.

lieutenant Gojkomir Glogovac, who was awarded the Maria-Theresa medal and a nobility rank—he was proclaimed as the first Bosnian knight with the title of baron. ① The 3rd BH regiment in Galicia was involved in battles near Lemberg from 9 to 14 September 1914. In the woods east of Szezerzec the regiment incurred great losses, and then with all other units retreated into the Carpathians. During the retreat, the units caught cholera and in a matter of days more than a quarter of the soldiers died. ② The 3rd BH regiment went through the most difficult times of war on 21 October 1914. That day the regiment received the order to attack the hill 688 on the side towards the east and the slope on the west towards the road Turku-Samobor. After the battle it was recorded that in the 4th battalion the 13th unit had only 24 soldiers, 14th unit 4, 15th unit 30, and the 16th unit only 15 soldiers. ③ In the second and third war year the BH units were arranged and engaged on the Balkan, Eastern and South-Western front. In the 48th infantry division, from a total number of $19\frac{1}{2}$ battalions, $8\frac{1}{4}$ came from the BH contingent. After the 5th battalion of the 3rd BH regiment took Solar and penetrated the Montenegrin positions on 9 January, the outcome of the battle for Cetinje was settled, and Montenegro capitulated on 13 January 1916. ④ On the Eastern front during 1916 the BH units fought with varying degrees of success, suffering great losses in the great Russian summer offensive. In the battles on the Italian fronts, the BH units stood out on account of their war efforts. The 2nd BH regiment took the well-

---

① Gandini, 1968, p. 29; Schahinger, 1996, pp. 55–57; *Kapetan Gojkomir baron Glogovac, prvibosanskivitezordena Marije Terezije*, Sarajevski list, No. 229, 19 September 1917, p. 1.

② Pero Blašković, 1939, pp. 119–122.

③ Blašković Pero, *Sa Bošnjacima u svetskom ratu*, Beograd 1939, p. 133.

④ Ö. St. A., KA-W, Nachlass Otto Wiesinger, Nr 13, *Der Kampf um das Lovćen 1914–16*, Wien, 1944, pp. 30–43.

fortified hill of Monte Melleta on 8 June 1916. ①

While on both sides the military efforts remained futile, the morale in the background weakened more and more. With greater impatience the public sought an answer to the question how long would the troubles last, placing themselves on the side of those who advised that the useless killing had to be stopped as soon as possible. Due to the difficulties in supplying of the Central Powers, the restlessness of population in the background grew. The death of Franz Joseph on 22 November 1916 opened a new epoch in the political history of the Monarchy. The war would, nevertheless, last for another two full years. The change on the throne was met with indifference and exhaustion. The population in the Monarchy had other worries. The war euphoria had already passed and all the attention was focused to the everyday fight for survival. ② The heir to Franz Joseph's throne, Charles, had a programme but not enough energy to implement it completely. As soon as he came to power he ended the regime of pressure which stifled the public life. Even though the requests of the national minorities had not yet been presented, the Emperor Charles felt the danger that they carried. The economic difficulties worsened, and Hungary, which could have offered help, chose to keep the existing supplies for itself. The solidarity between the two parts of the Monarchy did not exist any more. Charles was also unsuccessful in attempting to finish the negotiations with Great Britain and France, so the war continued with even more gloomy perspectives. ③ After general Sarkotić informed the

---

① Ö. St. A., KA-W, NFA Gefechts-Berichte, Bh IR 2, *Gefechtsberichtüber die Erstürmung des Mte. Melleta am 7/6 1916*, 85; Schachinger, 1996, p. 93; Gandini, 1982, pp. 41-42. The battle of Monte Melleta— day of special sacrifice became the traditional remembrance day for the 2nd BH regiment. The anniversary is marked every year thus surpassing the significance of a historic event. The only exception was made during the reign of national-socialists in Austria from 1938 to 1945. After the Second World War, the surviving members of the 2nd BH regiment continued the tradition of making the battle for Monte Melleta. This anniversary is marked every year in the Garrison church in Graz, on the first Friday in June which becomes the centre of gathering for Bosnians and Herzegovinians from all around the World. On this day, the perished and killed soldiers of the 2nd BH regiment are honoured and the Friday prayer is held. This traditional meeting is organized by the Austrian Society for Bosnian-Herzegovinian relations of the successors of the tradition of the 2nd BH regiment, the commanding battalion one with the Economy Chamber of Styria, with the basic principles to connect people, spread tolerance among races and religions and to search for the things that connect them and contribute to maintenance of peace. (Z. Šehić, 1999, p. 102).

② Wagner, 1995, p. 185.

③ Renouvin, 1965, p. 403.

k. u. k. Ministry of War in mid April 1917 that in the regions of Bileća, Trebinje and Rogatica public unrest was recorded, and as a precaution the High Military Command was ordered to move one battalion to that area. On the request of the High Military Command an investigation was carried out and it was established that the tense situation had diminished and that it was caused by the resonances of the Revolution in Russia, entering of the USA into the war, and thus a hope was born among the Orthodox Christians since they had difficulties in obtaining supplies. ①

The arid and fruitless year of 1916 had significant consequences on the events in Bosnia and Herzegovina during the following year. It was accompanied by hunger, especially among the population in urban areas, in passive regions and in villages. Thus there were recorded instances of people, and particularly children and the elderly, dying of hunger. ② In the spring of 1917 the reports of the regional representatives and the Police direction to the Provincial Government in Sarajevo spoke about the difficult situation in the land due to the bad nutrition of the population. The governmental reports for March and April of 1917 portrayed a defeating picture. Depression and war exhaustion appeared as direct consequences of this situation. ③During 1917 the condition in the nourishment of the Bosnian and Herzegovinian population worsened to such an extent that the very existence had been completely threatened. Due to the high snowfall, the delivery of food supplies, which were already short at the time, became even more challenging. General Sarkotić considered that the situation was very serious. On his emergent appeal for the delivery of food supplies, the Hungarian minister of economy answered with excuses citing transport difficulties as justification. By the end of February 1917 the gendarmerie reported about more death cases caused by famine. Due to malnutrition the population suffered general weakness and depression. ④ This situation had a negative effect on the discipline and public morale, and more cases were recorded of war profiteering.

---

① ABH, ZMF, Präs. BH 815, *Gärungunter der Bevölkerung der BezirkeBileća, Trebinje und Rogatica*. k. u. k. Ministry of War to the Common Ministry of Finances, Vienna, 25 May 1917.
② ABH, ZMF, Präs. BH 1917, p. 440. Cf. Kapidžić, 1959, p. 20.
③ ABH, ZMF, Präs. BH 1917, p. 573.
④ Signe Klein, *Freiherr Sarkotić von Lovćen: Die Zeit seiner Verwaltung in Bosnien-Herzegovina von 1914, bis 1918*, Neobjavljena doktorska disertacija odbranjena na Bečkon univerzitetu, 1964, p. 170.

During May the number of death cases due to malnutrition had increased. The repeated drought had a bad impact on the summer harvest and the situation kept worsening. The population only partially undertook measures of self-help, and those were mostly Orthodox Christians. The Muslims and Catholics fell into apathy, expecting the Provincial Government to undertake measures for providing help. In order to ensure the nutrition of the population, the Provincial Government of Bosnia and Herzegovina resorted to various measures of which some included irrespective requisitions, which caused bitterness among one part of the population. The low prices for the seized goods brought great losses to producers. General Sarkotić attempted to organize the distribution of supplies better in the interior of the land, trying to avoid austerity. The rationing of goods was small and kept decreasing with time. The small delivery from Hungary, four to six wagons daily, ended up almost completely in Herzegovina where the situation had become critical. The daily need for food amounted to 25 wagons. However, all the interventions of General Sarkotić remained unsuccessful. Eventually, on 4 December 1917 the Provincial Government could count on help from the Military Command amounting to 90 wagons of flour, with a delivery of three wagons per day.[①] The economic difficulties had significant consequences on the political life in the country. During 1917 livelier political movements in the Monarchy arrived, which had an effect on the activities in Bosnia and Herzegovina. The long duration of the war, the exhaustion of all the layers of population and the dangers of revolutionary activities under the influence from Russia, forced the political circles of the Monarchy to appeasement, so in certain states the parliaments were revived. In May of 1917 the parliament in Vienna was summoned, and somewhat later the Croatian parliament as well. The change on the throne made it somewhat easier, and this was also reflected on the political movements in Bosnia and Herzegovina. The resolution of the Yugoslav club in the Vienna parliament greatly contributed to the revival of political life. It was passed on 30 May 1917 and it concerned the unification of Yugoslav lands of the Monarchy under the sceptre of the Habsburgs. The May declaration posed the question of the unification of the South-Slavic lands, which was in contradiction with official standpoints of the Austrian and

---

① Signe Klein, 1964, p. 172.

Hungarian politicians.① The ideas contained in the May Declaration were considered as unsatisfactory by the Serb political circles, since they anticipated the creation of a state on the Habsburg South. However, the development of the political situation in the world, as well as the relations between the political groups in emigration were unfavourable for the political line of Nikola Pašić and the radical party in Serbia, because of the fall of imperialism in Russia and the breakdown of the Russian front, the main support of their foreign policy was lost. This meant that they were forced to compromise. On the meeting of Serb political parties and members of the Yugoslav committee on Corfu an agreement was reached about the future arrangement of the country. The Corfu declaration from 20 July 1917, defined that the future state would be organized as a unitarist, parliamentary monarchy with the name the Kingdom of Serbs, Croats and Slovenes. The principle of civil and religious equality, along with certain self-administration was emphasized. ②

Socially and politically, the soldier came more and more under the influence of events in the background. On one side, the images of distress of civilians, women standing in long queues for supplies, bread, and on other side the image of those who were not hit by war circumstances and who earned really well from it. ③ Because of that, a great number of desertions of soldiers at the front were recorded and against them certain legal measures were undertaken. Thus, it was foreseen that for those "who, as military servicemen, flee to the enemy or to foreign authorities that threaten the Austro-Hungarian Monarchy with war or who, during the war or threat of war or during internal turmoil, takes up arms against the Monarchy or against her allies, or who helps spying, or are in any other way available to the opposing army or who commit the crime of high treason, will be obliged for their deed to compensate the caused damage to the provincial budget." To secure the compensation for the provincial budget, personal property and real estate of the accused person could have been taken if based on trustworthy facts the suspicion was confirmed that a crime had been committed. The district court decided on the confiscation on the suggestion of the

---

① Kapidžić, 1968, p. 24.
② Fuad Slipičević, *Prvi svjetski rat i stvaranje države jugoslovenskih naroda*, Sarajevo, 1957, pp. 87-88.
③ Friz, 1931, pp. 71-72.

state attorney at the meeting of three judges and the conclusion was supposed to be published in the Official Gazette. ①

In the beginning of 1918 in Western states and in Italy there was a parole "victory by all means". In the Monarchy people only spoke about "peace by all means". The pacifistic manifestations met an ideal climate in the industrial areas of the Monarchy, where there was winter, famine and disease, and where the administration was powerless in the face of smuggling and corruption. ② The position of the Central Powers worsened, and the morale of the people in the background diminished. The expectation of a positive outcome of the war became unrealistic. The consequence was the dissolution of the army, especially where national and social ideas were accepted by the soldiers at the front, which manifested itself through revolts, desertion and the formation of gangs made up from deserters and soldiers who outstayed their allowed leave. In the last war year the number of desertions, and rebellions in the South-Slavic regions significantly increased. The first uprisings and revolts in Bosnia and Herzegovina happened on 10 February 1918 in Mostar, among the soldiers from Dalmatia of the 22nd infantry regiment, and soon in Čapljina and Konjic. ③ The rebellions and the breach of discipline had political, social and military causes. The national aims, strengthened by the propaganda of Entente forces, brought into question the existing legal system in the state. The spreading of Bolshevik ideas by the returnees intensified the bitterness against the state, especially among the soldiers who accepted the Bolshevik propaganda, which was not left without consequences. If the returnee established that back home misery and poverty reigned, or that his family life had been destroyed, his dissatisfaction grew, and this influenced his decision not to return back to the army after his leave, and to desert. Due to this cases of desertion multiplied, and the deserters were met with sympathetic attitudes

---

① The order of the k. u. k Common Ministry of Finances from 24 October 1917 on the response for the damage caused trough treason, approved in a decision from 18 October 1917, *Glasnikzakona i naredbiza Bosnu i Hercegovinu*, pp. 343–346.

② Ingomar Pust, *Die Steinerne Front: Auf der Spuren des Gebirgskrieges in den Julische Alpen, Von Isonzo zur Piave*, Graz, 1980, p. 286.

③ Plaschka-Haselsteiner-Suppan, 1974, I, pp. 148–156.

from the population which aided them and hid them from the authorities.① Further signs of breach of conduct was the increased number of desertions and exceeding of allowed leave. Accusations of trade with falsified documents were frequently heard of. The documents were sold at a price from 30 to 80 crones. The numerous controls, hired detectives and military patrols were of no help since the patrols often showed solidarity with the deserters. The awards announced for the capture of deserters did not help much because the deserters were protected and hidden by the population. Because of this emergency measures were undertaken through the formation of special control stations. Beside that, soldiers went for leave in an organized fashion in larger transport groups, under the supervision of trustworthy petty officers and under the strict control of papers, other propaganda materials and illegal possession of firearms.②

The diet of population during 1918 became a much more important factor which brought into question the legal system in the country. The delegation of the Council for the nourishment of peoples in Bosnia and Herzegovina submitted on 10 March 1918 in Vienna to Emperor Charles a Memorandum with the plea of the Bosnian and Herzegovinian population requesting that the food conditions and circumstances for the cultivation of land and sowing improve as soon as possible. In the Memorandum it was stated that for the fourth year of the war the people of Bosnia and Herzegovina with remarkable patience and dedication bore the heavy brunt of poverty and lived with a smaller diet of bread than any other people in the Monarchy, even though the great drought in the previous year destroyed crops in many parts of the land. Also, it was stated that the Hungarian government helped in these difficult circumstances, but that the help from that year could not, unfortunately, even come close to covering the most modest needs of the people, so that on average only 2 to 3 kilos of food were given per person, and when it is taken into consideration that the population of larger cities and working people had to be supplied with a complete and stronger meal, then the available food for the rest of the population was significantly diminished. Due to the drought the potato yield completely failed, so that the necessity for seeds could not be

---

① OULK, 1937, p. 44.
② Ibid., p. 78.

covered. At the same time, the population in Herzegovina and Krajina, and the Eastern regions of Central Bosnia which were directly hit by war, did not have seeds for barley, oats, corn and millet, requesting that the cattle requisitions cease or be reduced significantly until the cultivation of land was finished, so that the difference in price between the cost of the cattle that the military command paid in Bosnia and Herzegovina and other parts of the Monarchy be settled. Concluding that the people of Bosnia and Herzegovina came to the ultimate limits of their endurance and that they began dying from famine in greater numbers, the Council for nutrition requested that flour, corn and potatoes should be given to the people of Bosnia and Herzegovina for the following four months since they suffered the most at that moment, and that necessary amounts of seeds should be acquired in time. This request was presented to the Emperor with the emphasis that the people of Bosnia and Herzegovina bore all the difficulties of war with remarkable perseverance, that its soldiers fought on all battlefronts with outstanding courage and that they were still fighting for the defence of the Monarchy. ①

In the beginning of March 1918 the county office in Zvornik reported to the regional organs in Tuzla that lately the numbers of desertion cases and unauthorized overstay of allowed leave by military conscripts increased. It was stated that many individuals overstayed their leave without proper authorization for a matter of several months, and that they were again brought to their units only after the gendarmerie undertook certain measures. After the population was made aware on several occasions about the difficult consequences of hiding such persons, the deserters found a different way to escape returning to the front. In the forests on Majevica they found refuge and hid during the day, and during the night they would receive food from their supporters. In that way, the gendarmerie caught 18 deserters from 13 January to 27 February, apprehending them to the Military Command in Tuzla. Even though deserters were sent to quarantine in Doboj, they all soon appeared in their hometowns. ② The regional office in Tuzla reported that certain deserters escaped from

---

① ABH, Priv. Reg. 90/1918. *Memorandum der Deputation des Ernährungsratesaus BH überreichts am 10. mart 1918.*

② ABH, ZV BH Präs. 1918, 3.651. Deserteure, Umtriebe. The county office in Zvornik to the Regional organs in Tuzla, Zvornik, 9 March 1918.

the quarantine in Doboj on three or four occasions. Since the quarantine was closed due to the outbreak of epidemic disease, the deserters were sent to Tuzla before being allowed back to their units. One of the reasons for the unauthorized overstay was that the soldier did not receive food for his trip during the leave which lasted for four or more days. According to the information of the High Command, during January 360 individuals were sent to their units, and in February 420. The greatest number of deserters was recorded among the Muslims, somewhat less among the Orthodox Christians, and the least amount among the Catholics. From that it can be concluded that this problem was not politically motivated. The breach of law was recorded only in individual circumstances. ① One command of the "Streifskorps" was sent to Bosanski Petrovac and Bosanska Gradiška each. This remained without significant effect as was shown by the number of apprehended deserters. During May 1918 in Bosanski Novi and Dobrljin 392 were imprisoned, in Banja Luka 95 on 25 June, and on the same day in Tuzla 77 deserters, and in Brčko 44. The total number of imprisoned in Brčko until April amounted to over 400 persons. It was even reported that one petty officer in the uniform of a lieutenant took leadership of the rebels. ②

The most important difficulty was presented by the linking of deserters and soldiers who outstayed their allowed leave into armed groups, the "green cadre", becoming an important source of unrest and a true threat to the security in the background. The populace, without enough supplies, caught in national and socialist propaganda, was disturbed by the fact that it was constantly persecuted. Apart from this, all those who intended to desert or outstay their allowed leave, or were simply tired of war, knew that they would find a good reception and support among the "green cadre". ③

The formation of such groups in Bosnia and Herzegovina multiplied. The proof for this was one complaint of the Provincial Government of Bosnia and Herzegovina about these groups in North-Western parts of Bosnia, where they committed numerous criminal attacks and thefts of cattle, confronting the gendarmerie with arms. The

---

① Ibid., The regional organs of Tuzla to the presidency of the Provincial Government of Bosnia and Herzegovina in Sarajevo, 17 March 1918.
② ABH, ZMF, Priv. Reg. 264, 1918.
③ Signe Klein, 1964, p. 8.

largest number of attacks was recorded from the territory of Montenegro and Serbia, from where numerous incursions into border areas of Bosnia and Herzegovina were undertaken. Often these were purely bandit groups. Also, the committee units became important. Their goals were mostly of political nature. The Provincial Government in Bosnia and Herzegovina ordered that the gendarmerie stations should be strengthened and that punishment expeditions should be sent to the affected areas. Soon, the deserters formed gangs which began gaining significance and more and more resembling the "green cadre" in Croatia and Slavonia. The accompanying activity was smuggling of arms and weapons from the army to the background.① The formation of gangs from the deserters also had political consequences. The security situation in the background diminished the authority of the government and the army, which in turn had as a consequence the weakening of links with the Monarchy and the creation of the fertile ground for the spreading of national and socialist ideas. In a report directed to the High Military Command on 24 June 1918, General Sarkotić gave a general impression about mood in Bosnia and Herzegovina and the events that influenced the disturbance of public peace and order. Various combinations linked to the South-Slavic issue and especially the future destiny of the country, as well as the bad supply conditions, influenced the increased dissatisfaction of the population.

During 1917 the greatest number of Bosnian and Herzegovinian units was engaged at the Italian front where they played an important role in the autumn offensive of the Central Powers. In the composition of the 50th infantry division, the 1st Bosnian-Herzegovinian regiment moved in the direction of Volarje, where they penetrated the Italian positions in three places, moving deep into the background of their units. Soon they occupied all the important positions held by the Italians. The result of the 12th Isonzo battle was that in four days the front of a 160 km was broken, two Italian armies were destroyed and 60,000 soldiers were captured with 500 guns. The Italian army saved itself by retreating.② After the 4th battalion of the 3rd Bosnian-Herzegovinian regiment made a raid over the bridge across Tagliamento, allowing the

---

① ABH, ZMF, Präs. BH 1918, 510. General in command in Bosnia, Herzegovina and Dalmatia to the High Command, Sarajevo 8 June 1918.

② Ö. St. A., KA-W, Nachlass Otto Wiesinger, Nr 11. *Der Anteil des bh IR 1 am Siege von Karfreit*, 14-15.

penetration of numerous Austro-Hungarian and German divisions, and the conquest of Italian positions all up to Piava.

In the beginning of 1918, war fatigue, poor supplying of the military, and the bad health conditions caused a great number of death cases and illnesses among the soldiers, especially in the reserve units. It was concluded that sanitary measures should be undertaken emergently. The commission cited the circumstances which should be taken into consideration, and these were that the Bosnian and Herzegovinian population was at the lowest level of undernourishment, and that a large portion of the people suffered from tuberculosis. The general lack of life supplies did not allow the improvement of dietary conditions. The lack of shoes, clothes and underwear, prevented the implementation of the minimal sanitary measures. The aid workers and soldiers who performed guard service were under great strain, and from them the building engineering divisions were created. They were often burdened with heavier tasks than the troops which were at the front. The Bosnian and Herzegovinian populace was especially subject to all kinds of diseases due to the long lasting of war, which was linked with the portrayed situation. A particular problem was the returning fever of which 3 to 4 soldiers died per day, so a request was sent that these units be given the necessary medical staff. [1]

The supplying of the military on the front worsened every day. From 9 January 1918 the daily portion of salt was decreased to 1 gr, and from 6 March for the formations in the background and development troops one day in the week was without meat, and from 1 August 1918 this was extended to the second day as well. At the same time, the portion of meat was decreased to 100 gr. Not even such diminished portions could be ensured at all times. Often the portion of bread was only 350 gr for the fighting troops, and for the development troops 200 gr, only 71 gr of vegetables, 250 gr of meat, and food for livestock was only 1 kg per day. [2]

Beside the social situation, an important place in the complex of factors which complicated the circumstances in the Monarchy was played by the propaganda activities of the Entente forces. According to the project of its International commission

---

[1] ABH, ZMF, Präs. BH 1918, 187, 8 March 1918.
[2] Ö. St. A., KA-W, Ms, Carnegie Stiftung, 2, 46.

for propaganda, on the Congress of the Peoples of the Austro-Hungarian Monarchy, held in Rome from 8 to 10 April 1918, decisions were reached concerning the spreading of propaganda among the Austro-Hungarian troops. It was supposed to be implemented through proclamations, brochures and images, which would be thrown out of airplanes; by newspapers, revues and brochures which would be published in German, Hungarian, Czech, Polish and Serbo-Croatian language; by the sending of pacifists and defeatists who were able to influence the public; as well as by aiding various committees in Paris and London and the nationalistic agitation in the Habsburg Monarchy. The Yugoslav section of the Committee had to propagate the ethnic and linguistic unity of Yugoslavs, the Corfu declaration and the creation of the Yugoslav state, to write about the high treason trials, about Yugoslav sacrifices in order to satisfy German ambitions, about the crimes committed by the Austro-Hungarian government...[①] In the Yugoslav vanguard propaganda units, the scouts were armed with carabines and big knives, such as the ones used by the Bosnian-Herzegovinian units for fighting in trenches and caverns. They carried tromblones, in which they placed mines with leaflets; they had megaphones which they used to agitate with words and songs. Instead of printed flyers, they often threw written messages into trenches, especially if they wanted them to be written by Austro-Hungarian officers and soldiers who surrendered. The strongest propaganda means was the fact that Austro-Hungarian soldiers in trenches knew that the soldiers on the Italian side received better food. [②]

During August of 1918, moderate desertions were noticed among the Bosnian and Herzegovinian soldiers, exclusively of Orthodox Christians. The reason for this was dissatisfaction with the situation on the front rather than propaganda of the opponents. First of all, the soldiers were facing real famine. The food that the soldiers got was not sufficient and the meat was often useless for eating. Daily, soldiers received from 300 gr to 500 gr bread, and frequently, for breakfast and supper, only coffee. Officers were well supplied which caused great discontent among soldiers. The lately appointed Hungarian officers who did not speak the language of the soldiers influenced the growth of discontent. Almost two years of forbidden leave contributed to the bad mood

---

① Hrabak, 1980, pp. 166-167.
② Ibid., p. 181.

among the soldiers. Before each offensive, they had been promised allowed leave, only when they got to the reserve positions and submitted their requests, were they told that their requests were declined with the explanation that the ban on leave was in force. The news from home about the amount of aliment for families which had not been paid regularly or was stopped being paid completely additionally influenced the discontent of soldiers. Tobacco was not delivered regularly and the soldiers neither got new underwear nor aids for washing of the ones they possessed. ①

From the statements of Bosnian and Herzegovinian soldiers about the "green cadre", it can be concluded that the "green cadre" represented an organization of deserters, those who outstayed their allowed leave and who hid in the forests and lived from thefts and robberies. This organization functioned only during the summer months. In autumn they returned to their units to spend the winter in warmth. The groups were made of 10-15 people who spent together one week and then departed. The trade with falsified documents-permit for leave was a generally known issue. One soldier reported that he head heard two others arranging to steal the permits for leave from the comrades who were sleeping at the time. ②

Based on this summary about the organization of "green cadre", made up of deserters and those who outstayed the allowed leave, it was suggested to undertake, necessary measures and to pay attention to the evidence of leave, to always control people on the stations, to search in detail and conduct raids as well as to authorise the financial guards and gendarmerie to check military documents. ③ The general situation in the background created opportunities for the outbreak of unrest and circumstances which endangered the public peace and order, and when they spread to front, they significantly influenced discipline in military formations. The Provincial Government for Bosnia and Herzegovina passed an announcement about court, criminal and

---

① Ö. St. A., KA-W, KM, AOK, Op. 111.625. The Police direction to the Provincial Government of Bosnia and Herzegovina, Sarajevo 28 August 1918.

② Ö. St. A., KA-W, KM, AOK Op. 108.961, Resümmeüberdie Organisation des "Zeleni Kader" aus Deserteuren und Urlaubsüberschreitern, The Commanding General in BHD to the k. u. k. Ministry of War, Sarajevo, 5 July 1918.

③ Ibid., "Zeleni Kader." The High Army Command to the k. u. k. Ministry of War, Baden 15 July 1918, transcript.

administrative persecution of those who helped military fugitives and those who overstayed their allowed military leave. Providing help, hiding or nor reporting a bout military fugitives and those who outstayed their leave, as well as any other kind of helping those people was implied in the strictest court and criminal persecution. Apart from these measures, the families of military fugitives and also those who did not report the ones who had committed a punishable deed were deprived of the support. If there was founded suspicion that certain individuals, families or even whole municipalities helped the military fugitives and those who outstayed their allowed leave, hiding them or not reporting them to the authorities were punished with noticeable administrative penalties. ① In fear that deserters might connect with population, General Sarkotić introduced court-martial in bordering areas, in counties of Foča, Gacko, Bileća, Trebinje, Nevesinje and Stolac. All weapon certificates were proclaimed invalid and all arms should be submitted to police organs within eight days. Illegal possession of arms was severely punished. Also, threatening public security was harshly punished, the violation of military discipline in units, murder, public violence, destroying of housings and property as well as robbery if the value of the stolen items did not exceed 1,000 crones. The court-martial could have been established because of desertion without asking for a permission of higher organs, on the basis of an independent situation evaluation. ② Military forces stationed in the country were engaged for the immediate suppression of robbery in Bosnia and Herzegovina. In mid August, the High Military Command undertook measures to suppress desertion and soldiers were to be acquainted with the consequences for desertion and outstay of allowed leave. ③Also, all troop commands were ordered to stop the payment of aliments for families of deserters and to search for a suitable way to suppress help for deserters, chasing the fugitives. ④

---

① ABH, ZMF, BH 802. *Bekämpfung des Deserteurunwesens*, Provincial Government of Bosnia and Herzegovina, Publication of the order from 19 May 1918 about the judicial, penal and administrative prosecution.
② Ö. St. A., KA-W, KM, AOK, Op. 108.900. *Standes-Recht in BH*.
③ ABH, ZMF, Präs. BH 1918, 802. *Bekämpfung des Deserteur-unwesens*, The Provincial Government of Bosnia and Herzegovina to the Common Ministry of Finances, Sarajevo, 20 September 1918.
④ Ibid., *Deserteure und Urlaubüberschreiter, Bedrohung der öffentlichen und der Sicherheit des durchihr Unwesen*.

At the beginning of September 1918, the High command in Sarajevo announced the order which anticipated court and criminal persecutions and denial of help for the families of deserters. A telegram was sent by the Provincial government for Bosnia and Herzegovina to the county offices in Prijedor, Bosanska Dubica, Bosanska Gradiška, Prnjavor and Banja Luka, announcing court-martial in these places. This order implied the death sentence for the act of high treason, killing, arson, robbery, adding outlaws and theft.① In order to improve the control of military officers on their travels and for female workforce on military positions, special passes were introduced. For military officers who travelled, as travel documents served opened warrants with the inscribed final destination and permission to leave.

Tickets had to be clipped whereby the travel warrant should be shown on the request of military and civil controls. Every unauthorised change in the text of the travel document was strictly prohibited and every sale or giving it as a gift was punished and apprehension to the court-martial. Along with the permission for leave and the travel warrant the female workforce at the army also had to show their identification card with a photograph.② During 1918 the k. u. k. Ministry of War issued several instructions for the functioning of the official control for the travelling of military officers and the directives for watch patrols. The aim of these small departments was to prevent acts of sabotage, agitation and to capture and conduct deserters and war prisoners, to control travel documents of military officers and especially permissions for leave. These units were supposed to ensure order on the railway and postal stations, as well as in the trains, especially during the return of war prisoners from the Eastern front. The rules of the military service, way of conduct in cases of all felonies towards the offenders, were determined in the instructions, defining the command and organizational functioning of these patrols. The rights and

---

① Ibid., Transcription of the telegram issued by the Provincial Government for Bosnia and Herzegovina from 8 September 1918 to the county offices in Prijedor, Bosanska Dubica, Bosanska Gradiška, Prnjavor, county court in Banja Luka and county organs in Banja Luka, Provincial Government of Bosnia and Herzegovina, Sarajevo, 8 September 1918.

② ABH, ZV BH, 1918, 12.791. *Belehrungfürreisende Militär- (Landwehr-, Landsturm-) Personen und weibliche Hilfskräftebeimilitärischen Stellen*; *Behandlung von mil. Ausweispapieren*, The Provincial Government of Bosnia and Herzegovina to the Common Ministry of Finances, Sarajevo, 15 October 1918.

obligations of the members of these units were determined, along with their right to use firearms, the stations of the control organs, the way of controlling the valid travel documents, as well as the measures of their personal defence. Measures of cooperation with military and civil organs were also determined, the conduct in case of entering houses and shops of citizens in pursuit of felons. Also, the rules established the way of conduct in the internal service of these organs, the activities of command of road control in informing, apprehending and punishing of those who were arrested. In the end, the material rights of the patrol members were also defined. They received daily a ration of bread and tobacco, as well as a salary of 6 crones for the officers and aspiring officers, 5 for petty officers and 3 for soldiers. On their travels, the officers were accompanied by their batmen. Particular attention was to be paid to cases of agitation of socialist or revolutionary ideas among the populace. For the detained deserters rewards were handed out. ① The traveling supervision units had the same range of activities but not the supervision over the traveling control patrols. This patrols was made up of one officer and six people of which one was the clerk who noted the minutes. Their rules of service were stricter than of the ordinary road patrols. ② Particular rules were made for transport. The signs and consignment sheets for the commanders of transport and competent dispatchers in the stations were also established. The orders about the apprehended deserters were elaborated in detail. ③ The High Command in Sarajevo suggested to the Army high command on 4 September 1918 to abolish the court-martial for offences that do not surpass 1,000 crones, and only for Sarajevo and Mostar, since in other parts of the Monarchy no death sentences were proclaimed for petty thefts, which was accepted by the k. u. k. Ministry of War in Vienna on 2 October 1918. ④ During September 1918, gendarmerie in Bosnia and Herzegovina caught 619 deserters, 2,540 military servicemen who outstayed their allowed leave, and 524 runaway war prisoners, whereas the control organs detained

---

① ABH, ZV BH, Präs. 1918, 12.968. *Instruktionfür den ambulanten Reisekontrolldienst in Österreichdurch Militärpersonen*, 1–19. Cf. B. Hrabak, 1980, p. 73.

② Ö. St. A., KA-W, MKSM, 78-1/3, *Instruktionfürfahrende Überwachpatrouillen*, 1918.

③ Ö. St. A., KA-W, MKSM, 78 - 1/3, *Merkblattfür Transporteabfertigende Stellen und Transport-Komandanten*, pp. 1–20.

④ Milorad Ekmečić, *Stvaranja Jugoslavije*, II, Beograd, 1989, p. 798.

2,367 fugitives and 4,757 soldiers who outstayed their allowed leave. In order to prevent the support for the deserters coming from their families, the authorities imposed obligations in the submitting of cattle and food to those households which contained soldiers who outstayed their allowed leave. The lack of food and the dangers of famine within their families proved to be the most effective measures, especially in Herzegovina so that in Ljubuški a total of 149 fugitives voluntarily reported to the regional offices.① By mid-October of 1918 discipline measures in Bosnia and Herzegovina had waned significantly. General Sarkotić feared the "green cadre" in North-Western Bosnia, so his headquarters was regrouped in the military region of Sarajevo, proclaiming war zones in various areas, including the county of Banja Luka with the district of Derventa, county Tuzla, districts Žepče and Zenica from the Travnik county, county Sarajevo without the county Fojnica, and the whole county of Mostar without the district of Ljubuški. Within these war zones stricter regulations regarding traffic were in place and passports were obligatory. The k. u. k. Ministry of War paid particular attention to the "green cadre" in Bosnia and Herzegovina, fearing that they might link with the neighbouring areas in Slavonia and Dalmatia. After the inspection, a special officer of the High Military Command confirmed Sarkotić's opinion that there were no connections between the various groups and that the main motive for desertion was more social than political in its nature. The attacks were mostly attacked against the wealthy individuals, while they did not undertake any kind of action or sabotage towards the organs of government.②

After the June offensive in the Venetian valley, the political and economic situation in the background reflected on the army. July and August of 1918 were months of famine at the front. Units had not seen a piece of meat or received an ounce of fat for days. After the harvest the situation had improved to an extent, since there was at least enough bread at that time. Nevertheless, it was often the case that complete units in the first lines desert with their equipment, hoping to receive an ounce of food more from their adversaries. In the trenches of 82nd infantry regiment one morning a deserter left a written note: "Until now none of us recoiled from the

---

① Bogumil Hrabak, *Dezerterstvo i zeleni kadar*, Novi Sad 1982, p. 215.
② Ibid., p. 216.

enemy, but now we cannot endure it anymore because of famine..."① The situation was even worse regarding clothing. Sleeveless shirts were a usual garment for soldiers. Sick from malaria they had to stand almost naked in the wind, waiting for their washed clothes to dry. Uniform and shoes were made from poor materials and crumbled as if they had been made from paper. One officer of the general headquarters found a unit behind the first line dressed only in their underwear, preparing for their service. Uniforms were assigned only to those who were at the front line. Even the officers who went for leave used to loan their uniforms. The undernourished populace was exposed to diseases. In the lower Piava and in Albania, the malaria decimated the units, which were later hit by Spanish flu. Troops of 100 soldiers were the exception, while they were usually only half the size. It can only be presumed with what kind of bitterness did the soldiers, who were sent to leave from that hell, view the nouveau riche—war profiteers. This kind of body was very suspect to psychological activities. The enemy continued his propaganda which caught extra bodies in its net every day. ②

The supplying of the army had an important effect on the discipline. The soldiers lost the motive of fighting for the Monarchy that treated them in such a way. First of all, the petty and junior officers began renouncing their oath. One could not expect discipline from a hungry soldier. When the number of desertions increased, pure military formations were engaged, the so-called *Asistenz-trupen* (troops, battalions), for the suppression of unrest in the background. Felons in military units were punished by their own police departments. ③

During 1918 revolts and desertions became an important factor of the internal stability of the Monarchy. The military units had the task to support the organs of public security and prevent turmoil. Appropriate measures were undertaken which were grounded in the Penal Military Law: "Whosoever opposes his superior with arms or acts violently towards a person in service, or opposes a received official order... in

---

① Horstenau von Edmung Glaise, *Die Katastrophe: Die Zerstümerung Österreich-Ungarns und das werden der Nachfolgenstaaten*, Zürich-Leipzig-Wien (O. J.), p. 332.
② Ibid., p. 574.
③ Bogumil Hrabak, 1982, p. 72.

war and in peace is to be punished with death by shooting. Whosoever in times of war, tacitly or offensively declines to perform an official order, is also punished with death by shooting. A soldier who, with an accomplice, acts against the existing official order, against his superiors and their orders, or if they only agree, are guilty of rebellion. For instigators and leaders of the rebellion the stipulated punishment is death by shooting." In case of rebellion, every participant who did not return after the announcement of the court-martial, was sentenced to death by shooting. If there were more participants, this sentence was to be carried out one every tenth person who was selected by a draw, whereas all the officers and petty officers, who were involved in the conspiracy, were also punished. ①The emergency state and the court-martial were directed towards the quickest procedure. Basically, the verdict could be death by shooting or release from the accusation. During the execution of a death sentence, the "soul carer", doctor and executioner were supposed to be present. ②

The last great battle of the First World War started on 24 October 1918. The charging units of the Entente forces—the British, French and Italians—carried out the first attack in the region of *Seven provinces* in the hills between Brenta and on the Piava. The Italian plan anticipated that naval columns penetrate to the valley near Feltre and in that way disrupt the connection between Tyrol and Venice. The other, stronger column was supposed to move over the Piava, and penetrate the opposition lines near Vitorio Veneto, perform an encompassing manoeuvre and crush them. The facilitating circumstance for the Entente military forces was the fact that the Austro-Hungarian army faced dissolution. The reserve units refused to go to the front line, and when after the political circumstances in Hungary Emperor Charles consented to detaching the Hungarian armed forces, their units were the first to begin abandoning the sinking ship. In the last offensive, the Enente forces numbered 51 Italian divisions, 5 British, 2 French and a Czech and American regiment. The main attack strength was made up of 22 divisions of the first, and 19 divisions of the second line (with 4 cavalry units), and 4,500 guns of all calibres. ③ On the opposing side, on

---

① Plaschka-Haselsteiner-Suppan; 1974, Bd. I, p. 31.
② Ibid., p. 32.
③ Josip Horvat, 1967, p. 567.

the Western and Southern sector of the Tyrolian front was the 10th army under the command of General Krobatin. On the sector of the Seven provinces was the 11st army of General Scheuchenstule. The group of General Borojević held the mountain area between Brenta and Piava, the 6th army of Schönburg-Hartensten the areas on Isonzo, whereas the group of General Wurm held the region of Piava to its estuary. The Habsburg army had 57.5 divisions with 300,000 soldiers, and together with the background units it numbered around 1,500,000 individuals. The artillery was weaker than the one of the Entente by about 800 to 1,000 weapons. At 4:00 in the morning of 24 October began the artillery, and around 7:00 the infantry attack of the Entente. Even though in reality the Monarchy did not exist any more, the units of all nations offered strong resistance until the last day, not because of loyalty to the Monarchy but because the units in the front line had no other choice, resisting more due to the instinct of self-defence. At the same time, the units in the background followed the instinct of keeping alive, refusing to die in vain during the last hours of the war. Although Emperor Charles sent a proclamation to the soldiers before the battle, announcing immediate peace and return home, pleading with them to keep their discipline, this appeal never reached the soldiers in the first battle lines. [1] Two days before the great battle, the brigade of the Croatian home guard division refused to exchange the people of the remaining two brigades on the front line. A few hours later in the group at Bellun the 4th BH regiment deserted with the explanation that "in his manifest to the peoples of the Monarchy the Emperor forgot their homeland and thus they had no reason to continue fighting". Similar things occurred at other fronts as well. West from Brenta three Hungarian regiments revolted and refused to march towards the positions near Asiagio. Since the news spread that the Emperor consented that the Hungarian troops can return home, it was impossible to keep the soldiers in their positions. From the 24 to 27 October the decision was reached. Parts of the British 7th division suppressed the frontal forces of the Habsburg guards under the hill Montella on the Piava on 24 October, and two days later they performed a charge. The British forces of the 10th army and the French troops of the 12nd army, and between them the Italians of the 8th army, defeated during the night the lines on the Piava.

---

[1] Josip Horvat, 1967, pp. 568-569.

Until noon of 27 October the British penetrated the front which was 12 km in length, and moved 4 km deep into the defence system. This concluded the last operation on the Italian front. In the evening of 28 October, the forces of the Entente took firmly the area on the region on the left side of Piava. One last final attempt was made to force the most loyal Habsburg forces, the Tyrolian Hungers and the Imperial riflers, into counterattack. When they met the Honvéd units which were returning to their homelands and realized that they were supposed to bleed even further, fighting for a lost cause, they decided that the war was finished for them as well. They evaluated the situation much better than the Army High Command. In the morning of 28 October the strongest artillery attack of the Entente forces began and it had fatal consequences. The men of the elite 31st infantry division began waving white flags, which spread to the other parts of the front. The French bypassed the positions of the 3rd BH regiment and attacked them from behind. In the hopeless situation they were forced to surrender. Only a small number of soldiers managed to escape, while a part of the men were killed by machinegun fire when they were trying to flee the battlefield. ① The greater part of the regiment was taken into captivity. In the concentration camp in Vicenza they were visited by the Serb military attaché, the general headquarter major Nikola Hristić, expressing his wish to see these brave soldiers. As an active officer removed from politics he proudly stated that these brave Bosnians were future Yugoslavs. ②

The long duration of the war and the troubles that the soldier endured at the front, caused that desertion appeared even in those units which until that time performed all their tasks under the toughest conditions without objection. War fatigue and desire to return home were coupled with worry about the families of the soldiers and their uncertain future. Letters from the homeland informed the soldiers on the front about the unbearable sufferings at home that their families had to endure. ③ The Bosnian and Herzegovinian units were no exception. At the end of October 1918 there was a mass desertion of soldiers from the 4th BH regiment. After the regiment

---

① Ö. St. A., KA-W, NFA, Gefechts-Berichte, Pero Blašković, *Schlus-Kämpfe von Piaveim Oktober 1918*, Wien, 1936, pp. 143-145.

② Ibid., p. 148.

③ ULK, 1938, pp. 565-573.

assembled on 1 November in Cortina d'Ampezzo, the populace was placed into waggons and sent on 2 November through Villach to Ljubljana, where they were placed at the disposal of the People's council of the State of the Serbs, Croats and the Slovenes. The regiment which counted 2,700 armed and equipped soldiers, three complete machinegun troops with 36 hand machineguns and 400 horses, was disarmed and the soldiers were sent to their homeland. ① As for the arms, the evaluation of the military formation or the losses in the war, statistics play an important role. From a total of 1,783,453 inhabitants of Bosnia and Herzegovina, recorded in the 1910 census, during the war for military needs a number of 291,498 military conscripts were engaged, or 16.34% of the population. A total of 660,771 individuals were trained, while the percentage of military capable persons amounted to 40.6%. ②

The attitude towards the Monarchy can in a certain sense be evaluated according to the losses of individual nations. In the German lands of Austria 29 soldiers were killed per 1,000 inhabitants, in the Hungarian areas or in areas with a mixed Hungarian and German population, 28 per 1,000. The war mortality was also influenced by imprisonment, work units, epidemics, etc. According to the official data of the k. u. k. Ministry of War, the losses of the Bosnian and Herzegovinian units until the end of October 1918 totalled: 10,701 killed, 51,815 wounded, 18,088 imprisoned and 21,227 missing. ③ However, this data differs significantly from the real image. From the mobilized Bosnian and Herzegovinian military conscripts, 38,000 lost their lives during the war. The average losses for the whole of Bosnia and Herzegovina amounted to 12% of the total number of militarily engaged persons, but some regions suffered more than others (Banja Luka, Srebrenica, Bileća, Foča, Mostar, Bugojno, Prozor...). The greatest losses in Bosnia and Herzegovina were suffered by the city of Banja Luka, which from the 1,173 persons engaged in conflict lost 534, or 45.6 %. ④

---

① Werner Schachinger, *Die Bosniaken kommen, Elittentruppen der k. u. k. Monarchie 1879–1918*, Graz, 1989; *Bošnjaci dolaze: Elitne trupe k. u. k. armije 1879–1918*, Lovran, 1996, pp. 229-238.

② Ö. St. A., KA-W, KM, AOK, Op. 108.916, k. u. k. Ministry of War to the Common Ministry of Finances, Vienna, 6 July 1918.

③ Ö. St. A., KA-W, KM, AOK, Qu. M. Abt, Statistisches Bureau, Tafel VII. *Verluste*.

④ Winkler Wilchelm, *Die Totenverluste-u. Heeres nach Nationalit ten*, Wien, 1921, p. 33.

The awarding of decorations for war achievements had a great optimistic effect on units and individuals, and was also connected to certain privileges. Soldiers were awarded medals for bravery, while the officers were decorated with medals with stripes. Medals for bravery were made out of metal, mostly bronze, rarely from silver or gold, or they were silvered or gilded. [1] During the First World War, the BH infantry regiments and BH hunting battalions received a total of 35,637 medals for bravery. The members of the infantry regiments were awarded 27,245 medals, and infantry hunting battalions 8,392. The soldiers from Bosnia and Herzegovina were awarded 146 gold medals for bravery, of which 57 (39%) were awarded to the soldiers of the 2nd BH infantry regiment. [2] The information about the decorations of the soldiers from the BH regiments formed during the war were not recorded particularly, but were inscribed into the logbook about the decorations for four BH regiments. [3] The decoration was accompanied by a certain financial reward which was paid monthly. The bearer of the gold medal for bravery in 1918 received 197 crones and 93 hellers, the bearer of the great silver medal of the 1st class received 3 crones and 38 hellers, the bearer of the small silver medal 2 crones and 88 hellers, while the recipient of the bronze medal received 80 hellers. [4]

Of the BH units, the greatest number of decorations was given to the soldiers of the 1st BH regiment (7,768) and the 2nd BH regiment (6,880). Of the elite units of the k.u.k. army, Tyrolian imperial hunting regiments, the first received 7,081 medals for bravery; the second regiment 8,051, the third 5,187, and the fourth regiment 6,279 medals. From the Bosnian-Herzegovinian hunting battalions, the greatest number of medals for bravery was awarded to the 6th hunting battalion, 2,637, and then to the 3rd BH hunting battalion, 1,844. [5] The number of awarded medals for bravery to the Bosnian-Herzegovinian units is the best indicator of their services skills, answering the question why they were considered as the elite units of

---

[1] Sarajevski List, 6 January 1915, No. 6, p. 1.

[2] Ö. St. A., KA-W, KM, AOK, *Auszeichnungsgruppe. Statistiküber Verleihung von Tapferkeitsmedaillen an die Heeresinfanteriebis August 1918*, p. 443.

[3] Werner Schachinger, 1996, pp. 325–326.

[4] Ö. St. A., KA-W, Neue Feld Acten, Truppenköerpper, Karton 750.

[5] Ö. St. A., KA-W, Neue Feld Acten, Truppenköerpper, Karton 262.

the Austro-Hungarian army.

During the First World War in Bosnia and Herzegovina a number of 291,498 military conscripts were mobilized, of which 51,815 were registered as wounded or sick, i. e. in average one in six. ① Of this number, 12,726 remained disabled, or in average one in four. From the total number of Bosnian-Herzegovinian war invalids, 5,371 were Orthodox Christians (42.20%), 4,413 Muslims (34.68%), 2,586 Catholics (20.32%), 32 Jews (0.25%) and 356 others (2.55%), which closely mirrored the confessional structure of the population. ②

Conclusion

The international disagreements caused deep crises in the relations between the blocs of great powers, leading to the direct military conflict in 1914. From the beginning of August 1914 Bosnia and Herzegovina was a direct area of warfare. The war destruction on the territory of military operations, refugees, evacuations and interning of people, brought about great disorders in the economy of the land and increased requests for contributions to the war effort. After the mobilization in 1914, the Bosnian and Herzegovinian units were sent from their peace garrisons to different fronts. During the war, the soldiers from Bosnia and Herzegovina were arranged into eight Bosnian and Herzegovinian infantry regiments and eight Bosnian and Herzegovinian hunting battalions. They were also engaged within other units of the common army, fighting on the Balkan, Eastern and South-Western front. In January of 1916 the Bosnian and Herzegovinian battalions had an important role in the conquest of Montenegro, while the Bosnian and Herzegovinian units on the Eastern front had varying degrees of success, suffering many losses during the great Russian summer offensive. In the battles on the Italian front, the Bosnian and Herzegovinian units stood out on the account of their war exploits.

During 1918 the position of the Central Powers worsened, and the morale of the

---

① Ö. St. A., KA-W. KM, AOK, Qu. Abt 1918, Beillage VII.
② ABH, ZMF, Präs. BH 5.096, Broschure über die Kriegsinvalidenfürsorge, pp. 23-24.

population in the background decreased. The consequence of this was that the army began breaking up, especially in those areas where national and socialist ideas were accepted, which resulted in revolts, desertions and the creation of groups from the deserters and soldiers who outstayed their allowed leave. The number of desertions as well as revolts on the South-Slavic territory increased substantially. The rebellions and breaking of discipline had their political, social and military causes. The national requests, strengthened by the propaganda of the Entente forces, brought into question the existing legal system in the Monarchy. The general situation in the background created conditions for unrest and activities which threatened the public order and peace. When this situation spread to the front, it also influenced the discipline in the military formations.

The protracted duration of the war and the troubles suffered by soldiers on the front caused that desertion appeared even in those units which until that time performed all their tasks under the toughest conditions without objection. War fatigue and desire to return home were coupled with worry about the families of the soldiers and their uncertain future. Letters from the homeland informed the soldiers on the front about the unbearable sufferings at home that their families had to endure. The Bosnian and Herzegovinian units were no exception.

As for the arms, the evaluation of the military formation or the losses in the war, statistics play an important role. During the First World War in Bosnia and Herzegovina a total number of 291,498 military conscripts were engaged, or 16.34% of the population. Of the Bosnian and Herzegovinian military conscripts, 38,000 persons died in uniform. Average losses for Bosnia and Herzegovina were 12% from the total number of persons engaged in the military. Of the mobilized conscripts from Bosnia and Herzegovina, 51,815 were registered as wounded or diseased, in average one in six, of which 12,726 remained invalids, in average on in four. Of the total number of war invalids, 4,414 (34.68%) were Muslims, 5,371 (42.20%) Orthodox Christians, 2,586 Catholics (20.32%), 32 Jews (0.25%) and 356 others (2.55%), which closely mirrored the confessional structure of the population.

The awarding of decorations for war achievements had a great optimistic effect on units and individuals, and was also connected to certain privileges. During the First World War, the BH infantry regiments and BH hunting battalions received a total of

35,637 medals for bravery, which is the best indicator of their military skills, answering the question why they were considered as the elite units of the Austro-Hungarian army.

After the break up of Austria-Hungary in 1918, Bosnia and Herzegovina entered the new South-Slavic state, the Kingdom of the Serbs, Croats and Slovenes.

References:

Primary sources

A) *unpublished sources*

Archives of Bosnia and Herzegovina

Fonds of archival sources:

Provincial Government of Bosnia and Herzegovina, präs. BH 1914-1918.

Common Ministry of Finances, präs. BH, 1914-1918.

Common Ministry of Finances, general acts, 1914-1918.

Kriegs-Archiv Wien:

Fonds of archival sources:

Arméeeoberkomando Operations Abteilung (AOK, Op. Abt.).

Arméeeoberkomando, Heimkehrers-Gruppe 1918.

Arméeeoberkomando, Abt. VII, Verluste.

Arméeeoberkomando, Auszeichnungs-Gruppe, 1914-1918.

Kriegs-ministerium, Präs. 1914-1918.

B) *published sources*:

Bericht ber die Verwaltung Bosnien und der Hercegowina 1906-1914/16, Wien, 1907/1917.

Zbornik zakona i naredbi za BiH 1914-1918.

Fond of legacies in the Vienna Kriegs-Archiv: Oscar Potiorek, Otto Wiesinger, Pero Blašković.

Newspapers: Sarajevski list, Sarajevo 1914-1918.

Literature:

Books:

Bogumil Hrabak, *Dezerterstvo i zeleni kadar*, Novi Sad, 1982.

Bogumil Hrabak, *Jugosloveni zarobljenici u Italiji i njihovo dobrovoljacko pitanje 1915-1918 godine*, Novi Sad, 1980.

Charles Jelavich, *Južnoslavenski nacionalizmi: Jugoslavensko ujedinjenje i udžbenici prije 1914*, Zagreb, 1992.

Dževad Juzbašić, Zijad Šehić (ur.), *Lične zabilješke generala Oskara Potioreka o unutrašnjo političkoj situaciji u Bosni i Hercegovini*, Akademija nauka i umjetnosti Bosne i Hercegovine, Građa, Knjiga XXX, Centar za balkanološka ispitivanja, Knjiga 1, Sarajevo, 2015.

Dževad Juzbašić, *Politika i privreda BiH pod austrougarskom upravom*, ANU BiH, Posebna izdanja, CXVI/35,

Sarajevo, 2002.

Edmung Glaise von Horstenau, *Die Katastrophe: Die Zerstümerung Österreich-Ungarns und das werden der Nachfolgenstaaten*, Zürich-Leipzig-Wien (O. J.).

Ferdinand Hauptmann, Anton Prasch, *Dr. Ludwig Thallóczy: Tagebücher*, Graz, 1981.

Ferdinand Käs, *Versuchs einer zusamengefassten Darstellung der Tätigkeit des österreichisch-ungarisches Generalstabes in der Zeit von 1906 bis 1914. Unter besonderer Berüksichtigung der Aufmarschplanungen und Mobilmachung*, Disertation, Universität Wien, 1962.

Fuad Slipičević, *Prvi svjetski rat i stvaranje države jugoslovenskih naroda*, Sarajevo, 1957.

Hamdija Kapidžić, *Bosna i Hercegovina za vrijeme austrougarske uprave. Članci i rasprave*, Sarajevo, 1968.

Hans Friz, *Bosniak*, Waldhofen a. d. Ubbs 1931.

Inge Przybilowski, *Die Rückfürung der österreichisch-ungarischen Kriegsgefangene aus dem Osten in der letzten Monaten der k. u. k. Monarchie*. Neobjavljena doktorska disertacija odbranjena na Bečkon univerzitetu, 1965.

Ingomar Pust, *Die Steinerne Front: Auf der Spuren des Gebirgskrieges in den Julische Alpen, Von Isonzo zur Piave*, Graz, 1980.

Josip Horvat, *Prvi svjetski rat: Panorama zbivanja 1914-1918*, Zagreb, 1967.

Klaus Dorst, Wolfgang Wünsche, *Der Ersten Weltkrieg: Erscheinung und Wesen*, Berlin, 1989.

Manfried Rauchensteiner, *Der Tod des Doppeladlers: Österreich-Ungarn und der Erste Weltkrieg*, Wien, 1991.

Milan Zelenika, *Prvi svetski rat 1914*, Vojno delo, Beograd, 1962.

Milorad Ekmečić, *Ratni ciljevi Srbije 1914*, Beograd, 1974.

Milorad Ekmečić, *Stvaranja Jugoslavije*, II, Beograd, 1989.

Nusret Šehić, *Četništvo u Bosni i Hercegovini (1918-1941)*, Sarajevo, 1971.

Oskar Brendl, *Die Erstürmung des M. Melleta 7 juni 1916*, Wien, 1934.

Ottokar Landwer, *Hunger*, Zürich-Leipzig-Wien, 1931.

Pero Blašković, *Sa Bošnjacima u svetskom ratu*, Beograd, 1939.

Petar Tomac, *Prvi svetski rat*, Beograd, 1969.

Petar Tomac, *Ratovi i armije XIX veka*, Beograd, 1968.

Reinhardt Eugen Bösch, *Die Haltung des südslawischer Soldaten des-u. Heeres im Ersten Weltkrieg*, Neobjavljena doktorska disertacija odbranjena na Bečkon univerzitetu, 1971.

Richard Plaschka, Horst Haselsteiner, Arnold Suppan, *Innere Front: Milit? rasisistenz, Widerstand und Umsturz in der Donaumonarchie 1918*, Bd I-II, Wien, 1974.

Rudolf Hecht, *Fragen zur Hereserergänzung der gesamten Bewafnetenmacht Österreich-Ungarns während des ersten Weltkrieges*, Neobjavljena doktorska disertacija odbranjena na Bečkon univerzitetu, 1969.

Sigismund Gandini, *Das bosnisch-hercegovinische Infanterie-Regiment Nr 2 im Weltkrieg 1914 bis 1918*, Wien, 1968.

Signe Klein, *Freiherr Sarkotić von Lovćen: Die Zeit seiner Verwaltung in Bosnien-Herzegovina von 1914 bis 1918*, Neobjavljena doktorska disertacija odbranjena na Bečkon univerzitetu, 1964.

Vladimir Ćorović, *Crna knjiga. Patnje Srba Bosne i Hercegovine za vreme svetskog rata 1914-1918*,

Sarajevo, 1920.

Werner Schachinger, *Die Bosniaken kommen*, *Elittentruppen der k. u. k. Monarchie 1879–1918*, Graz, 1989; *Bošnjaci dolaze*: *Elitne trupe k. u. k. armije 1879–1918*, Lovran, 1996.

Wilchelm Deutschmann, *Die militärischen Massnahmen in Oesterreich-Ungarn während der Balkankriege 1912/13*, Disertation, Universität Wien, 1965.

Wilchelm Winkler, *Berufsstatistik der Kriegstoten der ö-u. Monarchie*, Wien, 1919.

Wilchelm Winkler, *Die Totenverluste-u. Heeres nach Nationalitten*, Wien, 1921.

Wilhelm J. Wagner, *Der Grosse Bildatlas zur Geschichte Österreich*, Verlag Kremayr & Scherian, Wien, 1995.

Zijad Šehić, *U smrt za cara i domovinu*: *Bosanci i Hercegovci u vojnoj organizaciji Habsburške monarhije 1878–1918*, Sarajevo Publishing, Sarajevo, 2007.

Österreich-Ungarns letztes Krieges *1914–1918*, *T. I* 1931–*T. VII* 1938.

Articles:

Bogumil Hrabak, *Operacije na srednjoj i gornjoj Drini i u Sandžaku avgusta 1914. godine*, Istorijski glasnik. Organ društva istoričara Srbije, 4, Beograd, 1964.

Božo Madžar, *Izvještaj vladinog komesara za glavni grad Bosne i Hercegovine Sarajevo o političkoj i privrednoj situaciji u Sarajevu od sarajevskog atentata do kraja januara 1915. godine*, Glasnik arhiva i Društva arhivskih radnika BiH, 26, Sarajevo, 1986.

Dževad Juzbašić, *Aneksija i stavovi austrougarskih vojnih krugova prema upravljanju Bosnom i Hercegovinom*, u: Naučni skup posvećen 80 godišnjici aneksije Bosne i Hercegovine (Sarajevo, 21 i 22 novembra 1988), Sarajevo, 1991.

Dževad Juzbašić, *Uticaj balkanskih ratova 1912/1913 na Bosnu i Hercegovinu i na tretman agrarnog pitanja*, Radovi, Filozofski fakultet u Sarajevu, Knjiga XII, Sarajevo, 2000.

Galib Šljivo, *Raspoloženje naroda Bosne i Hercegovine prema austrougarskoj politici i austrougarske političke protivmjere*, u: Zbornik radova s međunarodnog skupa: *Veleizdajnički proces u Banjaluci 1915 – 1916*, održanog 25–27. septembra 1986. godine u Banjoj Luci, Institut za istoriju, Banjaluka 1987, 117–145.

Hamdija Kapidžić, *Austrougarske centralne vlasti i omladinsi pokret u Bosni i Hercegovini neposredno nakon sarajevskog atentata*, Glasnik arhiva i Društva arhivskih radnika BiH, IV–V, Sarajevo, 1965.

Horst Haselsteiner, *Prozess Banja Luka 1916. Militärgutachten*, Zbornik radova s međunarodnog skupa *Veleizdajnički proces u Banjaluci 1915–1916*, Institut za istoriju, Banjaluka, 1987.

Oberst Eugen Redl, *Die Tagliamentoforcierung bei Cornino und das Baon IV/ bh 4*, Wissenschaftliche Technische Mitteilungen, Wien, 1924.

Wolf Dieter Bihl, *Die Beziehungen zwischen Österreich-Ungarn und den osmanischen Reich im ersten Weltkrieg*, Öst. Ost Häfte, Wien, 1982.

Zijad Šehić, *Sarajevski atentat 28. juna 1914. Dan koji je promijenio svijet*, u: Sarajevski dugi picnji 9 1914. Događaj-narativ-pamćenje, Zenica, 2015, 87–108.

Zijad Šehić, *Elitne jedinice iz Bosne i Hercegovine. Prva linija*, List federalnog ministarstva odbrane/obrane, april/travanj 1999, br. 66,

Zijad Šehić, *Lajos Thallóczy über die Ereignisse in Bosnien-Herzegowina nach dem Atentat von Sarajevo am 28 Juni 1914*, u: *Lajos Thallóczy der Historiker und Politiker*, Akademie der Wissenschaften und Künste von Bosnien-Herzegowina, Ungarische Akademie der Wissenschaften, Institut für Geschichte, Sarajevo. Staats Archiv Wien, 2010, 165-169.

Österreich-Ungarns letztes Krieges 1914-1918, Bd. I 193-Bd. VII 1938.

Abbreviations:

ABH—Arhiv Bosne i Hercegovine—Archive of Bosnia and Herzegovina

Ö. St. A.—Österreichische Staats Archiv—Austrian State Archives

k. u. k.—kaiserlich und königlich—Imperial and Royal

KM—Kriegsministerium—Ministry of War

保加利亚中学教科书中关于十月革命评价的变化

[保加利亚] 伊斯克拉·巴耶娃 著 马细谱 译

内容提要 20世纪80年代末的变革使保加利亚变成资本主义国家。保加利亚1989年的中学历史教材尚还能正面评价十月革命,但是1992年后塞姆科夫教授编写的《当代史讲义》对十月革命的意义完全否定。在《当代史讲义》之后的教科书中,虽然批评十月革命的言辞减少,但仍然认为其背离了民主的道路。

关 键 词 保加利亚 教科书 十月革命

作者简介 伊斯克拉·巴耶娃,保加利亚索非亚大学历史系教授

译者简介 马细谱,首都师范大学文明区划研究中心首席研究员,历史学院特聘教授

20世纪80年代末发生在保加利亚的变革对于其政治和社会经济都产生了深刻的转折性影响。其中,最主要的特点是否定共产主义的意识形态,代之而来的是自由主义、保守主义和其他思潮,并使保加利亚变成资本主义国家。这种新的意识形态范式要求修改保加利亚学校的教学大纲和社会科学教材,首先是修改中学的历史课本。

下面简要回顾一下1973年社会主义时期保加利亚出版的供9年级和10年级使用的世界近现代史课本与1989年出版的供9年级使用的世界近现代史课本的重要变化。1992年保加利亚没有统一的中学历史教材,只有塞姆科夫教授编写的《当代史讲义》。其后,在1996年和2001年根据教育部规定的教学大纲

编写的新教科书，都讲到十月革命的问题。

一、1973年历史教材对十月革命的记述与评价

在社会主义时期，保加利亚世界当代史教科书中，十月革命被称为伟大的十月社会主义革命，从此人类历史开启了一个新时代。保加利亚世界当代史教科书正是从这场革命开始讲起的。所以，保加利亚1973年的世界近现代史教材有一章就是《伟大的十月社会主义革命》，共25页，分为5课：1. 革命准备阶段；2. 革命运动在加速；3. 十月武装起义胜利；4. 组建苏维埃国家；5. 伟大十月社会主义革命的意义。第一课指出二月革命后俄国的民主化进程加速，俄国"成为一个最民主的国家"。列宁的《四月提纲》讲到两个政权并存。列宁建议土地国有化、监督银行、监督社会生产、保障居民供应，提出"全部政权归苏维埃！"俄国临时政府出现危机，1917年6月俄国第一次苏维埃代表大会召开并做出决议，7月彼得格勒工人、士兵举行游行示威。

第二课讲述一战战场俄军前线发生的事件。7月3日危机导致两个政权并存的局面结束，形势对临时政府有利，布尔什维克党第六次代表大会的决议通过武装起义的方针。科尔尼洛夫将军试图发动反革命暴乱及其遭到镇压。

第三课介绍俄国布尔什维克党通过武装起义夺取政权。其中包括苏维埃布尔什维克化、建立工人红色近卫军、列宁的起义计划，圣彼得堡武装起义、第二次苏维埃代表大会通过关于和平法令和土地法令、莫斯科起义、革命在前线胜利、《俄国各族人民权利宣言》。

第四课集中谈论俄国势力建立和维护苏维埃新政权经过。其中包括成立苏维埃国家机构——新的革命法庭、反革命势力负隅顽抗、成立全俄肃清反革命投机和怠工非常委员会（即"契卡"）、建立无产阶级与贫苦农民联盟专政、全俄苏维埃第三次代表大会（1918年1月10日）通过《被剥削劳动人民权利宣言》、宣布建立"俄罗斯社会主义联邦共和国"、开始社会主义建设、签订《布列斯特和约》。

第五课完全是讲十月革命的意义。其中认为十月革命是人类历史一个新时代的开端，将促使资本主义旧世界灭亡，确立社会主义新世界。工人阶级第一次成为统治阶级、人民成为所有财富的主人。俄国这个新国家将实行无产阶级专政，苏维埃是脱离了世界资本主义体系的新型国家组织，人民获得了发挥自

己创造性才干的机会；苏维埃是一种新型的民主，它为过去沙皇俄国的被压迫人民提供了平等。本课的最后强调十月革命的作用是把俄罗斯从世界帝国主义阵营中拯救了出来。以上是对俄国十月革命及其意义最普遍的看法。

二、1989年的历史教材对十月革命的记述与评价

1989年保加利亚面临制度变革，十月革命只是作为1989年历史教材第一章《第一次世界大战后的世界》里的一部分。这一部分与苏联直至第二次世界大战前夕的发展占26页，共6课。其中，十月革命占4课：1. 资产阶级民主革命转变成社会主义革命（1917年3月至10月）；2. 社会主义革命胜利和建立无产阶级专政（1917年10月至1918年7月）；3. 国内战争时期的苏俄和帝国主义国家的干涉；4. 伟大十月社会主义革命的国际意义和苏联建设社会主义。

第一课指出十月革命的几个基本前提条件、列宁对两个政权并存局面的论述、俄国布尔什维克党制定武装起义的方针。第二课讲述十月武装起义、苏维埃第二次代表大会的决议、建立苏维埃国家、与德国签订《布列斯特和约》、开始社会主义改造。本课结束时，对十月革命的世界历史意义做了如下评价："人类历史上最杰出的事件，标志着从资本主义向社会主义逐步过渡的新时代的开始。"这场革命突破了资本主义世界体系，使劳动群众革命化，推动了全世界民族解放运动向前发展，为人类社会的发展开辟了现实历史前景。

第三课讲述苏联爆发国内战争的原因。其中包括苏维埃政权所采取的一系列措施、联共（布）第八次代表大会的决议、苏维埃政权击败外国干涉和在国内战争中取得胜利。

第四课专门讲述伟大十月社会主义革命的国际意义和苏联的社会主义建设。这些事件被视为人类历史上第一次社会主义革命的凯旋胜利，消灭了地主资产阶级的统治，提出了社会主义改造的形式和方法，实现了不同社会制度国家之间的和平共处。

三、1989年之后历史教材对十月革命的记述和评价

1989年之后,前述评价在新的世界历史教科书中和1992年米伦·塞姆科夫的《当代史讲义》里已经消失,对俄国十月革命完全是负面评价。这场革命被看作一场建立在幻想基础之上的政变,并得到了德国的大量金钱资助。

作者塞姆科夫甚至说,布尔什维克保持政权的唯一手段是恐怖活动。"恐怖活动变成了苏联政府主要依据",苏俄"这种新政治体制建立了一种新型的极权主义社会"。

四、塞姆科夫后的教材对十月革命的记述和评价

在《当代史讲义》之后的保加利亚世界史教科书中,十月革命已经越来越被忽视。有的教材在讲到第一次世界大战、建立战后新秩序、欧美大国的历史之后才提到十月革命。而且,十月革命和两次世界大战之间苏联的发展被压缩为一堂课内容。虽然其内容已经与塞姆科夫的《当代史讲义》有所不同,那些负面的言辞少了,但仍然批评十月革命背离了民主的道路。在这些教科书中,十月革命的意义不再被提及,它的世界影响力更不被承认。有趣的是,多数教科书的作者在1989年之前和之后都是同一班人马,但他们对十月革命的评价却截然不同,其观点出现了根本的矛盾和对立。

1917年十月革命在保加利亚中学世界历史教科书中的演化,说明保加利亚社会对这个20世纪历史上具有划时代意义的事件的态度发生了巨大的改变。所以,2017年十月革命100周年时保加利亚几乎没有任何相关活动,只有部分大学组织了学术研讨会。

二战期间中国进步报刊
论巴尔干人民的反法西斯斗争和铁托
——以《新华日报》和《解放日报》为例

马细谱

内容提要 二战期间,中国人民一直密切关注着世界反法西斯斗争。本文主要以中国共产党在解放区延安和国民党统治区重庆公开发行的两大日报——《解放日报》和《新华日报》为例,考察南斯拉夫、保加利亚等国人民1941—1945年反法西斯斗争在中国的强烈反应。

关键词 巴尔干 保加利亚 南斯拉夫 铁托 反法西斯斗争

作者简介 马细谱,首都师范大学文明区划研究中心首席研究员,历史学院特聘教授

1941年德、意法西斯疯狂发动战争侵略南斯拉夫、希腊等巴尔干国家的时候,中国人民正处在抗日战争的艰苦年代里。中国人民从抗日战争一开始,就把自己的斗争同世界反法西斯斗争紧密结合在一起,不仅密切关注第二次世界大战全局的发展,而且还通过各种渠道介绍其他遭受法西斯侵略的国家人民的英勇斗争。其中,中国人民对巴尔干国家的反法西斯抵抗运动非常关心,并且给予极高的评价。

这里,我们主要以中国共产党在解放区延安和国民党统治区重庆公开发行的两种大型日报——《解放日报》和《新华日报》为例,考察南斯拉夫、保加利亚等国人民1941—1945年反法西斯斗争在中国的强烈反应。当我们展开

这一时期这两家报纸的时候，许许多多有关南斯拉夫、保加利亚等国的消息、报道、文章、评论和社论，以及巴尔干地形图和铁托的照片等，就像电影银幕一样闪现在眼前。

据粗略统计，仅《解放日报》从1941年至1945年就发表了近600条有关南斯拉夫人民反法西斯斗争情况的消息；共刊登了有关保加利亚人民的反法西斯斗争和建立人民政权消息463条，发表社论3篇、短评5篇和文章7篇。①

一、保加利亚在战斗

《新华日报》在1941年3月3日头版详细报道了保加利亚放弃中立政策、加入三国轴心的经过，以及西方世界的强烈反应。次日，该报在第1版据外电综合报道说，保加利亚正在"重蹈罗马尼亚覆辙"，国民议会在通过加入轴心国提案时，并非完全一致。同时，"保加利亚之加入三国同盟，等于德方之军事胜利"。《新华日报》在同一消息中第一次提到保加利亚共产党的武装在反对德军进入保加利亚，"保共的武装队伍反对德军占领保境"。

对于保加利亚成为轴心国附庸对巴尔干半岛局势带来的不利影响，中国的《晋察冀日报》做了全面的分析。该报在1941年3月8日评论说，开进保加利亚的德军已达13个师团，共20万人。"德国军队已占领了整个保国，保国人民已经遭受着亡国和战争的惨祸"。

该报在"国际时评"中写道："保加利亚加入三国同盟，使得德意在欧洲的气势，异常增强。"保加利亚政府投靠德意，使德国的巴尔干政策目标实现："保加利亚变成了德国在东南欧的战略基地，德国不仅扩大了对东南欧的控制，而且兵临土希边境……德国借以诱使土耳其中立，逼迫希腊屈服，加紧压迫南斯拉夫加入轴心集团。"该报还认为，保加利亚王室决定站在轴心国一边，对该国产生了灾难性后果。由于纳粹占领，保加利亚成了德国的"殖民地"和"兵营"，处于"地狱的边缘"。保加利亚被迫将许多粮食运往德国，结果"严重缺粮"。

《解放日报》在1941年8月9日的报道中指出：保加利亚人民对政府政策

---

① 详见马细谱：《南斯拉夫兴亡》，社会科学文献出版社2010年版，第186—194页；马细谱：《保加利亚史》，中国社会科学出版社2011年版，第213—216页。

之不满情绪日益增长，无数怠工，特别是铁道上，最近已形增多。保加利亚爱国志士所组织之战斗小组在全国秘密活动，彼等对其活动之掩护极为巧妙，且得人民之援助，而避免警察与秘密侦探之迫害。该报8月14日报道保加利亚人民反纳粹运动高涨，反抗事件普遍发展，消息称，"在保加利亚乡村散布着反抗德国希特勒的运动，例如组织武装部队……破坏事件异常普遍……法西斯之恐怖，使广大民众进行大规模的反抗……与保加利亚人民有着同样对反苏战争忿恨的情绪之保加利亚士兵亦参加示威"。

1942年，巴尔干各国人民的反法西斯抵抗运动采取了越来越有组织的武装斗争形式。年初，中国两报便指出"保国全境笼罩着恐怖""各地示威运动风起云涌""人民反对不义战争"。《解放日报》在1942年2月6日报道说："保加利亚人民有85%宁可对苏表示亲密，而不愿亲善轴心，保军若奉命攻苏，必弃械投降。"

1942年4月2日，《新华日报》报道说，保加利亚爱国者早在1941年就设立了秘密广播电台，号召人民反对法西斯。4月24日，《解放日报》摘要登载了保加利亚秘密电台"五·一"国际劳动节广播文章，号召人民组织游击队，规定5月1日为保加利亚人民反德起义日。

《新华日报》在1943年4月9日写道，希特勒德国"在巴尔干放了一把火，但如今没法子淹灭火焰了"。这一年，《新华日报》和《解放日报》着重介绍了保加利亚人民的反法西斯运动和祖国阵线的活动。4月20日，《新华日报》报道说，保加利亚国内情势紧张，人民反法西斯运动高涨，德军和菲洛夫政府甚感恐慌。在索非亚、布尔加斯、瓦尔纳、普罗夫迪夫及斯利文，反法西斯分子特别活跃。次日，《解放日报》的消息称，保加利亚不少军人具有反德情绪，有的军人已加入在山中活动的游击队，还有的军人参加了希腊和南斯拉夫游击队。

《新华日报》1943年11月26日发表《保国人民复仇的火焰》短评，称赞保加利亚人民的斗争和祖国阵线的纲领。短评指出："在巴尔干的东端，保加利亚人民现在应声而起，保国祖国阵线散发的纲领，正是根据要把一切力量为反对希特勒的战争而服务这一原则来进行反法西斯斗争的。"12月27日，《新华日报》全文刊登了保加利亚祖国阵线的12点纲领。12月29日，《新华日报》发表长篇文章称，"最活跃的反纳粹的政治行动，是保国工人的活动，是由共产党所领导的"。文章称赞祖国阵线发表了"一个辉煌的政纲，主张对外和苏英美合作，对内成立民主政府，来拯救保国"。它的"主要纲领已经获得各民主集团和党派的拥护"。

1944年是纳粹德国遭到惨败和保加利亚人民获得胜利的一年。这年1月6日，《解放日报》指出，"苏军愈胜，巴尔干保加利亚之和平示威运动亦愈烈……保境之反战情绪尤见高涨。索非亚已发生巷战，保总理已辞职，新阁亦已成立，摄政会议宣布保加利亚已入紧急状态"。

1944年1月8日，《新华日报》向读者介绍了保加利亚游击队的情况。报道认为，"据估计，游击队人数约在三千到七千之间"。消息还说，保加利亚共产党在各地散发宣传小册子，"号召民主及自由分子合作"。4月15日，《新华日报》发表舒翰写的《保加利亚的命运》长篇文章，回顾了保加利亚战时的对内对外政策，认为保加利亚当局已"临到最终结局"，"决定保加利亚命运的唯有人民"，"人民创造未来"。作者还指出，保加利亚共产党不仅领导祖国阵线，而且"自己组织有特别的游击队，经常袭击德军和保国警察"。作者在文章结尾表示深信："埋在雪底下的巴尔干半岛的冬天，已经过去……已经是绝大多数的保国人民在现在的祖国阵线的基础上，自己来创造民主自由的未来的时候了。"

1944年8月26日，《新华日报》以《保加利亚在彷徨中》为题的消息中，指出有种种迹象表明保加利亚资产阶级正处在徘徊中。8月28日，该报在第3版登载《巴尔干局势急转直下，保加利亚退出战争》的消息，称保加利亚政府已于8月26日宣布"完全中立"，下令解除在保加利亚境内的德军武装，并与同盟国商讨议和条件。

1944年9月13日，《新华日报》和《解放日报》同时发表消息，称保加利亚已经走上民主道路，恢复了宪法赋予人民的权利。接着，两报介绍了祖国阵线政府的对内对外政策，以及举行大选和审判战争罪犯的情况，尤其是对祖国阵线政府在1945年11月18日大选中的胜利给予了高度的评价。

1945年11月21日，《解放日报》发表《保国人民的胜利和干涉主义的破产》短评，专门评述保加利亚的大选及其意义。短评认为，"继南斯拉夫以后，保加利亚的大选又以祖国阵线占压倒多数而胜利结束了。这是东南欧新民主主义运动的又一次辉煌的胜利！""保国大选的胜利结束，宣告了英美方面对保国所采取的干涉政策已全部破产"，"同样地宣告了国内反动派的破产"。短评指出，帝国主义不管采取"不承认"政策，还是扶植保加利亚的反动势力，都不能动摇以祖国阵线为首的人民力量，都不能把人民拉回到黑暗的时代了。短评表示，"保国大选证明了：保国人民酷爱民主和坚持斗争的精神，决不是任何外来的威胁和恫吓所能压服的"。"保国祖国阵线在大选中的胜利,的确值得全世界和平民主人士庆贺!"

二、南斯拉夫是欧洲反法西斯斗争的光辉榜样

1941年4月7日,即德意法西斯入侵南斯拉夫的第二天,《新华日报》就在显著位置报道了这一消息,指出德国飞机轰炸南斯拉夫国土是"对南斯拉夫的战争"。4月11日,该报发表社论,对南斯拉夫和希腊沦陷后巴尔干半岛出现的严重局势做了这样的分析:德国在巴尔干地区的"春季攻势"已拉开序幕,"战争烽火将愈燃愈烈,愈烧愈广"。但是,巴尔干各国的命运取决于"巴尔干各国的人民",只有他们"才掌握了命运的最后决定权"。①

1941年7月初,塞尔维亚人民武装起义爆发后,南斯拉夫人民走上了有组织的武装斗争道路。从这时起,《新华日报》和《解放日报》开始系统地大量报道南斯拉夫的游击斗争,并指出这是"南斯拉夫人民反抗占领军的主要方式"。

1941年9月17日,《解放日报》发表题为《弥漫欧洲的反纳粹运动》,称赞南斯拉夫、希腊等地的游击战争已成为全世界反法西斯斗争的一个组成部分,代表反对希特勒侵略的"另一条强有力的战线"。这条战线"牵制着希特勒法西斯在东线的兵力,破坏着希特勒进行战争的经济、物资、原料的来源,扰乱着德国法西斯的后方,威胁着希特勒法西斯在欧洲的统治"。

1941年11月1日,《解放日报》刊登长篇文章《不屈服的南斯拉夫》,概括和总结了南斯拉夫人民半年来武装斗争的情况。文章认为,南斯拉夫游击战争迅速发展的一个重要原因在于南共的正确领导,"尤其是有南国共产党的领导与支持,及许多共产党员以身作则的参加。同时,更有南国人民普遍的拥护和帮助,所以,能够坚强的存在和胜利的发展"。

历史进入1942年,南斯拉夫成为重要的一个反法西斯战场,南斯拉夫各族人民反对外国侵略者和国内卖国贼的斗争已发展成为真正的人民战争。南斯拉夫人民的斗争已受到世界瞩目,中国人民称赞这场斗争为其他被法西斯侵略者占领的国家的人民做出了榜样。

---

① 《论巴尔干战争》,《新华日报》1941年4月11日社论。

1942年6月8日，《新华日报》在论述欧洲大陆被奴役国家人民反对德国法西斯斗争的社论中，首先列举了南斯拉夫和希腊的例子。社论认为，在战斗行动上，他们已从一般的破坏活动转入在大范围内完成"战略上更复杂的动作"；在解放区建立了"人民的民主政权"。①

1942年6月20日，《解放日报》发表署名文章《南斯拉夫的反德游击战》，强调指出南斯拉夫人民的斗争同苏联被占领区人民、挪威、法国、希腊、捷克斯洛伐克等国人民的斗争一样，有着"共同的战斗目标"，构成了"反法西斯的第三条战线，这是从后方打击法西斯最有力的一环"。

1942年11月20日，《解放日报》的社论写道："南国游击队的光辉胜利，在欧洲其他被奴役诸国人民前面，树立了有组织的武装斗争的模范。""我们对于站在欧陆被奴役人民的斗争前哨的南斯拉夫战友们，谨致热烈的敬意，并希望他们坚持战斗，再接再厉，取得不断胜利，把德、意寇军逐出南国国土之外。"②

1943年是世界反法西斯同盟取得巨大胜利的一年，也是南斯拉夫、希腊等国人民解放战争发生转折的一年。世界反法西斯同盟国家对巴尔干半岛上的人民解放军和游击队更加同情和钦佩，因为他们为反法西斯同盟的军事胜利做出了贡献。

1943年2月，《新华日报》在其社论中详细谈到南斯拉夫游击队的成长。社论说，"南斯拉夫的人民解放军，正是在坚持团结抗战反对分裂的斗争过程中坚强起来的，这可以成为举世反法西斯战争中的借鉴"。社论称赞"南国人民和他们的游击队，成为欧洲沦陷国人民的模范"。③

1943年3月中旬，《新华日报》在一篇评论中写道："在人民武装抗德的怒潮中，有南斯拉夫的人民解放军和希腊的解放军……毫无问题，这些武装是纳粹的心腹之患，是欧洲人民反法西斯统治的先锋，也就是根本摧毁法西斯统治的重要力量之一。"④ 该报还从南斯拉夫和希腊两国游击战争的规模和作用得出结论说，被占领国家里人民的反法西斯斗争已成为一支巨大的力量，正在从内部动摇德国法西斯的血腥统治。这支力量是打不垮、消灭不了的！

1943年9月8日意大利宣布投降，这对巴尔干地区的局势发展产生了积极

---

① 《欧洲大陆游击战争的烽火》，《新华日报》1942年6月8日社论。
② 《南斯拉夫游击队的胜利》，《解放日报》1942年11月20日社论。
③ 《南斯拉夫的游击战》，《新华日报》1943年2月10日社论。
④ 《援助欧洲的人民武装》，《新华日报》1943年3月18日短评。

的影响。《新华日报》撰文指出，这是对希特勒的一个"沉重打击"，这对东南欧被奴役人民的反法西斯斗争是个鼓舞。该报的社论预言："继在意大利人民之后，巴尔干的人民，南斯拉夫的人民，法兰西的人民，越过大海，跨过高山，是全世界的人民用民主的浪潮来冲毁巴土底监狱的时候了！"①

1943年10月下旬，《新华日报》发表一篇论南斯拉夫人民武装斗争的社论，全面介绍南斯拉夫人民解放战争两年多来在军事上和政治上所取得的重大成就。社论强调，南斯拉夫的武装斗争"已日益成为巴尔干局势发展当中一个重要的因素"。南斯拉夫人民"在全世界反法西斯各民族中，在中国之外，又树立了一个从事游击战争运动的光辉的模范"。②

在战争结束阶段，中国进步报纸和杂志对巴尔干局势的发展，特别是对南斯拉夫的报道，在数量上和质量上都达到新高度。据粗略统计，1944年上半年仅《文汇周报》就先后登载4篇专稿。它们是《南斯拉夫的铁托游击》《南斯拉夫之旗》《铁托元帅》《铁托与南斯拉夫》。

1944年10月贝尔格莱德战役后，《新华日报》发表长篇文章对1944年下半年的南斯拉夫战场形势做了如下评论："勇往无前的苏联红军和英雄光荣的南国人民解放军会师后，南斯拉夫大部分领土都从德寇奴役下解放出来了。在南国的山岗、森林、田园、村庄、都市……都飘扬起了人民的自由的旗帜，荡漾着人民的自由的歌声。一切的赞美，一切的荣誉，都属于南斯拉夫人民。"③

1945年3月9日，《新华日报》就希腊和南斯拉夫发生的事件评论说，希腊流亡政府同右翼组织勾结，反对和镇压希腊的人民解放运动，反动派正在"建立与雅尔塔会议精神违背的反民主军事国家"；与此相反，"南斯拉夫新的民主联合政府，已在铁托元帅主持下成立。南斯拉夫的民主团结完全实现了"。④不久，该报又把南斯拉夫联合政府同罗马尼亚民族民主阵线成立的联合政府比较，认为两国新政府都是由共产党领导的、有其他党派和爱国人士参加的民主团结政府。文章强调说，"两国人民反法西斯民族解放运动已是完成了本身的团结和统一。这不仅是南、罗两国人民的胜利，同时也是民主世界的胜利！"⑤

---

① 《意大利投降》，《新华日报》1943年9月10日社论。
② 《一个光辉的模范——论南斯拉夫人民的武装斗争》，《新华日报》1943年10月23日社论。
③ 茹纯：《自由南斯拉夫的雄姿》，《新华日报》1944年12月1日。
④ 《南斯拉夫和希腊》，《新华日报》1945年3月9日时评。
⑤ 《南罗两国的新政府》，《新华日报》1945年3月12日时评。

继 1945 年 3 月初南斯拉夫联合政府成立后，5 月中旬全南斯拉夫获得解放。《解放日报》在欢庆第二次世界大战胜利结束的社论中庄严宣告："由于欧洲反法西斯战争的胜利结束，欧洲人民翻了身。"11 月中旬，《解放日报》的短评写道："南国的大选胜利结束了，这是东南欧民主选举中的一个光辉范例，是巴尔干人民新民主主义运动的一面辉煌的旗帜。让我们欢迎新的正式的南斯拉夫民主政府诞生吧！"①

1945 年 11 月 21 日，《解放日报》发表《保国人民的胜利和干涉主义的破产》短评，专门评述保加利亚的大选及其意义。短评认为，"继南斯拉夫以后，保加利亚的大选又以祖国阵线占压倒多数而胜利结束了。这是东南欧新民主主义运动的又一次辉煌的胜利！""保国大选的胜利结束，宣告了英美方面对保国所采取的干涉政策已全部破产"。

三、铁托是一位传奇式英雄

铁托的名字是同第二次世界大战分不开的，也是同南斯拉夫各族人民的反法西斯斗争分不开的。还在战争中，他的名字便在整个南斯拉夫和国外传颂开了。

同样，中国进步报刊早在 1942 年底已公开提到铁托的名字，并开始报道他的战斗活动。例如，1943 年 1 月 4 日，《新华日报》在报道南斯拉夫反法西斯青年联盟第一次代表大会时，便讲道"南国人民解放军总司令铁托代表统帅部于第一次会议时到会"。

此后，《新华日报》和《解放日报》便经常提到铁托是"南国解放军领袖""共产党领袖"。例如，1943 年 9 月 23 日，《解放日报》在题为《共产党英明领导下，南游击队日益强大》的消息中，称"铁托是闻名于世的共产党领袖"。该报 11 月 17 日在《南斯拉夫》一文中，强调铁托是军队的缔造者："南斯拉夫人民解放军是在南斯拉夫共产党领袖铁托领导之下建立起来并壮大起来的。"再如，"阿夫诺伊"（南斯拉夫反法西斯人民解放委员会的简称）第二次会议召开后，12 月 19 日，《新华日报》报道说"铁托元帅被推为解放委员会

---

① 《向南斯拉夫人民致贺——祝南国大选中民族阵线的胜利》，《解放日报》1945 年 11 月 16 日短评。

的首长","南国各族人民和解放军在铁托元帅领导下团结着,并进行了不倦的斗争,牵制了轴心军力30个师团以上"。①

1944年2月25日和4月10日,《新华日报》和《解放日报》分别刊登了铁托的照片。《新华日报》在一篇社论中称铁托领导的武装斗争在巴尔干起着榜样的作用,并赞扬说:"请看铁托元帅不是以南国五金工人领袖、南国共产党领袖、南国各民族人民的领袖这三重荣誉的资格,受着南国全国上下内外一致热烈的爱戴么?"②

8月12日,《解放日报》刊登《铁托元帅略传》和照片。《铁托元帅略传》是这样开头的:"在南斯拉夫,今天有一个人是全国人民最崇信、最热爱的。这个人在他们心目中具有无比的勇敢与忍耐力。人们传说着,打起仗来,他总是骑着一匹白马,站在游击队的前面。他们有时叫他作元帅,有时又叫他'老人';希腊正教的牧师们甚至称他作'圣人'。这个人就是铁托。"

这一年,中国的几家进步报刊《群众》《文汇周报》《文摘战时旬刊》等,都发表或译载了歌颂铁托的文章。例如,1944年4月出版的《文摘战时旬刊》第117号上,发表了《游击队之王铁托元帅》一文,该刊物的第126号上刊登了《神出鬼没的铁托军》一文。

一旦一个领袖人物的名字和事迹传开,人们便渴望通过他的著作来学习他的革命理论,了解他的革命思想。还在战时,铁托论述南斯拉夫人民解放斗争的部分讲话和文章就传到了中国。

1944年3月20日,《新华日报》和《解放日报》摘要刊登了铁托的《南斯拉夫反法西斯人民解放委员会第二次会议的决议对于进一步发展我国斗争和建立联邦国家共同体的意义》(原文发表在1944年3月1日《新南斯拉夫》创刊号上)一文。

1944年上半年,铁托为美国《自由世界》杂志撰写了长篇文章《被奴役南斯拉夫人民的斗争》。7月19日和8月12日,《新华日报》和《解放日报》分别以《铁托元帅作:南国人民解放军的成长》为题,刊登了该文的内容摘要,并加了"编者按"。不久,这篇文章全文发表在《文摘战时旬刊》第127号附册上,标题改为《我们的奋斗》。特别需要指出的是,《新华日报》于1944年11月27日的"新华副刊"上,刊登了《人民的反法西斯力量是摧毁不

---

① 《祝南国临时政府》,《新华日报》1943年12月19日社论。
② 《检阅巴尔干人民的行列》,《新华日报》1944年4月2日社论。

了，蒙蔽不了的!》一文，向读者推荐该文，并详细介绍了这个小册子的主要内容和重要意义。文章说，铁托元帅的文章叙述了南斯拉夫人民解放军的兴起和壮大，"这自然是极可靠的信史"。它"鲜明地画出了人民的斗争和胜利的道路。所以，在这些朴素的报告文字中，没有一处，我们不能得到深刻的感应"。《新华日报》的文章最后指出，真理的声音是封锁不住的，铁托领导的人民解放军在敌人面前，已经成为"永不可摧毁的人民的伟大力量"。

1945年3月4日，《解放日报》报道了"阿夫诺伊"授予铁托"人民解放勋章"的消息，并援引授勋决议说，"因为铁托元帅是人民解放斗争中伟大的战略家、组织者和领导人，南国各民族友爱团结的组织者，民主联邦南斯拉夫的创造人，对人民解敢斗争有极大贡献"。

随着南斯拉夫人民解放战争的发展，中国人民对铁托的了解越来越多。1945年1月底，一位中国作者写下了《南斯拉夫人民的领袖——铁托》一文，全面介绍了铁托的经历和功绩。《解放日报》于3月11日发表了这篇文章，称赞铁托是"一个对于人民赤胆忠心的人"。他敢于斗争，又善于斗争，忠于祖国和人民。所以，"三年多血的战斗，使他变成南斯拉夫人民唯一的领袖，南斯拉夫人民的父母，他的名字成为南斯拉夫人中最崇高最光荣的象征"。

在当时中国作者的笔下，铁托既是一位军事指挥员和政治家，又是一位传奇式英雄，在南斯拉夫国内外流传着各种关于铁托的传说和逸闻。铁托的第一大功绩，是使南斯拉夫的游击战烽火燃遍整个南斯拉夫。"不仅如此，他的力量（指游击队）还超过了南国的边境……鼓舞了整个巴尔干的人民抵抗运动。"他的另一个功绩是正确解决了南斯拉夫的民族问题。由于根据各民族一律平等的原则建立联邦制国家，"这就第一次解决了历史上这个最大的问题"，实现了各民族之间的"兄弟团结"。

同年6月，另一位中国作者在《铁托——南斯拉夫各族人民的领袖》一文中，专门介绍了铁托作为革命家和领袖的优秀品质和模范作用。作者在文章一开头就指出，铁托之所以能在第二次世界大战中成为杰出的领袖人物，受到包括中国人民在内的许多国家人民的颂扬和爱戴，是因为他了解社会发展的规律，在风云变幻的战争环境中，"他把握住南斯拉夫历史变动的枢纽，给这种变动开辟了道路；给南斯拉夫人民指出了新的方向；同时，动员和组织了南斯拉夫人民为创造着新的国家而斗争"。

上述文章强调说，铁托是位卓越的指挥员，在战争中，"表现出军事天才与指挥战斗的能力"；他善于团结一切民主力量，"是个干练的政治家"。在南斯拉夫政党繁多和民族成分复杂的情况下,他采用各种不同的形式,成功地把各种力量动员和组织起来;"尽释前嫌,团结一致,为完成共同的任务而斗争"。在日常生活方面,有许多值得"人们向他学习的细节"。例如,他生活俭朴,忘我无私,以身作则,关心他人;在工作作风方面,他是"实事求是"的模范。他要求工作人员少说漂亮话,多做平凡事。"他处理公文非常迅速,随到随批"。他指示青年干部"要向群众学习,细心研究群众斗争的实际经验,理解群众的行动"。

最后,作者得出结论:铁托建立了军队和人民政权,执行了正确的民族统一政策,团结了全南斯拉夫的所有反法西斯力量。"这一切便奠定了新南斯拉夫的民主政治基础。铁托所做的,替欧洲所有被奴役的人民,创造了最光辉的模范!"[①]

[①] 该文为石啸冲编著的《新南斯拉夫》(读书出版社1945年版)一书的附录一,第199—212页。

波黑：失落的"出生证明"

陈慧稚

内容提要 位于西巴尔干的波斯尼亚和黑塞哥维那是一个"古老而年轻"的国家，作为其近千年历史见证的是1189年8月29日当时的波斯尼亚统治者库林巴昂对邻国颁布的一纸宪章。宪章篇幅简短，但是措辞被认为体现出波斯尼亚的国家性。宪章存世有数个版本，但均散佚在外国。让宪章回到波黑的努力被认为维系于波黑政府，但是波黑内战造成的民族裂痕和至今民族主义政治话语盛行的政治局面，让波黑人多年来对于自己国家的"出生证明"只能是望眼欲穿。

关键词 波黑 库林巴昂宪章 巴尔干 中世纪历史

作者简介 陈慧稚，《上海日报》记者，首都师范大学文明区划研究中心兼职研究人员

波斯尼亚和黑塞哥维那作为一个独立国家首次在1992年被联合国承认并接纳为成员国，但是，在今波黑所在之地建立的最古老的国家可以追溯到1000多年前，在中世纪欧洲复杂的地缘竞合之下还一度成为西巴尔干的最大国家。这段令波黑人足以引以为荣的光辉历史有个重要见证，那就是1189年8月29日当时的波斯尼亚统治者库林巴昂对邻国颁布的一纸宪章（povelja）。这则宪章因其文字表述中体现出的波斯尼亚的国家性，被有的波黑学者称为波黑的"出生证明"。

这份历史文件对波黑如此重要，但它的原件和其他几个版本都并不掌握在波黑人手里，而是保存在克罗地亚和俄罗斯的档案馆里。波黑民政部2015年底向俄罗斯提出将俄方掌握的库林巴昂宪章归还波黑的请求，但至今未能如

愿。经历了20世纪90年代初内战和仇恨洗礼的波黑仍在挣扎着寻找民族和解之路,当民族主义政治话语依然盛行,找寻共同的身份标记恐怕很难被真正提上议事日程。

一、宪章的由来

斯拉夫人在公元6世纪末7世纪初和阿瓦尔人(Avar)一同迁徙到巴尔干地区,有历史学者认为,塞尔维亚人和克罗地亚人是在第二波斯拉夫人迁徙浪潮中最后来到此地的,而在他们建立起自己的巴尔干国家之后,从帕诺尼亚的斯拉沃尼亚经波斯尼亚①南至杜布罗夫尼克一带长期是一片"中立的斯拉夫地区"。②

历史上,波斯尼亚首次被提及是在公元949年。关于波斯尼亚国名的源起史学家们众说纷纭,有的认为斯拉夫人迁徙至此之后沿袭了原住民对这一地区的称呼,也有人认为,波斯尼亚和克罗地亚以及塞尔维亚一样,是一斯拉夫部落名。有学者认为,当时波斯尼亚是塞尔维亚国家的一部分,在塞尔维亚统治者死后一度成为独立国家,但在公元10世纪下半叶和11世纪上半叶先后又并入克罗地亚王国、拜占庭帝国和泽塔国(Zeta)③。从公元11世纪末到12世纪末,波斯尼亚的统治者或和拜占庭帝国或和匈牙利结盟。④

到公元12世纪末时,波斯尼亚的疆域已经显著扩大,将北面的乌索尔(Usor)和索利(Soli)等小国纳入,地域范围已包括今波斯尼亚的大部,直至和塞尔维亚的界河德里纳河。当时的波斯尼亚统治者叫库林(Kulin),他是拜占庭帝国的一个诸侯,1180年拜占庭君主死后,他治下的波斯尼亚再次成为一个独立国家。库林的头衔叫"巴昂"(ban),这是一个来自阿瓦尔人语言的词,意思是"富有的人""地主"。"巴昂国"(banovina)是中世纪很多中东欧斯拉夫人国家的名称。

---

① 最初的波斯尼亚国家的地域只是局限于波斯尼亚河上游地带,也即今天的萨拉热窝、维索科和泽尼察一带。
② Bakir Tanović, *Historija Bosne u okviru Osmanskog carstva*, Sarajevo: Svjetlost, 2010, p. 10.
③ 中世纪时期的黑山国家。
④ Husref Redžić, *Srednjovjekovni gradovi u Bosni i Hercegovini*, Sarajevo: Sarajevo Publishing, 2009, pp. 9–10.

研究者认为，从 1180 年到库林巴昂去世的 1204 年，波斯尼亚内政较为稳定，封建体制得到发展，和海滨城市尤其是杜布罗夫尼克贸易往来频繁。位于亚得里亚海东岸的杜布罗夫尼克因其得天独厚的地理位置，从公元 7 世纪建立之始就在巴尔干地区有着独特的政治和经济地位。和其他克罗地亚海滨城市不同的是，杜布罗夫尼克的腹地深入内陆，而没有被山脉阻隔，因此得以和波斯尼亚、塞尔维亚等内陆国家发展商贸往来。[①]

1189 年 8 月 29 日，库林巴昂对杜布罗夫尼克颁布了一则宪章，宣布允许杜布罗夫尼克商人在波斯尼亚境内自由经商、通行无阻。宪章全文如下：

> 以圣父、圣子和圣灵之名，我，波斯尼亚的巴昂库林，承诺你，科尔瓦什王子，以及所有杜布罗夫尼克的公民，从现在起做你们真正的朋友，直到永远。我将保证你们的权利，真正信任你们，只要我在世。
>
> 所有在我统治的地方经商的杜布罗夫尼克人，不论他们想去哪里，将去哪里，我将真正信任他们，并全心全意保护他们，不征收任何税负，除了他们出于自己的意愿要献给我的礼物外；我的官员们不会对他们使用暴力，只要他们在我国领土上，我就将帮助他们，就像帮助自己，尽我所能，毫无任何恶意。
>
> 愿上帝和神圣的福音助我。
>
> 我，拉多耶，巴昂的执笔人，于基督诞生第 1189 年的 8 月 29 日写下这本巴昂宪章，（今天是）施洗者约翰的殉道日。

二、宪章的国家性

库林巴昂宪章虽然简短，但不少波黑学者认为，它清楚地体现了波斯尼亚的国家性，故有人将其形象地称为波黑的"出生证明"。波黑著名政法学者穆斯塔法·伊马莫维奇（Mustafa Imamović）如此评价："作为波斯尼亚的统

---

① Mustafa Imamović, *Historija države i prava Bosne i Hercegovine*, Sarajevo: University Press, 2014, pp. 47–48.

治者，（库林巴昂）许诺杜布罗夫尼克人在他'统治'的领土内自由经商和流动。在巴昂身边已经存在一定的政府和暴力机关，因为库林许诺杜布罗夫尼克商人保护他们免受其'官员们'的暴力。最后，还有他的宫廷办公室，这通常是代表着一个封建国家体系完整性的最后一环。宪章的文本毫无疑问地体现出，在其被颁布的年代，即公元12世纪末，在波斯尼亚的领土上已经存在一个有着特定政府组织和相应司法系统的封建国家。"①

萨拉热窝大学政治学教授塞纳丁·拉维奇（Senadin Lavić）也认为，当一个统治者对某人发布宪章，允许这个人在他的国家通行无阻，那么这个统治者一定是在当地建立了某种形式的政府。他表示，当时波斯尼亚处在拜占庭帝国和匈牙利王国之间，两国都意欲使库林巴昂臣服于己，在如此复杂的国际环境之下，库林巴昂以自己的智慧成功地维护了波斯尼亚的独立性。②

库林巴昂宪章也被认为是所有南斯拉夫民族和国家留存下的最早的国家文件之一。它的独特之处还在于，它是由被称为bosančica的波斯尼亚的西里尔文字写成，尽管克罗地亚和波黑克族历史学家大多称之为"克罗地亚西里尔文字"或"西西里尔文字"。一般认为这种文字从公元10世纪开始就在达尔马提亚克罗地亚、杜布罗夫尼克共和国和今波黑地区被使用，是西里尔字母的一种变体。除了库林巴昂宪章，bosančica还见于波黑和克罗地亚中世纪的石碑、墓碑、经书和其他公文中，在波斯尼亚被奥斯曼帝国征服之后才逐渐被拉丁字母取代。

波黑历史学家伊布拉西姆·帕希奇（Ibrahim Pašić）研究了这篇宪章的词汇，他指出，一些塞尔维亚和克罗地亚学者试图赋予库林巴昂宪章塞尔维亚或克罗地亚色彩，但是这篇宪章的独特之处在于其使用的词汇词源不完全是斯拉夫语，160个单词中有26.6%的词词源是哥特人的语言。"根据一家瑞士研究机构的研究，20%的波黑人有哥特人基因，所以我基本的结论就是，这则宪章是波黑多元文化的丰碑。"③

库林巴昂所在的年代只是波斯尼亚作为中世纪国家发展的开始。到公元14世纪20年代，在匈牙利和克罗地亚之间周旋的波斯尼亚已经将领土范围拓展至亚得里亚海边。在被奥斯曼帝国征服之前，波斯尼亚国土范围在特弗尔特科

---

① Mustafa Imamović, *Historija države i prava Bosne i Hercegovine*, p. 66.
② "Lavić: Ban Kulin je znao sačuvati brod koji se zvao Bosna", klix. ba, 29. 8. 2012.
③ Ibid.

一世·科特罗马尼奇（Tvrtko I Kotromanić）统治时期最大，获得部分塞尔维亚领土的他于1377年10月26—27日加冕为"塞尔维亚、波斯尼亚和滨海的基督上帝的国王"。到1390年，他又成功地在克罗地亚攻城略地，于1390年加冕为"蒙上帝之恩的拉什卡（Raška）①、波斯尼亚、达尔马提亚、克罗地亚和滨海的光荣的国王"。因此，称特弗尔特科一世是"第一个南斯拉夫国王"② 并不为过。

时至今日，在波黑民间仍有一句俗语叫"自打库林巴昂和好日子开始"（od Kulina bana i dobrijeh dana），意指某些事物由来已久。

三、宪章的现状

目前已知库林巴昂宪章有三个存世的原本，两件位于克罗地亚国家档案馆的杜布罗夫尼克分馆（Državni arhiv u Dubrovniku），另一件保存在圣彼得堡，由俄罗斯联邦科研机构管理局（FASO）保管。③ 不过，杜布罗夫尼克档案馆的一名高级研究员认为，其实宪章有四个版本，但是第四个版本已经遗失了。④ 关于这三个版本哪个才是正本，目前并没有定论，但有学者认为，杜布罗夫尼克档案馆保存的两个版本并不是1189年8月29日当天颁布的宪章的正本，而是分别早于和晚于正本成文，俄罗斯人手里的才是正本。据说19世纪时，俄国驻杜布罗夫尼克的领事在一个集贸市场上发现了这一纸珍贵的古老宪章，带走后觐献给俄国沙皇，保存在当时的彼得堡科学院。而现杜布罗夫尼克档案馆保存的两个版本在19世纪时曾一度流落维也纳，二战之后根据当时南斯拉夫和奥地利两国政府的协议才被归还给杜布罗夫尼克。

现存的三个版本在排版上有差异。保存在俄罗斯的版本有12行拉丁文和20行波斯尼亚西里尔文，而杜布罗夫尼克人保存的两个版本分别有9行拉丁文、25行波斯尼亚西里尔文和7行拉丁文、22行波斯尼亚西里尔文。⑤

---

① 早期塞尔维亚国家的名称。
② Mustafa Imamović, *Historija države i prava Bosne i Hercegovine*, p. 75.
③ "Povelja Kulina bana danas slavi 828. rođendan: Svjedočanstvo suverenosti i samostalnosti BiH", klix. ba, 29. 8. 2017.
④ "Kako je ruski konzul ukrao Povelju Kulina bana iz Dubrovnika", klix. ba, 19. 4. 2013.
⑤ Ibid.

波黑人一直想让头号"国宝"回家。每年的 8 月 29 日，都有高等学府、档案馆或民间组织举办纪念宪章的活动，公开呼吁波黑取回库林巴昂宪章的有学者、媒体人士和政客。2013 年，一名波黑联邦议会代表院的波族议员曾试图推动议会讨论要求俄罗斯向波黑归还库林巴昂宪章之事，但后来不了了之。这名议员当时表示，提出这份动议正是因为"很多人否认波黑的国家性，有些人甚至要破坏这个国家，用尽一切办法制造争议，对它的文化历史宝藏却毫不关心，他们隐藏、毁灭或是无视波黑历史悠久的国家性的所有符号"。①

波黑人想要在家门口亲眼看一看这份宪章，没有政府出面恐怕不行。图兹拉大学前校长、波黑前驻俄罗斯大使恩维尔·哈利洛维奇（Enver Halilović）曾表示，库林巴昂宪章被俄罗斯人看作是斯拉夫人最重要的历史文献之一，对于这一无价之宝，波黑必须由政府出面才有可能要回来。他说，尽管他 2005—2008 年任驻俄大使期间曾和包括俄总统普京在内的多名政府要员和俄宗教领袖提及过此事，但是"这样的要求在波黑国家层面从来没有得到真正的支持"。②

波黑内政部长、波黑波族最大政党民主行动党（SDA）的阿迪尔·奥斯马诺维奇（Adil Osmanović）2015 年底和俄罗斯文化部长会谈时提出俄方向波黑归还库林巴昂宪章的主张，后俄方由俄联邦科研机构管理局处理该请求。波黑内政部 2017 年时表示，在 2016 年下半年收到过俄方相关机构的回复。该机构称，库林巴昂宪章是 1832 年俄国副领事耶雷米亚·加吉奇（Jeremija Gagić）向一名烟草商购买的，因此是通过合法途径获得的，宪章被保存在俄罗斯科学院图书馆已经 170 多年，已经被登记为图书馆手稿部门的馆藏，属于俄联邦国家所有。收到俄方回复之后，波黑内政部回函称，希望俄方考虑将宪章在波黑临时展出的可能性，但还没有收到对方答复。波黑内政部称，将再次就这一请求敦促对方，希望对方能理解波黑人想亲眼看一看库林巴昂宪章原本的愿望。③

对于克罗地亚保存的宪章版本，波黑联邦档案馆馆长、波黑前主席团波族成员阿利雅·伊泽特贝戈维奇的顾问阿达米尔·耶尔科维奇（Adamir Jerković）2008 年曾致信克罗地亚政府，请求对方将保存在杜布罗夫尼克的库林巴昂宪章临时归还给波黑，但是遭到拒绝。耶尔科维奇认为这与克罗地亚主政的克罗地址民主共同体（HDZ）对波黑作为独立国家的消极立场有关，"他们把波黑视

---

① "Mehmedović traži povrat Povelje Kulina bana iz Rusije", klix. ba, 26. 3. 2013.
② "Država godinama neradi ništa na vraćanju Povelje Kulina bana BiH", klix. ba, 27. 8. 2012.
③ "I pored najave, Rusi još nisu odgovorili namolbu da Povelja Kulina bana privremeno bude izložena u BiH", klix. ba, 29. 8. 2017.

作一个临时性的国家，没有什么上千年的历史"。而杜布罗夫尼克馆方表示，库林巴昂宪章对杜布罗夫尼克也很重要，因为其内容涉及当地历史。①

从目前看来，呼吁宪章回归波黑的主要是波族和克族人士，并没有塞族人士。

四、寻回宪章的困境

今日波黑有三个法定主体民族——波什尼亚克族、塞尔维亚族和克罗地亚族，相应地有三大主要宗教——伊斯兰教、东正教和天主教。根据波黑2013年人口普查结果，波黑总人口为3,531,159人，其中50.11%为波族，30.87%为塞族，15.43%为克族。波黑三个民族、三种宗教共生共存数百年，却被南斯拉夫解体时期的民族主义政治荼毒。波黑战争已经结束20多年，但是波黑民族和解之路还相当漫长，民族主义政治话语仍然甚嚣尘上。虽然三个民族都是波黑历史的参与者、见证者，但很难想象同床异梦的波黑民族主义政党会在与俄罗斯或者克罗地亚商谈归还库林巴昂宪章一事上达成一致。

波黑波族当中历来有种说法，称波黑穆斯林都是前鲍格米勒派异端基督徒，本来就受到天主教和东正教的两头打压，所以在奥斯曼帝国入侵后改信伊斯兰教，希望借助这种"更高级"的信仰摆脱来自天主教和东正教的打压。但历史事实是，伊斯兰教在波黑的传播历经约250年，而且改宗的不仅有自称bosanski krstjani的鲍格米勒派异端基督徒，也有天主教徒和东正教徒。② 研究者认为，异端的"波斯尼亚教"（Crkva bosanska）在波斯尼亚巴昂国和王国时期有着包括不少诸侯在内的大量追随者，波斯尼亚的统治者虽然面临罗马教廷的巨大压力，但是也无法撼动波斯尼亚教会，这让波斯尼亚经历了数次十字军的洗劫。如今，波斯尼亚教这段中世纪历史被一些波黑人，尤其是波族人视为波斯尼亚人的历史身份标记之一。

虽然波斯尼亚巴昂国和王国均为基督教国家，在当时波斯尼亚的很多核心城市如今信仰伊斯兰教的波族人口也是占绝对多数，这并不妨碍波黑波族纪念本国中世纪的光辉历史。2012年，图兹拉市的市立公园就矗立起特弗尔特科一

---

① "Kako je ruski konzul ukrao Povelju Kulina bana iz Dubrovnika", klix. ba, 19.4.2013.
② Mustafa Imamović, *Historija države i prava Bosne i Hercegovine*, p.125.

世·科特罗马尼奇的雕像以及一块刻有库林巴昂宪章的石碑。耐人寻味的是，这块石碑上所刻的库林巴昂宪章"去基督教化"色彩严重，把文中所有指向基督教的词汇和句子都删去了。此事引发图兹拉州波黑克族民主共同体（HDZ BiH）州委会主席的抗议。他表示，"这是在试图以歪曲的方式呈现历史，特弗尔特科一世国王和库林巴昂是历史的一部分，如果有人要做出改动，那问题会很严重，这不是一个善意表示"。①

波黑克族主要信仰天主教，但是天主教在中世纪波黑的广泛传播被认为是在公元 13 世纪末期。此前天主教的多明我会传道士试图在异端横生的波斯尼亚传播正统天主教未果，在当时塞尔维亚国王的请求下，罗马教皇再派出方济各会传道士，希望波斯尼亚人"改弦易辙"。在波斯尼亚，方济各会传道士不做宗教裁判，而是善于亲近百姓，还通过主动承担参谋和外交斡旋等角色逐渐接近波斯尼亚王侯，从而极大地推动了天主教在波斯尼亚的传播，甚至挤压了本土波斯尼亚教的空间。② 波黑的方济各会天主教修士数百年来热爱祖国、深明大义、极力维护民族团结，受到波黑波族和克族共同的极大尊重。

波黑战争之后民族分布出现明显变化，形成民族大聚居的格局。波黑克族人口在波黑实体之一波黑联邦的西黑塞哥维那州、第 10 州、黑塞哥维那—内雷特瓦州和中波斯尼亚州较为集中。前三个州都位于西黑塞哥维那，且克族人口数量多于波族人口。

公元 14 世纪上半叶，立足于西黑塞哥维那的胡姆国（Hum）巴昂斯捷潘二世（Stjepan Ⅱ）宣布效忠波斯尼亚。一个多世纪之后，斯捷潘·科萨查（Stjepan Kosača）一统今波黑伊万山（Ivan Planina）以南、克罗地亚科纳弗莱（Konavle）以北、黑山尼克希奇（Nikšić）以东和克罗地亚伊莫茨基（Imotski）以西的领土，并自称"黑塞哥"（herceg③）。这片地区于是史称黑塞哥维那，意即"黑塞哥的领地"。胡姆国的古都是在今莫斯塔尔附近的布拉加伊（Blagaj），奥斯曼帝国统治时期黑塞哥维那的政治中心曾长期位于黑山的普列夫利亚（Pljevlja），19 世纪初黑塞哥维那帕夏谋求自治时迁往莫斯塔尔。现在，在莫斯塔尔市中心有一座叫"黑塞哥斯捷潘·科萨查克族宫"（Hrvatski dom Herceg Stjepan Kosača）的建筑，在外立面上还刻有波斯尼亚西里尔字母的斯捷

---

① "Povelji Kulina Bana nedostaju elementi o kršćanskoj povijesti Bosne", klix. ba, 22. 9. 2012.
② Mustafa Imamović, *Historija države i prava Bosne i Hercegovine*, pp. 71-72.
③ 准确音译为"赫尔采格"。

潘·科萨查的名字。这座建筑是在南联邦时期的 1960 年完工，建筑设计者是来自萨拉热窝的著名建设师雷乌夫·卡迪奇（Reuf Kadić），落成后曾长期被叫作"文化宫"（Dom kulture）。①

波黑克族津津乐道的另一位波斯尼亚王国时期的人物是卡塔琳娜·科萨查-科特罗马尼奇（Katarina Kosača-Kotromanić），她是黑塞哥斯捷潘·科萨查的女儿，嫁给了当时统治波斯尼亚王国的科特罗马尼奇家族的王储，这两大家族的联姻也标志着波斯尼亚和黑塞哥维那的正式合体。卡塔琳娜·科萨查·科特罗马尼奇后成为波斯尼亚的女王，有些历史学家认为她是波斯尼亚最后一位女王。

波黑战争时期，波黑克族右翼政党波黑克族民主共同体以西黑塞哥维那为据点建立黑塞哥—波斯尼亚克族共和国（Hrvtaska Republika Herceg-Bosna），虽然战后这一政权不复存在，但是"黑塞哥—波斯尼亚"的名称从未消亡，而且以波黑克族民主共同体为首的克族右翼政党至今仍在每年的 8 月 28 日这天庆祝黑塞哥—波斯尼亚克族共和国的"生日"。波黑主席团克族成员、波黑克族民主共同体党魁乔维奇 2017 年在莫斯塔尔举行的纪念活动上称，所纪念的是那些"为了波黑能作为国家存续下去而开创这一宏大事业的所有亲爱的人们"。② 克族右翼政客曾扬言要在波黑建立克族的"第三实体"，其对波黑政治秩序的挑战被波族视作为波黑政治稳定的一大威胁。

信仰东正教的人口大量进入波黑被认为是发生在黑塞哥斯捷潘·科萨查一统东西黑塞哥维那之后，或者是奥斯曼帝国征服波斯尼亚之后一段时期人口导入的结果。东正教在奥斯曼帝国治下的波黑得以发展，教徒分布在波黑各地。

波黑塞族右翼政党 1992 年 1 月 9 日宣布成立"波黑塞族人民共和国"（Republika Srpskog Naroda u Bosni i Hercegovini），3 月 1 日，当时作为南斯拉夫共和国之一的波黑公投决定脱离南斯拉夫成为独立国家，但投票遭到塞族抵制，波黑战争同年打响。1995 年 12 月 14 日《代顿和平协议》的签署标志着波黑内战结束，协议给予了波黑塞族政治实体——塞族共和国。波黑塞族共和国总统、独立社会民主人士联盟（SNSD）主席多迪克 2017 年 8 月 4 日在波黑塞族共和国和塞尔维亚共同纪念 1995 年克罗地亚"风暴"（Oluja）行动中遇难

---

① http://kosaca-mostar.com/web/onama.php.

② " Čović na obljetnici Hrvatske republike Herceg Bosne: Zadatak je sjećati se svih koji su pokrenuli jedan veliki projekt da bi BiH uopće preživjela", hrvatska-danas.com, 28. kolovoza 2017.

塞族的活动上说:"我相信,本世纪塞族将因其历史上遭受的苦难而有权利合为一体,我们在一起这也是非常自然的事情……我指的是在领土和国家意义上的在一起,这毫无疑问,因为我们反正都在一起。"① 多迪克政府还推动"去波斯尼亚语化",声称波黑宪法规定的三种官方语言之一波斯尼亚语不存在,称波族的语言为"波什尼亚克语"。

2017年10月多迪克接受一家波黑电视媒体专访,当对话他的记者说"这个国家(波黑)有一千年历史"时,他冷冷地回应道"我没活过那一千年",对波黑是三个民族共同的国家这一说法嗤之以鼻,表达了对波黑目前政治安排的失望。② 有意思的是,在波黑塞族共和国的"国徽"底部就赫然有个金百合花装饰的王冠——这正是波斯尼亚王国统治者科特罗马尼奇家族的象征。

如果让俄方归还库林巴昂宪章或允许宪章在波黑展出的努力在短期内没有长足进展,那么未来波黑的这一"国宝"能否回家恐怕更是未知数。

---

① "Dodik: U ovom vijeku Srbija i Srpska će biti jedno", oslobodjenje. ba, 4. avgusta 2017.
② "Dodik u CD-u: Pravim državu! Hadžifejzović: Neće moći bez rata!" https://www.youtube.com/watch? v=4eGGZCe6dQg, 15.10.2016.

斯洛文尼亚分离主义活动的宣传话语

杨 东

内容提要 在分裂活动中,动员宣传对民族关系有着重要的影响,宣传的内容直接影响动员的效果。二战后分裂活动的动员框架基本可分为民族安全、民主、经济三个类型。动员宣传通常是这三个类型的交叉,或按时序分布。巴尔干地区国家独立过程体现了这一假设。其中,斯洛文尼亚在独立公投时,经济话语成为优势话语,这也是斯洛文尼亚走向分离时没有引发大规模暴力冲突的原因之一。

关 键 词 分离主义 宣传话语 斯洛文尼亚

作者简介 杨东,中央社会主义学院学报编辑

话语指已经动员起来的民众共同使用的、却不是指向单一目的的一系列言语表达。话语是一种描述性语言框架,它是人们对于事件、行为、机构的认识,而且是已被人们通过各种媒体表达出来的诉说。如果说一种话语变成了优势话语,那么意味着它提供的解释成为公众看待某事物的普遍想法。政治家必须用一套话语描述和解释正在发生的事件,影响乃至引导舆论,让自己的话语成为优势话语。

分裂活动的话语,就是说明分裂必要性的话语集合。在多族群的背景下,就分裂活动而言,政治宣传比日常政治活动更具决定性作用。在分裂活动中,动员宣传对民族关系有着重要的影响,宣传的内容直接影响动员的效果。通过观察南斯拉夫的分裂,可以发现分裂活动的动员宣传话语并非单一,而是多种且经常变化。那么,分裂活动的领导者选取宣传话语体系的根据是什么?本项研究根据斯洛文尼亚独立的历史过程,给上述问题提供一种解释。

20世纪80年代末斯洛文尼亚发生的每一项重大事件都被政治人物当作提出主权的机会,他们通过各种具体的言论支撑自己的话语动员框架。这些话语框架借鉴了独立运动之前在斯洛文尼亚已经存在的话语——经济、民族主义、民主。这些人物运用这三种框架解释各种事件,宣传话语和舆论也随之被这些政治事件所塑造。不过,普遍的公开辩论大大限制了政治活动家可选择的宣传话语。

一、斯洛文尼亚独立之前的宣传话语

在斯洛文尼亚独立动员开始之前,三种民族认同话语共存并相互竞争:经济、种族—民族主义、民主。

(一)经济话语

经济问题是斯洛文尼亚1990年独立的重要论据。斯洛文尼亚具有经济民族主义的传统,经济话语能够吸引人们,强化自我形象,是斯洛文尼亚国家认同的重要组成部分,因为斯洛文尼亚人对本国在南斯拉夫联盟中是经济发达地区而感到自豪。而经济问题与财政问题有关,在讨论经济改革时,必然会在联邦一级引发斯洛文尼亚主权问题的讨论。

20世纪80年代初,斯洛文尼亚社会中就蔓延着如下看法:南斯拉夫的经济危机拖累了斯洛文尼亚的经济发展,如果没有贝尔格莱德的联邦官僚机构,斯洛文尼亚可以更有效地发挥其经济潜力。不过,当时没有人论及独立,但弱化与联邦联系的愿望确实存在。这种看法并不是20世纪80年代才出现的新鲜事物,早在60年代末,斯洛文尼亚共盟自由派对经济不平等的愤慨就浮现出来。当时,克罗地亚和斯洛文尼亚都提出了改革的要求。在克罗地亚,这引发了民族主义运动,甚至是独立的要求;而在斯洛文尼亚,则因为"道路事件"①,引发了领导人中的共和派和邦联派的对抗。1987年和1988年的民意调查显示,斯洛文尼亚的大多数人认为,斯洛文尼亚如果不在南斯拉夫的框架

---

① 1969年,斯洛文尼亚得到世界银行的资助,扩大其公路网络,但这笔资金由联邦领导层重新分配给了其他共和国的公路项目,这引起了斯洛文尼亚公众的高度关注,斯洛文尼亚政府与民众都认为这是联邦权力的滥用。

内，经济发展前景会更好，但绝大多数人（71.2%）不希望斯洛文尼亚与南斯拉夫分离。

在斯洛文尼亚流传广泛的一种情绪是，"如果我们自己，就没有经济问题，我们可能成为东方的瑞士或列支敦士登，或是达到意大利、奥地利的水平"。这种不满情绪，为斯洛文尼亚人认为自己是南斯拉夫经济政策的牺牲品的悲情打下了基础。《新周刊》（Nova Revija）在1987年发表了所谓的斯洛文尼亚国家计划，描述了分裂的愿景，"考虑到斯洛文尼亚拥有南斯拉夫人口的7%……生产了南斯拉夫社会产品的18%，出口的27%……在未来，我们不再需要在更大的国家的羽翼下爬行……正如数字所证明的那样，我们现在已经在经济上被定义为一个国家"。[1]

对经济不公正的看法反复引发"斯洛文尼亚在联邦中的作用"的讨论。参与这种讨论的主要是斯洛文尼亚的政治精英，他们以经济理由寻求更多的自治权。由于联邦一致性的规定，如果决策不能得到每一个共和国的同意，联邦总统是不能签署的。每个共和国对联邦的制衡作用使得斯洛文尼亚得以保护自己利益。

南斯拉夫关于权力下放与集权化的争论也诱发了对经济改革的憧憬。塞尔维亚希望联邦更加集权，而斯洛文尼亚、克罗地亚希望各共和国能有更多的自主权。塞尔维亚的立场是增加联邦的权力可以确保南斯拉夫市场的统一，并保证政策在全联邦的贯彻执行。为此，塞尔维亚希望改变联邦议会的投票制度，主张多数制，限制共和国和自治省院的一致性原则。[2] 相比之下，斯洛文尼亚和克罗地亚政治家和知识分子则认为"集中制将导致行政控制，遏制经济主动性"，他们认为南斯拉夫地区发展不平衡使得实施中央领导的经济稳定和改革政策是不可能的。这场争论扩大了斯洛文尼亚、克罗地亚一方与塞尔维亚一方之间的分歧。

1987年，斯洛文尼亚和克罗地亚政府拒绝支付联邦军费，并且从联邦政府的税收中扣除了税款。从此，除了外国贷款的获得权和分配权之外，各共和国获得了事实上的财政自主权。

1987年至1988年间，不仅米兰·库昌（Milan Kucan）等斯洛文尼亚领导

---

[1] "Nova Revija again weeps over the fate of Slovenia in Yugoslavia: Smoke bombs of 'democracy'," *Borba*, 18 January 1988.

[2] Lenard J. Cohen, *Broken Bonds: The Disintegration of Yugoslavia*, Boulder, CO: Westview Press, 1993, pp. 57-58.

人，还有许多外国评论家将斯洛文尼亚的自治要求解读为经济问题。虽然经济话语能够吸引大众表达不满，但并不能激发人们参加抗议活动或群众运动。

（二）种族—民族主义话语

除了经济方面的不满之外，在斯洛文尼亚社会中斯洛文尼亚语言和文化受到威胁的观点也非常普遍。这一问题在1979年首次引发公开讨论。产生这种社会心理和相关政策的原因在于移民。有大量的民众从南斯拉夫联邦其他共和国和自治省迁居到斯洛文尼亚，对移民的敌意源于斯洛文尼亚人担心移民影响自己的就业。1979年，卢布尔雅那市9%的人口是非斯洛文尼亚人，而到1981年，达到16%。20世纪80年代初，来自南斯拉夫南部各共和国的移民与斯洛文尼亚人之间的紧张局势不断加剧，大多数斯洛文尼亚人希望限制移民。根据80年代初期的民意调查，斯洛文尼亚44%的受访者认为他们的语言受到移民数量上升的威胁。1982年春天，斯洛文尼亚共盟代表大会甚至也讨论了语言保护问题。本民族语言的传承和保护问题也促成了斯洛文尼亚新闻工作者和知识分子关于斯洛文尼亚是否存在民族主义的辩论。

民族主义话语的舆论阵地《新周刊》所刊发的文章，强调民族国家，强调家庭、语言、基督教传统价值观的重要性，是一种民族主义话语，这与20世纪上半叶斯洛文尼亚的政治话语相似。这种民族价值观的抬头伴随着强烈的反共意识。[1] 不过，80年代末民族主义话语被边缘化，民主和人权话语成为动员人们的新工具。因为，绝大多数移民是出于纯粹的经济原因而来，与塞尔维亚或南斯拉夫没有任何政治联系。

（三）民主话语

20世纪80年代经济话语、民族主义话语都已存在，但到了80年代后期最有影响力的话语是民主话语。这一话语将斯洛文尼亚人视为公民，从而为国家认同建立了比种族更为包容的解释。[2] 民主话语的动员能力很强，它不仅能够动员一小部分政治或文化精英，而且能以可见的方式动员群众。当然，在斯洛文尼亚，经济、民族主义话语也能吸引大众的信仰和不满，但它们并未能激励

---

[1] Baranka Magas, *The Destruction of Yugoslavia: Tracking the Break-up, 1980–92*, London: Verso, 1993, p. 132.

[2] John K. Glenn, *Framing Democracy: Civil Society and Civic Movements in Eastern Europe*, NY: Stanford University Press, 2002.

人们参加抗议活动或群众运动。民主话语将不公正定义为侵犯人权。人权观念体现在公民的集体认同中,而共盟政权则代表着认同的"他者"。支持这一话语框架的人并不关心斯洛文尼亚的主权问题,而且是反民族主义者。恰是该话语在确立斯洛文尼亚国家认同的过程中,引导斯洛文尼亚的公众舆论,值得玩味。

20世纪70年代中期,伴随斯洛文尼亚社会的多元化,民主、人权话语开始浮现,出现了朋克运动,以及各种艺术和文化活动。从20世纪80年代初,斯洛文尼亚出现了一些自发组织的团体,如环保人士、和平运动、新时代精神运动,还出现了女权主义和同性恋权利活动。托马斯·马斯特纳克(Tomaz Mastnak)把这些新的社会运动称为"替代场景",它们共同代表了一个"民主阵线",都反对共产主义制度。不过,这个"替代场景"不是一个统一的政治反对派,而是"一些为了具体、日常、特殊事情的复合体"。[1]

起初,斯洛文尼亚共盟认为,这些新的社会运动只是对西方类似活动的"赶时髦模仿",会自行消散。此外,共盟利用葛兰西的新马克思主义将民主纳入马克思主义政治语言的解释范围,以此证明民主问题本质上与自治社会主义有关,自治模式实际上是真正能够实现的民主,因此民主就成为党的纲领中的目标之一。共盟内部也开始将新社会运动视为一种可以理解的、正面的社会现象。关于"民主"的党内讨论持续了数年。1985年,斯洛文尼亚学生组织起来,抵制在贝尔格莱德举行的第二次世界大战胜利四十周年纪念活动。斯洛文尼亚共盟意识到,民主问题绝不是单纯的观念和理论问题,而是一场"争取青年"的较量。将一些新社会运动纳入社会主义青年联盟进行管控,虽然是十分精明的决定,但这项政策却没有产生预想的效果,社会主义青年联盟实际上未能争取到青年人。[2] 1986年,米兰·库昌当选斯洛文尼亚共盟中央主席团主席,党内自由派取得党的领导权。斯洛文尼亚共盟转向容忍乃至支持各项民主的倡议。1987年1月,斯洛文尼亚青年领袖在卢布尔雅那组织请愿签名活动,要求停止庆祝铁托生日的仪式、优待政治犯、投票决定核工厂的建设、舆论自由。《青年报》(Mladina)是斯洛文尼亚政治活动中民主话语的代言者。《青年报》发表了许多当时禁忌主题的文章,如铁托和南斯拉夫军队等。由于斯洛文

---

[1] Jill Benderly and Evan Kraft, eds., *Independent Slovenia: Origins, Movements, Prospects*, Basingstoke: Palgrave Macmillan, 1997, p.95.

[2] 何海根:《民主与斯洛文尼亚的政治转型》,《当代世界社会主义问题》2014年第1期,第72—81页。

尼亚共盟当局存在一种容忍的气氛，这些运动逐渐改变了斯洛文尼亚的政治气氛，公开的讨论和异议都变得平常。

南斯拉夫当局认为斯洛文尼亚政府容忍对贝尔格莱德和南人民军的敌视是危险的，最让南斯拉夫保守派感到头疼的是，斯洛文尼亚的领导人不镇压这些行为。斯洛文尼亚的多元化，助长了联邦领导层、南人民军、塞尔维亚人与斯洛文尼亚共盟之间的对抗。1988年初，塞尔维亚修改自己的宪法，加强了对塞尔维亚共和国、科索沃、伏伊伏丁那省份的控制，并力图限制部分共和国的自治权，建立一个更强大的联邦政府，这引起了斯洛文尼亚的恐慌。直到1988年末，斯洛文尼亚的领导层仍不干涉民主活动，同时在联邦一级强烈捍卫斯洛文尼亚的利益。在面对贝尔格莱德压力的情况下，斯洛文尼亚共盟容忍不同政见，分离倾向日益明显。对斯洛文尼亚领导层和民主运动的攻击，反而强化了"只有走向多元化和自由化才能保护共和国主权"的观念。结果在1988年，讨论分裂的可能性成为知识界的一种普遍现象。《新周刊》号召保卫斯洛文尼亚人民自决权和独立权。1988年4月，讨论修改南斯拉夫宪法时，斯洛文尼亚作家和社会学家要求政治多元化，认为斯洛文尼亚有权"加入国家联盟或脱离该国家联盟"。1988年6月，500名知识分子在卢布尔雅那集会，讨论斯洛文尼亚在南斯拉夫中的地位问题，一些人提出斯洛文尼亚有权分离。这表明分裂的舆论准备基本完成，只是需要事件将其转化为行动。1988年夏天对《青年报》记者的审判成为了导火索，这是斯洛文尼亚最重要的动员事件，标志着分裂运动的开始。

二、斯洛文尼亚走向分离与社会舆论

（一）"四人受审"事件

1988年春，在斯洛文尼亚军官的帮助下，《青年报》的三位记者披露了一份秘密军事文件。文件是一份宣布紧急状态的计划，在紧急状态下，南斯拉夫人民军可以接受的保守派将代替斯洛文尼亚的自由派领导人。计划还包括一份逮捕名单。这份军事文件公开后，导致三名记者和一名军官受审。经过联邦军事法庭的审判，四人入狱。审判不是在斯洛文尼亚，而是在塞尔维亚和克罗地亚举行，诉讼程序没有向公众公开，被告也不能申请平民律师辩护。这在斯洛文尼亚引发了一系列大规模的示威活动，从 1988 年 6 月开始一直持续到 1989 年春。斯洛文尼亚共盟领导人也抗议这种违反共和国宪法权利的做法，并要求在斯洛文尼亚进行审判，南斯拉夫联邦主席团拒绝了这一呼吁。这一事件促进了斯洛文尼亚的团结并将斯洛文尼亚推上了独立的道路。

这场审判开庭前，民主话语是群众运动的主流声音，公众的视线集中于被告能否得到公正的审判。1988 年 6 月，在卢布尔雅那有大量人群举行抗议活动，要求释放记者。除此而外，抗议者的要求远远超出了与记者命运有关的内容。他们呼吁"南斯拉夫的更大的自由，民主和人权，遏制军队的权力"，提出军方对三名男子的处理"实际上损害了斯洛文尼亚国家的主权"。动员是通过基于民主话语框架发生的。

开庭后，公众发现法庭上使用的是塞尔维亚—克罗地亚语而不是斯洛文尼亚语，公众的关注点就转移到斯洛文尼亚语的地位问题。一旦语言问题出现，社会活动家就依托民族主义话语，这一类的话语在斯洛文尼亚各界都有强大和广泛的情感号召力。在 1988 年抗议活动中，语言问题成为最强大的动员主题，"沉默的多数"被民族主义意识形态所驱动。

总之，在示威活动中能听到两种话语：一种是民主话语，强调应该以人权为主导，重视整个国家的自由平等；一种是民族主义话语，强调种族文化安全。民主话语被斯洛文尼亚领导层所接受，反而导致该话语的边缘化，种族安全舆论提升。斯洛文尼亚共盟领导人最初不愿论及审判，远离国内的反人民军情绪和活动，并试图通过对该事件做务实的解释来表现自身的中立性。他们提出应关注经济和社会问题，"工业生产下降、斯洛文尼亚经济结构调整和现代化进度太缓慢、流动性不足、通货膨胀，由此引起的一系列社会问题，引起了人们的关注，才导致安全和政治事件恶化"。[①] 但这种表态遭到多方反对。南斯拉夫其他共和国和媒体要求斯洛文尼亚领导人对允许示威活动负责。同时，在斯洛文尼亚国内，一方面，退休的国防部长布兰科·马穆拉（Branko Mamula）批评库昌放宽开放的经济政策；另一方面，抗议者批评斯洛文尼亚领导人允许这种"耻辱和屈辱"的审判，军事法庭"侵犯斯洛文尼亚人民和国家的主权"。斯洛文尼亚共盟领导人压力倍增，他们需要国内支持，才能继续坚持开放政策，才能应对贝尔格莱德和军队的压力。如何获得这种支持？显然容忍民主发展和务实的政策不足以维护新形势下的国内合法性，斯洛文尼亚共盟领导

---

① "Slovene presidency discusses situation", Tanjug news agency, Belgrade, 14 July 1988.

人转向民族语言问题,利用民族主义情绪,最终实现与抗议者结盟。斯洛文尼亚共盟领导人开始强调以斯洛文尼亚语作为国家语言的权利,提及"斯洛文尼亚国家的独特性和文化、历史合法性",从而拥有国家认同的民族定义版本。库昌在斯洛文尼亚共盟中央委员会会议上完全致力于斯洛文尼亚语的问题,他说:

> 斯洛文尼亚认为语言同斯洛文尼亚人和其政治主权密切相关。正是由于自身的文化、语言受到意大利人、德国人、匈牙利人的威胁,斯洛文尼亚国家才开始形成。到目前为止,我们还没有自己的国家来保护这种语言。因此,为一个新的社会主义南斯拉夫而进行的斗争……也是为我们的语言而斗争。斯洛文尼亚不是那种不能保证自由使用斯洛文尼亚语和语言平等的国家,而且也不能被视为不能保障斯洛文尼亚人民的自由,主权和平等的国家。①

斯洛文尼亚共盟领导人的态度,表明他们认同庭审时是否使用斯洛文尼亚语与共和国主权直接相关。审判结果宣告后,库昌说"判决篡夺了共和国的主权"。总而言之,领导层通过民族主义话语加强其合法性,争取民众支持。斯洛文尼亚共盟与南人民军的这场冲突,让"斯洛文尼亚公共舆论与背后的共盟和政府领导层得以统一,却又不破坏政治多元化的种子"。②

为什么斯洛文尼亚共盟领导人选择民族主义话语来解决问题?尽管斯洛文尼亚早有自由主义倾向,但共盟毕竟是共产主义组织的一部分,接受民主框架,以反共产主义的人权活动家的面目示人,是一个尴尬的选择。而强调民族和文化主题则没有这些顾虑,庭审期间的语言问题已是公众不满的重要来源,这能有效赢取民心。捍卫斯洛文尼亚人的国家和文化权利对于共盟而言不仅仅是空洞的言论,因为共盟仍然是执政党,拥有政府权力,也就负有保护国家和文化的责任。斯洛文尼亚共盟在南斯拉夫联邦中维护本国的权利,增强了自己在斯洛文尼亚民众中的威信。在对抗贝尔格莱德的过程中斯洛文尼亚共盟的执政合法性得到巩固。选择民族主义言论在当时看来最有可能增加斯洛文尼亚共

---

① Slavko Gajevic, "A dispute grows into a political trial," *Borba*, Ljubljana, 28 July 1988.
② Susan L. Woodward, *Balkan Tragedy: Chaos and Dissolution After the Cold War*, Washington, DC: Brookings Institution, 1995, p. 96.

盟在国内的信誉和合法性。斯共盟在1990年第一次大选之前就开始使用民族主义话语,以此表明他们在保护斯洛文尼亚,而不是南联邦的代言人。虽然他们既不能让记者免于起诉,也不能确保这一审判在斯洛文尼亚进行,但他们在1989年秋天设法修改宪法,在法理上保证了如若没有斯洛文尼亚政府的同意,联邦领导层和军队不能干预斯洛文尼亚,这为防止联邦策动政变打下了基础。

(二)斯洛文尼亚修宪

1988年初,南斯拉夫联邦主席团打算实施联邦宪法改革,旨在集中南斯拉夫的政治权力,以便解决经济问题。斯洛文尼亚反对联邦修宪的政治动员随之开始,这一举措再次来自下层,主要是来自保守派知识分子,其中许多后来成为反对党的创始人。2月,斯洛文尼亚出现了一个新的联盟,由《新周刊》《青年报》和作家协会组成。他们担心宪法修正案会遏制斯洛文尼亚的自治权,要求对联邦宪法修正案进行全民投票。3月,《青年报》刊发了5万人签署的支持全民投票的请愿书。迫于压力,斯洛文尼亚共盟决定不接受联邦宪法修正案。11月,在第三次抗议"四人受审"的浪潮中,再次出现对联邦宪法进行全民公投的要求,并把这一要求与保护斯洛文尼亚主权关联起来。斯洛文尼亚作家协会是这个议题最大的推动者,他们要求在联邦宪法修正案通过之前,先修订斯洛文尼亚宪法。

修宪促成了新的党派联盟。1989年5月,一些党派组成斯洛文尼亚民主反对派——"德莫斯"(DEMOS),它们共同签署了《1989年5月宣言》,号召建立了一个"斯洛文尼亚人民的主权国家",同时也提出了民主化的要求。同月,"四人受审"事件的当事人之一亚内兹·扬沙(Janez Janša)突然被捕,引发了斯洛文尼亚城市的第四波抗议活动。抗议者指责领导人没有保护好被监禁的记者。

斯洛文尼亚民主反对派内部对主权和人权的关系存在两种意见,一种是基于民族的政治传统,另一种则以国家的民意为基础。社会主义青年联合会、《青年报》等虽支持主权,但他们认为主权是为了确保尊重人权,人权才是最重要的。保守的知识分子则采用相反的逻辑,认为独立是首要事项,其后才是民主和尊重人权。这反映了"斯洛文尼亚主要知识分子已分裂成民族主义派和自由派"。随着主权得到越来越多的民族主义解读,自由主义者失去了对这一问题的热忱,只能不情愿地在竞选中支持独立,民主话语框架逐渐边缘化。

最终,斯洛文尼亚共盟屈服于反对派的压力,接受斯洛文尼亚宪法修正案，兑现了他们捍卫国家免受贝尔格莱德压力的承诺。宪法修正案提出了政治多元化，保证斯洛文尼亚的分离权力，并禁止联邦对斯洛文尼亚领土进行任何干预。修正案的功能是法律意义上的国家自卫，其中的逻辑是种族—民族主义话语所表达的内容。

（三）"经济战争"

1989年9月，斯洛文尼亚宪法修正案通过。11月，斯洛文尼亚政府禁止塞尔维亚人和黑山人到卢布尔雅那抗议集会。针对这一禁令，塞尔维亚政府中断了与斯洛文尼亚的经济关系。此后的两个月，两个共和国之间的经济交流大大减少，这就是塞尔维亚和斯洛文尼亚之间所谓的经济战争。

斯洛文尼亚一方的普遍观点是，抗议集会和禁运是为了推翻斯洛文尼亚现有领导集体。因此，斯洛文尼亚官方将主权当作保护本国经济利益的方法，以减少"经济战争"的损失。这使斯洛文尼亚与联邦之间的关系越来越对立。斯洛文尼亚共盟将禁运描述成"塞尔维亚政权最新的疯狂行动"，强烈要求斯洛文尼亚的经济主权。斯洛文尼亚共盟内部已有人宣传"应该预防对斯洛文尼亚的经济掠夺……取消援助不发达地区的基金，发行国家货币"。米兰·库昌说："在对斯洛文尼亚实施禁运之后，南斯拉夫不再是，也不可能是曾经的南斯拉夫。我们要重新确定各国在联盟中的相互关系……有一件事是肯定的，南斯拉夫作为大塞尔维亚的概念……我们是不能接受的。"① 这场冲突不久之后，1990年1月，联邦主义者和邦联主义者之间的谈判破裂了。斯洛文尼亚代表团退出南斯拉夫共产者联盟会议，原本将南斯拉夫共盟改为"自由和独立的共和主义共产党"的建议也被彻底否定了。

三、1990年的竞选与公投——话语的混合与竞争

参加1990年斯洛文尼亚二战后第一次多党制大选的有三个主要政治团体：前共产主义者重组为民主革新党、由保守的反对党组成的"德莫斯"、由之前的社会主义青年联盟组成的自由党。整体而言，独立议题主导选战。不仅是政

---

① "Kucan opens Belgrade congress", Tanjug news agency, Belgrade, 22 December 1989, FBIS-EEU, 8 January 1990.

治家,连普通百姓都认为"独立"是主要的政治问题。值得玩味的是,独立的实际内涵是模糊的,可以指从联邦到全面分裂之间的任何状态,因此,尽管每个党和候选人都提倡斯洛文尼亚"主权",但他们之间存在巨大差别。德莫斯经常暗示独立就是全面分裂,它的总统候选人普奇尼克(Jože Pučnik)赞成在未来的南斯拉夫联盟内部建立一个享有主权的斯洛文尼亚。不过,对这一点他觉得塞尔维亚能否接受仍是未知数。因此,要准备分裂南斯拉夫联盟,建立独立国家。前共产党人也倡导争取主权,但他们更希望组成一个邦联,"斯洛文尼亚独立可以,但分裂不行",这是他们的口号。而民主革新党采取务实和温和的语言,提出"尊重人权、自由选举、缓解与科索沃的紧张关系、要求南斯拉夫各共和国的自决权",工作的重点是经济问题、民主转型。民族主义话语实际上已从该党的宣传话语中消失。但曾经大肆宣扬的外部威胁并没有消失,为什么要放弃这个能够动员民众的话题?之所以产生这种话语转变,是因为德莫斯的竞争,前共产党人即便坚持种族安全话语也很难与德莫斯竞争,德莫斯的许多领导人都是《新周刊》的活跃人物,被认为是代表了民族主义的"最真实"的声音。这一宣传话语的主导权已经被德莫斯占有。

民族主义在德莫斯的动员话语中占据显著地位,德莫斯的政治人物都谈及"担心对斯洛文尼亚认同和文化的威胁",把南斯拉夫描述成一个人造的帝国主义产物,宣称斯洛文尼亚曾经公开遭受到克罗地亚人、塞尔维亚人同化的威胁。在此基础上,它们要求建立独立的国家。因此,德莫斯的国家认同是基于种族排他的观点之上,也是基于所谓南斯拉夫其他人民对斯洛文尼亚的威胁之上的。这一观点与《青年报》所倡导的国家认同形成鲜明对照,《青年报》强烈谴责新生的各党是在"放纵民族主义言论",对斯洛文尼亚的国际政治形象感到焦虑,嫉妒地注视着中欧和东欧其他地区的民主化,同时严厉批评德莫斯,害怕它"正在推动斯洛文尼亚成为一个民族国家"。

经济主权是独立运动的重要组成部分,竞选各方都提出经济独立,这一议题成为各方共识,说明经济问题在斯洛文尼亚群众中有着广泛的影响。斯洛文尼亚人普遍认为斯洛文尼亚在联邦中支出过高,联邦经济政策伤害斯洛文尼亚的经济。因此,只有联邦重组,斯洛文尼亚才可以留在南斯拉夫境内。这种观点有事实依据。20世纪80年代后期到90年代,斯洛文尼亚经历了一个经济衰退期,当时国内的产品供应下降,失业率上升。斯洛文尼亚指责联邦经济政策有问题,如不切实际的汇率、限制性货币政策、利率不足等。但正当联邦政府终于设法遏制住通货膨胀时,经济话题已走入舆论的中心。1989年11月开始的"经济战争",也使经济成为斯洛文尼亚群众关注的焦点,并如上文所述催生了斯洛文尼亚争取主权的动机。1990年3月,斯洛文尼亚宪法修正案中包含"经济独立"的条文。因此,参与竞选的各方都在讨论经济、斯洛文尼亚的物质利益。

竞选的结果是,德莫斯在240席议会中获得了126席的相对多数席位,并获得了最多17.3%的选票,表明选民对独立的谨慎态度,他们没有把全部权力都交给主张分离的民主反对派。

总的来说,相比之前的各项事件,以单一问题吸引公众关注不同,竞选活动提供了一个相对开放的空间。竞选成为1988—1989年出现的所有话语框架之间的公开竞赛。选举结果显示了话语的相对共鸣。只有德莫斯选择用排外主义版本的民族安全话语传播国家认同,并得到了略多于一半选民的支持。经济话语为各方所共有,民主话语也是如此,但在各方言论中并不突出。经济话语框架是以民族包容的方式构建国家认同的适当工具,能够吸引那些偏爱公民身份和节制的群众,他们不喜欢激进的民族主义。因此,在此后的竞选活动中,为了说服尽可能多的人赞成独立,各方必须运用经济话语。在竞选期间,各方强调分歧,为了在民众面前表现自己的不同,德莫斯这种新成立的党,需要极端的言论吸引选民,同时也要撕裂民众的共识,才有机会战胜共产党人。而执政后,它需要团结民众,为独立争取民意。这就解释了为什么德莫斯随后发生根本性转向。

德莫斯组建新一届政府后,开始推动独立公投。反对党则认为新政府是不能应付经济困境,才发起独立公投。《青年报》严厉批评新一届领导人"反民主、歧视、无理",指责这是"疯狂地扫除斯洛文尼亚共产主义社会的巫术",指责斯洛文尼亚政府正在伤害"斯洛文尼亚作为民主的天花板"的形象。对于《青年报》来说,共产党人下台后的新敌人是国民沙文主义,这表明国家认同的争议仍在继续。[①] 事实上,所有主要的政治行为者,包括执政党和在野党,都支持独立。而且,双方所使用的话语也没有显著差异。总的来说,以经济和威胁论为主,而民族主义的议题几乎消失。这意味着公民身份对选民的吸引力大于种族排他性。

然而,经济利益才是公投的主要理由。斯洛文尼亚议会发表声明,概述举

---

① Patrick Hyder Patterson, "The East is read: The end of communism, Slovenian exceptionalism, and the independent journalism of Mladina," *East European Politics and Societies* 14, No. 2 (2000), pp. 411-459.

行公民投票的原因。该文件仅讨论经济原因，并详细说明了预期的经济优势，结论是："斯洛文尼亚的自治将有助于更迅速地出台适合斯洛文尼亚经济的正常经济政策。"① 库昌认为，举行公民投票的经济原因是非常重要的，"南斯拉夫的经济正在加速混乱，可能产生不可预见的经济、社会和政治后果"。"斯洛文尼亚经济基础正在受到破坏"，因此，斯洛文尼亚的独立刻不容缓。

总的来说，竞选活动中最为突出的是经济话语框架和对军事干预的恐惧。公投是亲独立阵营的一大成功，投票率为93.5%，88.5%的投票赞成"斯洛文尼亚独立和自治国家"。

四、结论

直到1991年6月宣布独立为止，斯洛文尼亚的政治人物都在强调，争取主权是因为经济问题。然而，通过总结斯洛文尼亚独立运动的话语动态，可以发现，话语框架存在变化，并受到情境化事件的强烈影响。"四人受审"事件，《青年报》的记者被捕，在没有平民律师的情况下即被军事法庭审判，影响这一事件的话语框架是民主话语。当人们获悉，审判时不能使用斯洛文尼亚语后，民主话语很快就边缘化，强调斯洛文尼亚语言、文化和民族的重要性的民族主义话语框架成为主流舆论。而民族主义话语框架有着悠久的历史渊源，甚至被看作"天生"的。早在1988年，民族安全就是斯洛文尼亚民众话语中最突出的话题。1989年，民族主义话语成为是推动修改宪法的理想工具，而追求独立的政治人物都以民族主义话语动员群众。在与塞尔维亚的"经济战争"中，经济话语又上升为优势话语。因此，是各种相互关联的事件推动动员过程中哪些话语框架成为优势话语，这种情况在竞选和独立公投期间再次出现。总之，由于早期的多元化和自由化，政治家们有机会试验不同类型的话语框架。自由的政治气候、各种问题的探讨形成了活跃的公共空间。三年间，三种话语框架互相竞争，政治家、社会活动家有时间和机会来培养集体团结，找到共同点，最终促成了三种话语框架之间融合，从而形成一个较少对抗性的独立话语框架。到全民公投时，哪些话语能割裂选民，哪些能整合选民已经很明显。大

---

① "Slovene Executive Council approves plebiscite", Tanjug news agency, 30 November 1990, FEBIS-EEU, 3 November 1990.

部分斯洛文尼亚人否定了种族—民族安全话语，经济话语成为最大多数人可以接受的观点。

此外，在动员过程中同时出现包容性和排他性的国家认同。在整个动员期间，这两个版本的国家认同相互竞争，到运动结束时，包容性解释已成为主流。除了全民公投外，整个动员期间，民族安全始终存在于话语领域，成为一股潜流。自由党和《青年报》聚集的知识分子维护民族的公民观念；而德莫斯的政治家则坚持排他性的解释；在选举的前期，前共产主义者将国家认同态度从族裔角度转变为公民角度。斯洛文尼亚领导人意识到，公民身份而不是民族认同才是国家的共同特征，他们建立了一种基于公民意识而不是民族观念的国家认同。因此，斯洛文尼亚独立运动的一个特点是，动员进程中没有针对内部少数群体（特别是移民）的种族排斥或仇外心理，这在巴尔干地区是难能可贵的。虽然各项事件决定了哪些话语框架在某一时间点获得优势地位，但总体动员过程倾向于包容性框架，把少数民族当作内部威胁的看法没有出现。据此，可以说，如果生活在分离主义实体中的少数群体与受到威胁的中央政权没有政治联系，那么就不会被公认为是内部威胁，并有望在民族包容的基础上构建集体认同。在这种情况下，由于经济问题的相对非对抗性，经济话语更适合构建集体认同。如同斯洛文尼亚，这种适度的动员就很有效。

学术论坛

我译《保加利亚中短篇小说集》

余志和

作者简介 余志和,新华社高级编辑,历任新华社索非亚分社记者、参编部主任、《参考消息》总编辑、经济信息编辑部主任等职

2018年4月,人民文学出版社出版了我翻译的《保加利亚中短篇小说集》(上下册)。6月2日,保加利亚驻华大使馆在北京朝阳公园金台艺术馆为小说集举办了推荐会;6月30日,人民文学出版社和"北京阅读季"联合举办了题为"保加利亚及其文学历程"的文学公益讲座。

《保加利亚中短篇小说集》收集了保加利亚不同时期、不同风格的18位经典作家的41篇作品,是对保加利亚中短篇小说创作完整过程的真实记录。这些精心筛选的作品以其深邃的思想、浓郁的乡土气息和鲜活的人物形象,展现了保加利亚人100多年来不断变幻的生活场景,以及他们的爱与恨、欢乐与忧愁……

一、译事缘起

2009年年初,中国社会科学院世界历史研究所研究员马细谱博士转给我一份保加利亚文化部的文件——《关于申请翻译保加利亚文学作品的一般条件》,我喜出望外,针对我国译介保加利亚文学作品的短板,开始选译该国历代经典中短篇小说。2010年4月,当翻译工作告一段落时,我发现,其时已超过了保方规定的申请截止日期。无奈,我在6月上旬把部分译稿交给了人民文学出版

社。出版社很快就答复我说，译稿质量符合出版要求。此后，我一面继续翻译，一面设法解决出版经费和某些作品的版权问题。光阴荏苒，一晃六年。

面对部分国人"一切向钱看"的境遇，不止一个朋友对我翻译保加利亚文学作品感到困惑，甚至有人对我说："在保语界，数你最傻，现如今，谁还在搞翻译啊？"我往往莞尔一笑，简短地回答："值得，值得！"

我坚持翻译，起码有三个理由。

一是情缘。中国和保加利亚相隔天渊。我作为新华社记者，曾三度赴该国履职，共计13年，对这个美丽的国度及其友善的人民充满了眷恋之情。

二是责任。保加利亚经典作品较难翻译，我虽才薄智浅，仍愿大胆尝试，茕茕孑立而不畏寂寞，想以我的绵薄之力填补一点两国文化交流的空白。

三是爱好。我自幼膜拜文学，参加工作后又同翻译结下了不解之缘，久而久之，我把翻译视为我的一种生存状态、一种乐趣，往往废寝忘食，甘之如饴。

二、保国文学

保加利亚学者断定，该国文学是最早的斯拉夫文学。其理由是，它发端于9世纪，即在圣徒基里尔和梅托迪创造了斯拉夫字母，翻译了首批宗教典籍之后。9—10世纪，由于基里尔的门徒克利门特·奥赫里茨基等启蒙者和神职人员的潜心研究，以及诸多学派的积极活动，古保加利亚文学取得了杰出的艺术成就，进而传入俄罗斯、塞尔维亚、瓦拉几亚（罗马尼亚）和摩尔多瓦。

10世纪末，世俗和反正统教会的文献陆续问世。13—14世纪，古保加利亚文学再度繁荣，《博里洛夫追荐亡人名簿》《索非亚圣诗》等相继产生，特尔诺沃学派的代表还广泛从事语言、文学和翻译活动。许多保加利亚手抄本对罗马尼亚文学和俄罗斯文学产生了较大影响。17—18世纪，政治、社会和生活题材进入文学殿堂，约450册手抄本中就有许多布道稿、人物传记和历史故事。最有代表性的文学现象是出现了宗教格言录。热法罗维奇的《圣贤图文集》一书浸透了文艺复兴思想，并促进了保加利亚人、塞尔维亚人和其他斯拉夫人的民族意识的形成。

在奥斯曼帝国长达五世纪的统治期间，保加利亚的文学活动主要在修道院中展开。出生在该国西部班斯科的帕伊希·希伦达尔斯基完成了第一部民族复兴的文学作品——《斯拉夫保加利亚史》。这部作品反映了民族意识的觉醒，成为当时的一篇文学和政治宣言。帕伊希虔诚的追随者索夫罗尼·弗拉昌斯基撰写了保加利亚新文学的第一本印刷书籍《礼拜日》和自传体回忆录《罪人索夫罗尼苦难的一生》。

18世纪下半叶和19世纪初，保加利亚文学具有明显的启蒙性质，其代表人物有编著《识字课本》的贝龙，完成《保加利亚语语法》的里尔斯基，撰写《贫穷的母亲保加利亚的哭泣》的博兹维利，创作保加利亚第一部长诗《斯托扬和拉达》的格罗夫。其时，学者们对民间文学情有独钟，米拉迪诺夫两兄弟出版了《保加利亚民歌集》。此后，保加利亚文学迈出了雄健的步伐，创造了保加利亚新的书面语言，在体裁和文学性方面大大超越了前人。卡拉维洛夫首开先河，推出了一批保加利亚真正意义上的中短篇小说。保加利亚"文学之父"伐佐夫则创作了22卷各种体裁的文学作品。

1878年摆脱奥斯曼帝国的统治后，普罗夫迪夫、索非亚两座城市的文学活动最为活跃。许多定期出版物，如文学刊物《曙光》和《启明星》，对保加利亚文学的发展发挥了重要作用。斯托扬诺夫、拉德夫是文学鼎盛时期的两位巨匠。著名的现实主义小说家有金切夫、弗拉伊科夫、格奥尔基耶夫和斯特拉希米罗夫。

19世纪末产生了社会主义文学，代表人物有布拉戈耶夫、基尔科夫和波利亚诺夫。

20世纪初，保加利亚文学以《思想》杂志为中心，以欧洲文学为榜样，开始了现代化的变革进程，这一时期，小说创作在格·斯塔马托夫和埃林·彼林的作品中结出了硕果。

1912—1918年的巴尔干战争和第一次世界大战结束后，保加利亚小说充分反映了本民族的深重灾难。小说在传统现实主义中增添了抒情风格、心理描写、风土人情和历史厚重感，其中约尔丹·约夫科夫成为经典作家。

1923—1944年，社会小说和无产阶级革命小说独占鳌头，代表作家有奥·瓦西列夫、克·维尔科夫、格·卡拉斯拉沃夫。

1944年以后，社会主义现实主义的创作方法在保加利亚文学中居于统治地位。尽管当时存在教条主义，但是，塔列夫、迪莫夫、斯塔内夫等作家仍然创作了优秀作品。维任诺夫、海托夫、拉迪奇科夫等作家则独辟蹊径，赋予短篇小说特殊的审美价值，他们的作品在保加利亚国内外至今仍畅销不衰。

三、选材重点

我在翻译《保加利亚中短篇小说集》的过程中，选材所用的时间实际超过了翻译所用的时间。100多年的保加利亚中短篇小说汗牛充栋，选什么，弃什么，颇为踌躇。我最终确定突出两条原则：连贯性、通俗性。

关于"连贯性"，是说既然作品的时间跨度超过百年，即从1872年（我国清代同治十一年）至1980年（我国改革开放初期），那么，每10年都应有相应的经典作家及其作品入选。换句话说，每个10年都应有一张展示保加利亚人生活场景的幻灯片，总共10张幻灯片相互独立又相互联系，构成一个整体，使得读者有可能清晰地看到保加利亚人不断演进的世态、苦乐和愿景。

为了实现"连贯性"，书中的某些作品虽算不上经典，但其作者却在保加利亚文学史上占有重要地位，不可或缺。例如，阿列科·康斯斯坦诺夫的长篇小说《加纽大叔》等代表了一个时代，我必须在本书中收录他的《时过境迁》和《订婚》两个短篇。迪米特尔·迪莫夫曾因其长篇小说《烟草》等蜚声保加利亚文坛，我也在本书中收录了他的《狂欢》。

近年来，我国作家言必称卡夫卡、马尔克斯、昆德拉，但是说实话，对一般读者来说，他们的作品很难理解。为了取得较好的社会效果，我在翻译《保加利亚中短篇小说集》时，尽可能选取通俗易懂的作品，尽管要理解这些作品的深刻含义，也需要认真思考一番。

四、译者感受

保加利亚是欧洲传统的农业国，因此，作家们对农村题材可谓驾轻就熟。本书收集的作品，大多展现了农耕文化的风貌，相比之下，城市题材的作品就显得较少，而工业题材的作品则只有《飞燕》一篇。文学是生活的一面镜子，本书这面"镜子"里不乏田园牧歌式的细腻描写，如埃林·彼林的《割草人》，开篇一段就极具诗意：

迷人的夏夜降临大地，凉爽，清新。广袤的色雷斯平原隐入黑暗，仿佛在青蛙和蛐蛐单调的鸣叫声中躲藏起来，放心休息。星汉灿烂，四周寂然，安闲恬静。大地深情地敞开胸膛，陶醉在快愉之中。

在创作方法上，保加利亚近现代作家囿于相对狭小的环境，大多尊崇现实主义，尤其是社会主义现实主义，而同浪漫、象征、抽象、魔幻等保持着一定距离。当然，文学创作是一种特殊而复杂的精神生产，是作家对生命的审美体验，现实主义并不等于对生活的刻板复制。

书中收集的作品，相当一部分呈现出沉郁灰暗的色调，这无疑是保加利亚历史的真实写照。奥斯曼土耳其人统治保加利亚500年，这在保加利亚人心中投下了难以抹去的阴影。本书中的柳本·卡拉维洛夫的《硬汉一去不复还》、伊凡·伐佐夫的《一个保加利亚农妇》、尼古拉·海托夫的《山羊角》等，都描绘了奥斯曼帝国时期保加利亚人的极其恶劣的生存状态。

此外，《小说集》中的作品，充塞着"教会""教堂""神父""牧师""祈祷""圣餐"等字眼。这是因为，保加利亚居民约85%信奉东正教，在他们的日常生活中，宗教无处不在、无孔不入。可以说，基督信仰成了整个保加利亚社会的精神支柱，它为人们提供道德资源和共同的价值观，是人们心灵稳定的家园。

五、特别推荐

埃林·彼林（1877—1949年）以保加利亚农村为题材的中短篇小说，在世界批判现实主义文学中占有重要地位。几十年来，保加利亚教育部门一直把他的作品编入语文教材。高尔基说："你从他的每一行字中都能感受到，你的这位小说大家是保加利亚的一寸美丽的土地。"埃林·彼林的作品已被译成包括汉语在内的40多种文字，他在创作生涯的后期所写的童话《扬·比比扬》及其续篇《月亮上的扬·比比扬》，至今在中国仍拥有广大读者。

作家的中篇小说《格拉克一家》，被评论界称为保加利亚具有重要意义的伟大作品，它在欧洲文学史上占有一席之地。在这篇小说里，埃林·彼林通过对一个农村大家庭从兴盛走向衰败的描写，展示了农村宗法制度在资本主义的冲击下逐步瓦解的过程。小说情节紧凑，情感丰富，语言生动，人物鲜明。

诺贝尔文学奖获得者莫言2014年9月在接受索非亚大学授予的荣誉博士学

位的仪式上发表演讲说,他25岁时第一次读到的翻译成汉语的保加利亚文学作品,就是埃林·彼林的作品,而在埃林·彼林的这些作品中,他印象最深的是《格拉克一家》和《土地》。他说,埃林·彼林在自己的作品中描绘了保加利亚农村最广阔的场景。他还说:

> 实际上我遇到过许多像埃林·彼林小说中的主人公一样的人,他们耕作土地,关心收成。埃林·彼林的小说让我了解到保加利亚农民的生活,那个时代农村人之间淳朴的感情;另一方面,我觉得,那里的富农、地主对普通农民的态度和当时我故乡的情况没有实际区别。我想,如果一个人有机会了解这个国家的文学作品,他实际上就有了最好的机会了解这个国家和它的文化。在文学这片田野里我有很多的导师,很多老师,可以说埃林·彼林就是他们中的一位。

尼古拉·海托夫(1919—2002年)曾任保加利亚作家协会主席,并曾获得季米特洛夫文学奖金。本书收录的《山羊角》等四篇作品,均选自作家的短篇小说集《野性故事》。

《野性故事》1967年问世时,其"道德基础"曾遭到广泛质疑。某些评论家甚至认为作家在作品中宣扬了消极的"宿命论"。为此,保加利亚科学院文学研究所于1968年开展了一场历时数月的关于《野性故事》的思想和伦理问题的辩论。但是,谁也没有料到,这场辩论反倒促使小说在国内外连续再版,其印数达到保加利亚小说集的巅峰。

《野性故事》几近一半的小说后来被改编成了电影,其中《山羊角》先后被制作成黑白片和彩色片,并斩获多项国际大奖。

1982年5月一期的《广州文艺》在发表我翻译的《山羊角》时,还配发了编辑蔡怀励的评论《悄悄拨动心弦的悲歌》,其中说:

> 以《山羊角》的原始生活素材而言,事件那么复杂、人物那么多、时间跨度那么大,要是落到别的小说家手里,请恕我冒昧揣测,也许有人就会把它繁衍成为中篇以上的大作。不是吗?请看看这篇《山羊角》:什么都简单得不能再简单似的。人物肖像描写,大都只有一两个字词,顶多是一句话;心理活动描写,难找;对话呢,也可以说没有,因为只有结尾的一句,不称其为"对"。小说从头到尾,大

都是纯粹动作性的描写,而且还是粗线条的勾勒。总之,乍一看起来,几乎是一个中篇的梗概。在好些地方,只要来一番想象加工,要生发开去,似易于探囊取物。说《山羊角》像一个中篇梗概,仅仅是"乍一看"而已。细看呢,则又大别于中篇梗概。麻雀虽小,五脏俱全,《山羊角》以它的简约和精巧,显示了作家即使在弹丸之地也能翻腾跳跃,使出十八般武艺的深厚功力。

关于巴尔干的七个观点

[英] 蒂莫西·雷斯* 著
邓灿、马浩然、童佳雯、徐睿、刘蕴玚、李心语** 译

作为剑桥大学地缘政治论坛的研究员,我大部分时间都在思考地缘政治,以下七点是我对巴尔干地缘政治的看法。

第一,也是最基本的观点,巴尔干地区的政治是由内部和外部势力交互作用的结果。当然,当地人也有一些自己的政治目标,首要目标就是要建立独立自主的民族国家,并且他们一直为实现这个目标而不懈努力。但作为相对弱小的国家,他们能否实现这个目标,在很大程度上取决于周边大国的态度和意愿——支持或阻挠。

第二,在过去10年的大部分时间里,巴尔干一直处于大国同盟也就是西方国家的控制之下——先由美国后由欧盟主导。出于各种可分析的原因,西方国家坚持"冻结"从旧南斯拉夫继承下来的边界,而不顾母国的沮丧和被分离出

---

* 蒂莫西·雷斯(Timothy Less)是负责东欧政治风险评估的"新欧"(Nova Europa)智库的主任。他毕业于伦敦大学斯拉夫和东欧研究学院政治学专业,在剑桥大学进修过国际关系。他曾任教于肯特大学,教授过东欧政治课程。他还是剑桥大学达尔文学院的成员。他曾在英国外交部做过为期十年的分析师、外交官和政策制定者,其主要外交生涯是曾担任过英国驻巴尼亚卢卡领事馆欧盟机构司长以及英国驻斯科普里大使馆的政治秘书。他2017年在《外交事务》杂志上发表了一篇对西巴尔干政治局势分析的文章,该文章在西巴国家学界和媒体中掀起了一场大规模讨论,甚至引发一些批评者的强烈反驳。根据他的观点,西方在西巴尔干应当放弃目前"培育多元伦理"的政策,要开始重视"少数民族的民族愿望"。他认为,这种政策方案将导致"大塞尔维亚""大克罗地亚"和"大阿尔巴尼亚"的建立,但同时也将为西巴尔干带来长期的和平与稳定。这篇探讨解决西巴尔干问题的文章只是抛砖引玉,对西巴尔干问题的理解和探讨从未止步。首都师范大学文明区划研究中心在此介绍他2018年12月发表的另一篇文章《关于巴尔干的七个观点》,由读者自行判断他对西巴尔干局势的理解是否妥当。该文曾发表于以下网址:https://www.danas.rs/dijalog/licni-stavovi/sedam-tacaka-o-balkanu/。

** 邓灿、马浩然、童佳雯、徐睿、刘蕴玚、李心语为北京第二外国语学院欧洲学院学生。

去的少数族裔的焦虑——如波斯尼亚的塞尔维亚族人和克罗地亚族人、马其顿阿尔巴尼亚族人和其他发现自己"滞留"在别国的少数族裔。西方没有解决根本问题，只是把精力集中在通过提供欧盟和北约成员资格来发展巴尔干的政治经济上。总的来说，该地区的人民接受了它，进而暂时放弃未实现的民族主义，虽然，他们可能从未有太多的选择。

第三，我认为这段历史已接近尾声，因为西方已经失去了促进巴尔干地区发展的能力和意愿。原因之一就在于欧盟的内部危机。它在过去的10年中持续变化，从金融危机开始，转变为多层次的政治危机。究其根源则是自由主义意识形态的严重丧失，而这一意识形态正是欧盟建立的基础。危机对巴尔干地区的直接影响就是加入欧盟的计划实际上已经终止了——这一结果在今年夏天举行的一场又一场首脑峰会后逐渐明朗。尽管官方表示扩大政策仍继续存在，西方的政治家们也说有足够的理由继续保持入盟期待，但作为一个政治现实，扩张政策已经宣告破产，这也意味着欧盟成为巴尔干地区真正唯一的"杠杆"不可能实现了。与此同时，美国基本上对巴尔干地区失去了兴趣。虽然它还在这里继续宣扬民主、市场改革和一体化的思想，但由于全球重要战略地区出现了很多更大的问题，美国早已不愿在巴尔干投入大量的人力、物力和军力。欧盟危机给美国出了难题——华盛顿很难说服那些不愿意与西巴尔干一体化的欧盟成员国。

第四，很显然，欧盟内部危机将变得更为复杂，且未来几年经济将再次陷入衰退。自最近的一次经济危机爆发以来，欧洲国家的领导人都错失了纠正欧元区结构性错误，尤其是建立财政联盟的良机。同时，欧元区并没有任何一个缓冲地带能够抵御后续危机的爆发。利率已经降为零，并阻碍了货币刺激。地中海地区的借贷水平已经远远超出过去10年，这同样阻碍了财政刺激，况且在移民危机所造成的痛苦氛围下，并不存在"富裕国家拯救穷苦国家"这样的机会，就如同上一次经济危机时那样。所以，我预计脆弱的欧元区将无法在下一次金融危机中幸存，这也将会导致欧盟自身的存在危机。

第五，俄罗斯可能将控制其在乌克兰的战略缓冲区——恰因为其看到欧洲正处于混乱状态。这将是美国必须面对的主要政治难题。当前有两种可能性，即美国牺牲乌克兰，因为乌克兰在上周的刻赤冲突中做出了一个不妥的回应；或者美国保卫乌克兰，帮助其坚定地回归东欧，但与此同时俄罗斯也会努力中和并控制乌克兰的边缘地区。

第六，至高无上的欧盟如今已无法再继续压制巴尔干的民族主义。或许，该地区会像 20 世纪 90 年代初那样再次出现权力真空，一些民族继续其未竟的民族国家建设；或许，该地区将成为俄罗斯和美国之间的战略竞争带，同时也伴随着土耳其、英国、德国等其他大国的加入。若是第二种情况，科索沃、马其顿、波斯尼亚等巴尔干冲突问题都将无法再保持"冻结"状态。

第七，该怎么做？作为一名分析者，我不会过多涉足政治领域。但是，如果巴尔干倾向于重新组建民族国家，因为居住在这里的人把它看作安全、权利和机会的先决条件，那么明智的领导人就应该阻止事态朝着混乱、肆意乃至暴力的方向发展，并最终通过谈判协商而达到重组。在这一点上，我赞赏武契奇总统和塔奇为"重新规划"科索沃边界所做的努力。我相信波什尼亚克族务实的领导人能与塞族和克族就新的国家结构达成一致。这种新结构既能让波什尼亚克族从波斯尼亚中脱离出来，也能为形成中的波什尼亚克民族国家带来尽可能多的保障。我也在佐兰·扎耶夫身上看到了政治家对欧洲、巴尔干，以及最终对马其顿的事态发展视而不见。

这并非我的地区，所以我不会再多言。我会重新把精力集中在我自己国家的重大问题上。我希望巴尔干人民像欧洲其他地区的人民一样，警惕外部威胁并做出正确选择。

史料选译

意大利、巴尔干与二战之始：
法文档案选编

杨紫桐 编译[*]

[编译者按] 1939年9月1日第二次世界大战全面爆发，英国、法国、意大利、德国、苏联等围绕巴尔干问题也展开了角逐。其中，法国外交的一项主要议题是，如何保持意大利的中立。编译者从《法国外交文件集》（DDF）中选编7份档案，以反映这一时期大国的各种考虑。

19390910, FD000315

政治司致英国驻法大使备忘录[①]
（1939年9月10日）[②]

1. 英国大使馆9月9日的备忘录里关于意大利中立以及英法需要避免在巴尔干地区采取任何可能影响到这一中立地位的行动的考虑，已经引起了外交部的全部注意。尽管外交部认为两国政府应该就该问题的不同方面进行彻底的调查并从这一共同研究中得出结论，但外交部相信现在可以给英国使馆提交一些它对英国备忘录的初步思考。

---

[*] 杨紫桐，首都师范大学历史学院硕士研究生。本组档案的编目得到首都师范大学历史学院硕士研究生窦云婷的协助，特此致谢。

① 文献来源：DDF, 1939 (3 septembre-31 décembre), pp. 55-56。
② 文件没有注明日期。拟出的时间是根据上下文推算的。——原编译者注

2. 外交部认同英国关于目前,现阶段,保持意大利中立并且避免一切可能导致意大利倒向德国的不成熟的举动。不能忽视这一中立中带有的保留,也不能忽视预防其脆弱性。我们绝不能忽视任何东西,以便使这个中立状态继续延长,也不能为了其态度向我们转变的可能性而使得意大利当局采取一种比现在更犹豫、更不长久的态度。

3. 英法可能在巴尔干地区采取的任何行动都不能以一个敌对的意大利为前提。只有在一种特殊的情况下才能立即考虑这个问题,即关于我们在罗马尼亚安置防御性装置的安排计划。我们对这一国家所做的承诺并不能免除我们对我们希望使其有效的道路和方法的审查。正因如此,考虑到现存的所有外交形势,这个问题看起来应该加以研究。

4. 外交部长认为如果事态的发展使我们担心罗马尼亚所面临的外部威胁,出于不被令我们的援助失效的消极措施抢先的需要,我们可能会被迫在巴尔干地区建立一些基地。这将取决于法国和英国政府事先同意大利政府进行必要的外交行动,以突出我们行动的真正意义和合理理由。应该向罗马表明,这一倡议中的任何内容都不会掩盖意大利的敏感问题,也不会对其利益造成任何损害;归根结底,我们的目标只是在巴尔干保持一种平衡,其为罗马带去的利益绝不比我们现在所见的少;一旦罗马尼亚落败,这一平衡将被打破;最终,我们除了使自己能够有效地协助罗马尼亚预防其独立所引发的威胁(总有一天这个威胁将会紧迫地爆发)之外,没有其他目的。

5. 基于这些迫切的理由,这一行动就算是被包围在罗马政府合理要求到的所有保障中,也至少需要得益于意大利政府的默认。英国政府不可避免地发现,如果在这种情况下我们拒绝这一同意,我们将看到意大利的重大反击:通过间接或直接援助促进德国在东欧和巴尔干地区的霸权计划。然后,将由法国和英国政府从这样的意大利立场中承担可能带来的后果。①

6. 外交部还计划,如果发生了第4段提到的意外情况,应与希腊政府接触,以便向其充分保证,防御其面临的风险,在其领土建立对罗马尼亚的援助基地。

7. 外交部认为,必须进一步强调,上述考虑只是为了澄清它认为构成问题的某些方面。对问题的实质审查,当然应根据军事和外交事件的演变,留给两

---

① 一条垂直线将第5段与一段手写符号隔离:由部长删除。——原编译者注

国政府共同审议。①

19390912，FD000316

马西利致博内急件（第 s. n°1 号）②
（1939 年 9 月 12 日）

我感谢阁下在 1939 年 9 月 6 日的信函③中给我的指示，因为我没有一天不被问及巴黎对意大利问题的看法，这些指示对我来说更有价值。在苏联局势不明的情况下，这是这个国家领导人最关心的问题。

在战争的早期，所谓的"逃避的意大利"让人们感到困惑和愤怒：我们非常渴望与一个我们既畏惧又鄙视的国家进行清算的机会会消失吗？法国和英国不打算强迫意大利公开自己的立场吗？随后，情绪发生了一些变化：我们发现，至少在一段时间内，罗马的中立是有一些好处的；地中海的航运将保持开放。商业已经隐约看到了恢复的可能性，军队也得到了他们等待的物资；最后，在德国的宣传所到达的区域里传播着这样的一个观点，即元首实际上控制着政治，而他不会允许做傻事。

精神因此镇定下来。但领导人们对那些不信任的细节总是倍加关注。大家都认为意大利的政策是由一系列对冒险的成本与预期收益的精密计算决定的；没有人相信这种情况能持续很长时间；因此，我们随时都有发现其他事实的可能。

法国和英国可能会承认这种不确定性会持续下去吗？这由它们来决定；目前，人们承认的是，只要西方国家承诺的战争物资没有到达土耳其港，局势总之是对土耳其有利，人们同样认为，波兰与地中海的自由交通非常重要。

---

① 由于担心法国在地中海以及巴尔干地区的计划，尼维尔·张伯伦 9 月 11 日在战时内阁宣布了他会见爱德华·达拉第的打算。这是英法 9 月 12 日在阿贝维尔仓促举行第一次盟国最高军事会议的直接原因。——原编译者注

② 文献来源：*DDF*, 1939（3 septembre - 31 décembre），pp. 81 - 82。勒内·马西利（René Massigli），法国驻土耳其大使。乔治·博内（Georges Bonnet），时任法国外长。

③ 这份信件在 1939 年 9 月 7 日由罗马发给巴黎，后转发至安卡拉。他特别指出：无论如何，在我们与意大利的争论中，重要的是要保障一切可能有利于朝着符合我们愿望的方向发展的东西。——原编译者注

然而在大多数人看来，意大利的中立仍然是和柏林合作的，在任何时候，如果柏林需要，只要在德国的军事局势没有恶化前，意大利都可能在我们面前耍把戏。

这一德国与意大利相互勾结的信念，我们不应该只（将其）视为一种存在于所有关于意大利事务上的先验的偏见。当然，这算是本能反应，但也有一些事实证明，这其中是有一些价值的。

例如，早在今年7月，冯·帕彭先生就对他的一些同胞说，如果德国在这里输掉了第一局，那将是因为与意大利的同盟（关系），而重要的是要让土耳其对意大利放心。正如我的通信中所反复提到的那样，德意志大使曾多次为萨拉吉奥卢先生打开德国在罗马和安卡拉之间调解的方便之门。①

这是一个事实，我已经提醒人们注意过：意大利特工在德国的知情下在这里工作；在贝尤鲁，意大利大使馆和领事馆的机关刊物在德国情况最不利的时候报道国际政治事务和军事事件，且应意大利总领事馆的邀请，该刊物现在免费发给所有土耳其议员。最后，我们不能不注意到目前的形势给德意志帝国带来的好处，这既是因为向其提供供给的便利性，也是因为意大利的中立为那些支持土耳其中立的人即日耳曼主义党提供了强有力的论点。

总之，无论意大利是否参与罗马和柏林之间的谈判，人们只能对德国外交机构如何迅速和果断感到惊讶。如果意大利加入战争，即使它的军队不会立即进入阿尔巴尼亚，这里的人也不会相信德国的和平抗议——德国大使到处重复说，它在巴尔干地区什么也不想要。但是，在意大利退出游戏的那一天，冯·帕彭先生的信仰声明就算没有变得更真诚，也显得更可信一些。如果我们承认，柏林的巴尔干政策目前主要倾向于放松（对手的）警惕，以便在波兰最终被打败的那一天，能够把它的意志残酷地强加给恐惧的政府，我们可以相信，无论其原因是什么，意大利的放弃会消除战争在巴尔干地区蔓延的威胁，而这与柏林的作用密不可分。冯·帕彭先生承认，意大利的盟国两个月前劣迹已加重，今天如果还认识不到意大利助其行动成功后会遭到多少"背叛"，是非常不合适的。

---

① 见 *DDF*, 1936-39, XIX, document n°275。——原编译者注

19390914，FD000317

科尔班致达拉第电（第 3151—3158 号）[①]

(1939 年 9 月 14 日)

我刚刚与哈利法克斯伯爵交谈过巴尔干的情况。外交办公室的情报与我们掌握的差不多一致。尽管如此，根据英国驻贝尔格莱德的公使所言，南斯拉夫政府已经决定从今开始在索非亚采取行动，与土耳其人达成一致，为的是预防保加利亚一方的任何突发情况。

在这几天，战时内阁的会议上讨论了巴尔干问题。哈利法克斯伯爵提出了主张巴尔干国家保持中立的论点，并在您最近与英国首相的会晤中阐述了这一点。[②]

此外，英国驻巴黎大使馆将向部里发出照会，答复本月 12 日的信函。[③]

但是，从那时起，又有了新的情况。首先是罗马尼亚面临的威胁。很明显，德国想要切断罗马尼亚与波兰之间的联系，为的是在转向对抗罗马尼亚前完全地孤立和削弱波兰。

从那时起，可以利用波兰领土对罗马尼亚采取行动。但是在匈牙利执行行动更方便，尽管布达佩斯抵制，这条道路最终也很可能被选择。

罗马尼亚公使在向外交大臣讲述现状时，对于受到德国攻击时（会得到）土耳其人的援助显得很确定，尽管与土耳其人沟通时困难重重。在他看来，土耳其可能得到了苏联政府不进攻罗马尼亚的保证。这个保证并没有给布加勒斯特带来任何信心，但布加勒斯特对土耳其政府的声明非常重视，这个声明的条款激发了很大的信心。

至于罗马尼亚的物质需求，英国军方的审查结果表明，唯一可以给罗马尼

---

① 文献来源：文献来源：*DDF*, 1939 (3 septembre – 31 décembre), pp. 99 – 101。夏尔·科尔班 (Charles Corbin)，法国驻英国大使。

② 达拉第和张伯伦 9 月 12 日在阿贝维尔举行的盟国最高军事会议上会面。

③ 9 月 9 日，英国在备忘录里谈及了罗马尼亚中立的好处以及因其政治和战略局势而必须保护罗马尼亚的问题，法国在 9 月 12 日的备忘录里对此表示异议，认为盟军既没有办法促使罗马尼亚放弃中立，也无法在它能这样做的时候给予帮助，此外罗马尼亚很可能在遭受"突然的打击"时，很快就对德国妥协。——原编译者注

亚的物资就是现在正在生产中的给英国自己部队的物资。同盟国政府应该来考察在这种条件下是否适合满足罗马尼亚的要求。

据哈利法克斯伯爵所知，卡罗尔国王①也向巴黎提出了同样紧迫的请求。②

接下来说南斯拉夫政府的态度，外交大臣不认为他能使索非亚转而认同我们宣布的活动。他分析，事实上除非保罗王子对意大利没有足够的放心，他是不会走这条道路的。还有一点依然存疑，就是为尽力满足一些保加利亚的需求，在多布罗加对罗马尼亚采取行动，比如交换人口，是否合适。哈利法克斯伯爵倾向于什么也不做，为的是不使布达佩斯太过猜疑或失望。

如果我们被告知的这些事情是真实发生的，这些很可能会强迫意大利表态。英国大使和齐亚诺伯爵的对话持续到目前为止情况令人满意。意大利政府看起来很欢迎大使给出的关于供给和封锁的建议。

美国驻伦敦大使指出，就他而言，联邦政府可以照顾意大利一些商业上的好处以影响其偏向。

但哈利法克斯伯爵不愿意在意大利问题上过于乐观。他知道在墨索里尼心里，有强有力的理由站到德国一边。

我们特别应该注意，是否在巴尔干地区开启冲突提供了刺激意大利舆论的论点，使他们相信自己的利益受到了威胁。

外交大臣希望与罗马的谈判结束于明确一些意大利的意图。他注意到，与安卡拉的谈判总是建立在对意大利入侵的恐惧上，如果罗马倾向于采取对我们友好的中立立场的话，土耳其人将发现自己陷入悖论。

在向外交大臣道谢完毕后，我认为我必须向他指出，他没有触及问题的一个核心方面：在巴尔干国家建立一个援助基地。这个可能性在我们相信东南欧保持中立时被暂时搁置了。在不久的将来这些都要改变了。然而，法英联合行动的焦点毫无疑问地会对小国和土耳其的政治产生可观的影响。

我补充说，对我们来说，这可能是唯一维持双重战线的办法，而在德意志帝国司令部中，这一直都是如此令人生畏。哈利法克斯伯爵回复我说显然这个问题要全部重新考虑，而他将会把这些建议告知战时内阁，但是，在他看来，决定的适当性归根结底还是取决于意大利的态度。他也不排除在正在进行的与

---

① 卡罗尔二世（Carol II），1930—1940 年任罗马尼亚国王。

② 这个活动，如果真的存在，在档案中并未发现。见 *DDF*, 1939 (3 septembre-31 décembre)，第 62 号文件注释 3。——原编译者注

意大利的谈判中查实他们这方面安排的可能性。

19390916，FD000318

弗朗索瓦-蓬塞致达拉第电（第3750—3760号）[①]
（1939年9月16日）

今天早上，我和齐亚诺伯爵进行了一次愉快的交谈，当时，这位部长的语气不仅没有任何拘束，而且非常自由、直接，让人感觉是坦率和可信任的。

齐亚诺伯爵向我保证意大利的态度不会在我缺席时有任何改变。[②]

在他看来，现在情况已经稳定下来了。我们可以认为这个情况是持续性的。诚然，意外事变、令人不快的创举总是有可能损害这种状态。但这就是该我们，也就是部长本人和他有着长久联系的法国大使和英国大使来避免和排除的了。

在这些致命的错误中，齐亚诺伯爵列举了那些坚持要通过逼迫意大利表明自己"是敌是友"而把它逼近墙角的举动。

在他们看来，一个没那么严重的错误是把政治人物送到意大利来大声地公开谈判的意图。

目前的情况需要的是老练、灵巧、过渡和谨慎的磋商。

伯爵没跟我说任何关于解决法意争端的事。

我没有跟我的对话者隐瞒两个可能使我感到担忧的事情。第一个是墨索里尼先生情绪的急转直下；第二个是伴随德意志威胁而来的压力。

齐亚诺伯爵认为这些恐惧是没有基础的，他说墨索里尼先生并不像表面上看起来那样冲动和善变。在内心里，他是谨慎、明智、极周密的。意大利目前的态度是基于坚实的基础之上的；这是经过严格的审查、丰富的思考之后的结果；这是有着坚实的政治和司法基础的；这里不可能有突然的、生硬的大转折。

为了证明他前面跟我说的那些，部长向我建议准备重新把在罗马的法国高

[①] 文献来源：*DDF*, 1939（3 septembre - 31 décembre）, pp. 134 - 136。安德烈·弗朗索瓦-蓬塞（André François-Poncet），法国驻意大利大使。

[②] 见 *DDF*, 1939（3 septembre-31 décembre），第41号文件。

史料选译

中开放成正常状态,同样地,他也打算在法国的非战争区域重新开放意大利学校。为了回复我向他提出的问题,他同样向我建议允许居住在意大利的法国家庭返回。

至于德国的压力,他向我保证现在没有,以后也不会有。他补充说:如果它造成了(压力),德国和任何其他国家一样,都不会对此感到高兴。

齐亚诺伯爵表示自己对意大利与英法关系的现状满意。对于伦敦和巴黎向他传来的善意的表示他显得很感动。他顺便告诉我他与哈利法克斯伯爵交换了私人信件。他还向我询问关于法国政府的改组。① 我回答他说在(改组)中可以看到一种为了增强战时内阁而想要集中权力的表现。这些被实施的改变并不包括任何有关对意大利政策的调整。瓜里利亚大使②在对阁下访问时已经对此被说服,他也已经将这告知了齐亚诺伯爵。法国非常珍视意大利的不参战状态:法国希望这种克制是可以持续的,也是最终的。

齐亚诺公爵看起来像是被说服了。他补充说:"我们能做的最好的就是继续以同样的方式做我们已经开始做的事。"

部长问了我一些很有象征意义的问题,关于巴黎的风貌、首都的生活、法国人民的精神状态等一些问题。他充分赞扬了一部法国的宣传片,影片里向他展现了动员的一幕,在两行(文字)里看到了希特勒先生的承诺与行动。

轮到我提问时,我询问了关于德国对于罗马尼亚的打算。德国打算为了占领其石油和小麦而染指这个国家吗?齐亚诺伯爵对我说,他一无所知。于是我向他解释说,我们愿意尊重巴尔干地区的和平;但是,如果德意志把战火带到了这里,我们将会与之作战。我们已经做出了承诺。③ 我们将会把我们的参战视为荣誉。至于其他的,包括土耳其在内的巴尔干协约国不能再无所作为了。关于这些,在行动前,我们乐于适时与意大利交换意见。齐亚诺伯爵回答说,他已经准备好了,应该这样做。他同时暗示,阁下曾经出于预防目的向瓜里利亚大使建议,把法国军队派驻到黎凡特地区。

此外,部长看起来对苏联和德国的计划都知之甚少。他绝对不相信苏联想

---

① 法国政府的改组起始于9月13日,乔治·博内离开了,外交部由爱德华·达拉第接手,联合尚普捷德里布作为副国务秘书。他首先考虑的是埃里奥,但意大利人讨厌埃里奥。在部长的命令下,这位大使于同日由第3774号电报里说及"关于政府的安排和法国人民"。齐亚诺伯爵知道剩下要坚持的是什么。——原编译者注

② 拉斐尔·瓜里利亚(Raffaele Guariglia),意大利驻法国大使。

③ 1939年4月13日英法两国向罗马尼亚做出保证。——原编译者注

要插手波兰。他声称,德意志帝国也没有通过下一次"和平攻势"的计划夺取罗马,领袖墨索里尼在这方面非常谨慎。如今,他没有信心保证一场同样的攻势的成功。他只对真正值得的事情感兴趣,他不愿意把留到以后用得上的信用提前用在一个可能会被批判的事情上。

"事实上这是有用的",齐亚诺伯爵宣称,有人守卫着高于欧洲的概念,关注着高于欧洲的利益。意大利的态度对本国无疑是有益的。但这个态度对全体欧洲国家同样有益。

齐亚诺伯爵不相信英法德之间剩下的战争有军事上的出路。他说,"这将是漫长的!将会是沉重的!德国是块难啃的骨头!"他也看不出有那种和平能消除日耳曼的危险。他看起来尤其担心一场旷日持久的战争将会导致共产党的蔓延、虚无主义和人民的反抗。

19390916,FD000319

科尔班致达拉第电(第 3199—3201 号)[①]

(1939 年 9 月 16 日)

回复您第 2175—78 号电报[②]。

对于阁下让我向哈利法克斯伯爵表达的看法,伯爵表示大体赞同。他了解,我们向罗马尼亚提供援助的重要性不只在物质上,也在道义上。

关于英国政府必然十分有限的军事物资是否应该被运送到罗马尼亚或者土耳其的问题已经在战争内阁中被讨论过了。

英国参谋部倾向于认为这些武器在土耳其人手里会更有用。事实上,关于罗马尼亚部队,没有特别高度的评价。

我已经向外交大臣解释说如果我们不满足罗马尼亚军队的需求,我们将会冒使贝尔格莱德和布达佩斯表现出的善意受挫的风险,并且德国向东南方向的行进将会对土耳其自身的布局起很大影响。我的对话者明白这个意见的分量。

在这一方面,他提问如果出现波兰军队不得不进驻罗马尼亚领土的情况,布达佩斯政府将会是什么态度。我回复说,我曾就这个问题详细地向罗马尼亚

---

① 文献来源:*DDF*,1939(3 septembre-31 décembre),pp. 138-139。

② 见 *DDF*,1939(3 septembre-31 décembre),第 80 号文件。

部长提问过，他认为波兰部队将会被暂时扣押，而私下的算盘其实是当情况迫使罗马尼亚自卫的时候利用它。

外交大臣担心德国政府要求交出部队，或者至少交付武器。但是我们认为最重要的是，在波兰政府不得不流亡罗马尼亚的情况下，能获得欢迎。事实上，让一个正常组阁的波兰政府继续存在，并且能够继续行使权力是很有用处的。

如果罗马尼亚，或者可能是土耳其，对此有疑义，则法国和英国应该让波兰政府代表知道，法英两国很乐意收容他们。

19390925，FD000320

博内致达拉第电（第3390号）①

（1939年9月25日）

我今天（9月25日）与齐亚诺伯爵的对话聚焦于一些最近发生的最重要的事件，首先是罗马尼亚议会主席被暗杀一事。②

齐亚诺伯爵承认，他也想知道是什么缘由造成了这一罪行。他不是不知道希特勒先生让卡罗尔国王产生厌恶和敌意的情绪。在他看来，在镇压铁卫队的活动和科德雷亚努被粗暴地处决后，卡里内斯库先生种下的仇恨足够解释杀人者的举动。③ 罗马尼亚议会主席对那些把"一切为了党"当作口号的人太无情了！鉴于这种狂热的爱国主义，也许他曾经可以以更明智、更公正的方式人道地对待他们？刺杀卡里内斯库先生的杀手自己也挣扎在最艰险的生存条件下。阿尔菲耶里先生曾向伯爵展示过一些照片，这些照片真的属于我们所能见到的最令人反感的、可怕的照片之列。④ 关于袭击对罗马尼亚内政的影响，我的对

---

① 文献来源：*DDF*, 1939 (3 septembre-31 décembre), pp. 238-242。

② 阿尔芒·卡里内斯库先生（Armand Calinesco）9月21日被刺杀。关于此，参见 *DDF*, 1939 (3 septembre-31 décembre), 第133号文件。——原编译者注

③ 阿尔芒·卡利内斯库先生，米隆克里斯蒂主教（patriarche Miron Cristea）政府中的内政部长，于1938年4月7日以叛国和密谋颠覆政府的罪名下令逮捕法西斯政党"铁卫队"精神领袖科尔内留·泽莱亚·科德雷亚努（Corneliu Zelea Codreano），后者在布加勒斯特军事法庭被判决十年劳改。科德雷亚努与他的13名同伙于1938年12月30日在所谓"试图越狱"时被守卫击杀。——原编译者注

④ 刺杀卡里内斯库的凶手于当晚在行凶地被当众处决。据称，自从1938年2月被解散之后，292名"铁卫队"成员在布加勒斯特被处决，原因是出席非法集会。——原编译者注

话者表示他现在没有足够的信息来评估。我同样提请他注意这方面问题可能引起的后果。八天来，我们可能担心德国入侵罗马尼亚领土，以及在此之后战火可能蔓延到整个巴尔干地区。目前，苏联的部队在德国和罗马尼亚之间调停。但如果后者在没有外部袭击的情况下试图从内部摧毁国家，则已经排除的危险又会重现。假设罗马尼亚陷入了混乱和无政府状态，苏联将会是什么态度呢？在这方面，我应该重复我对意大利部长所说的话。同盟尊重巴尔干的中立；但是如果有其他人干涉这种中立，我们不会因同盟重拾采取行动的自由而吃惊。

提及苏联的影响，使我想起我的对话者曾表达过的对于这些事件将使地中海人民团结起来的共同利益愈发突出的信念。地中海是希腊—拉丁文化的继承者，现在面对着在古典时代被人们称为"蛮族"的日耳曼人和斯拉夫人的压力。

齐亚诺伯爵没有排斥这个看法；相反，这次他如以往一样让我感受到他积极开放的态度。

我们接着对墨索里尼先生向博洛尼亚人发表的讲话交换了意见。[①] 齐亚诺伯爵对我说，他认为我没有理解错这个讲话的意义：意大利在9月1日确定下来的政策将不会改变。为了确认我正确地理解了他的意思，我还是补充说，领袖对更远的未来提出了一些保留，我们没有忽视这些保留。部长反驳道，"事实上！当邻居家发生火灾，我们永远也不知道自己会不会被波及！"然而，齐亚诺伯爵看起来相信，未来将在很长的一段时间内是被确定的。在我向他表达我们愿意相信意大利，并且我们愿意重新送回我们定居在半岛的同胞时，他赞同了我的意见。

此外，我注意到，尽管从某种程度上领袖对德国和德国事业的持续同情是可以想象的，但他如此轻易地支持所谓的"波兰清算"出人意料。另一方面，在英法政府首脑反复声明之后，他怎么还能认为英法两国能在波兰的尸体之上接受一个立刻和平的结论？在这之中我没有看到对法西斯主义素来很强调的荣誉和英雄主义崇拜的担忧。

齐亚诺伯爵回复我说他充分理解英法不赞同的动机。然而不幸的是，要着眼现实。而事实是，德国和苏联坐在波兰的尸体上跺脚。如何把它们赶走呢？

[①] 这个讲话在9月23日发表。关于这个话题，见9月23日罗马发给部里的第374号电报和9月2日的第3907号电报；"墨索里尼先生昨天发表的讲话确定了意大利的中立立场；他（确认）了它的中立状态，他延长了它。""从今天起，除非联盟发生很严重的军事挫折，否则我们可能有着不是几日，也不是几周，而是好几个月的时间。"——原编译者注

如何自夸说为一个伟大的国家画下了完美的句号？"只有经历才能告诉你，是否这个国家真的如您所说的那样伟大。很多今天没有想到的元素都可以为我们所用。"我们没有理由把我们提前看作没有实力的。

我向我的对话者提问，德国是否坚持波兰内部划定一个分界线，或者是否它一直就有把波兰作为它和苏联之间的一个拥有1200万国民①的缓冲国的企图。

齐亚诺伯爵向我保证他对此一无所知，除了十几天前他与里宾特洛甫先生的一通简短的电话对谈以外，他已经很久没有与德国领导人们直接对话了。

重新谈到墨索里尼先生在对他的官员的演讲中所强调的，以及在他激励下报纸对"立即和平"的结论的主张时，我请部长告诉我：领袖是否期待着下一次希特勒先生再搞出这样的结局。

齐亚诺伯爵回复我说，他绝对不知道什么明确的信息。但他暗示他确实有感觉，希特勒先生希望阻止战争的发展，并准备在这方面采取下一步行动。

这是部长说的，墨索里尼先生既想鼓励元首的意图，又想为他开辟道路。由于我重申了我的保留意见和警告，齐亚诺伯爵立即补充说，领袖不会冒险，他将保持高度谨慎，只对认真和有效的尝试感兴趣。

无论是这时，还是我们对话中的任何一个时候，我都没有听到我的对话者对其"钢铁盟约"盟友的任何同情的语气。与此相反，在其盟友的问题上，他的态度完全开放。他还提到了里宾特洛甫的智慧，他认为其就像天边的明星。关于盖世太保的领导人希姆莱，他用最挖苦、最严厉的方式评价他。在我说到希特勒总理看起来天生就没有能力履行承诺或者当我明确表示元首在但泽的讲话既不慎重也不合理时，他没有像意大利媒体自称的那样反对我或者抗议，相反的，他显得前所未有的不屑、武断、愤懑和狂怒。

在我们对话的结尾谈到了法意正在进行的经济谈判。虽然齐亚诺公爵显然没有被告知总体情况，但他说对进展满意。他提到了法国订购机车和火车车厢的可能性，这他已经被告知了。他对此表示祝贺。就我而言，我向他通报了第1017号电报②的实质内容，并强调了将依赖意大利的供应方案的重要性，该方案如果得到某些保障和控制，可能会达到相当大的数字。我的对话者同意了。

---

① 德国与苏联的第一个分界线应用了之前8月23日的秘密协定，确定于9月22日。不久后，9月28日《苏德友好与边界条约》在莫斯科签订，边界问题最终解决。——原编译者注

② 未找到该份电报。——原编译者注

但他补充说预防措施是必不可少的。目前,直接向法国提供战争物资是微妙的,而且会造成困难。应该从日用类产品开始。火车头或者船只的交付不会引起反对。军用飞机的交付则很可能会引起反对。目前,我们应该满足于建造飞机或者发动机,一点点地,我们将会发现扩大贸易圈的方式。趋势已经形成了,我们会更加近距离地观察我们将会如何。①

齐亚诺伯爵用一句典型的话总结了他的想法:"有一些心理上的过渡需要照顾!"

在目前的阶段,虽然没有明说,他显然担心,引起不满并且引得德国的指责。但看起来,他承认,随着时间发展,意大利将会越来越不在乎德国的指责。

于是,在这一领域,就像所有我们谈到的领域一样,他用了一种含蓄的表达,让我感到他在内心深处站在我们这边,他将会努力帮助我们;他像9月16日②曾经做过的一样,制订出了一个默许的计划,这并不是25日的谈话中最不引人注目的地方。

当我走进他的办公室时,外交部长正在浏览法国的杂志《竞赛画报》和《玛丽安娜》,"我读这些,我依靠这些,因为这些逗我笑。然而,这些报刊不再谈论我了……他们不再写我被德国收买了;他们不再披露我妻子的举止或我请贵国大使吃饭菜单的细节了!"

我问他:"您希望法国的书报审查重新焕发活力吗?"

他看起来想了片刻:"不,这样最好。"

---

① 关于法国提案的准备,见《商业部9月20日周三15时30分由对外贸易主管阿尔方出席主持的会议纪要》,1940达拉第文件第四卷(文件*DDF*未收录):其中包括申请使用意大利商人总吨位200万吨(的船舶),从意大利购买原材料(硫黄、汞、浮岩)和制成品(毯子、帐篷、取暖设备;1000辆罐车,10辆液货船,500—800吨硬铝条、铝)。为了与之联合,航空局宣布采购计划的金额:7.75亿法郎以购买飞机发动机和零件。——原编译者注

② 见19390916,FD000318。

19391013，FD000321

弗朗索瓦-蓬塞致达拉第急件（第 506 号）[①]

（1939 年 10 月 12 日）

尽管罗马政府在西欧的事务中态度消极，但相反的是，法西斯的外交政策在巴尔干作用独特。就像我多次重申的，意大利的政策致力于防止战火燃及巴尔干半岛。在罗马，我们很清楚，（战争）从巴尔干很容易快速蔓延到意大利。同样，意大利为了拉紧不同的巴尔干国家也展开了最大的努力，并且把它们安放在以意大利为首的中立立场上，而这个中立立场，从某种程度上，是受到意大利的保护的。

我在这些新闻分析中指出，意大利报纸是怎样地欢迎匈牙利和罗马尼亚之间签订的协定，根据其条款，两国边境间之前集结的军队撤离了 35%。随后的报纸继续报道着来自布达佩斯、布加勒斯特以及贝尔格莱德的新闻。据它们说，意大利想要在巴尔干巩固和平，于是担任起在贝尔格莱德和布加勒斯特，以及在贝尔格莱德和布达佩斯之间的调解员。人们清楚地指出，正是在意大利的建议下，南斯拉夫不仅决定大幅改善与圣艾蒂安的王国[②]的关系，准备了一份关于 10 万居住在南斯拉夫边界线以内的匈牙利人的条约，而且尝试改善匈牙利和罗马尼亚的关系。我们看到了匈牙利、南斯拉夫和意大利缔结三国协约的可能性。意大利外交部新闻发言人说，如果说南斯拉夫担任着布达佩斯和布加勒斯特之间的调解人，只能是因为意大利—南斯拉夫条约的存在和意大利—南斯拉夫之间的强大的友谊。意大利部长会议 9 月 1 日的会议第一次讨论的结果是防止冲突蔓延到巴尔干半岛，如果没有法西斯政府的支持，战争就会立即爆发。[③]

现在应该要巩固巴尔干起初的中立，意大利正在尽最大努力。墨索里尼在罗马的政客中说，想要把巴尔干和多瑙河国家集中起来。这就是我们乐见每一个表明匈牙利和南斯拉夫，匈牙利和罗马尼亚关系改善的现象的缘由。

[①] 文献来源：*DDF*，1939（3 septembre–31 décembre），pp. 406–409。
[②] 圣艾蒂安（Saint-Etienne），即艾蒂安一世，公元 1000 年他创建了匈牙利王国。
[③] 推测可能是指由意大利部长会议声明，在欧洲的战争中，"意大利不会采取任何军事行动"。见 *DDF*，1936–1939，XIX，第 317 号文件。——原编译者注

由于《苏德互不侵犯条约》的缔结，意大利清楚，事实上，它冒着明确失去它曾长期在欧洲的巴尔干地区所坚持的立场的风险。苏联现在拦着德国的路。但布尔什维克在巴尔干半岛的渗透对罗马来说就像日耳曼人在这些土地上的扩张一样令人担忧，甚至可能更担忧。我们非常清楚罗马尼亚面临的严重威胁，它几乎没有办法逃开德国和苏联的联合指令，可能轻易就被当作猎物瓜分了。法西斯领导人还认为，在不久后，布加勒斯特政府将会在充分的利益驱动下，与布达佩斯政府交好。自从意大利—南斯拉夫友好条约①签订以来，罗马好几年都想带罗马尼亚以这样或那样的形式加入这个条约。布达佩斯政府的态度令这个计划搁浅了。现在，我们认为罗马尼亚有充分的理由不那么顽固。另一方面，意大利的中立使得土耳其可以不介入冲突。现状中最棘手的是保加利亚政府的态度；只要保加利亚政府拒绝加入罗马所设想的中立区，巴尔干的和平就无法实现。有人称，在意大利的主动下目前正在索非亚进行会谈，但要预言一个好结果还为时尚早。因为保加利亚还是索求者。显而易见，我们认为在台伯河岸，罗马尼亚应该像其邻国做些让步，特别是向多布罗加。只有这样我们才能克服索非亚政府内阁的勉强和犹豫。

　　简而言之，对泛斯拉夫主义扩张的恐惧是意大利在巴尔干行动的动力。一些法西斯分子甚至担心苏联对保加利亚的控制，并怀疑克里姆林宫的统治者已经接管了之前沙皇对君士坦丁堡的计划。苏联军队现在对匈牙利朋友的威胁引起了罗马极大的不安。同样令人担忧的是，德国在这些地区的影响力可能会扩大。意大利把南斯拉夫和匈牙利当成直接处于其影响范围内的国家。齐亚诺伯爵甚至向我保证（见我第4062号电报②），在他访问柏林时负责不拐弯抹角地告知德国政府。意大利向希腊迈出了示好的第一步，并试图通过从阿尔巴尼亚边界撤出部分部队来改善其关系。（意大利）与保加利亚的关系很好，保加利亚修正主义者可以依靠法西斯外交友好的支持。只有土耳其仍置身其外，但我们可以希望，通过在一些事件上施压，因为意大利的期待态度，土耳其将在成形的中立区并且按照罗马领导人的想法，加入巴尔干协约。

　　这个组合的弱点显而易见是在罗马尼亚。因此，意大利试图在政治上尽可能地保护它，同时促使它在经济上服从第三帝国的要求。因此在罗马尼亚问题

---

　　① 这是1924年1月27日由帕奇奇与墨索里尼签署的"罗马条约"，其中承认意大利对弗伊梅的主权，南斯拉夫对巴洛斯港的主权。到1925年7月的聂图诺协议，明确了从扎拉到达尔马提亚成为意大利的飞地。——原编译者注

　　② 1939年12月1日。——原编译者注

上，罗马可能会做出最大让步；因为它不会忽视这个国家的现状有多么困难，不能听之任之地让这个国家陷入火海。这就是为什么意大利的防御线从某种程度上绕过了罗马尼亚，意大利对匈牙利、南斯拉夫和保加利亚的防御最为严密。然而只要意大利能够避免将罗马尼亚分割，它就会这样做：事实上，它并不能掩饰可能随之而来的严重后果。

苏联在中欧的扩张，苏维埃在波罗的海的重新现身，都让罗马尼亚统治者感到不安。他们在看到苏联军事占领立陶宛、爱沙尼亚和拉脱维亚时非常震惊。他们认为，这些国家很快将会被要求改组成共和国与苏联联合。日耳曼人在波罗的海沿岸的撤退给整个半岛留下了深刻的印象。安萨尔多先生[①]在《电讯报》（见我的第4222号电报）上发表的文章就是很好的证明。这场苏联—芬兰争端现在引起了政治界的广泛关注。他们对斯堪的纳维亚国家，特别是瑞典的反应很感兴趣，他们也想知道，美国的态度是什么样的。就在刚刚为英国的影响力被打破而欢欣鼓舞后，他们很难接受波罗的海正日益成为苏联的活动范围。

意大利越来越关心苏联在欧洲各地扮演的角色。但因为它不想跟德国搞僵，所以它比较想与西班牙一样，向柏林施加足够的压力使得德国政府与苏联合作的程度不会太深，并且使德国政府反思这个合作将带来的危险。罗马—柏林轴心很难与柏林—莫斯科轴心调和。仅仅德国保持国家社会主义，苏联保持共产主义，并不意味着先前布尔什维克在欧洲造成的危险就消除了。意大利试图提醒其他伙伴关注德苏勾结的危险，以及柏林与莫斯科之间过度接触可能在罗马引起的不可避免的反应。

这就是为什么我们看到意大利可能是在德国的首肯下正在着手，在东南欧建立第一道屏障，为的是拖延或者说阻止苏联在巴尔干地区的扩张。德国最终将发现其自身优势。事实上，无论德国从罗马尼亚、黑海还是苏联充分接收其所需的战争物资，苏联入主巴尔干并在此引起混乱都不符合德国的利益。另外，柏林并不希望，同盟国可以趁乱开辟一个萨洛尼基战线，这是德国一直以来就有理由担心的。在这个情况下，意大利在巴尔干的政策的展开有着德国的支持，或者至少是默许。在现在，巴尔干半岛是法西斯外交的主要甚至是唯一地区，在这里法西斯努力恢复和加强其地位，这并非没有取得成功。

议会主席先生，请接受我最高的致敬。

[①] 胡安·安东尼奥·安萨尔多（Juan Antonio Ansaldo），西班牙社会活动家。

学术信息

罗马尼亚东南欧研究所简介

武 垚

作者简介 武垚，首都师范大学历史学院博士研究生

罗马尼亚东南欧研究所（Institute for South-East European Studies，ISEES），简称东南欧研究所，是罗马尼亚科学院下属的研究机构。东南欧研究所致力于系统研究古希腊文明、古罗马文明、拜占庭文明、斯拉夫文明、东正教文明、奥斯曼文明、欧洲现代主义等对东南欧世界的影响，旨在促进巴尔干乃至整个东南欧地区科学研究的发展，增进地区各国人民的相互了解，强调其历史和文化的共性。

尽管罗马尼亚从地理位置看其只有一小部分领土（位于多瑙河南岸的多布罗查地区）处于巴尔干半岛，但从地缘政治、历史和文化的角度看，罗马尼亚一直被视为巴尔干国家。基于这种巴尔干半岛地理界线和一些国家边界的不相重合，罗马尼亚历史学家和政治家倾向于认为自己的国家属于东南欧，而不是巴尔干半岛。同时，罗马尼亚政治家和知识精英们还强调，罗马尼亚人属拉丁民族，是古罗马帝国达契亚人的后裔。

但是，在历史研究领域，罗马尼亚学者早就对巴尔干学表现出了浓厚的兴趣。20 世纪初，罗马尼亚的巴尔干研究与知名历史学家尼古拉·约尔加（Nicolae Iorga, 1871-1940）的名字密不可分。今日罗马尼亚科学院历史研究所仍冠以"尼古拉·约尔加"的名字。约尔加既是学者，又是社会活动家。第一次世界大战后，约尔加作为国家民主党的领袖一度曾担任首相职务。作为历史学家，他和考古学家瓦西尔·帕尔万（Vasile Parvan）早在 1913 年在布加勒斯特就创立了罗马尼亚东南欧研究所（Institul de Stutii Sudost-Europene）。这是一

所由私人投资建立的研究所，它的建所目的是：第一，激励、领导和帮助开展喀尔巴阡地区和巴尔干地区以及整个东南欧地区领土和民族的研究，尤其是罗马尼亚古代传统的研究；第二，在政治层面，支持研究罗马尼亚与东部地区，特别是巴尔干地区的民族利益。1913年约尔加的代表作《巴尔干国家当代史》问世。第一次世界大战结束时，约尔加完成了另一部专著《巴尔干半岛上罗马尼亚人史》。1916年该所正式成为国家级研究所，约尔加当选为所长。

约尔加在其著作中特别强调，如果不研究地区史，就无法理解每个民族国家的历史。每个民族都为地区史做出了贡献，所以，应该鼓励地区史研究。他号召对地区的历史和文明进行比较研究。加强对东南欧地区的研究，于该地区每个国家，于整个世界史都大有裨益。通过东南欧国家过去类似经历和命运的研究，有助于克服彼此之间的"仇恨"和"冲突"，达到东南欧地区的谅解和团结。

不过，应该看到约尔加强调罗马尼亚属于东南欧国家，而非巴尔干国家。他认为，罗马尼亚是亲西欧、特别是亲法国的国家，它的地理位置属于东南欧。所以，约尔加创办的研究刊物也都冠以"东南欧"的名称。1914年东南欧研究所出版期刊《东南欧研究通讯》（*Bulletin de l'Institut pour l'Europe Sud-Orientale*）。1924年该刊改名为《东南欧历史评论》（*Revue historique du Sud-Est europeen*）。为了全面研究巴尔干地区，1926年约尔加建立了拜占庭研究所（Institul de Studii Bizantine）。

1940年约尔加去世后，罗马尼亚巴尔干学研究进入一个新的阶段，其代表人物是历史学家维克托·帕帕克斯特（Victor Papacostea，1900–1962）。1937年，帕帕科斯特筹集私人资金，建立了罗马尼亚巴尔干研究所（Institul de Studii si Cercetari Balcanice，1937–1948），次年出版《巴尔干》（*Balcania*，1938–1948）杂志。1943年该研究所转变为国家级研究所，1948年该所并入罗马尼亚科学院历史研究所。罗马尼亚这个阶段的巴尔干学研究，开始着重整理和公布文献资料，与现实政治保持一定的距离。一批年轻的历史学家更加关注历史问题，而很少涉及国家政治和民族问题。

帕帕科斯特将罗马尼亚的巴尔干学研究提高到了一个新的高度。他在主持巴尔干研究所期间，提倡要对巴尔干国家的历史、文化、地理和政治按国别和年代进行多领域的比较研究。他指出，巴尔干研究应该摆脱各国的民族主义因素，消除历史上的误解，客观评价错综复杂的过去。他还强调说，巴尔干各国的巴尔干学研究中心和学者应该加强团结，彼此合作，不排除共同研究一些学术问题。为此，他对巴尔干研究所提出了两点要求：第一，鼓励对巴尔干各国的历史、文明和文化进行学术研究和比较研究；第二，提倡罗马尼亚文化机构与巴尔干国家的学术研究中心进行学术合作。

第二次世界大战后，罗马尼亚巴尔干研究获得了较快的发展。在"人民民主时期"（1944—1948）约尔加和帕帕科斯特创建的两个研究所关闭了。因为苏联强调"无产阶级国际主义"，不希望巴尔干国家之间政治上和学术上紧密合作。20世纪50年代末和60年代初，随着1957年苏军撤出罗马尼亚和其他东欧国家，罗马尼亚工人党独立自主的倾向加强，巴尔干国家开展地区合作的思想日益强烈，罗马尼亚希望在巴尔干地区发挥更加大的作用。1957年起它向阿尔巴尼亚、保加利亚、希腊、土耳其和南斯拉夫发出倡议，主张改善和缓和巴尔干国家之间的关系，召开地区领导人峰会，号召建立巴尔干无核区。但这些倡议没有得到希腊和土耳其的响应。

1962年10月古巴导弹危机结束，东西方的军事政治"冷战"开始缓和，这也影响到学术领域。与此同时，罗马尼亚与苏联的关系却因经互会里的经济分工问题而紧张起来。正是在这个历史时刻，罗马尼亚建议巴尔干研究领域加强国际合作。

1962年，罗马尼亚联合国教科文组织全国委员会和罗马尼亚科学院在联合国教科文组织的协助下举行了巴尔干国家学者第一次会晤，决定在联合国教科文组织的协助下成立一个国际组织。1963年在罗马尼亚首都布加勒斯特召开了国际东南欧研究学会（Association internationale des Edudes du Sud-Est Europeen，AIESEE）创立大会。这个国际非政府组织在布加勒斯特设立了常设秘书处，与巴尔干国家的巴尔干研究学者和西方巴尔干问题研究的机构与学者保持经常性联系。从此，每四年召开一次国际东南欧学代表大会。随后，各国的巴尔干学研究机构轮流举办代表大会，一直延续至今。

在这次代表大会的前夕，罗马尼亚科学院率先成立了东南欧研究所（Institutul de Studii Sud-Est Europene），出版所刊《东南欧学评论》（*Revue des Etudes Sud-Est Europeennes*），这意味着罗马尼亚恢复了1948年之前的巴尔干研究所及其刊物。此时，帕帕科斯特经过多年的监禁之后，被安排担任研究所东南欧杂志的副主编。1962年帕帕科斯特去世后，一直承认他是该杂志的编委。1978年出版的罗马尼亚历史百科认为，帕帕科斯特是罗马尼亚"巴尔干研究的真正奠基人"。

但是，罗马尼亚的巴尔干研究仍然没有摆脱约尔加的东南欧研究模式。这说明一方面罗马尼亚从传统上对巴尔干地区保持一定的距离；另一方面罗马尼亚从外交政策上与苏东集团相对独立。这也是 20 世纪 60 年代起罗马尼亚强调独立自主和开始亲西欧的必然反映，其结果导致 70 年代罗马尼亚的巴尔干研究在齐奥塞斯库政治和意识形态的影响下出现倒退。这一现象持续到整个 80 年代，此时罗马尼亚巴尔干学研究所依然存在，但民族主义思潮上升，对其他巴尔干国家的研究明显削弱，研究巴尔干问题的人才短缺，国际学术交流减少。

1989 年罗马尼亚社会制度转轨后，它与其他巴尔干国家的联系加强，地区合作开始活跃。罗马尼亚宣布，它在动荡不定的巴尔干地区对任何巴尔干国家没有政治、经济和领土诉求。相反，它是地区的稳定器，希望成为地区和平和稳定的因素。罗马尼亚积极参加了 1996 年的东南欧合作进程，即东南欧的政治和外交对话论坛；它与美国和欧盟一起提出了东南欧合作倡议；罗马尼亚是《1999 年东南欧稳定公约》倡议国之一，2008 年该公约转变成东南欧地区合作委员会。2007 年罗马尼亚加入欧盟后，它的巴尔干研究或者说东南欧研究越来越关注巴尔干国家之间的团结，关注和平解决巴尔干地区出现的冲突和危机，加速该地区国家融入欧洲一体化的进程。

东南欧研究所现有研究人员 25 人，现任所长为安德烈·蒂莫汀（Andrei Timotin）。研究所下设的研究室包括古代史、拜占庭研究、历史学、东南欧研究、国际关系等。2018 年东南欧研究所的主要研究项目有：

1. 海外的罗马尼亚著作及外国作品中对罗马尼亚人的记载，出版 8 卷（2008—2018）；

2. 巴尔干半岛的种族特点及社会经济实践（2016—2018）；

3. 东南欧传统文化、社会及语言史（2017—2019）；

4. 《东南欧研究》及《东南欧历史》杂志的评论著作（2018—2019）；

5. 16 世纪至 20 世纪欧洲一体化与东南欧的现代化（2017—2019）；

6. 19 世纪至 20 世纪东南欧的政治与文化（2017—2019）；

7. 历史记载，回忆与想象（文化、政治与身份认同）（2017—2020）；

8. 希腊古代的学院、宗教与殖民化（2017—2020）；

9. 阿勒颇的保罗（Paul of Aleppo）——东方旅行者的罗马尼亚各公国和俄国之旅（2018—2020）；

10. 东南欧研究所图书馆，包括东南欧研究所研究员及合作者的著作和其历史上一些重要人物的研究著作（2018—2019）。

保加利亚巴尔干学研究所成立 50 年及其学术活动

马细谱

作者简介 马细谱，首都师范大学文明区划研究中心首席研究员，历史学院特聘教授

保加利亚巴尔干学研究所走过了半个世纪的艰难历程，已经成为一个在欧洲乃至国际上颇负盛名的研究机构，在国际东南欧近现代史研究和巴尔干地区的现状研究领域取得了值得称道的成绩，为保加利亚国家和社会的发展做出了贡献。

今天，巴尔干学已经是一门综合性的社会科学，包括历史、哲学、语言学和其他相关学科，主要研究巴尔干半岛各国及其人民的过去和现在，重点是巴尔干各国的历史。保加利亚巴尔干学研究所的科研项目和学术水平在国内外日益体现了创新性和竞争性，在东南欧确立了自己组织协调和学术研究的地位和作用，拥有重要的国际话语权。

一、研究所成立恰逢其时

保加利亚科学院巴尔干学研究所成立于 1965 年，那年我正在当时的国立索非亚大学哲学历史系读四年级。一天，我们的巴尔干史专业课老师尼科拉伊·托多罗夫教授在课堂上说，保加利亚将建立巴尔干学研究所，成立大会将在科

学院小礼堂举行，欢迎感兴趣的同学们出席。4月的一天下午，我怀着好奇的心情去了，因为这个所的组织者和领导人是深受我们欢迎的托多罗夫教授。我也特别爱听他讲课，因为他经常访问巴尔干国家的首都，时常向我们介绍巴尔干各国的见闻，如当时的南斯拉夫、土耳其、希腊等我非常陌生的国家。

时间一晃过去了50年。2015年，我参加了在索非亚举行的由巴尔干学所举办的第11届国际东南欧学代表大会。会议茶歇时，我采访了现任巴尔干学研究所所长、国际东南欧研究学会主席亚历山大·科斯托夫教授。他赠予我保加利亚巴尔干学研究所成立50周年纪念册，并邀请我访问了他们研究所，还与各研究室负责人举行了座谈会。他们热情地给我介绍了巴尔干学研究所50年所走过的光辉道路。

1964年1月15日，保加利亚部长会议做出决议正式成立巴尔干学研究所，足见当时保加利亚政府对巴尔干地区研究的重视。时任保加利亚科学院院长柳博米尔·克勒斯塔诺夫院士在成立大会上说："巴尔干各国的历史发展密切相连，如果不研究它们彼此之间相互联系的历史，就无法解决社会经济、政治和文化的基本问题。"他还讲道，巴尔干学研究所的基本任务是研究各国的历史、生活和文化，促进巴尔干国家的接近和发展，实现本国的政治任务。

20世纪的60年代初，在保加利亚出现了有利于巴尔干学研究的国内外条件。这个时期，东西方冷战和对峙的局面有所改善，巴尔干国家之间的关系开始缓和。这一切都有利于加强巴尔干国家各个领域（包括学术领域）的合作。任何一个巴尔干国家不仅要热爱本国的历史，还要关注其他国家发展的共同趋势。1963年罗马尼亚倡议成立了国际东南欧研究学会（Association Internationale des Edudes du Sud-Est Europeen, AIESEE），保加利亚学者参加了成立大会。1963年在保加利亚成立了国际东南欧研究学会全国委员会，得到联合国教科文组织的支持，而在巴尔干各国则成立了历史学、考古学、人口学、语言学、文学、艺术、民俗学等研究中心。在东欧和西欧的一些国家也建立了研究巴尔干国家的研究所或者中心，如德国的"东南研究所"（Südost-Institut）和奥地利的"奥地利东欧和东南欧研究所"（Osterreichisches Ost-und Südosteuropa-Institut）。它们从事学术和相关国家外交政策的研究。

在保加利亚，研究巴尔干国家的历史和现状具有传统和一定的基础。到20世纪60年代初，保加利亚已经建立南斯拉夫、罗马尼亚和希腊等研究中心。在巴尔干学研究所成立之前，保加利亚科学院的历史研究所有一个巴尔干各国历史研究室，研究地区发展中的某些问题。保加利亚人民图书馆（国家图书馆）和一些大学也有一些人研究巴尔干地区的问题。

所以，1965年成立巴尔干学研究所在是水到渠成的事。随着它正式登上科学院的科研舞台，保加利亚巴尔干学研究进入了一个新的阶段，开启了东南欧研究的先河。

二、研究室设置与研究课题

巴尔干学研究所成立初期，尼科拉伊·托多罗夫院士连续25年是所长。全所设有4个课题组："巴尔干各国人民的起源和历史地理"，研究巴尔干国家自古代色雷斯至19世纪的发展时期；其他三个课题组是：奥斯曼学、巴尔干国家近现代史和巴尔干国家文化史。几年后，课题组改为研究室。

20世纪70年代，巴尔干学研究所的组织结构根据形势需要进行了调整，扩大了研究范围，确定了新的研究方向，研究室的名称也发生了变化：拜占庭和巴尔干国家、奥斯曼帝国统治巴尔干时期与民族解放运动、资本主义时期的巴尔干国家、第二次世界大战后的巴尔干国家、巴尔干国家文化史和学术情报室。各个室都有自己的重点课题。

1989年巴尔干学研究所及其学术活动进入了一个非常艰难的阶段，其面临严峻挑战，被推到了崩溃的边缘。在转轨初期，保加利亚科学院和整个国家一样，处于混乱和无政府状态，科研经费奇缺，人心涣散，工作人员被解雇，科研工作停滞。有的研究人员离开了研究所，还有的到国外去谋生，研究所处于瘫痪状态。

在新的条件下，坚守下来以及新进所的研究人员不再像过去那样严格按计划进行研究。选择课题的自主性更大了，但所里研究的基本方向仍然是围绕巴尔干国家的社会经济、政治和文化发展问题。1989年确定了4个基本研究方向：巴尔干国家的社会政治发展和结构、巴尔干国家的国际关系和联系、巴尔干国家的民族解放与社会运动和巴尔干各国文化史。从专题研究来看，所里研究人员40%的论文集中于整个巴尔干的问题，另有40%的研究成果集中反映巴尔干国家之间的相互关系和大国的巴尔干政策，只有20%的文章涉及与保加利亚相关的在全巴尔干具有重要政治和文化意义的重大历史事件。

特别是20世纪90年代，巴尔干地区成为学术界、媒体、国际政治和社会关注的焦点，它的核心区就是前南斯拉夫地区。在整个90年代，与南斯拉夫相关的事件是各国报纸的头版头条，展现在人们眼前的是硝烟四起的农村、颓垣断壁的城镇、成片的墓地、逃难的人群。学者们不理解为什么一个好端端的南斯拉夫成了大国争夺和内战的场地，成了流血冲突和任人宰割的战场。有人说，这是侵略性民族主义大爆发的结果；也有人说，这是欧美大国出卖了南斯拉夫。客观地讲，这两个方面的原因都不能排除，但有一点十分清楚：南斯拉夫解体与西方大国对南斯拉夫的横蛮干预和它们的错误政策是分不开的。当然，除此之外，南斯拉夫解体还应该有一些深层次的原因。

在 90 年代，保加利亚巴尔干学研究所的科研人员克服难以想象的困难，坚持下来了。1999 年在罗马尼亚召开了第 8 届巴尔干学代表大会。一位出席大会的保加利亚学者做了题为《巴尔干学还活着吗?》的发言，她说："我们可以平静地认为，尽管前进的道路上困难重重，但巴尔干学还存在，它活着。我们不仅有了新的技术和新的研究方法，而且为了我们共同的学科大家在努力进行持久的合作。"

2010 年保加利亚科学院因经费拮据将 1972 年成立的色雷斯学研究所撤销，并作为一个中心并入巴尔干学研究所。色雷斯研究中心的"加盟"，使研究所的研究范围涉及公元前和公元后 2000 年，包括色雷斯学、拜占庭学、奥斯曼学、东南欧国家近现代史、地中海地区，以及巴尔干文化、语言、政治和欧洲化等新的领域。

今天，研究所学者们的注意力集中于巴尔干地区的政治、经济、外交和文化以及色雷斯学、拜占庭学和东方学。近年，欧洲学，即欧盟东扩和欧洲一体化也是研究所关注的重点之一。这些研究和学术活动旨在对历史事实进行重新思考，鼓励运用比较研究的方法在东南欧多元文化和多种族的背景下研究本地区的历史。

三、重视自己培养人才，努力出版研究成果

随着学术研究活动的扩展，巴尔干学研究所里的人员结构亦发生了较大的变化。1978 年全所有 75 人，而到 1989 年全所已有 81 人，其中有 1 名院士、1 名通讯院士、12 名研究员和 18 名副研究员。1989 年 4 月所里的创始人和所长托多罗夫院士退休。不久，保加利亚社会制度发生剧变，所室各级领导几乎都换了新人。

在培养人才方面，研究所一开始就注意培养巴尔干学方面的年轻人。一个重要途径是研究所自己带培研究生（主要是博士生）。这些研究生毕业后绝大部分都留在所里工作，他们是所里高素质人才的主要来源。1990年以来，所里培养了40名博士生，其中大多数人获得了博士学位。

2004年研究所里剩下不足40人，其中有6名研究员和16名副研究员。2010年色雷斯学研究所作为一个中心并入后，该研究所的全称为巴尔干学研究所和色雷斯学研究中心（简称巴尔干学研究所）。所和中心合并后，2014年5月全所共有49人，其中有8位研究员、13位副研究员和26位助理研究员。研究人员中，有8位具有理学博士学位、39位具有哲学博士学位。2010年以来的所长是亚历山大·科斯托夫教授，另有1位副所长和1位学术秘书。研究所和中心分别在两个地方办公，各有自己的图书馆和出版物。

巴尔干学研究所从一开始就关注出版研究人员的成果。20世纪60年代成立之初，出版杂志《巴尔干研究》（*Études balkaniques*）和《史料》《巴尔干》。研究所还出版了《巴尔干学》和《第二次世界大战后的巴尔干国家》等系列丛书。

研究所非常重视文献资料的收集、整理和出版。由于该所在研究一些重大问题上取得了重要成果，并在国际上享有崇高的威望，所以巴尔干与地中海史料和文献国际信息中心（Centre international d'information sur les sources de l'histoire balkanique et méditerranéenne，CIBAL）设立在该所。这是一个得到联合国教科文组织帮助和支持，有国际档案委员会（Conseil international des archives）积极参加的组织。该中心1976年起有巴尔干、地中海、西欧国家以及美国和苏联等近20个国家参加。巴尔干学研究所的所长托多罗夫兼任该中心的主任。从成立之日起，中心就重点关注收集和发布本地区之外的国家所保存的巴尔干史料的信息。中心出版了多卷巴尔干外交文献索引，其中既有原始文件，也有复印件。到1989年，该中心收集了几十万份文件，做成了缩微胶卷。这对巴尔干学研究者是一个很大的帮助。这个中心与巴尔干学研究所共同出版了巴尔干学研究分类论文索引。1967—1976年期间一直出版《巴尔干研究论丛》（*Bibliographie D'études Balkaniques*）。此外，还联合出版了一批有关巴尔干国家的图书目录。如《保加利亚文学中的阿尔巴尼亚1878—1978》（1979）、《保加利亚文学中的土耳其1878—1978》（1979）、《希腊与保加利亚著作中的保希关系1878—1980》（1983）、《罗马尼亚与保加利亚文学中的保罗关系1806—1981》（1985）等。

尽管出版经费十分紧张，研究所仍继续出版过去的杂志和丛书，并在近年开始出版保加利亚文版《巴尔干》杂志。近十几年来，所里出版了一大批专著和论文集。2012年和2015年研究所分别编辑出版了《21世纪第一个十年的巴尔干》和《21世纪第二个十年的巴尔干》两本书，集中探讨当代巴尔干国家面临的问题、挑战和前景。

四、积极开展国内外学术交流

50年来，巴尔干学研究所与联合国教科文组织下属的国际东南欧研究学会紧密合作，与布加勒斯特、萨格勒布、贝尔格莱德、卢布尔雅那、地拉那、采蒂涅、萨洛尼卡、雅典和莫斯科的有关东南欧研究所或巴尔干研究所以及欧洲和世界上其他学术研究机构建立了经常性的合作。其中，有美国哈佛大学、意大利罗马大学、中国首都师范大学文明区划研究中心等。

巴尔干学研究所成功地举办了各种国际讨论会和学术会议。其中，特别组织了第一届（1966年）和第六届（1989年）国际东南欧研究代表大会（又称巴尔干学代表大会）；还在2011年召开了第22届拜占庭学代表大会和第13届国际色雷斯学代表大会（2017年）。研究所每年还与国内相关研究机构组织和召开全国性的或双边的（如与罗马尼亚）学术研讨会。2015年，研究所在联合国教科文组织的赞助下组织了题为"东南欧和欧洲一体化：政治、社会经济和文化问题"的第11届国际东南欧研究代表大会。来自世界上26个国家的250多名巴尔干问题研究的代表与会，展示了专家们的研究成果，彰显了最高水平学术会议的影响力。中国几名巴尔干学研究者出席了大会。

国际东南欧研究学会对保加利亚巴尔干学研究所的组织能力给予高度的评价，所以，该所的三位所长先后担任国际东南欧研究学会的主席达十五六年之久。他们是：弗拉迪米尔·格奥尔基耶夫院士（1965—1967）、尼科拉伊·托多罗夫院士（1975—1979；1989—1994）和亚历山大·科斯托夫教授（现任主席）。他们为国际东南欧研究学会的建立和发展做出了公认的贡献。

同时，2010年并入巴尔干学研究所的色雷斯研究中心也在国际上拥有举足轻重的发言权。1988年成立的印欧研究和国际色雷斯学研究委员会就设在色雷斯研究中心。前两届国际色雷斯学研究代表大会分别在土耳其和罗马尼亚举行，而第13届大会于2017年在保加利亚举办。色雷斯学研究中心与土耳其、希腊的多个研究中心以及大学有广泛的合作。

保加利亚巴尔干学研究所和色雷斯学研究中心的专家学者一直活跃在国际舞台上，他们的研究工作和学术活动受到国际同行的肯定。他们与一系列的国际组织和机构交流频繁，其中包括联合国教科文组织、国际东南欧研究学会（AIESEE）、国际拜占庭研究学会（AIES）、中世纪研究所国际联合会（FIDEM）、国际印欧研究和色雷斯学研究委员会，等等。

与此同时，研究所继续邀请保加利亚和国外学者举办系列讲座，如"谈谈巴尔干""巴尔干大使谈""半岛文学漫谈"等。研究人员走出研究所，广泛参与社会和国家项目，开展合作研究，如参与文化部、教育部、国防部和外交部以及议会相关委员会和首都有关部门的研究课题。研究所还积极参加国家档案局、一些州的历史博物馆、古典语言和文化中学、外交部的外交学院和国家文化研究所、外交部邻国司、军事科学院等的活动。可以说，1989年后，巴尔干学研究所在国家学术和文化生活中发挥了显著作用。研究所组织了几十次不同专题的国内和国际学术会议、展览和其他活动。另外，研究所还与国内大学的有关教研室和非政府组织，与国外的研究所（如美国的研究所）以及其他巴尔干国家和意大利、法国、德国、奥地利、匈牙利等国家驻索非亚大使馆或文化中心保持联系和合作关系。

事实证明，小所也能办大事。保加利亚巴尔干学研究所之所以能够在国际上拥有一定的学术高度，获得较大的话语权，下面几个因素值得关注。

第一，它继承了办所的传统。它是巴尔干地区成立最早的巴尔干研究机构之一，从一开始就成为国际东南欧研究学会创始成员单位，并开展了有效的合作。2010年色雷斯学研究所作为一个中心并入该所后，使该所在欧洲拥有更加雄厚的实力和更加广泛的发言权。

第二，它积极参与国际学术活动。在2007年保加利亚加入欧盟之后，研究所进一步扩大了合作范围和研究领域，不仅加强了与原来的合作单位的联系，而且与巴尔干国家、西欧和其他洲的研究机构建立了联系，签订了新的协议，开辟了共同研究的新课题。

第三，它充分发挥国际东南欧研究学会的组织和领导作用。研究所走向国际化，使历史、政治、法学、经济、语言、文学和文化诸领域的研究出现了新的气象。尤其是色雷斯学研究所并入后，使其研究跨度涵盖了自古至今的整个历史时期。近年，研究所加强对当代政治和国际关系问题的关注和研究，诸如欧盟和北约在巴尔干地区的扩张、西方与俄罗斯地缘政治的对峙、中东事件和东南欧的难民危机等现实问题。这也促进了巴尔干学研究所的合作伙伴越来越多，学术氛围也越来越浓厚。

参考资料：

1. *Половин век институт за Балканистика & Център по тракология АЛМАНАХ*, София, 2014.

2. A. Kostov, "Fifty Years and the Last Ten of Them: International Activities of the Institute of Balkan Studies & Centre of Thracology," BAS, *Etudes balkaniques*, 2014, pp. 7-21.

3. Василка Тъпкова-Заимова, "45 години балканистика," *Двувековният път на едно понятие* "*БАЛКАНСКИЯТ ПОЛУОСТРОВ*"（*1808-2008*）, София, 2014, с. 19-25.

4. Екатерина Никова, "Балкани, балканистика, балканскатаполитика," *Двувековният път на едно понятие* "*БАЛКАНСКИЯТ ПОЛУОСТРОВ*"（*1808-2008*）, София, 2014, с. 201-215.

喜读《巴尔干百年简史》

李建军

作者简介 李建军，首都师范大学历史学院副研究员

2018年12月，马细谱和余志和二位先生的《巴尔干百年简史》由中国青年出版社出版。这是我们国内第一本用通俗易懂的语言系统介绍和论述20世纪巴尔干国家历史的专著，实为2018年中东欧研究学术界的幸事。

该书作者马细谱先生和余志和先生是国内巴尔干研究的著名代表人物。其中，马细谱先生是中国社会科学院世界历史研究所研究员，现任首都师范大学历史学院特聘教授、文明区划研究中心首席专家。他多年来一直从事巴尔干国家的历史和现状问题研究，多次承担国家重点科研项目，已发表近300多万字的论文和著作，合译著作7部。专著代表作有《巴尔干各国人民反法西斯战争史》《巴尔干纷争》《南斯拉夫兴亡》《保加利亚史》。而余志和先生是新华社高级编辑、资深翻译家，曾任新华社驻索非亚分社首席记者、《参考消息》总编辑、经济信息部主任，已出版散文、小说、传记、时政类自撰和翻译作品30多部。专著代表作有《玫瑰国之都索非亚》《二战大事记》《圆桌旁的顶级谋算：揭秘二战期间国际会议及大国外交》等；译著代表作有《轭下》《保加利亚中短篇小说集》等。两位作者都有多年驻外从事外交或新闻工作的经历和经验，擅长把握和写作时政方面的文章和书籍。

两位作者一直关注巴尔干的历史和现实，那里发生的历史事件和人物比较突出，在世界历史中占据重要地位。巴尔干半岛历史悠久，是人类文明较早的发祥地之一。地理学家使用这个名词的本意是创造一个和亚平宁半岛、伊比利亚半岛并列的地理名词，并没有政治意涵。随着时间的推移，巴尔干地区从19

世纪晚期开始政治动荡，成为世界关注的焦点，这一术语才逐渐带有地缘政治意义。巴尔干半岛的最大特点是其多元性和复杂性：在相对狭小的面积上，杂居着塞尔维亚人、保加利亚人、马其顿人等众多种族；世界三大宗教天主教、东正教和伊斯兰教在这里碰撞、互动和发展，每个巴尔干国家的宗教和教会又各有特色；巴尔干长期处于拜占庭帝国、奥斯曼帝国、奥匈帝国和沙皇俄国的统治和影响之下，又是一个多元文化的地区，且文明程度差异较大。由此，巴尔干各国的政治、经济、社会、文化、语言、文字、宗教信仰都属于不同的范畴，存在明显的差别。这虽是多民族国家的普遍现象，但在巴尔干地区尤为突出。

我们对巴尔干国家了解甚少，同样巴尔干国家对我们也知之不多。我们对巴尔干国家历史的研究成果更是少之又少，同样巴尔干国家对中国历史的研究著作也是凤毛麟角。显然，造成这一结果的一个重要原因是缺乏这方面的专家学者和历史书籍，尤其是缺乏以介绍巴尔干国家历史上重大事件和人物以及巴尔干当代正在发生的现实进程的书籍。当我们正在践行"一带一路"倡议和"17+1"合作机制，倡导建立"人类命运共同体"的时候，确实需要一本中国人自己写的、介绍巴尔干地区历史和社会发展的书籍。

从这种意义上说，《巴尔干百年简史》的出版如降甘霖。两位先生发挥自身优长，使《巴尔干百年简史》这本书融历史学和新闻学于一体，将历史与现实相结合，用通俗易懂的笔墨，再现了20世纪巴尔干波澜壮阔的历史画面。这里既有鲜活的历史人物，又有惨烈的历史事件，但是，作者在书中始终以严谨的学风和"第三者"的客观态度引领读者客观公正地去阅读和理解巴尔干国家的不同命运。当我们阅读该书时，从字里行间可以看出，作者用他们多年在巴尔干国家学习和工作的经历在讲娓娓动听的故事，在无拘无束地与读者聊天。而实际上，正如马细谱先生所说，他们是用自己多年的学术成果和经验、用自己的心血写作，再用读者易于接受的文字表述出来。因此，本书的真实性、学术性、知识性、普及性显而易见。本书在结构方面打破了以往的惯例，章节设计引人入胜，标题新颖，直观性和可读性强，值得细细品味。

首先，本书真实地再现了20世纪巴尔干国家的百年历史，重点描述了百年巴尔干历史进程中的重大事件（如巴尔干战争、一战、二战、冷战和南斯拉夫解体后的战争等）和人物（如凯末尔、季米特洛夫、铁托、日夫科夫等），以及几次战争和重大政策给社会和人民带来的深刻影响。

其次，本书使我们获得了关于巴尔干国家的大量信息和知识，既满足了社会对外国历史，包括国别史、地区史和世界史的需要，又为"一带一路"在巴尔干地区落地开花展示了依据和前景。

再次，本书为我国巴尔干史和巴尔干问题的研究开创了先河。两位先生对20世纪巴尔干国家的历史和国际、国家之间的问题有着独特的见解，为我们进一步关注和了解巴尔干问题做出了表率，对我们认识和研究今日的巴尔干问题提供了钥匙。

最后，本书将助力于在我国普及巴尔干国家的历史和现状。马细谱先生说过，作为严肃的世界史专业研究者，一般强调引证规范，资料翔实，常常不愿意为广大群众，尤其是为青少年写通俗易懂的读物。这次两位作者是应中国青年出版社之约，第一次尝试，应该说是成功的。

百年烽烟和风雨，百年丰碑和记忆，这就是巴尔干百年兴衰荣辱史的写照。一个世纪，巴尔干国家多灾多难，巴尔干人民饱受艰辛痛苦。连绵不断的冲突和战乱既缘于巴尔干国家自身的固有矛盾，更与外部势力的介入和离间密不可分。值得庆幸的是，巴尔干百年风雨飘摇的年月已经翻过一页，历史开启了新的篇章。如今的巴尔干已今非昔比。部分巴尔干国家不管加入欧盟和北约与否，彼此之间相互尊重，共谋发展，已经成为共识。

当然，演绎百年巴尔干的不仅有冲突战乱、争权夺利，也有和平共处、联合协作；不仅有诡异离奇的政治和经济兴衰，也有多样性的社会和文化；不仅有野心勃勃的政客权要，也有追求安逸的普通百姓。这些都是构成巴尔干引人瞩目、魅力四射的不可或缺的部分。二位作者也认同这一点。但是由于篇幅限制，二位在此方面着墨不多，加上本书封面的设计，可能会造成读者加深巴尔干是"火药桶"的印象，而不能全面地理解巴尔干的魅力，这算是本书的一小点遗憾。但瑕不掩瑜，在长期缺乏厚重作品的中东欧研究学术界，二位先生能够奉献高质量的开创之作绝对属于惊喜！我们谨向马细谱和余志和两位老先生表示深切的敬意，向他们的大作问世表示热烈的祝贺！让我们怀揣《巴尔干百年简史》，认识巴尔干，理解巴尔干，研究巴尔干。

Katalog Osmanskih Dokumenata（Ⅰ）/ Catalogue of Ottoman Documents, prepared by Azra Gadžo-Kasumović, Gazi Husrev-Bey Library in Sarajevo, 2018, 448 pg.

[波黑] 尼哈德·多斯托维奇[*]

　　The archival material that originates from any period and region of Ottoman Empire anywhere in world today is counted among the most trustworthy sources, be it in science and research or publicist writing and journalism. Ottoman archives contain various kinds of documents. From those documents we can learn different information, be it information about some microgeographic region like village or street or be it macro geographic region which presumes some administrative or military unit. In the same manner from this archivalia it is possible to reconstruct daily life of a community or an individual. Regarding the importance of Ottoman documents for historians we should not forget that Fernand Braudel, as one of the most important historians, considered his works on Mediterranean and civilizations as uncompleted due to the fact that Ottoman archives were not open for scientific public when he was writing those works.

　　In one of the oldest institutions that operates in Bosnia and Herzegovina in

---

* 尼哈德·多斯托维奇（Nihad Dostović），波黑萨拉热窝大学东方学院研究人员。

continuity, for over 480 years, the Gazi Husrev-Bey Library, various collections of oriental manuscripts in Arabic, Persian, Ottoman Turkish and Bosnian language are preserved. Together with manuscripts there is also very rich collection of archival documents from Ottoman period. It should be also mentioned that those collections which are hosted in the Library are among the richest and the most appreciated in the world. After series of 18 catalogues of manuscripts that are being preserved in this library, first book of Catalogues of Ottoman documents [*Katalog osmanskih dokumenata* (Ⅰ)] was published in Bosnian language during 2018. The Catalogue includes diplomatic documents, various kinds of administrative and judiciary documents, but also documents of private and public correspondence be it at local or international level that are preserved in the various archival collections of the Gazi Husrev-Bey Library.

Structurally the Catalogue is divided into two parts: first part included single original documents, while the second part is consisted of the documents from Sarajevo *sidjills*. In the first part the documents are ordered in hierarchic, a sequence firstly come *fermân*s-documents issued by sultan, than *berâts* and after them *buyuruldus*. The editor endeavoured to include all original documents from higher levels of government that are found in the archival collection, i. e. the documents sent from the higher administrative instances are almost all included. This is understandable, taking into account the fact that documents from lower levels of government (*tezkire*, *hüccet*, circular letters) are very numerous therefore could take place in the Catalogue, and many of those documents are written in a template frame where sometime only names and dates are changed. The second part of the book covers documents registered in the court protocols (*sdjills*) of Sarajevo court period 973/1565-66 to 1192/1779. Same as it is case with the first part, in second part of the book registers of original documents in the *sidjills* are ordered in the hierarchical order, i. e. firstly the ones issued by sultan and his office down to the lowest ranking office of *kadı* and *nâib*.

The main characteristic of this catalogue is peculiar approach to every catalogued document. In the introductory part the editor together with basic information on used archives gave also an essential information and definition for every sort of documents used in the book. In this respect we can say that the Catalogue is a remarkable guidebook in Bosnian language for understanding of the Ottoman archives. For each document catalogued together with a call number it is stated to which kind of documents it belongs and short summary in Bosnian language is provided. All of this will make research easier for anyone who is interested into this archieve. For a researcher immersed into field of Ottoman history such a professional catalogue represents in exhaustible source of topics that should be explored. It is very hard to mention all topics that are found in the Catalogue in one short review as this one is. Besides the topics on attitude of centre and periphery that pervade through the whole Catalogue there are also the following topics: tīmār possessions and their succession by heirs or transfer to third parties (pg. 44, 105, 170, 204, 247), protection of priests who have *a hidnāme* of Sultan Mehmed Fatih (pg. 82-83), protection of rights of the Orthodox Church (pg. 168, 228, 235, 236, 240), abolishment of janissary corpses (pg. 128-9, 130, 134), and many other topics that appear in different document like women in Ottoman provincial courts, *vakıfs*-endowments and their role in economy of Ottoman province, trade of Ottoman State with neighbours (Venetian Republic, Austro-Hungarian Empire), and many other topics. Very professional and informative arrangement of a catalogue of Ottoman archival sources will find admirers not only among historians, but also among researchers and experts from other scientific areas. It also should be noted that the Catalogue covers archival material stored in Gazi Husrev-Bey Library from very first days of the Ottoman rule in the region up to the very last day of the existence of the Empire. Very simple approach of the editor, professional explanations and summaries of the documents will be very interesting to a wider public and journalism. As a supplement to the Catalogue at the end vocabulary of specific terms is given, what will make this book more understandable for many researchers, be it from academia or wider public, to write about different periods of the Ottoman Empire. Together with the vocabulary, as the second supplement there are also facsimiles of the documents. It would be improper and out of place to criticise a work like this, which will ease work to many researchers, especially if we know that editor is among the most experienced experts on Ottoman archival materials, not only Bosnia and Herzegovina, but also in wider region.

评艾莱兹·比贝莱的《阿尔巴尼亚与中国：不对称的联盟》

[克罗地亚] 白伊维

作者简介 白伊维（Ivica Bakota），首都师范大学历史学院世界史专业副教授

在中国与中东欧国家建交 70 周年之际，研究中东欧与中国关系的一些学者回顾和梳理了当代东欧社会主义国家与中国之间政治、经济和社会关系的发展与演变。从双方关系的发展历程上来看，其内容、角度发生过巨大的变化。其中，东欧剧变是一个大的节点，中国倡导的"17+1"合作机制的建立可以作为一个小的节点。这两个节点的影响使得曾经以社会主义为基础特征的关系在今天不再发挥作用，甚至被人们遗忘。这种状况在中东欧国家特别明显。东欧剧变后，除了短期陷入政治动荡的南联邦之外，每一个中东欧国家都在对外关系上开始另起炉灶，且几乎彻底放弃"旧制度"下的对外关系方针以及与大国经营起来的联系。可以说，中东欧 1990 年以来的对华关系是目前对外关系研究的组成部分，而 1990 年前的对华关系早已成为历史。

然而，美国阿族裔知名历史家艾莱兹·比贝莱所著的《阿尔巴尼亚与中国：不对称的联盟》（Elez Biberaj, *Albania and China: An Unequal Alliance*, AIIS, Tirana, 2016）是一个把中国与阿尔巴尼亚历史关系看作具有现实意义的研究成果。虽然这本书第一次出版是 1986 年，但是其探讨中阿两国关系的视角和对大小国之间关系的聚焦点使得出版 30 年后被再版。

近年俄罗斯与欧盟之间关系紧张，欧、美、俄等大国为了追求更大的影响

力在中东欧进行被学界称为"冷战式的"博弈。在这种背景下，小国的反应及其对全球实力制衡发挥的作用依然容易被忽视。那么，为什么小国与大国会结盟？小国在与大国发展关系中又如何获取自己的利益？比贝莱从新现实主义理论出发，探讨从1964年到1978年阿尔巴尼亚和中国建立盟友关系的时期。作为阿族人，他从阿尔巴尼亚的角度对中阿友好关系的研究，弥补了主流学界探讨"大国与小国典型关系"的不足。

该书对20世纪60年代初期中国与阿尔巴尼亚共享同样的"斯大林式马列主义"的意识形态进行了详细分析。作者认为这些意识形态的相似之处让两个截然不对称的国家聚集在一起，但这并不是两国友好的主要原因。共同的意识形态被视为两国相互友好的基石，但比贝莱分析认为，对于阿尔巴尼亚来说，意识形态的重要性远远比不上经济需求的战略利益。

本书第一章概述了阿尔巴尼亚与中国成为盟友之前与其他大国的交往。这有助于理解为什么两国领导人进行后来的接触，并形成一个"几乎被所有政治分析人士认为不可持续的联盟"。据作者分析，无论阿尔巴尼亚是如何孤独并走独立的发展道路，其外交政策一直倾向于与大国建立牢固的关系。

在与中国结盟之前，阿尔巴尼亚处于二战后获得独立不久，它与南斯拉夫和苏联都建立了伙伴关系。该国的地理位置和动荡的历史、与邻国的领土争端以及对外援的依赖，使它不得不与强国建立友谊。因此，在20世纪60年代，阿尔巴尼亚与苏联分裂的时候，阿尔巴尼亚急需经济援助。作者称，该国50%的外贸都是与苏联实现的，导致与苏关系破裂后阿尔巴尼亚失去了一个巨大的市场以及大量的资金和军事援助。

那时的阿尔巴尼亚需要一个强大的新盟友来填补苏联的空缺。作者认为，对于阿尔巴尼亚来说，中国经历了与苏联的冲突，也谴责了苏联与美国的和解，并认为苏联实行自由市场政策背离了共产主义。对中国来说，阿尔巴尼亚在巴尔干的战略地位及其与苏联的决裂使它成为一个值得交友的国家。

阿中关系是一个在大国与小国关系中小国利益多于大国利益的一个少见的例子。除了经济援助外，阿尔巴尼亚需要一个能保护它的边境安全，但同时不威胁到它独立的盟友。阿尔巴尼亚认为，阿中联盟足以阻止其他国家入侵以及确保中国也不会侵犯阿尔巴尼亚的主权。维护阿尔巴尼亚的独立和共产党执政的合法性以及得到经济援助是阿尔巴尼亚与遥远的中国合作的主要原因。然而，正因两国间的政治联系比较薄弱，外交政策方面的沟通有限，两国最终分手了。

总之，对于阿中关系的兴衰以及两个国土遥远且国情差异很大的国家组成的联盟，《阿尔巴尼亚与中国：不对称的联盟》提供了一个有趣的分析视角。

新书速递（九本）

一、《南斯拉夫社会主义的社会不均与社会不满》（Social Inequalities and Discontent in Yugoslav Socialism）

【出版社】Routledge, New York, USA
【ISBN】9781472459541
【出版时间】2016 年
【作者】Rory Archer, Igor Duda and Paul Stubbs

【主要内容】作为社会主义国家的南斯拉夫通过诉诸社会平等获得了合法性，然而，社会分层是南斯拉夫社会的特征，并且随着国家的存在而强化。到了 20 世纪 80 年代，南斯拉夫在社会经济与国家体制方面出现了分歧。通过一系列关于社会背景的案例研究，本书希望"将阶级重新纳入"南斯拉夫史学，探索社会阶层的理论如何为社会流动的政治和政策提供信息。反过来，社会或基层对阶级的理解又如何影响了政治和政策。本书并不关注南斯拉夫各共和国和各省之间的区域差异，而是将重点放在特定社区内的社会分化和不满。这些历史研究的作者来自不同的学科背景，将社会主义时代的学术与基于最新材料的当代研究联系起来。本书包含了各个阶层的声音，从工厂工人和自耕农到虚构的电视角色，还有流行、乡村音乐的巨星。

【目录】

List of Tables ······ vii
Acknowledgements ······ ix
Notes on Contributors ······ x
1. Bringing Class Back In: An Introduction ······ 1
2. What nationalism has buried: Yogoslav social scientists on the crisis, grassroots powerlessness and Yugoslavism ······ 21
3. The gastarbajteri as a transnational Yugoslav working class ······ 38
4. "Paid for by the workers, occupied by the bureaucrats": housing inequalities in 1980s Belgrade ······ 58
5. Education, conflict and class reproduction in socialist Yugoslavia ······ 77
6. Roma between ethnic group and an "underclass" as portrayed through newspaper discourses in socialist Slovenia ······ 95
7. Of social inequalities in a socialist society: the creation of a rural underclass in Yugoslav Kosovo ······ 112
8. "They came as workers and left as Serbs": the role of Rakovica's blue-collar workers in Serbian social mobilisations of the late 1980s ······ 132
9. "Buy me a silk skirt Mike!" Celebrity culture, gender and social positioning

in socialist Yugoslavia ·· 155

10. When capitalism and socialism get along best: tourism, consumer culture and the idea of progress in *Male misto* ·· 173

二、《裹挟正义：巴尔干历史问题的处理》（*Hijacked Justice: Dealing with the Past in the Balkans*）

【出版社】Cornell University Press, New York, USA
【ISBN】9780801448027
【出版时间】2009 年

【作者】Jelena Subotic

【主要内容】在《裹挟正义》中,Jelena Subotic 追溯了为解决南斯拉夫战争留下的暴力而建立的机构的设计、实践和政治影响。她发现,追究前南斯拉夫战争罪行责任的国际努力被用来追求非常不同的地方政治目标。迫于国际压力,塞尔维亚、克罗地亚和波黑实施了各种"过渡司法"(transitional justice)机制来系统地处理过去的罪行。然而,三个国家其实背后都有不可告人的政治动机:摆脱国内政治对手、获得国际金融援助、进入欧盟。作者认为,过渡司法被这种政治战略劫持时,会助长国内的抵制势力,加剧政治不稳定,甚至创造另类的、政治化的历史观。战争罪行的审判(如海牙的审判)和真相委员会(如南非)是必要且可取的,这是关注于冲突后社会重建的人们的主要信念。各国现在都会在体制内部处理这些问题,而不是大赦或者胜者即正义,但这种期望产生了矛盾的结果。作者认为,为了避免裹挟正义的陷阱,国际社会应该把重点放在冲突后更广泛和更深刻的社会转型上,而不只是去逮捕战犯。

【目录】

Preface and Acknowledgments	ix
List of Abbreviations	xvii
Introduction: The Importance of Dealing with the Past	1
1. The Politics of Hijacked Justice	15
2. The Past is not yet Over	38
3. The Truth Is in Croatia's Favor	83
4. Who Lives in Your Neighborhood?	122
Conclusion: Hijacked Justice beyond the Balkans	166
Index	193

三、《种族冲突后：冲突后波黑和马其顿的政策制定》(*After Ethnic Conflict： Policy-making in Post-conflict Bosnia and Herzegovina and Macedonia*)

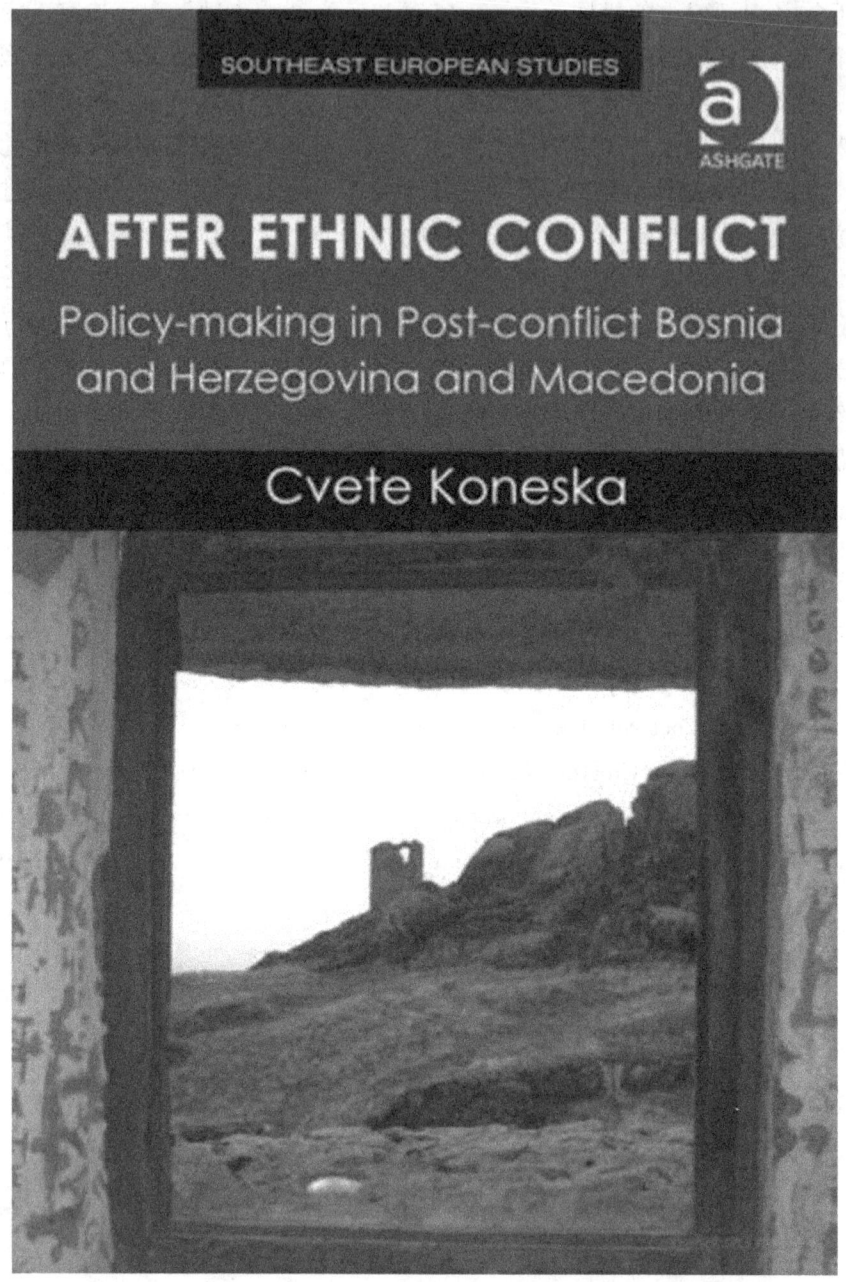

【出版社】Ashgate Publishing, Farnham, Surrey, United Kingdom
【ISBN】9781472419798（hbk），9781472419804（ebk - PDF），9781472419811（ebk-ePUB）
【出版时间】2014年
【作者】Cvete Koneska

【主要内容】为了更好地理解是什么使得政治精英能够克服种族冲突的遗留问题，引导政治走向更加相互合作与和平的政治竞争，本书从政策层面研究了冲突后政治领导人之间的民族和解与抵抗。各章讨论的问题是：冲突后种族分裂国家的政治精英为何选择跨越种族界限相互包容或对抗？通过探讨权力分享制度、非正式实践和跨领域的政治身份如何影响民族和解，本书还探讨了什么时候和在什么条件下民族和解更有可能发生。它侧重于波黑和北马其顿，分别在第三和第四部分对这两个巴尔干国家进行了分析和比较。

【目录】

Part I Introduction

1. After Ethnic Conflict: Why Look at Post-conflict Recovery? ……… 3
2. Explaining Ethnic Accommodation ……… 19

Part II Historical and Institutional Background

3. Bosnia 1991-1996: From Communism to Ethnic Conflict ……… 39
4. Macedonia 1991-2001: Simmering Ethnic Tensions ……… 59

Part III What Makes Post-conflict Politics Work

5. Military Reform in Bosnia: A Single Joint Army ……… 79
6. Decentralisation in Macedonia: Designing Municipal Mapsand Funds … 97

Part IV Continuing Challenges: Persisting Ethnic Tensions after Conflict

7. Police Reform in Bosnia: Ethnicity above Effciency ……… 119
8. Minority Education in Macedonia: Recurring Ethnic Tensions ……… 137
9. Conclusions ……… 157

Bibliography ……… 169
Index ……… 185

四、《暴力作为一种生成力量——身份认同、民族主义与一个巴尔干社区的记忆》(*Violence as a Generative Force: Identity, Nationalism, and Memory in a Balkan Community*)

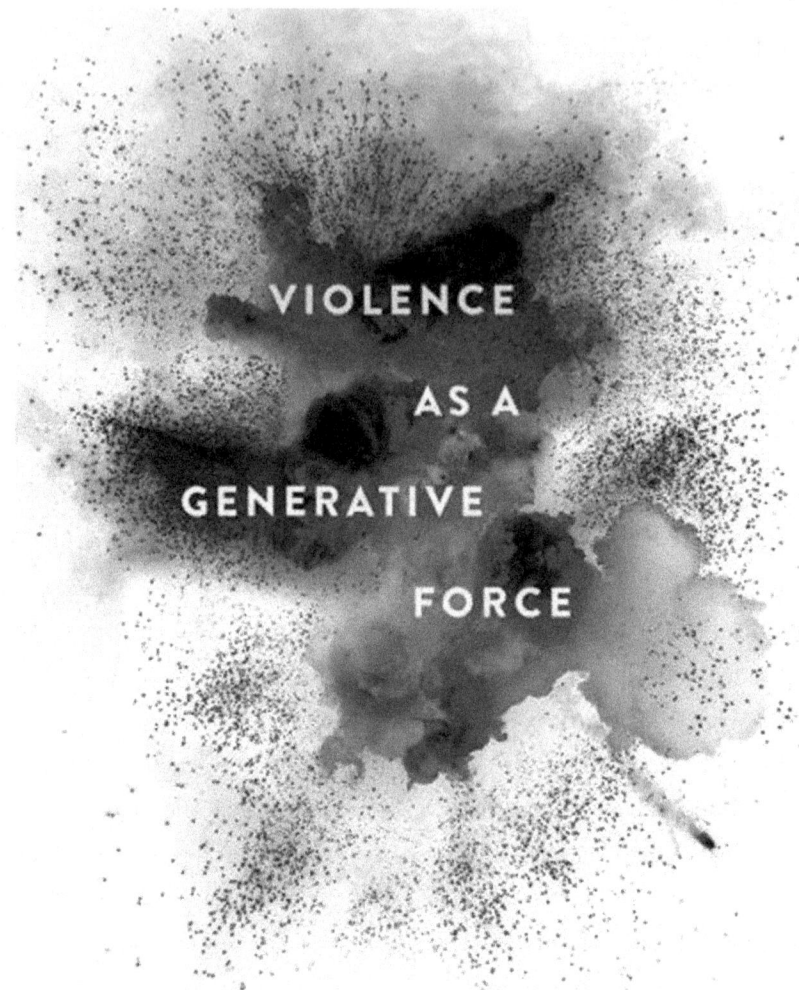

【出版社】Cornell University Press
【ISBN】9781501704925
【出版时间】2016 年
【作者】Max Bergholz
【主要内容】本书利用政治暴力、种族和民族主义领域的问题和调查结果，讲述库伦·瓦库夫（Kulen Vakuf）在 1941 年前后的故事。然而，随着时间的推移，这个故事丰富的经验将成为批判性地参与这些领域关键辩论的一种手段。因此，这本书揭示了当地社区间暴力的动态及其在巴尔干农村社区的影响，这是一个在政治暴力文献中明显缺失的主题。这个巴尔干社区的故事为我们提供了一种扩展政治暴力研究的方法——其中许多研究与非种族内战有关。这里的目标是通过将其扩展到一种本书中较少分析的暴力类型来加强这项工作：即许多人可能认为的"种族暴力"。

【目录】

List of Illustrations	ix
Acknowledgments	xi
List of Abbreviations	xv
Part I History	
Introduction	3
1. Vocabularies of Community	21
Part II 1941	
2. A World Upended	61
3. Killing and Rescue	100
4. Rebellion and Revenge	145
5. The Challenge of Restraint	183
6. Forty-Eight Hours	217
Part III After Intercommunal Violence	
7. Sudden Nationhood	267
Epilogue: Violence as a Generative Force	297
Notes	323
Bibliography	409
Index	431

五、《种族与南斯拉夫地区：后社会主义、后冲突、后殖民?》（*Race and the Yugoslav Region：Postsocialist，Post-Conflict，Postcolonial?*）

【出版社】Manchester University Press, Manchester, United Kingdom
【ISBN】1526126621, 9781526126627
【出版时间】2018 年
【作者】Catherine Baker

【主要内容】这是第一本将前南斯拉夫的领土和集体特征纳入种族政治的书，其不仅仅是关注族裔政治，以及种族差异的思想在全球转化的历史。这本书将批判种族研究、全球历史社会学的"翻译中的种族"与东南欧文化批判联系起来，表明南斯拉夫地区深深地植根于全球种族形态之中。在这样做的过程中，它考虑到了大众文化的日常地缘政治想象；族裔、民族和移徙的历史；包括不结盟运动在内的国家社会主义之前和期间的跨国种族形态；以及后南斯拉夫关于安全、移徙、恐怖主义和国际干预，包括反恐战争和目前的难民危机的论述。

【目录】
Series editor's introduction
Preface
List of abbreviations
Introduction: what does race have to do with the Yugoslav region?
1. Popular music and the "cultural archive"
2. Histories of ethnicity, nation and migration
3. Transnational formations of race before and during Yugoslav state socialism
4. Postsocialism, borders, security and race after Yugoslavia
Conclusion

六、《巴尔干错综复杂的历史》（第一卷：民族主义和语言政策）（*Entangled Histories of the Balkans*, Volume One: National Ideologies and Language Policies）

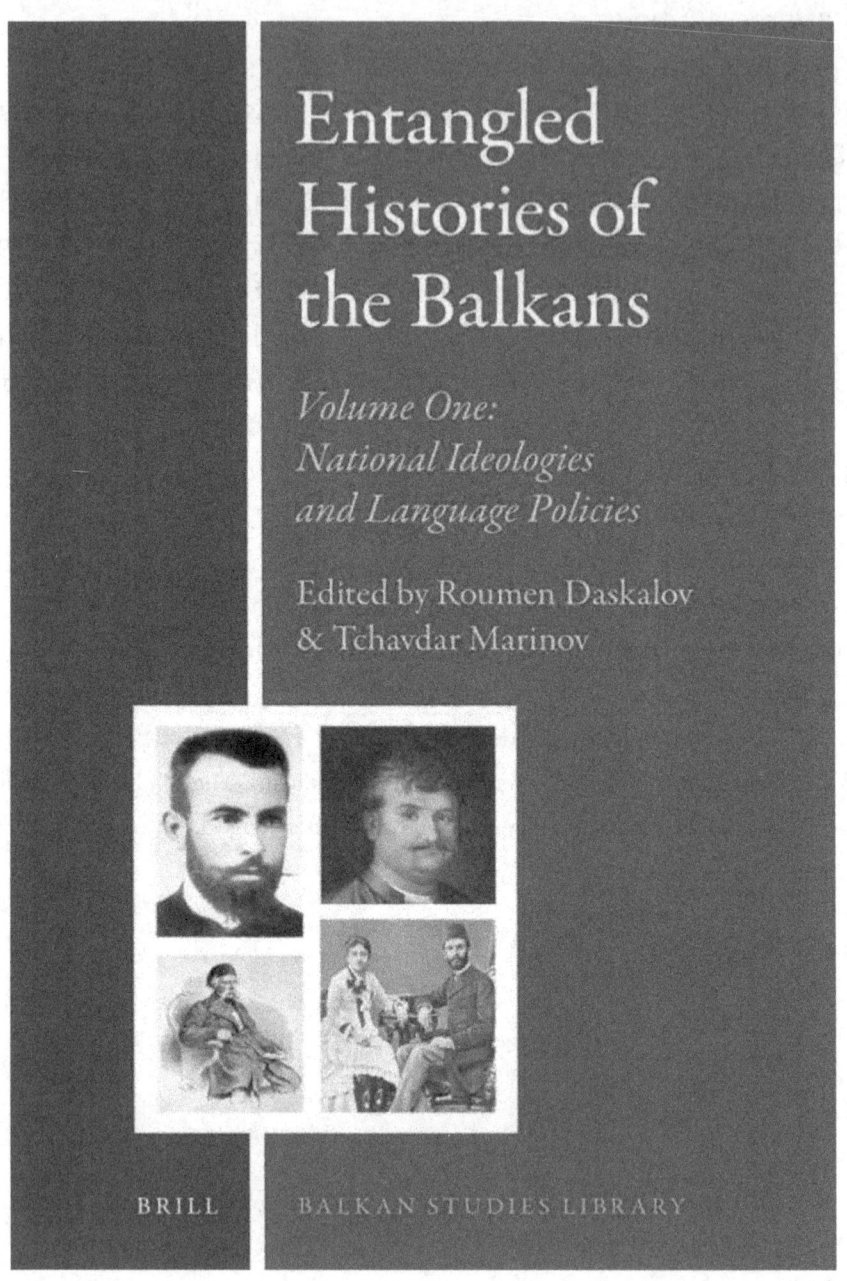

【出版社】Koninklijke Brill NV, Leiden, The Netherlands
【ISBN】9789004250758
【出版时间】2013 年
【作者】Roumen Daskalov and Tchavdar Marinov

【主要内容】本书是有关巴尔干地区历史研究重要项目的一部分。它以一种全球的、联系的视角，将巴尔干地区国家的历史作为一个文化交融和分离的整体进程，书写巴尔干各国人民共同的、相互联系的、错综复杂的历史。全书包含两部分内容，第一部分为巴尔干地区的民族和民族主义，第二部分为巴尔干地区的语言和语言政策。第一部分以"巴尔干地区的前民族国家认同"开篇，主要研究的是两个或者两个以上巴尔干地区国家间不断相互作用的国家意识形态和特征的形成，以及他们之间的文化认同、分离和领土争端。如罗马人与希腊人和保加利亚人之间的相互作用和纠葛与建立一种广泛认同的奥斯曼主义的失败尝试，后期形成马其顿民族意识形态与保加利亚、希腊和塞尔维亚的民族主义激烈的争论。第二部分着眼于民族国家形成进程中的中心环节，即语言和语言政策的形成带来的区别于邻国的思想。如塞尔维亚—克罗地亚命运、马其顿语的标准化和阿尔巴尼亚语问题。本书通过选取具有高度代表性的案例，表明巴尔干国家的国家建设进程和语言政策的关联性。

【目录】

Note on Transliteration ……………………………………… vii
Notes on Contributors ……………………………………… ix
List of Maps ……………………………………………… xi
Preface ………………………………… *Roumen Daskalov* xiii

Section One: Nations and National Ideologies in the Balkans
Introduction to Section One: Nations and National Ideologies in the Balkans ……………………………………… *Tchavdar Marinov* 3
Pre-National Identities in the Balkans ……… *Raymond Detrez* 13
From Imperial Entanglements to National Disentanglement: The "Greek Question" in Moldavia and Wallachia, 1611–1863 ……… *Constantin Iordachi* 67
Bulgarian-Greek Dis/Entanglements ……… *Roumen Daskalov* 149
Formulating and Reformulating Ottomanism ……… *Alexander Vezenkov* 241
Famous Macedonia, the Land of Alexander: Macedonian Identity at the

Crossroads of Greek, Bulgarian and Serbian Nationalism ……………………………………………………………… *Tchavdar Marinov* 273

 Section Two: Languages and Language Policies in the Balkans

 Introduction to Section Two: Languages and Language Policies in the Balkans ……………………………………………… *Alexander Vezenkov* 333

 Language and Identity: The Fate of Serbo-Croatian … *Ronelle Alexander* 341

 In Defense of the Native Tongue: The Standardization of the Macedonian Language and the Bulgarian-Macedonian Linguistic Controversies ……………………………………………… *Tchavdar Marinov* 419

 The Albanian Language Question: Contexts and Priorities …………………………………………………………… *Alexander Vezenkov* 489

 Index ……………………………………………………………… 523

学术信息

七、《同时的渴望:"正常生活"和萨拉热窝综合类公寓中的状况》(*Yearning's in the Meantime*:*"Normal Lives" and the State in a Sarajevo Apartment Complex*)

【出版社】Berghahn Books,New York,USA
【ISBN】9781782386506
【出版时间】2015 年

【作者】 Stef Jansen

【主要内容】 基于对萨拉热窝郊区一栋综合类公寓的调查，作者试图以人类学的角度，研究二战后当地人们对于正常生活的渴望和与之相关的政治因素。由于人们普遍认为"正常的生活"总是需要正常的状态，作者着眼于社会政治秩序中的生活轨迹。通过对萨拉热窝城市交通、学校教育、建筑维护、裙带关系、战争和地缘政治等方面经历的详细描绘，本书一次又一次地回到这些看似不言自明的陈述中提出的问题，即人们有过"正常的生活"并且所有人都想过上"正常的生活"，没有比这更重要的事情。

【目录】

List of Illustrations ·· vii

Preface ··· ix

Acknowledgements ·· x

Introduction〔or, Towards an Anthropology of Shared Concerns〕············ 1

Part I：Figuring "Normal Lives"

Chapter 1 "Normal Lives"〔or, Towards an Anthropology of Yearning〕··· 33

Chapter 2 Waiting for a Bus〔or, Towards an Anthropology of Gridding〕··· 59

Chapter 3 Wartime Gridding for "Normal Lives"〔or, Towards an Anthropology of Hope for the State〕·· 87

Part II：Diagnosing Daytonitis

Chapter 4 First Symptom："There Is No System"〔or, Towards an Anthropology of an Elusive State Effect〕·· 123

Chapter 5 Second Symptom："We Are Patering in Place"〔or, Towards an Anthropology of Spatiotemporal Entrapment〕··································· 157

Part III：Living With Daytonitis

Chapter 6 Conviviality in the Meantime〔or, Towards a Critique of Dayton Non-Politics〕··· 189

Epilogue：Shovelling and Numbering for "Normal Lives" ··············· 221

References ·· 233

Index ·· 243

学术信息

八、《南斯拉夫与后南斯拉夫国家的民族与公民：百年的公民身份》
(*Nations and Citizens in Yugoslavia and the Post-Yugoslav States*: *One Hundred Years of Citizenship*)

【出版社】Bloomsbury Academic, London and New York
【ISBN】9781474221528
【出版时间】2015 年
【作者】Igor Štiks

【主要内容】1914 年至今，巴尔干的政治随着国际和国内边界不可预测的变化而被无情地改变。在这些边界之间以及跨越这些边界，各种政治实体形成、共存、相互摩擦。通过分析百年间南斯拉夫以及后南斯拉夫国家现代公民身份的发展历程，作者表明，公民身份的概念和实践对于理解政治实体是如何被构建、摧毁和重建是十分必要的。他认为，现代公民身份在整合和重新统一分裂民族的工程中是一种可以用于不同甚至相反目标的工具。对作为"实验室"的巴尔干地区公民身份的研究不仅提供了一个叙述另类政治历史的原始视角，而且提供了对现代政治的精细机制以及重复故障的洞察力，适用于欧盟及其他国家的现状。

【目录】

Preface and Acknowledgements ………………………………………… x
Introduction: A Balkan Laboratory of Citizenship ……………………… 1
A century of dis/integrations ……………………………………………… 1
Citizenship and citizenship regime ……………………………………… 4
In Yugoslavia, and after: Citizenship as research field, Citizenship as battlefield
 ……………………………………………………………………………… 11
Citizenship as a political history of Yugoslavia and the post-Yugoslav states …
 ……………………………………………………………………………… 17
Part 1 From National Integration to the First Disintegration …………… 23
1. Brothers United: The Making of Yugoslavs …………………………… 25
Brothers as aliens: From Yugoslavism to Yugoslavia …………………… 25
Brothers as citizens: The belated birth of Yugoslav citizenship ………… 30
Precarious birth, fragile existence and the brutal death of the first Yugoslavia
 ……………………………………………………………………………… 34
2. Revolutionary Brothers: The Communist Formula for Yugoslavia …… 37
Yugoslav communists: Solving the national question …………………… 38
Wartime: Enemies or brothers? ………………………………………… 47
From brothers in arms to federated citizens …………………………… 50

Part 2 From Socialist Re-Integration to the Second Disintegration ……… 53
3. Brothers Re-United! Federal Citizenship in Socialist Yugoslavia ……… 55
　Centralist federalism, 1945–1967 ……… 55
　Bifurcated citizenship ……… 62
　Self-management, decentralization and citizenship ……… 66
4. Brothers as Partners: Centrifugal Federalism, Confederal Citizenship and Complicated Partnership ……… 71
　Centrifugal federalism, 1967–1974 ……… 71
　From federal to confederal citizenship ……… 79
　Broken partnership: From confederal citizenship towards crisis ……… 82
5. The Bridges Over the Miljacka: The Long Farewell to Yugoslav Citizenship ……… 89
　Yugoslavism: Fading of an idea ……… 90
　Yugoslavia: Only a matter of interests? ……… 93
　Code red: Turning citizens into enemies ……… 97
Part 3 From Nationalist Disintegration to War ……… 101
6. Partners into Competitors: Divisive Democracy and Conflicting Conceptions of Citizenship ……… 103
　Democracy and nationalism ……… 104
　Citizens as voters: Democratize and divide ……… 110
　A secret handshake between nationalism and electoral democracy ……… 116
7. Where is My State? Citizenship as a Factor in Yugoslavia's Disintegration ……… 119
　So, why did it happen? ……… 119
　Relevant factors of Yugoslavia's disintegration ……… 121
　The citizenship factor ……… 128
8. Enemies: Citizenship as a Trigger of Violence ……… 133
　The dark side of 1989: Violence in post-socialist Europe ……… 133
　Triggers of violence: Citizenship, borders and territories, and the role of the federal military ……… 138
　Conclusion: The price of war ……… 146
Part 4 From Ethnic Engineering to European Re-Integration? ……… 149

9. From Equal Citizens to Unequal Groups: The Post-Yugoslav Citizenship Regimes …… 151

 The citizenship conundrum in post-socialist Europe …… 152

 Ethnic engineering after Yugoslavia: The included, the invited, the excluded and the self-excluded …… 156

 Enemies into neighbours: Unconsolidated and overlapping citizenship regimes …… 165

 Concluding remarks: From ethnic engineering to ethnic democracies …… 168

10. Partners Again? The European Union and the Post-Yugoslav Citizens …… 173

 The EU's direct and limited influences …… 174

 Five ways to (mis) manage the post-Yugoslav citizenship regimes …… 176

 Partners, or just neighbours? …… 183

 Epilogue: The Citizenship Argument—Why Are We in This Together? …… 187

 Notes …… 194

 Bibliography …… 203

 Index …… 215

学术信息

九、《乌玛公社再释读：巴尔干地区民族主义与跨国主义之间的穆斯林》
(*Rediscovering the Umma*: *Muslims in the Balkans between Nationalism and Transnationalism*)

【出版社】Oxford University Press, New York, USA

【ISBN】9780199964031

【出版时间】2013 年

【作者】Ina Merdjanova

【主要内容】在重新释读乌玛公社时,作者讨论了伊斯兰教在后奥斯曼时代国家建立时期、共产主义时期和巴尔干地区后共产主义时期发展方面的条件和作用,并特别关注穆斯林群体。冷战结束后,他们在多元化的社会结构和文化转型中作为基督教社会中的主要少数群体,寻求重新定义他们的地位,并在正式的世俗法律和规范环境中重新获得他们的伊斯兰身份。东南欧穆斯林日益增强的政治和文化自我意识经常通过国内和国际两个参考框架来表达。尽管这两种观点之间存在一定程度的紧张关系,但它们紧密相连。跨国伊斯兰教的影响往往加强了穆斯林的民族认同。作者在国内和全球因素的影响的基础上探讨了该地区穆斯林身份的转变,同时也探讨了解决当前复杂的历史纠葛的方法。此外,她还研究了穆斯林妇女在其宗教社区和更大的社会中不断变化的地位和作用。

【目录】

Map of the Balkans ··· ix

A Note on Pronunciation and Transliteration ····················· xi

Preface and Acknowledgments ··· xiii

1. Islam and National Identities in the Balkans ··················· 1

1.1. Historical Overview ··· 2

1.2. Muslims in Bulgaria ··· 11

1.2.1. Turks in Bulgaria: From Religious Community to Ethnic Minority ······ 11

1.2.2. Pomaks in Bulgaria: Identities in Flux ····················· 21

1.3. Islam and the Building of a Bosniak Nation ················ 29

1.4. Islam and Albanianism ··· 37

1.4.1. Albania: A Country of Tree Religions and Two Muslim Communities ······ 38

1.4.2. Albanian Muslims in Kosovo ···································· 42

1.4.3. Albanian Muslims in Macedonia ····························· 45

1.5. Conclusion ··· 49

2. Muslim Transnationalism and the Reclaiming of "Balkan Islam" ……… 51
2. 1. Defining Transnational Islam ……………………………… 54
2. 2. The Umma—Rhetoric and Reality ……………………………… 56
2. 3. The Wars of Yugoslav Secession: Shehids and Mujahideen ………… 60
2. 4. Collision over the Interpretation of Islam ……………………… 64
2. 5. The Specter of Islamic Radicalism in the Balkans ………………… 68
2. 6. The Role of Turkey ……………………………………… 76
3. Islam and Women in the Balkans ……………………………… 82
3. 1. The Balkan Context ……………………………………… 84
3. 2. The Family ……………………………………………… 86
3. 3. The Veil ………………………………………………… 90
3. 4. Religious Education ……………………………………… 96
3. 5. Participation in the Public Sphere ……………………………… 100
4. Balkan Muslims and the Discourse on a "European Islam" ………… 103
4. 1. Muslims in Western Europe: A Brief Overview ………………… 103
4. 2. The Discourse on a "European Islam" ………………………… 107
4. 3. "Balkan Islam" as "European Islam" ………………………… 116
Conclusion: Divergent Trajectories of Islam in the Balkans …………… 130
Notes ……………………………………………………… 133
Selected Bibliography ……………………………………… 181
Index ……………………………………………………… 191

(本部分由首都师范大学文明区划研究中心学生助理王欢、王晶莹、陈寒冰、邵申申、周旭东整理)

征稿启事

《巴尔干研究》是首都师范大学文明区划研究中心创办的学术辑刊。本辑刊的宗旨是创立致力于推进中国巴尔干学发展的学术交流平台,促进中外巴尔干研究最新学术成果的传播,推动中外巴尔干研究机构、研究人员之间的学术对话。

本辑刊侧重从历史与现实的双重视角来解读巴尔干的方方面面。内容主要分为三大类,包含历史研究、热点追踪和信息传递。辑刊同时收录中英文稿件,每年一辑。每辑都围绕一个主题征稿,主题的设定围绕巴尔干地区关注的问题和外界聚焦巴尔干的领域。

本辑刊设定第二期的历史研究主题是"巴尔干与第二次世界大战",现实问题主题不限,计划于2020年出版,现面向广大致力于巴尔干研究的中外学者、专家征文。要求如下:

一、请围绕主题写作,文字精练,每篇稿件字数在8000—15000字。

二、关于论文格式,中文稿件请参照《世界历史》的编辑技术规范。

三、为便于读者阅读,中文稿件请提供300—500字中英文摘要,英文稿件请提供1000词的英文摘要。同时提供3—5个关键词。

四、请写明作者真实姓名、性别、出生年、籍贯、单位、职务、职称、通信地址、邮编、联系电话、联系邮箱等。

第二辑征稿截止日期为2019年12月31日。

收稿邮箱:civilized@163.com

联系地址:北京市西三环北路105号首都师范大学本部文明区划研究中心

邮编:100048

联系电话:010-68901620

联系人:李建军

首都师范大学文明区划研究中心

2019年1月29日